COLD WAR II

COLD WAR

COLD WAR II

HOLLYWOOD'S RENEWED OBSESSION WITH RUSSIA

EDITED BY
TATIANA PROROKOVA-KONRAD

University Press of Mississippi / Jackson

The University Press of Mississippi is the scholarly publishing agency of
the Mississippi Institutions of Higher Learning: Alcorn State University,
Delta State University, Jackson State University, Mississippi State University,
Mississippi University for Women, Mississippi Valley State University,
University of Mississippi, and University of Southern Mississippi.

www.upress.state.ms.us

The University Press of Mississippi is a member
of the Association of University Presses.

Copyright © 2020 by University Press of Mississippi
All rights reserved

First printing 2020
∞

Library of Congress Cataloging-in-Publication Data available

LCCN 2020036669
ISBN 9781496831095 (hardback)
ISBN 9781496831101 (trade paperback)
ISBN 9781496831118 (epub single)
ISBN 9781496831125 (epub institutional)
ISBN 9781496831132 (pdf single)
ISBN 9781496831149 (pdf institutional)

British Library Cataloging-in-Publication Data available

CONTENTS

Introduction: Cinematic Reimagining of the Cold War in the 2010s 3
Tatiana Prorokova-Konrad

PART I. ENDURING CLICHÉS

The Warm Glow of Cold War Nostalgia 29
Vesta Silva & Jon Wiebel

Big Rewards for the Small Screen: *The Man from U.N.C.L.E.*
during Both Cold Wars 49
Helena Goscilo

The Westernization of Stalin: Late Hollywood Readings of
Real-Existing Socialism 70
Lucian Țion

PART II. NEW AESTHETICS OF THE OLD PAST

The Coldest City: Berlin and the Remapping of Cold War
Movie Aesthetics 95
Ian Scott

"Your Body Belongs to the State": The Mobilization
of the Action Heroine in Service of the State
in *Red Sparrow* and *Atomic Blonde* 112
Dan Ward

The Shape of Water and the Cold War Revisited 129
Cyndy Hendershot

Laughing at the Early Cold War: Communism, the USSR, and
the Comedy of *Hail, Caesar!* and *The Death of Stalin* 140
Lori Maguire

PART III. OF PATRIOTISM, CORRUPTION, AND OTHERNESS

Of Mothers and Motherlands: Figurations of Parenting
and Patriotism in *The Americans* 159
David LaRocca

Conservative Understanding and Nationalist Exclusion:
Moral Equivalency as Contested Concept in *Bridge of Spies*
and *Tinker Tailor Soldier Spy* 182
Christian Jimenez

Unacknowledged Realignment: Representations of US-Russia
Relations in Recent American Cinema 203
Thomas J. Cobb

Red Sparrow: Cold War Redux and the Treatment of Corruption 223
Donna A. Gessell

About the Contributors 247

Index 251

COLD WAR II

INTRODUCTION
Cinematic Reimagining of the Cold War in the 2010s

Tatiana Prorokova-Konrad

The Cold War, with its bald confrontation between the United States and the Soviet Union, has been widely depicted in films. Starting even before the conflict actually began with Ernst Lubitsch's portrayals of communism in *Ninotchka* (1939), and ranging from Stanley Kubrick's openly "Cold War" *Dr. Strangelove* (1964) to Fred Schepisi's *The Russia House* (1990), Hollywood's obsession with the Cold War, the Soviets/Russians, communism, and the political and ideological differences between the US and Russia was pronounced. Although there have been far fewer films about the Cold War since the fall of the Berlin Wall and the breakup of the Soviet Union, Cold War tropes continue to be (ab)used, as can be seen in multiple representations of evil Russians on screen, including Wolfgang Petersen's *Air Force One* (1997), Jon Favreau's *Iron Man 2* (2010), Phillip Noyce's *Salt* (2010), Brad Bird's *Mission: Impossible—Ghost Protocol* (2011), John Moore's *A Good Day to Die Hard* (2013), and Antoine Fuqua's *The Equalizer* (2014), to name just a few. All these films portray Russians in a rather similar manner: as members of the Mafia or as plain criminals. Yet recently, Hollywood cinema has made a striking turn regarding its portrayals of Russians, returning to the explicit images of the Cold War. This turn and the films that resulted from it are what the collection examines.

The sanctions imposed on Russia during the Ukrainian crisis in 2014 by several Western countries, including the United States, along with Donald Trump's admiration for Vladimir Putin, Russian attempts to influence the 2016 American election, as documented in the Mueller Report (2019), the poisoning in the UK, etc., have led to a tense relationship between Russia and the Western world. At the same time, over the past few years, several Hollywood films have evoked events from the Cold War and have brought back the memory of that confrontation between the USSR and the US, Russians and Americans, communism and capitalism. The collection examines these films—among them Guy Ritchie's *The Man from U.N.C.L.E.* (2015), Steven Spielberg's *Bridge of Spies* (2015), Ethan Coen and Joel Coen's *Hail, Caesar!* (2016), David Leitch's *Atomic Blonde* (2017), Guillermo del Toro's *The Shape of Water* (2017), and Francis Lawrence's *Red Sparrow* (2018)—as well as TV series, including *Comrade Detective* (2017) and *The Americans* (2013–18), that either explicitly tackle the issue of the Cold War or deal with it as a subplot. Well informed about established Cold War tropes, the collection expands the existing scholarship on Cold War cinema by looking at the most recent portrayals, comparing them to the older ones or studying them independent of the "classic" Cold War examples. The book explores the reasons for Hollywood's sudden renewed interest in the Cold War and argues that these recent examples attempt to interpret the tightened political relations between the United States and Russia, cinematically suggesting the beginning of a Cold War II. By proposing to characterize the current relationship between the US and Russia as Cold War II based on the films released, the collection by no means *equates* the political situation that dominated the second half of the twentieth century with the current uptick in political tension. Indeed, during the Cold War, American policy was directed toward defeating (or at least containing) communism, and Russian policy sought to defeat capitalism, but now in the twenty-first century the rivalry has been figured in anti-Russian/anti-American terms. The contention between powers today is not, as it was during the Cold War, between communism and capitalism but between oligarchy and liberal democracy. The complex, tortuous events that produced this shift took place over a long period, which reveals that the emergence of what I call "Cold War II" had been a steadily approaching phenomenon rather than an unexpected political turn. Being aware that the Cold War and "Cold War II" differ considerably, this collection examines the sudden boom in Russia-related films as well as the effectiveness of understanding the current US-Russia political crisis through the lens of recent Cold War films and TV shows. *Cold War II* thus pinpoints the necessity of acknowledging the change that took place in the political arena between the two countries, and Russia and the West in general, and the swift recognition of this change by filmmakers who then transferred it to our screens.

The essays in this collection investigate the revival of the Cold War movie genre under multiple angles, including questions of patriotism, national identity, otherness, gender, and corruption. They are sensitive to the cinematic aesthetics and ethics of these representations in the service of understanding the contribution made by the most recent examples to the Cold War movie genre in general and how they shape audiences' understanding of the Cold War as well as of the relationship between the US and Russia in particular. Hollywood rarely offers positive portrayals of Russians. From the images of communists whose ideology endangers fragile American democracy to those of brutal Mafia criminals, the Soviets/Russians are usually presented as embodying some form of menace, with views entirely different from those of Americans. *Cold War II* investigates whether this stereotype persists in current Cold War cinema and, through an examination of the portrayals of Russians, scrutinizes the images of and the relationship between the US and Russia today. All essays in this collection pay attention to the question of so-called national identity and its centrality to the Cold War movie genre. Through the prism of identity, the contributors look at the current Cold War examples to see how identity informs and transforms the genre, offering new insights into the understanding of who Russians and Americans are and of the various misunderstandings between the two peoples and the two nations. Establishing differences and finding similarities, the collection not only enriches the conventional understandings of the Cold War but also acknowledges the intricate relationship between the two countries during the Obama presidency as well as meditates upon the current political systems created and sustained by Trump and Putin. In doing so, it denies any simplistic interpretation of recent cinema on the Cold War as mere examples of the genre, insisting that the interest of Hollywood has been sparked and continues to be directly influenced by the complex political situations in both countries. What do these examples have to tell their viewers about *new* heroes and villains, about transformed notions and manifestations of femininity and masculinity, about the two nations in the *twenty-first* century, about corruption and morality? And how do these issues inform the visual, audio, and verbal aesthetics of Cold War films, which have come together to create a new type of Cold War cinema? The present collection, therefore, defies the traditional definitions of the Cold War film and invites readers to discover the new phase in the Cold War movie genre: Cold War II.

The History of the Cold War

Hardly ever were the US and Russia true friends during the twentieth and twenty-first centuries, except for the years during World War II when their important political alliance helped defeat Nazism. The Russian Revolution in 1917 toppled czarist autocracy and established the world's first communist nation, the Soviet Union, and thereafter Russia (for most of the twentieth century the heart of the Soviet Union) became synonymous with communism. The figure of the Russian/Soviet has become a metaphor for someone who threatens Western values, including and especially democracy, and thus has been perceived as the enemy. Yet Hitler's attack on Europe and the spread of Nazism throughout the continent made the nonfascist West tolerate communism during World War II. Nazi Germany, along with its Axis allies Japan and Italy, faced the armed opposition of the Allied nations, which meant that by 1942 the Soviet Union and the United States were fighting on the same side. Until the end of the war in 1945, the two countries remained allies, whatever the tensions below the surface.

On February 4–11, 1945, the Yalta Conference brought together the political leaders of the US, the UK, and the USSR to decide how postwar Europe would be reorganized. As a result of these deliberations, Berlin was divided among the four main Allied countries (those listed above, and France), and although the chief decision made at the conference was to install democratic regimes throughout Europe, the Soviet Union occupied Poland and over the next four years exercised full control over several other eastern European counties. This led to the creation of the so-called Eastern Bloc, which enlarged the territory under communist influence. During that time, the involvement of the US in Stalin's plans resulted in the declaration of the Truman Doctrine in 1947, which helped suppress the spread of communism (and the possibility of communist governments) in Greece and Turkey so that the two countries could join NATO in 1952, and later, in 1948, the Marshall Plan, an American allotment of $13 billion to help restore the economies of Western European countries.[1] Although there is no scholarly consensus about a definite start date to the Cold War—"was it 1917, 1944, 1947 or 1948?"[2]—it is plausible to argue that the Yalta Conference was a key inflection point in the relations between the Soviet Union and the West, including the US, since in its wake the situation began to rapidly worsen due to polarized ideologies and the emergence of certain political intentions. Defining the Cold War, Jonathan Auerbach specifies what the conflict signified:

> Rather than armed conflict fought in a clearly demarcated geographical region or regions, the Cold War refers to an ideological struggle between two different "ways of life," to borrow the president's phrasing from his famous 1947 "Truman Doctrine" speech. Having as much to do with competing ideas, values and patterns of behaviour as physical force, this was a perceived clash between capitalism, or "the free world," and communism, or "totalitarianism," that lasted from the end of World War II to the collapse of the Soviet Union in 1991.[3]

The Soviet government, despite its clearly totalitarian control over its population and its promises for a better future, could not prevent the migration of a considerable number of people who did not want to live under a communist regime. Thus, between 1949 and 1961, over ten million people in Berlin "fled west to escape communism." Ultimately, "to stop that embarrassment," the Soviet leader Nikita Khrushchev decided to build a wall through the city, dividing it into West Berlin and East Berlin. The Berlin Wall, however, not only divided Berlin physically; it ideologically divided Germany and the whole world into opposed camps of communists and noncommunists. Even the so-called Non-Aligned countries were nonetheless defined by this bipolarity. The wall existed for almost thirty years and thus became "a central image of the Cold War."[4] Underscoring the scale of the Cold War, Jeffrey A. Engel and Katherine Carté Engel claim that it "manifested itself in every facet of life, in industrial and developing nations alike, East and West, urban and rural, on the periphery of the international system and throughout every stratum and region of the superpowers themselves."[5]

While the Cold War was a war of ideologies and never saw actual *fighting* between the US and the USSR directly, James W. Peterson claims that "in a sense, Cuba became one important surrogate that acted as a kind of substitute for actual war between the United States and the Soviet Union." In 1961, the US conducted the infamous Bay of Pigs invasion in a failed attempt to overthrow Fidel Castro's communist regime. This, in turn, strengthened the relationship between the Soviet Union and Cuba, and "during the next year, Soviet leader Khrushchev reacted by beginning to place nuclear missiles covertly into Cuba." Once the missiles were found, President Kennedy had "enough evidence to issue an ultimatum requiring that they be dismantled." Although the missile site was close to the US—as little as ninety miles from Florida—the Missile Crisis standoff was ultimately won by the US.[6]

The 1970s are characterized as the period of "détente," a time when the major goal of both countries was "to limit the weapons." Peterson states: "While their leaders had profoundly different visions of the world and global politics, they did agree to work together to restrict the weaponry in the name of a larger good." The key events of that decade include the signing of SALT I and SALT II (Strategic Arms Limitation Talks), in 1972 and 1979 respectively. The first treaty was "an agreement that addressed both defensive and offensive weapons," whereas, according to the terms of the second treaty, the superpowers were supposed to "limit the size of the nuclear arsenal." In 1987, the two countries' leaders, Ronald Reagan and Mikhail Gorbachev, "decided to eliminate all intermediate nuclear weapons in Europe."[7] Nuclear war between the US and the USSR, a prospect that the whole world feared as the arms race unfolded, never took place, though the US and the Soviet Union's successor, Russia, still possess vast stockpiles of nuclear weapons.

Calling the Cold War "World War III," Andrew J. Bacevich singles out its two main periods. He defines the first phase "as the period of Soviet-American competition that could have produced an actual rather than apocryphal World War III," and notes that it "essentially ended in 1963." During the second phase (i.e., between 1963 and 1989), "both of the major protagonists [were] pursuing inane adventures on the periphery," a reference, of course, to the wars in Vietnam and Afghanistan.[8] The Cold War effectively ended with the fall of the Berlin Wall on November 9, 1989—an event that Peterson calls "the key sign that the Cold War was indeed over."[9] With the collapse of the Soviet Union in 1991, the reign of communism in Russia, the post-Soviet countries, and the European countries that were members of the Eastern Bloc came to an end.

Post-1990s theories on the Cold War interpret the conflict differently. For example, some see "the Cold War as having been created in the U.S. in order to ensure a climate that would allow for the expansion of the government both in economic reach, as it became the grantor of billions of dollars in defense contracts, and in the lives of American citizens, as fear of communism allowed for all manner of surveillance and intrusion." Yet, "the dominant interpretation of the Cold War as America and her allies coming together to protect the world from Soviet aggression has remained."[10] Cynthia Weber characterizes this phenomenon as a "moral grammar of us/capitalists versus them/communists" in the Cold War, which "'ensures' the eventual victory of us over them."[11] In turn, Bryn Upton concludes: "This understanding has been the basis for much of American popular culture, films, books, and television, about the Cold War as well as its collective memory of the Cold War and its origins."[12]

It is true that the Cold War was primarily "a conflict of competing social and political visions." However, these visions were not an immediate reaction to the Yalta Conference and the events that followed it. John V. Fleming, for example, urges that we also look at the Cold War from the perspective of the 1930s–40s in order to understand the roots of the confrontation. From its emergence, the Soviet Union had been "the object of great and often sympathetic interest in the West," yet because of the distance that separated it from the Western world, Westerners have never fully understood the culture of the Soviets—their knowledge came only from works of literature, art, music, etc.[13] One can therefore view the Cold War as the result not only of political disagreements but also, in part, of longstanding cultural noninteraction. The difference between the two nations that is so feverishly foregrounded, particularly in cultural texts on the Cold War, in principle, has been formulated because of cultural isolation. And although Western capitalism won the fight against Eastern communism in the Cold War, it is correct to argue that "at the level of abstraction the conflict was never resolved, and it probably will never be resolved."[14] The portrayals of Russians by Hollywood (and surely of Americans in Soviet/Russian cinema) prior to but especially during the Cold War have generated countless stereotypes that continue to dominate cultural consciousness, positioning Russians as the Other (which is frequently equated with "danger" or "enemy").

It is correct to state, as Thomas Doherty does, that "Soviet communism posed a menace to human freedom."[15] The collapse of the USSR indeed symbolized the victory of the Free World. But it is also crucial to note that this collapse left the United States as the sole superpower. Joseph S. Nye Jr. ambitiously designates 1991 as "the beginning of the American century."[16] And although the US has experienced numerous tragic events, including 9/11, and episodes of instability such as the financial crisis of 2007–08, and has conducted various unsuccessful and/or controversial military interventions in Somalia, Iraq, Afghanistan, and elsewhere, the country remains a powerful nation. Whether its preeminence will continue and the US will fulfill the prognoses of the National Intelligence Council and become (or, many would argue, remain) "the most powerful country in the world" by 2030[17] can now be questioned, in light of the 2016 election. As events of the twenty-first century demonstrate, American democracy and the values that are so important for the nation and the Free World continue to be threatened internally and externally, even after the defeat of communism.

The Cold War in Film

Although the long confrontation between the US and the USSR in the Cold War was widely reflected on screen during the conflict, Hollywood saw Soviet communism as a threat prior to it, too. In his brilliant discussion of the changing portrayal of Russians on screen, *Russians in Hollywood, Hollywood's Russians: Biography of an Image*, Harlow Robinson notes: "It is . . . a most curious historical coincidence that the Bolshevik Revolution of 1917 . . . occurred precisely at the moment when the American film industry was entering a rapid period of development, moving westward from New York toward Hollywood. . . . The overthrow of the Romanov dynasty and the creation of the USSR was one of the biggest and most shocking stories of the century, so it is hardly surprising that films about Russia constituted a significant part of the output of the Hollywood studios from the very beginning of their existence."[18] Tony Shaw makes a similar observation: "*Ninotchka* did not appear out of the blue in 1939. The American film industry had effectively been at war with political extremism, and with communism in particular, for two decades."[19] Finally, Daniel J. Leab argues that Cold War films "incorporated political, social, and cultural attitudes that had surfaced in American films decades earlier."[20] The cinematic examples preceding the Cold War years doubtless contributed to the formation of the dominant images of the Soviet Union, its ideology, and its people, and arguably facilitated the process in which these images evolved and new images were created during the Cold War.

Tony Shaw and Denise J. Youngblood single out five major periods between 1947 and 1990 of Hollywood's Cold War cinema: "1947–1953 (dominated by hard-line negative propaganda); 1953–1962 (soft-core, positive propaganda mixed with the beginnings of negotiated dissent); 1962–1980 (pro-détente propaganda); 1980–86 (New Right propaganda); 1986–1990 (a call for peace)." Yet the scholars note that these divisions are rather flexible, and what they propose does not represent a strict arrangement of Cold War films according to their years of production; rather, it is one of the ways to approach the vast pool of examples created during a period that spanned more than forty years.[21]

In one of the most recent explorations of Cold War cinema, *The Screen Is Red: Hollywood, Communism, and the Cold War*, Bernard F. Dick outlines the necessity of examining Hollywood's stance on communism in the 1930s, a time when both communism and fascism were vigorously discussed in films and it was not yet clear which sort of regime would be more threatening. Interestingly, communism appeared less of a menace than fascism, according to those early films. Yet it was obvious that for Hollywood itself, both ideologies were dangerous: either "would have subverted the free enterprise system on which the industry was founded."[22]

Nevertheless, Cold War cinema dealt with more than just communism. Different events that took place during the war influenced the scenarios being written, the characters that became iconic and recurred in various forms in many films, and the emergence of so-called Cold War tropes that today help us easily identify a film as a product of the Cold War and locate it within the conflict's discourse.

Thus, there are several key themes raised in Cold War cinema. "The Bomb" was perhaps one of the most prominent. Fear of the Bomb was triggered even before the end of World War II, when it became known that the Nazis were conducting research into nuclear weapons. Having obtained this information, the US started to finance its own program to develop atomic weaponry, in the initiative known as the Manhattan Project. The situation escalated, however, in 1945, when the US dropped atomic bombs on the Japanese cities of Hiroshima and Nagasaki. Since then, the Bomb has become one of the world's greatest fears, and this has been widely reflected in popular culture. The nuclear arms race between the US and the USSR and the possibility of nuclear war were perhaps the key dangers threatening the two nations and the world in general. Therefore, the issue of the Bomb was widely discussed in Cold War films. Some examples include *Notorious* (1946), *Flight to Nowhere* (1946), and *The Beginning or the End* (1947).[23] Even these films' titles indicate the apocalyptic aura that surrounded the Cold War, as for a long time the possibility of nuclear war was feared as an inevitable reality.

"Science" is another important trope in Cold War films. Dick argues: "Science was put to demonic use in the B movies of the 1940s, strangely mirroring the equally demonic experiments being conducted in the Nazi death camps." In the 1950s, too, the issue of science was conspicuously present in numerous films. Its most famous type of manifestation is perhaps the mutations that can occur as a result of nuclear activity, which gave rise to all sorts of fantasies. The examples here include *Them!* (1954), *Creature from the Black Lagoon* (1954), *Tarantula* (1955), *It Came from Beneath the Sea* (1955), *Forbidden Planet* (1956), and *The Deadly Mantis* (1957).[24]

"In 1946, the year the Iron Curtain fell on Eastern Europe, unidentified flying objects were reportedly seen in the skies over Scandinavia. Then, in early July 1947, aliens were sighted in Roswell, New Mexico." With these events, the trope of "aliens" entered Cold War cinema, as can be seen in, for example, *Flight to Mars* (1951) and *It Came from Outer Space* (1953).[25] Yet it is also plausible to argue that the alien as such was a metaphor for the Soviet, used to designate the cultural, linguistic, ideological, and political differences between the US and the USSR. An alien invasion can therefore be metaphorically interpreted in the context of Cold War cinema as a dangerous and clearly unwelcome intrusion of Soviet communists in the land of democratic freedoms.

Certainly communism itself was reflected in films during the Cold War, as is evident from examples like *State Department File 649* (1949), *I Married a Communist* (1949), *The Red Menace* (1949), and *Red Snow* (1952).[26] Noteworthy here is the scholars' unanimous claim that the unambiguous fear of communism reflected in Cold War films was "paranoiac" and "hysteri[cal]."[27] From the very outset via these films' titles, which use words like "communist," "menace," and "red," the cinema attempted to spread fear among viewers, as well as accentuate the differences between the two nations, whose hostility toward each other was, on both sides, deep and overt.

Hysteria, however, manifested itself not only through fictional portrayals on screen but also through real stories that happened to people in Hollywood. Thus, the excesses of the McCarthy era, the time "when producers were forced into making dozens of lurid 'red-baiting' movies and when scores of filmmakers' careers were ruined by bogus accusations of communist subversion."[28] Because the thought of a "communist penetration of the entertainment industry" was particularly scary, there were numerous film-industry figures interrogated by the House Un-American Activities Committee (HUAC).[29]

Many films also commented on the problem of espionage, identifying spying as one of the means used to fight the Cold War. Consider here, for example, the James Bond films *Dr. No* (1962) and *To Russia with Love* (1963).[30] Simultaneously, the patriotism inspired by John Wayne's roles reinforced Americans' faith in the righteousness of their country's actions.[31]

There are several films that can be considered particularly important to Cold War cinema. For example, *Red Danube* (1949) "illustrates vividly just how radically and quickly Hollywood's representation of the USSR and Russians changed after World War II."[32] *Dr. Strangelove* (1964) "show[s] the genre [of comedy] reforming to meet the needs of current audiences fearful of Communism but in need of humorous release from that fear."[33] *The Russians Are Coming! The Russians Are Coming!* (1966) "helped break down cultural barriers, giving support to those promulgating détente between the superpowers."[34] *The Hunt for Red October* (1990) is identified as "Hollywood's last major contribution to the Cold War."[35] But there are of course numerous other examples from different genres that helped illustrate the conflict as well as the state of fear and insecurity that the world found itself in over the course of the Cold War.

The Cold War was so energetically reflected on screen not only because it was the dominant political reality of its time but also because cinema was (and still is) a tool through which to communicate ideology. Michael H. Hunt argues that "ideology is central, not incidental, to policymaking."[36] The promotion of a certain ideology was therefore essential to securing the support of the American people over the war's lengthy and evolving course. According to Andrew J. Falk, "People expressing conflicting ideologies . . . seek to exert power over the production, distribution, and exhibition of popular culture. By doing so they indirectly help define the national identity that those forms of culture represent."[37] One can hence confidently conclude: "The Cold War influenced how films were made, which films were made, and how audiences understood the films they watched."[38]

At the time when "a military confrontation would have become mutually suicidal" (given the nuclear arms race), cinema became one of the ways to fight the war. It is unsurprising, then, that the Cold War is frequently referred to as "a conflict of ideas and images."[39] The films "not only reflected the Cold War; they also projected it."[40] The abundance of Cold War films and the repetition of similar tropes resulted in the creation of "an instrumentalized stream of consciousness that insinuates itself into a shared national narrative."[41] After all, as Peter Biskind claims in *Seeing Is Believing: How Hollywood Taught Us to Stop Worrying and Love the Fifties*, "movies are peculiarly well suited to translate social values into felt needs that seem as authentic as the memories of childhood. Although we may not always agree with them, or even recognize that they are courting our consent, we tend to accept the frames of reference they supply. They speak our language, and we learn to speak theirs."[42] Cinema has thus proved itself to be a "powerful [weapon]," particularly powerful in its ability to generate a "strong anti-Soviet consensus."[43] Film, among other cultural media, "was bound to be politically charged,"[44] and Hollywood film was. That their cinematic productions were supposed to reach wide audiences indeed made the filmmakers filter their works so that they could achieve the most refined expression of their stance on the war. Lori Maguire specifies the audiences to whom Hollywood was trying to display the American way of life as a "better" one (certainly the Soviets adopted a similar strategy, trying as well to show in film that *their* way of life was better): "First of all, to their own citizens, then to the citizens of their sphere of influence (notably in Europe), then to countries with great numbers of sympathizers (such as France or Italy in the West with their large communist parties or most Eastern European nations with their anti-Russian feelings), then to inhabitants of the developing and often recently decolonized nations and finally to each other's population."[45] Part of the war between the ideologies was based on a cultural re-creation of truths and myths that, on the American side, would facilitate a perception of communism as corrupt and dangerous, and would sustain anti-communism as the only right political course. As I argue in *Docu-Fictions of War: U.S. Interventionism in Film and Literature*, the appeal to various "cultural myths and memories regarding wars" has been a prominent tool to deal with historical reality.[46] It proved effective during the Cold War era, too, when in the fight against communism the US found it as necessary as ever to stress its status as "a land in which life should be better and richer and fuller for every man, with opportunity for each according to his ability or achievement," as James Truslow Adams did in 1931, introducing the concept of the American Dream. Indeed, the notion is strikingly in contrast to the Soviet leadership's oppression of its people under communism.[47]

Russia and the US in the 2010s: Cold War II?

Several times since the end of the Cold War, the US has considered resetting its relationship with Russia, yet such a reset has never really happened.[48] And while since 1991 the US and Russia have never enjoyed "good" political relations, the situation sunk to a low during the Obama presidency and has continued to slide. Putin's vision of democracy (read "authoritarianism") has never coincided with Western ideals of freedom. Moreover, his military activities in Ukraine and Syria, which one can interpret as attempts to expand Russian political power and the country's sphere of influence, received particular condemnation from the West, the US included.

Scholars argue that for Russians the fact that "Americans consistently denied them a sphere of influence along their historical borderlands" (consider Georgia and Ukraine) was highly problematic. Russia believes that it would not be able to guarantee its regional security in the event that Georgia and Ukraine were to become members of NATO.[49] The annexation of Crimea in March 2014 was a way for Putin to demonstrate his political dominance over Ukraine and thus keep this post-Soviet nation on his side (particularly after the overthrow of the pro-Russian Ukrainian leader Viktor Yanukovich). Yet the Crimea case was a clear violation of key democratic principles as they have been articulated in the international sphere; for the West it was arguably the last straw, leading to Russia's full isolation from the Western world.

Nonetheless, any hopes for a reset had already collapsed before the Ukrainian crisis, in the wake of the 2011 Russian legislative elections. Putin's United Russia Party would have lost had he not performed the trick of blaming the US for financing the opposition and thus lifting anti-Putin sentiment during the elections; in fact, Putin's team simply underestimated the strength of the opposition. Hillary Clinton was among those blamed for the alleged interference. And afterward the relationship between the two politicians was irrevocably spoiled. In one of her memoirs, Clinton confirms that "Putin deeply resented her public ridicule of his manipulation of Russia's parliamentary elections of December 2011."[50]

The Russian interference in the 2016 US presidential elections can therefore be interpreted as an attempt to compromise Clinton, for due to the years of strained relations that followed the 2011 elections, Putin understood that "there was little to hope for and perhaps much to fear from a Hillary Clinton presidency." In addition, scholars speculate that Clinton most likely agreed with President Obama in 2014, when the latter "publicly identified the three major threats facing the United States" as follows: "Ebola (in effect to be eradicated), ISIS (to be annihilated), Russia (. . . ?)." The interference, however, was arguably conducted "*not* to elect Donald Trump," and the victory of Trump was most probably as big a surprise for Putin as it was for millions of Americans and others around the globe; moreover, it would have simply been too risky for Putin to hope that Trump would win. Hillary Clinton was the expected winner, and Putin, notably, thought quite correctly that "a President Hillary Clinton would launch a new campaign of pressure against his government and Russian client states in the name of human rights and democracy."[51]

While a candidate, Donald Trump considered it a necessity to improve the relationship between the US and Russia, but the "Russian interference in the election itself has made such a warming of relations politically impossible in the United States."[52] By the end of 2017, relations between the two countries have been characterized as being "at their worst level since the height of the Cold War." Russia continues to be under American sanctions for its intervention in Ukraine and its interference in the 2016 American elections in the form of "hacking and publicizing emails from the Democratic National Committee and other political actors," which revealed that "the party's national officials had tried to subvert the prospects of Hillary Clinton's rival, Senator Bernie Sanders"—the story was in the news up until Trump's victory.[53] In the end, despite Trump's inability to restore peace with Russia, he has never really behaved as the country's adversary but rather has been Putin's puppet. He has never acknowledged Russian culpability for their interference in the election but instead has attacked the FBI and the US intelligence agencies (for various issues, including the Russia investigation). Trump has also openly questioned the necessity of NATO, which Douglas Kellner comments on as follows: "It appeared that the U.S.-Europe alliance which had kept the peace and guaranteed 60-plus years of stability was threatened for the first time as Vladimir Putin and Trump's Russian and pro-Russian comrades chortled with glee."[54] But while scholars call the current phase in the relationship between Trump and Putin a "honeymoon,"[55] for indeed Putin's aggressions seem to evoke rather tacit (and sometimes active) support from Trump, it is obvious that politically the two countries remain opponents.

Unlike in 2011, Putin's victory in the 2018 presidential elections was easily predictable: "The Kremlin demonstrated quite effectively its ability to suppress the protests that erupted in large Russian cities following the last presidential election in 2011 [*sic*: Russia's parliamentary elections had been held in December 2011, followed by the presidential election in March 2012]. Since that time, Putin has further consolidated his control over Russian television and other media sources. In April 2016, he also created a new national guard under his direct command, employing up to 400,000 troops."[56] Moreover, since his previous presidential term, Putin's political tactics have changed, for the primary tool with which he now manipulates the Russian people is patriotism—a vivid shift "from a technocratic autocracy to a regime based on populist nationalism."[57] Interestingly, Putin usually makes his appeals to the patriotic feelings of Russians through references to World War II and the Soviet people's glorious fight for freedom from Nazi oppression. But it is also through allusions to the Cold War times, when the Soviet Union was one of the world's two superpowers, that Putin reaches the hearts and minds of the population. Kimberly Marten correctly pinpoints his strategy: "For several years Putin has been building up the Russian military and advertising Russia's nuclear might—powerful symbols of the country's Cold War glory days."[58] He skillfully employs anti-Americanism, making the population frequently forget about the deep economic trouble that the country finds itself in, obviously due to endemic corruption and oligarchy, and adopts the discourse in which the US is hated, reminiscent of the rhetoric of the Cold War. In doing so, Putin creates an image of himself as a true leader who knows best how to confront the West. And yet, although in 2011 Helena Goscilo could observe that "no Russian or Soviet head of state since Stalin has inspired the widespread hero worship that irradiated Putin's presidency,"[59] Putin's leadership and his political decisions seem to be questioned by many more Russians at present.

Trump's election in 2016 truly was "an American nightmare." That was the first time in American history when "the legitimacy of the presidency [had been starkly] ... questioned," and "the first time that a Russian leader had ever publically denied that a U.S. president was a Russian asset."[60] With Trump as the head of state, it is easy to question statements like "America will remain the world's only superpower for the foreseeable future,"[61] a sentiment that seemed to dominate the pre-Trump twenty-first-century scholarship. As for the US-Russia relationship, it is difficult to make prognoses. Several months after the 2016 election, scholars claimed that such a "level of unpredictability has not been seen since the later 1980s, when it was not clear who would be running the Soviet Union a few months hence—or even, it turned out, whether there would be a Soviet Union at all."[62] It is clear that the current situation is not the same as it was during or right at the end of the Cold War. While the US and Russia are definitely not in the warmest phase of their relationship, there is a level of "uncertainty" on "*both sides* of the relationship."[63] Yet the advice of scholars that today "the focus of U.S. Russia policy should be to avoid the worst instead of achieving the best"[64] indeed echoes what was heard during the Cold War era and inevitably invites comparison of the situation as it was *then* and as it is *now*.

Hollywood's Return to Cold War Images

Bernard F. Dick convincingly claims: "The Cold War may not be a war for all seasons, but it will always find its season—on either the big or the small screen." Cold War cinema will continue to explore issues pertinent to the war, including "the repatriation of citizens from countries under communist control, atomic spies, HUAC, the blacklist, the bomb, the missile race, nuclear war with or without doomsday."[65] While the recurrence of certain events—especially those with particular significance, such as the Cold War—in various cultural texts from different decades and centuries is a regular phenomenon, these sorts of reimaginings of history should be treated carefully. Addressing Cold War films released in the 2010s, this collection argues that these examples not only help envision the Cold War anew but also comment profoundly on the current political tensions between the US and Russia. Using *the Cold War*—"the most crucial and defining aspect of American culture from the late 1940s until the early 1990s"[66]—as a trope or a metaphor to speak about the political situation today, however, is a powerful, if not dangerous, way to suggest how irrevocably bad the relationship has become. These films by no means try to argue that the current situation is literally the same as it was during the Cold War, thus reducing the political, social, economic, and cultural significance of the past thirty years and the attendant transformations; but it is apparent that this strong metaphor allows these films to tell us much about the two countries in the 2010s. Each essay in this collection suggests that "films are more than process or propaganda, more than business or industry; films have meaning beyond the stories they are trying to tell. Each tells a story—this is the text of the film—but it also tells a story about the time in which it was made." We see as well that films are "products of particular places and times . . . [and] reflections of those places and times."[67] In addition, the essays explore the ways through which these recent films on the Cold War arrive at their meanings, borrowing the approach in analyzing Cold War cinema adopted by Jeff Smith, who believes that instead of "trying to answer the question of *what* these Cold War-era films mean," it is more productive to ask "*how* they came to mean."[68]

The emergence of films about the Cold War in the 2010s is a particularly curious phenomenon, considering that after the end of the Cold War the number of films that referred to Russia/Russians, in the words of Robinson, "declined significantly," and that the issue of the Cold War has literally "vanished."[69] And although the last statement can be debated, films about the Cold War have been released rarely and rather sporadically, and there has not been great interest in them—until the 2010s, particularly the decade's second half. It is true that "outsiders" are an important part of Hollywood films, and although in the twenty-first century terrorism poses a much larger threat than Russia, Russians continue to be othered, and Russia remains "an unstable and dangerous place."[70] The discussions related to the Cold War, communism, and the instability and uncertainty characteristic of that era offer a unique way to tackle the current political issues roiling both the US and Russia, as well as examine the *cold* relationship between the two countries.

★ ★ ★

This book is divided into three sections—"Enduring Clichés," "New Aesthetics of the Old Past," and "Of Patriotism, Corruption, and Otherness"—to discuss the most recent portrayals of the Cold War and the relationship between the US and Russia on screen.

Section one, "Enduring Clichés," focuses on portrayals of the US and the USSR/Russia, centered on various stereotypes that surrounded both countries as well as their policies during the Cold War. The section opens with Vesta Silva and Jon Wiebel's "The Warm Glow of Cold War Nostalgia," which examines the image of the US as it has recently been expressed. The authors argue that the resurgence in the late 2010s of films set during or focusing on events of the Cold War allow American audiences to buy into a nostalgically purified vision of America as morally and militarily superior to our allies and to our enemies—contributing to a new victory culture untroubled by the actual events of history. In *Atomic Blonde* (2017), the weaknesses and treachery of the Russians, East Germans, and even the British are juxtaposed with the power, panache, and triumph of the American triple agent playing them all for fools. In *Bridge of Spies*, Steven Spielberg's 2015 romantic retelling of an American Cold War triumph, Tom Hanks's character is even directly referred to as the "standing man," or the man who stands for what is right. These narrative fantasies resecure and re-create a comforting and comfortable image of Americans in a world simplified into the binary distinctions (right and wrong, good and evil) that have become central to our nostalgic retellings of the Cold War.

The section continues with Helena Goscilo's "Big Rewards for the Small Screen: *The Man from U.N.C.L.E.* during Both Cold Wars." President John Kennedy's suggestion to the UN General Assembly that the US and the USSR embark on a joint expedition to the moon, though no such partnership ever materialized, was symptomatic of the liberalism of Soviet and American attitudes during the early 1960s and adumbrated the appearance of a highly successful American TV series: NBC's *The Man from U.N.C.L.E.* (1964–68). Its scenarios hinged on the cooperation of the two superpowers as a joint spy weapon against international enemies: the cool, sophisticated American, Napoleon Solo (Robert Vaughn), and his intellectual, enigmatic Soviet counterpart, Illya Kuryakin (David McCallum). The popular series unexpectedly triggered audience fascination with the Ukrainian Kuryakin and elevated the Scottish McCallum to star status. Spawned by the first James Bond film, *Dr. No* (1962), it had Ian Fleming's input and contributed to the small-screen spy-mania of the sixties: *The Avengers* (1961–69), *The Saint* (1962–69), *I Spy* (1965–68), *Mission: Impossible* (1966–73), and *The Prisoner* (1967–68), all predated by *Danger*

Man (1960–68), from which Bond's famous self-introduction ("Bond, James Bond") is borrowed. What, one may ask, prompted the successful British director Guy Ritchie in 2015, when relations between Russia and the US were at a nadir, to reprise and revamp the 1960s series in a film with the same title? To what extent does Ritchie's film revise the earlier situation and the symbiosis between the two spies from the 1960s, even as he re-creates that period? How do the Anglophone directors (multiple for TV, Ritchie for the film) represent Kuryakin's Sovietness/Russianness? Does the film reflect the political tensions of the 1960s or of the 2010s—or both—long after the fall of the Berlin Wall? If Ritchie succeeds in capturing the sixties (in the mise-en-scène, sartorial style, dialogue, etc.) more than a half century later, how does his success in doing so correlate to the currently "renewed" Cold War paradigm? These constitute some of the key questions that Goscilo addresses in a comparative, politically contextualized analysis of *The Man from U.N.C.L.E.* on the small and big screens, the former and latter manifestations separated by a half century.

Finally, Lucian Țion's "The Westernization of Stalin: Late Hollywood Readings of Real-Existing Socialism" explores how late Hollywood has mounted a defamatory political campaign against not only the authoritarianism of the former Soviet regime but the entire past of the "socialist bloc." Țion argues that examples like *The Death of Stalin* (2017) and *Comrade Detective* (2017), set in the Soviet Union of the 1950s and socialist Romania of the 1980s, respectively, condemn communist ideology *a posteriori* for the sole purpose of colonizing the postsocialist space with Western notions of "democracy," which purportedly precludes the postsocialist world from fully embracing the values of liberalism. Moreover, Țion claims that the new turn in Hollywood cinema not only represents a false progressive view on behalf of a deceptively "leftist" Hollywood, but also reinstates America's neocolonial film practices vis-à-vis the postcolonial world, as seen in 1950s hits like *The King and I* (1956) and *South Pacific* (1958), to the postsocialist space. This turn represents the beginning of the erasure of the local histories of Russian and Eastern European socialism, subsuming them to a necessarily Western interpretative frame.

Section two, "New Aesthetics of the Old Past," examines the new ways of reimagining Cold War past. Thus, in "The Coldest City: Berlin and the Remapping of Cold War Movie Aesthetics," Ian Scott claims that Cold War aesthetics on TV and film have never been more lauded, taking part of a wider nostalgic visitation upon the 1970s–80s era especially. But this exercise in reminiscence also acts as a contemporary cultural precursor to a newly emergent Cold War, rising up like a phoenix in the secretive, wildly volatile Trump-Putin era of the late 2010s. This aesthetic pretension and the concurrent attention to visual landmarks and ephemeral details have become the calling card of films rekindling the look and feel of those times, as can be seen in Tomas Alfredson's updated adaptation of *Tinker Tailor Soldier Spy* (2011) and Steven Spielberg's *Bridge of Spies* (2015). What has become more apparent, though, Scott claims, is not just the way the Cold War has been historicized in the mode of these movies, but also how in other texts it has increasingly been filtered through the lens of nostalgic pop-culture referents. The locations are not simply backdrops but active signifiers, the characters less archetypes than reassembled studies in cinematic RPGs, the soundtracks no longer somber diegesis but more a mixtape of your favorite hit songs. In *Atomic Blonde* (2017), such aesthetic conceits collide very handily in a bombardment of graphic novel vignettes punctuated by ironic modern dialogue and lashings of violence and sexuality. This essay, therefore, argues that, over the course of the 2010s, from *Tinker Tailor* to *Atomic Blonde*, art as the unconscious face of politics has never been more important. Reminiscence has thus shifted from a mode of nimble historical furnishings to one that contains a jumble of ideological contradictions designed to accentuate—and critique—the reassembled Cold War mentality of the Trump-Putin age.

Dan Ward's "'Your Body Belongs to the State': The Mobilization of the Action Heroine in Service of the State in *Red Sparrow* and *Atomic Blonde*" is an exploration of Russian female spies. Ward examines two examples of recent Cold War films that also constitute part of another increasingly prominent format within popular cinema, the female-centered action thriller. *Atomic Blonde* (2017) is a stylized period piece that depicts a tough, street-smart American undercover agent outmaneuvering and outlasting regressive, misogynist KGB agents (along with their British counterparts) in Berlin. *Red Sparrow* (2018) updates the setting to the present day, but the familiar tropes of Hollywood's imagining of Cold War Russia remain conspicuous: the state is omnipotent and all-controlling, its corrupt officials and security apparatus ruthlessly wielding their repressive power against civilians. In both films, Russian men are portrayed almost without exception as brutal, abusive, and malicious beasts who (we are told by an American character) "all look like toads." One particular area of interest here is not just in the familiar forms of dehumanization invoked to reinforce the inherent othering of the rival nation, but also in how Hollywood interpolates the ostensibly progressive image of the self-reliant female action hero in working to shore up perceptions of institutions such as the CIA (with its long and ongoing record of collusion with some of the most reactionary militant and political groups across the globe). The CIA agents in *Red Sparrow* are dedicated but humane, reacting by turns with courage or empathy when an asset is put in harm's way. They use violence only when necessary, and in defense of others. By contrast, members of the Russian security services revel in torture and murder. While women can and do ascend the ranks of the FSB and GRU, those who do are well aware that a woman's body "belongs to the state," and that she must be willing to use it in the service of her (male) superiors in order to succeed. The essay examines these two films within the context of the broader resurgence of Cold War imagery and ideology in contemporary Hollywood.

Cyndy Hendershot's "*The Shape of Water* and the Cold War Revisited" analyzes Guillermo del Toro's Oscar-winning film and its relation to Cold War nostalgia. According to Hendershot, *The Shape of Water* reimagines Cold War America while paying homage to classic tropes of the 1950s. To specify, the film reimagines the classic horror/SF film for a twenty-first-century audience. While the same pathos for the creature exists as in the original that inspired it—*Creature from the Black Lagoon* (1954)—del Toro adds pointed social commentary that would not have been permitted in Hays Code America. The love story between human and creature is central to the film, but the heroine is not a typical fifties woman. She is a mute janitor possessing unique beauty and intelligence. Also, the film allows for a mythical, but satisfying, ending to their love story, suggesting that the impossibility of this love in the original can now be imagined as possible. Moreover, del Toro reveals once-taboo subjects that the original film could only skirt metaphorically. For example, the heroine's roommate is gay and sympathetic as a character. The film also addresses racial inequality through scenes at the diner where both the gay man and African Americans encounter discrimination. Finally, *The Shape of Water* humanizes the Soviet scientist who sacrifices his life to save the creature from the insidious forces of both the Americans and the Soviets. Thus, the essay explores how *The Shape of Water* pays tribute to *Creature from The Black Lagoon* while serving as a statement and an update for twenty-first-century filmgoers.

The concluding essay in this section, Lori Maguire's "Laughing at the Early Cold War: Communism, the USSR, and the Comedy of *Hail, Caesar!* and *The Death of Stalin*," examines two recent films, both set in the early 1950s, that use black humor to consider two very serious events. Both are based on real events and include among their characters real people or, at least, characters based on real people. The first, *Hail, Caesar!* (2016), directed by the Coen brothers, concerns the second Red Scare in the United States and in particular its infamous attack on Hollywood. It takes place during the filming of the biblical epic *Hail, Caesar! A Tale of the Christ* (a clear reference to the 1959 film *Ben-Hur*, which has the identical subtitle), whose star is kidnapped by a communist cell. The second, *The Death of Stalin* (2017), as its title indicates, follows the events that occurred after the demise of the USSR's leader and the rise of Nikita Khrushchev. Set two years apart (the first in 1951 and the second in 1953), both films use laughter to explore a particularly stressful period in the histories of the respective superpowers. The essay places the films in the context of the 2010s and shows how their darkly humorous re-envisioning of the past, particularly of Cold War tropes, fits into a period of renewed tensions between Russia and the United States.

Section three, "Of Patriotism, Corruption, and Otherness," is devoted to the problem of morality and the representation of otherness and patriotism in recent Cold War films. The section opens with David LaRocca's "Of Mothers and Motherlands: Figurations of Parenting and Patriotism in *The Americans*." Coming to terms with the contemporary moment—defined as it is, in part, by the arrival of chilly winds announcing a new Cold War—our eyes and ears are drawn to distinctive instances of art that may shed light on the cultural and intellectual orientation of the time. Into a landscape with many prominent instances of "Russians on screen," it comes as something of a (pleasant) surprise to discover *The Americans*, an FX series (2013–18) that depicts "the enemy" as a married couple with children who run a small business and live in the suburbs of 1980s Washington, DC. These people may be foreigners or enemies, but they are also spouses, friends, neighbors, bosses, and parents. The question for us, then, is how a show that is squarely focused on the "first" Cold War might have something to say to our current reckoning with the "second" Cold War. LaRocca suggests that *The Americans* provides a deeply human and humane portrait of parents and patriots, who happen to be loyal citizens of the Soviet Union, and in this way orients us to the not-always-clear distinctions between the personal and the political.

In "Conservative Understanding and Nationalist Exclusion: Moral Equivalency as Contested Concept in *Bridge of Spies* and *Tinker Tailor Soldier Spy*," Christian Jimenez focuses on the issue of "moral equivalence" (invented by neoconservatives during the Cold War), which attempts to discredit virtually any criticism of US policy, foreign or domestic, in novels, films, and books, to show how it continues to be utilized today. Jimenez compares *Bridge of Spies* and *Tinker Tailor Soldier Spy* and argues that, far from equating the West and Russia, these films try, repetitiously, to suggest that there is no equivalence whatsoever between these entities, for Russia is continuously framed as some bestial Other without freedom and normality against the essential healthiness, even the life—through the use of bright colors—of Western countries. The essay showcases how the films attempt to contain criticism to only a few selected areas and disallow any other, perhaps genuinely difficult, criticisms of world politics, as represented in the Cold War cinema.

The section proceeds with Thomas J. Cobb's "Unacknowledged Realignment: Representations of US-Russia Relations in Recent American Cinema." Trump's inauguration in January 2017 prompted an ideological reconfiguration in American politics. Collusion with Russia was a political sin attributed to the Democrats at the heights of the Cold War in the McCarthy era of the 1950s and under Reagan in the 1980s. It recently became a millstone around the Republican Party, owing to reports of Russian hacking of Democratic Party emails during the 2016 presidential election. Although Cold War narratives have returned in American cinema, portended by the pre-Trump releases of *Bridge of Spies* (2015) and *Hail, Caesar!* (2016), it is uncertain, Cobb claims, whether Hollywood will address the Trump era's ideological unorthodoxies. *The Shape of Water* (2017) excoriates the social illiberalism and paranoia that blighted early Cold War America. Yet its magical realist narrative avoids critique of the Realpolitik central to Trump's statecraft. It instead adopts a stance of anti-McCarthy liberalism by embracing the Russian Other, averting the liberal antipathy toward modern Russia lampooned by the pro-Trump alt-right. The critically lambasted thriller *Red Sparrow* (2018), which concerns the subject of Russian "sexpionage," also declines to interrogate the recent changes wrought to East-West relations. Despite its storyline possessing affinities with the lurid allegations against Trump posed by the Christopher Steele dossier, Francis Lawrence's film avoids invoking the current state of US-Russia relations and even refuses to reference Vladimir Putin. Evaluating these two disparately received films, Cobb argues that the ideal cinematic representation of Cold War II has yet to arrive and is precluded from doing so because of bewildering new ideological reconfigurations. Concluding with a reflection on the impact of *Black Panther* (2018), a film that considers issues of idealism and realism relevant to US-Russia relations, Cobb posits that allegory might be the most probable method of addressing new international relations dynamics.

Finally, this section, and the book itself, concludes with Donna A. Gessell's "*Red Sparrow*: Cold War Redux and the Treatment of Corruption," which examines *Red Sparrow* as commentary on current US politics. In a time when traditional identity values are at stake, the two current governments of Russia and the US both operate at the expense of the individual. As a "second" Cold War film, *Red Sparrow* acts a mirror, manipulating American fascination with Russia to direct Americans' gaze at themselves. In the process, the film evokes a reevaluation of how Americans maintain traditionally held values, including concepts of duty and patriotism, even if that loyalty demands contesting America's own corruption. Thus, this essay argues that *Red Sparrow* compels its viewers to reevaluate their values in light of how the "new" Cold War is being fought: not conventionally, but on a much more personal level compelling individual choice.

★ ★ ★

The Cold War as such has become the subject of large and continuous scholarly debates. Along with providing meditations on the political aspects of the war, numerous scholars have investigated its particular cultural representations, specifically in film. While the existing books provide detailed analyses of Cold War cinema, none considers the most recent films, some of which deal with the Cold War only briefly, others quite extensively. This collection thus not only examines the most recent representations of the Cold War on screen from cultural, cinematic, and political perspectives, but it significantly broadens the existing scholarship on the Cold War, singling out an important era in the US-Russian relationship—defined here as "Cold War II"—a period that film and television have so promptly responded to. *Cold War II* is thus the first book to scrutinize the renewed tensions between the US and Russia as represented on screen. We hope that along with academics and students working in the fields of Cold War studies, popular culture, war studies, and film studies, the book will appeal to readers interested in the cinematic portrayals of the Cold War, the Soviets/Russians, and Americans caught up in fighting the ideology deemed alien to their country's values, as well as to those who have enjoyed watching the award-winning films of the past few years that have happened to tackle the issue of the Cold War in their plots.

Notes

1. James W. Peterson, *American Foreign Policy: Alliance Politics in a Century of War, 1914-2014* (New York: Bloomsbury, 2014), 43.

2. Cyril Buffet, "Preface: Visual Reflection of the Cold War," in *Cinema in the Cold War: Political Projections*, ed. Cyril Buffet (London: Routledge, 2016), xi.

3. Jonathan Auerbach, "Cold War Films," in *Edinburgh Companion to Twentieth-Century British and American War Literature*, ed. Adam Piette and Mark Rawlinson (Edinburgh: Edinburgh University Press, 2012), 172.

4. Peterson, *American Foreign Policy*, 46-47.

5. Jeffrey A. Engel and Katherine Carté Engel, "Introduction: On Writing the Local within Diplomatic History—Trends, Historiography, Purpose," in *Local Consequences of the Global Cold War*, ed. Jeffrey A. Engel (Washington, DC: Woodrow Wilson Center Press, 2001), 3.

6. Peterson, *American Foreign Policy*, 47-48.

7. Peterson, *American Foreign Policy*, 55-58.

8. Andrew J. Bacevich, *The New American Militarism: How Americans Are Seduced by War* (Oxford: Oxford University Press, 2013), 177-78.

9. Peterson, *American Foreign Policy*, 47.

10. Bryn Upton, *Hollywood and the End of the Cold War: Signs of Cinematic Change* (Lanham, MD: Rowman & Littlefield, 2014), 8.

11. Cynthia Weber, *Imagining America at War: Morality, Politics, and Film* (London: Routledge, 2006), 40.

12. Upton, *Hollywood and the End of the Cold War*, 8.

13. John V. Fleming, *The Anti-Communist Manifestos: Four Books That Shaped the Cold War* (New York: W. W. Norton & Company, 2009), 9, 10, 12.

14. Fleming, *The Anti-Communist Manifestos*, 9.

15. Thomas Doherty, *Cold War, Cool Medium: Television, McCarthyism, and American Culture* (New York: Columbia University Press, 2003), viii.

16. Joseph S. Nye Jr., *Is the American Century Over?* (Cambridge: Polity Press, 2015), 2, 7–8.

17. Nye, *Is the American Century Over?*, 97.

18. Harlow Robinson, *Russians in Hollywood, Hollywood's Russians: Biography of an Image* (Boston: Northeastern University Press, 2007), 3.

19. Tony Shaw, *Hollywood's Cold War* (Edinburgh: Edinburgh University Press, 2007), 11.

20. Daniel J. Leab, "How Red Was My Valley: Hollywood, the Cold War Film, and *I Married a Communist*," *Journal of Contemporary History* 19, no. 1 (1984): 59, https://www.jstor.org/stable/2604255.

21. Tony Shaw and Denise J. Youngblood, *Cinematic Cold War: The American and Soviet Struggle for Hearts and Minds* (Lawrence: University Press of Kansas, 2014), 18–19.

22. Bernard F. Dick, *The Screen Is Red: Hollywood, Communism, and the Cold War* (Jackson: University Press of Mississippi, 2016), 4, 8; Shaw, *Hollywood's Cold War*, 44.

23. See Dick, *The Screen Is Red*, 44–57.

24. See Dick, *The Screen Is Red*, 58–76.

25. See Dick, *The Screen Is Red*, 77–95.

26. See Dick, *The Screen Is Red*, 104–34.

27. Russell E. Shain, "Hollywood's Cold War," *Journal of Popular Film and Television* 3, no. 4 (1974): 334; Cyndy Hendershot, *Anti-Communism and Popular Culture in Mid-Century America* (Jefferson: McFarland, 2003), 18; Cyndy Hendershot, "Anti-Communism and Ambivalence in *Red Planet Mars*, *Invasion USA*, and *The Beast of Yucca Flats*," *Science Fiction Studies* 28 (2001): 246.

28. Shaw, *Hollywood's Cold War*, 1.

29. James Smith, "The MacDonald Discussion Group: A Communist Conspiracy in Britain's Cold War Film and Theatre Industry—or MI5's Honey-Pot?," *Historical Journal of Film, Radio and Television* 35, no. 3 (2015): 454–55.

30. See Dick, *The Screen Is Red*, 192–209.

31. See Dick, *The Screen Is Red*, 210–22.

32. Robinson, *Russians in Hollywood, Hollywood's Russians*, 146.

33. Matthew Sorrento, "The Service Tragicomedy: From Woody Allen to *Full Metal Jacket*," in *A Companion to the War Film*, ed. Douglas A. Cunningham and John C. Nelson (Oxford: Wiley Blackwell, 2016), 75.

34. Tony Shaw, "*The Russians Are Coming! The Russians Are Coming!* (1966): Reconsidering Hollywood's Cold War 'Turn' of the 1960s," *Film History* 22 (2010): 236.

35. Shaw and Youngblood, *Cinematic Cold War*, 36.

36. Michael H. Hunt, *Ideology and U.S. Foreign Policy* (New Haven: Yale University Press, 2009), 3.

37. Andrew J. Falk, *Upstaging the Cold War: American Dissent and Cultural Diplomacy, 1940–1960* (Amherst: University of Massachusetts Press, 2010), 9.

38. Upton, *Hollywood and the End of the Cold War*, 1.

39. Tony Shaw and Sergei Kudryashov, "The Cold War on Film: Then and Now," *Historical Journal of Film, Radio and Television* 36, no. 1 (2016): 1.

40. Buffet, "Preface," xi.

41. J. Hoberman, *An Army of Phantoms: American Movies and the Making of the Cold War* (New York: New Press, 2011), xviii.

42. Peter Biskind, *Seeing Is Believing: How Hollywood Taught Us to Stop Worrying and Love the Fifties* (New York: Henry Hold and Company, 2000), 2.

43. Shaw, *Hollywood's Cold War*, 1; Tony Shaw, *British Cinema and the Cold War: The State, Propaganda and Consensus* (London: I. B. Tauris, 2001), 10.

44. Lori Maguire, introduction to *The Cold War and Entertainment Television* (Newcastle upon Tyne: Cambridge Scholars Publishing, 2016), 1.

45. Maguire, introduction to *The Cold War and Entertainment Television*, 2.

46. Tatiana Prorokova-Konrad, *Docu-Fictions of War: U.S. Interventionism in Film and Literature* (Lincoln: University of Nebraska Press, 2019), 273.

47. Howard Schneiderman, "Introduction to the Transaction Edition: James Truslow Adams and the American Dream," in *The Epic of America* by James Truslow Adams (New Brunswick: Transaction Publishers, 2012), xvi.

48. Allen C. Lynch, "Putin and Trump," *Diplomatic History* 42, no. 4 (2018): 583.

49. Lynch, "Putin and Trump," 584.

50. Lynch, "Putin and Trump," 584.

51. Lynch, "Putin and Trump," 584–85; italics in original.

52. Lynch, "Putin and Trump," 585.

53. Kimberly Marten, "Trump and Putin, Through a Glass Darkly," *Asia Policy* no. 23 (2017): 36, https://doi.org/10.1353/asp.2017.0005; Peter Rutland, "Trump, Putin, and the Future of US-Russian Relations," *Slavic Review* 76, no. S1 (2017): 46.

54. Douglas Kellner, *American Horror Show: Election 2016 and the Ascent of Donald J. Trump* (Rotterdam: Sense Publishers, 2017), 141.

55. Marten, "Trump and Putin," 41.

56. Marten, "Trump and Putin," 40.

57. Rutland, "Trump, Putin, and the Future of US-Russian Relations," 42.

58. Marten, "Trump and Putin," 42.

59. Helena Goscilo, "Russia's Ultimate Celebrity: VVP as VIP *objet d'art*," in *Putin as Celebrity and Cultural Icon*, ed. Helena Goscilo (New York: Routledge, 2013): 6.

60. Kellner, *American Horror Show*, ix, 136, 143.

61. Ian Bremmer, *Superpower: Three Choices for America's Role in the World* (London: Portfolio Penguin, 2015), 1.

62. Rutland, "Trump, Putin, and the Future of US-Russian Relations," 41.

63. Rutland, "Trump, Putin, and the Future of US-Russian Relations," 41; italics in original.

64. Lynch, "Putin and Trump," 585.

65. Dick, *The Screen Is Red*, 6, 250.

66. Upton, *Hollywood and the End of the Cold War*, 1.

67. Upton, *Hollywood and the End of the Cold War*, 1–2; Ronnie D. Lipschutz, *Cold War Fantasies: Film, Fiction, and Foreign Policy* (Lanham, MD: Rowman & Littlefield, 2001), 5.

68. Jeff Smith, *Film Criticism, the Cold War, and the Blacklist: Reading the Hollywood Reds* (Berkeley: University of California Press, 2014), 18; italics in original.

69. Robinson, *Russians in Hollywood, Hollywood's Russians*, 264.

70. Robinson, *Russians in Hollywood, Hollywood's Russians*, 5, 272; Dick, *The Screen Is Red*, 250; Tony Shaw, *Cinematic Terror: A Global History of Terrorism on Film* (London: Bloomsbury, 2015), 2.

PART I
ENDURING CLICHÉS

THE WARM GLOW OF COLD WAR NOSTALGIA

Vesta Silva & Jon Wiebel

> We are likely soon to regret the passing of the Cold War.
> —John Mearsheimer, *The Atlantic*, 1990

> Without the Cold War what's the point of being American?
> —Rabbit Angstrom, *Rabbit at Rest*, John Updike, 1990

> Christ, I miss the Cold War!
> —M, *Casino Royale*, 2006

It seems that almost since the November 1989 day when the Berlin Wall fell, some were missing the global order it symbolized—or at least missing the ways that the Cold War had allowed them to make sense of the world. The appeal of a simplified Cold War story is not difficult to see. From the American perspective, we firmly occupied the role of the "good guys" fighting for freedom and democratic ideals, battling the scourge of communism and tyranny. That such a story bears little resemblance to the moral quagmires and ethical missteps of key Cold War events (think McCarthy, Korea, Vietnam, the Cuban Missile Crisis, etc.) matters less and less as time goes on and Americans become increasingly sure of our romantic retellings of our bipolar past.

As early as 2000, George W. Bush argued, "This is a world that is much more uncertain than the past. In the past we were certain, we were certain it was us versus the Russians in the past."[1] In 2014, James Inhofe, the ranking Republican on the Senate Armed Services Committee remarked, "I look back wistfully at the Cold War. There were two superpowers, they knew what we had, we knew what they had."² These sentiments—that the Cold War was an era of certainty and stability—have gained increased traction in the twenty-first century as we lament a world of rogue states, terrorist cells, suicide bombings, and social media attacks. The enemy we knew (or at least thought we knew) is a comforting image when many contemporary threats seem hard to locate or pin down.

Against the backdrop of new and emergent threats, the second decade of the twenty-first century has seen an explosion of Cold War stories in American films and television series that highlight a nostalgic desire for a return to the more "certain" past referenced by President Bush and Senator Inhofe. But nostalgia should not be thought of simply as a desire to return to some lost time. It is always as much about reconstructing ourselves in the present as it ever is about remembering our past. As Michael Pickering and Emily Keightley argue, nostalgia is "not only a search for ontological security in the past, but also a means for taking one's bearings for the road ahead in the uncertainties of the present."³

In this essay, we look in detail at two recent films, *Bridge of Spies* (2015) and *Atomic Blonde* (2017), in order to explore the specificities of Hollywood Cold War nostalgia in the 2010s. These two films, the first featuring the construction of the Berlin Wall and the second set on the eve of its collapse, reveal the ways in which Hollywood films use nostalgic representations of the Cold War to recapture a feeling of what Tom Engelhardt terms American "victory culture."⁴ Engelhardt suggests that victory culture is a way of combining American military might, moral right, and divine exceptionalism to create a sense of the world in which our wars are all justified and glorious and our victories are all assured. We argue that Cold War nostalgia narratives are a way of resecuring a sense of American exceptionalism and victory in a time of uncertainty and fear. In other words, nostalgic Cold War narratives help reassure contemporary Americans that we are still the good guys (and gals) fighting on the right side to protect the world.

Although other genres of war/conflict films can contribute to a re-creation of victory culture, Cold War narratives are exceptionally well positioned to be effective in generating nostalgic power in the social and political climate of the 2010s. The 2018 Edelman Trust Barometer indicates that only about a third of Americans trust our government "to do what's right," the lowest level ever recorded in the eighteen-year history of the survey.⁵ Unlike nostalgic World War II narratives, Cold War narratives focus on heroic individuals (the spy, the negotiator, etc.) and thus do not require audiences to believe that our military or our leaders are trustworthy or will do the right thing. Our faith is in the clever and strong individual American who stands up not only against the enemy but also, if needed, against our supposed friends and allies who fail to fulfill their part of the mission.

We begin by briefly considering the importance of film as a way of constructing popular understandings of war and conflict. Then we turn to a consideration of the twenty-first-century global political context out of which the new Hollywood Cold War narratives emerge. We then look at nostalgia as a critical frame and apply it to a close reading of the films, considering especially the themes of American exceptionalism and the contrast between East and West.

Hollywood Film and War

Research from a wide array of disciplines has established the influence of cinema and the role of Hollywood in "the production, reproduction, and transformation of everemerging US individual, national, and international subjectivities."[6] While stories continue to circulate about the decline in cinema,[7] theaters are still able to attract millions of viewers each week. Cinema, therefore, remains a critical site where an "understanding of particular events, national identity and relationships to others" is forged and reforged.[8] Of particular interest to this project is the role of film in developing popular understandings of global politics and historical events. Cinema has been, and continues to be, a "space involved in the process of actively forgetting and actively producing history."[9] That process of (re)producing history is far from a neutral form of storytelling. Bracketing for the moment the notion that all storytelling is political insofar as it entails intentional and unintentional expressions of extant systems of power and privilege, it is also the case that Hollywood has a long "tradition of using history for political purposes."[10] Two of those purposes are of particular interest to this project: the maintenance of the culture of victory and Hollywood's contribution to the "cultural Cold War."[11]

In his treatment of American victory culture, Engelhardt notes the function of film in reinforcing victory culture, particularly among the youth of America. Although not the originator of the war story on which victory culture was predicated, Hollywood used America's martial past as a way to reinforce a larger story of progress that served as America's defining mythos. For example, the function of the Western was to reinforce an "unforgettable history" of America's "westward progress to dominance."[12] Hollywood used the logics that subtended the Western to help the public make sense of events in the present. Thus Engelhardt notes that not long after the US entered World War II, "Hollywood's film studios began producing war movies in which . . . a savage, nonwhite enemy ambushed and overwhelmed small groups of outnumbered American soldiers."[13] These films, like the Westerns that preceded them, sought to advance a triumphalist narrative that constituted a critical element of what it meant and means to be American.

In terms of the Cold War, Tony Shaw offers a detailed assessment of the "American film industry's unique contribution to the cultural Cold War."[14] Attending to questions of political economy, Shaw explores how the "relationship between Hollywood's Cold War coverage" and the "US political establishment" and its views on the conflict functioned to influence domestic and global perceptions of the conflict.[15] In his comprehensive survey of Hollywood during the Cold War, Shaw does note moments where Hollywood challenged the dominant narrative advanced through US policy and governing institutions; yet even then Hollywood filmmakers reified and promoted key elements of "Cold War orthodoxy."[16] This relationship has continued beyond the Cold War with Hollywood filmmakers producing films that reinforce dominant ideas about September 11, 2001, and the American fight against global terrorism. Given this history, it is not surprising that Hollywood filmmakers are returning to stories of the Cold War at the very moment policymakers, national security and foreign policy experts, and academics are warning of the existence of a new Cold War. And just as they did in the past, filmmakers in Hollywood are turning to history to speak to contemporary anxieties and insecurities.

America and Conflict in the Twenty-First Century

At the onset of the Global War on Terrorism, President George W. Bush declared to the American public that this war would be "a lengthy campaign, unlike any other we have ever seen,"[17] and in the nearly two decades since, the US has seemingly come no closer to bringing the War on Terror to a successful close. Our experiences in Vietnam taught policymakers that public support for conflicts abroad could be maintained only if interventions met at least one of three specific conditions: (1) they were "short, sharp operations" that demonstrated "decisive use of force," such as the first war in Iraq; (2) they were conducted through the use of proxy forces; or (3) they consisted primarily of air operations, such as those in Kosovo.[18] From the outset, it was recognized that the War on Terror violated these conditions. Indeed, in his joint statement to Congress at the start of the conflict, President Bush cautioned his listeners that the War on Terror would not "be like the war against Iraq" or the "air war above Kosovo" and pledged that the US would deploy "every necessary weapon of war," making it clear that it would not be a war by proxy.[19] It should not be surprising then that many of the critical words and phrases associated with Vietnam, such as *quagmire*, soon became part of the public discourse of the Global War on Terror.[20]

The American public's weariness with the War on Terror is perhaps best exemplified by the growing belief among Americans that our military involvement in Afghanistan was a mistake. While a Gallup poll in October 2001 showed almost universal support for the military intervention in Afghanistan,[21] by 2014 polls showed that roughly half of the American public (48 percent) characterized the intervention as a "mistake."[22] After seventeen years in Afghanistan, fewer than half of the American public (45 percent) believed the US made the "right decision" to use military force in Afghanistan, and nearly half (49 percent) believed that the United States had "mostly failed" in "achieving its goals in Afghanistan."[23]

Sixteen years after President Bush pledged to use whatever military force was necessary to win the War on Terror, President Trump appeared before the nation to discuss his administration's approach to Afghanistan. Even as he acknowledged that the war in Afghanistan was emblematic of Americans' weariness of a "war without victory" and claimed to share "the American people's frustration," President Trump affirmed a commitment to a war with no foreseeable victory, promising that America would "never let up" until the terrorists were "dealt a lasting defeat."[24] Yet a year later, the US Department of Defense concluded that "terrorist and insurgent groups continued to present a formidable challenge to Afghan, U.S., and coalition forces."[25]

Americans' sense that the War on Terror has become a war without much hope of victory is also evidenced by the belief many Americans hold that they are no safer from terrorism today than they were prior to September 11, 2001. This sentiment persists despite the trillions of dollars spent and thousands of lives lost attempting to defeat global terrorism. Since 9/11, any number of factors arguably could have precipitated a decline in public anxiety about the threats posed by global terrorism; however, a study of polling data since 9/11 reveals that although other issues have taken center stage, there has been little change in the "degree to which Americans voice concern" about the danger posed by global terrorism.[26] The study argues that the most plausible explanation for the ongoing anxiety is the characterization of Islamic terrorism as "part of a large and hostile conspiracy that is international in scope and rather spooky."[27] Epitomizing this discourse is a recent report from the RAND Corporation which declares that even as al-Qaeda's ability to launch 9/11-style attacks has been eroded, al-Qaeda is "unquestionably a dangerous organization" that in becoming "more decentralized" relies on "its affiliates and allies" and its ability to "inspire homegrown recruits to carry out terrorist attacks."[28]

Thus, even as the Department of Defense articulates its successes in limiting the capabilities of al-Qaeda, it nonetheless reinforces the very characteristics of Islamic terrorism that bear directly on Americans' ongoing anxiety: In becoming more decentralized and thus harder to locate, terrorism seems more threatening. And as it doubles down on cultivating "do-it-yourself" forms of terrorism, the reach of "Islamic terrorists" becomes ever greater. Given this framing, it is no wonder that more Americans now than in 2003 believe that terrorists have increased their capabilities for launching another major attack on the United States.[29]

The New Cold War

At the same time that Americans grapple with the uncertainties of global terrorism, we are also encountering the re-emergence of Russia as a real or potential enemy. Journalists, former diplomats, and security experts have for years now been warning of a new Cold War. Some of these analysts assert that the actions of Russia and Vladimir Putin have created the context for a new Cold War,[30] while others claim that the post–Cold War policies of the United States are the key factor in the growing hostilities.[31] Both sides, however, agree that once again Russia and the US are on opposite sides in a larger global conflict.

American media institutions have repeatedly characterized the tensions between the United States and Russia in the 2010s as a new Cold War. For example, since early 2013 *The Nation* has published numerous articles by Stephen Cohen warning of the advent of this new Cold War, claiming that it may be even more dangerous than the last and even warning that an armed conflict with Russia is a real possibility. A Nexus search of the *New York Times* and *Washington Post* between October 16, 2015 (the release date for *Bridge of Spies*), and July 28, 2017 (the release date for *Atomic Blonde*), reveals dozens of articles either warning of or describing a new Cold War with Russia. While there are also stories during that time that argue that the tensions between the United States and Russia are not tantamount to a new Cold War, it is nonetheless the case that major news outlets are participating in the circulation of these renewed Cold War narratives.

Perhaps no text exemplifies the new Cold War discourse more than Edward Lucas's *The New Cold War: Putin's Russia and the Threat to the West*. First published in 2008 and updated twice since, *The New Cold War* is targeted not just toward experts, policymakers, or academics. Writing in accessible prose, Lucas seeks to convince a more general readership of the "direct menace that Russia poses, not only to its citizens, but also to outsiders" and to the United States in particular.[32] Acknowledging that many of the factors that defined the Cold War no longer exist, Lucas nonetheless contends that "the rosy sentiments"[33] that followed the end of the Cold War have also disappeared. He argues that while the current situation is not analogous to the original Cold War, a new conflict that seeks to undermine the West is being waged by Russia and is thus best described as a *new* Cold War. Lucas's text was acclaimed by the *Wall Street Journal* as one of the best books of 2008[34] and was positively reviewed by multiple popular press outlets, including *Time* and *Newsweek*. In addition, Lucas appeared on CNN and NPR to discuss the release of the book and the ideas it advances. Well before the release of *Bridge of Spies* and *Atomic Blonde*, discourses extolling the existence of a new Cold War circulated across the American media landscape.

The potential existence of a new Cold War and the global uncertainties of the War on Terror provide a unique context for Hollywood to revisit stories and themes from the original Cold War. We argue that such films do particular cultural work for a public long asked to accept a never-ending war in the Middle East and presented with the specter of an old enemy who may once again be threatening our very existence. In returning to the Cold War, Hollywood is able to construct a nostalgic retelling of a familiar story of American exceptionalism to advance a national narrative of victory that reminds Americans of the need to wage an ideological battle against global terrorism. Nostalgia offers a powerful frame through which to recast the past and make new sense of the present.

Nostalgia and the Twenty-First Century

First used in the seventeenth century by Swiss physician Johannes Hofer, the term *nostalgia* originally referred to an illness—an extreme homesickness characterized by depression, lack of appetite, anxiety, and a host of other physical and psychological symptoms.[35] Over time, the medical usage of the term began to wane, and nostalgia became associated more broadly with individual or societal longing for lost places or times. Scholars have taken up the idea of nostalgia as a useful critical framework for interpreting a wide range of responses to political, social, and economic changes. In this essay, we define nostalgia as a collective spirit of longing for a prior time perceived as better than the present in some crucial way. Not as simple as merely remembering or reminiscing, nostalgia is "a particular way of ordering and interpreting the various ideas, feelings, and associations we experience when thinking of the past,"[36] or "a longing to recapture a mood or spirit of a previous time."[37]

Thus, nostalgia is not and never can be a literal reconstruction of the past. Because nostalgia is always already linked to a particular interpretation of the past, it is necessarily a re-visioning of that past. "The logic of nostalgia dictates that nothing can really be recovered, only re-collected, re-imagined."[38] In one sense, nostalgia simplifies the past in order to make it instantly recognizable and desirable. In film especially, the symbols of the past must be familiar and must connect firmly to the particular emotions or understandings that are part of the dominant reading of the narrative. Feature films do not have much time to explore conflicted signifiers or nuanced expressions of political uncertainty. When the goal is to appeal quickly to a large audience, nostalgic stories "exhaust the past by paring down its heterogeneity for effortless recognition and streamlined exhibition."[39] That is to say, nostalgic stories empty out much of the complexity of the past in order to position it clearly as an object of longing and desire.

However, nostalgia is not necessarily about a literal desire to return to the past—even a commercially romanticized one. When we look at twenty-first-century representations of the Cold War or hear political leaders sigh wistfully about the certainty of a world defined by the possibility of mutually assured destruction, it is important to recognize that part of what nostalgia gives us is the safety to dream about times that we cannot return to. Unlike depictions of other times and conflicts, Cold War narratives allow us to explore tensions and global conflicts with the comfort of knowing that American ideals will come out safely on the other side. Like a particularly good roller coaster, we can experience the anxiety and fear of being at risk without ever entering into any real moral or narrative danger. As David Lowenthal explains, "Few admirers of the past would actually choose to return to it—nostalgia expresses longings for times that are safely, rather than sadly, beyond recall."[40]

Rather than a literal return then, nostalgia gives us a sense of the past as a way of feeling better about the present. Nostalgic audiences do not necessarily think that such filmic representations are true, but truth is not the goal. The goal is recognizability and a recapturing of that which was admirable—particularly in times when such feelings or qualities seem lacking. As Janelle L. Wilson explains, "The head knows that what is being fondly recalled wasn't really that way, but the heart finds comfort in the feeling. Nostalgia realigns cognition and emotion to produce comfort and security."[41]

Hollywood and Cold War Nostalgia

For this analysis, we have chosen two films that, at first glance, have little in common. *Bridge of Spies* (2015) pairs longtime collaborators Steven Spielberg and Tom Hanks in a historical drama based on actual events. The film centers on the story of James Donovan (Tom Hanks), an insurance lawyer tasked with defending captured Soviet spy Rudolf Abel (Mark Rylance) in New York

City in 1957. Despite those around him urging a perfunctory defense, for Donovan, the ideals of American justice and his insistence that "every person matters" mean that Abel deserves his best work.[42] Despite Donovan's efforts, Abel is convicted and sentenced to death, but Donovan successfully argues for the sentence to be commuted to life in prison. Three years after the trial, an American U-2 pilot is captured in East Germany and Donovan is brought in again—this time to go to Berlin to broker a deal to exchange Abel for the pilot, Francis Gary Powers (Austin Stowell).

Based on a 2012 graphic novel, *The Coldest City*, 2017's *Atomic Blonde* is an action film directed by David Leitch, the director of the ultraviolent 2014 film *John Wick*. The story is told from the perspective of MI6 agent Lorraine Broughton (Charlize Theron), who is sent to Berlin to retrieve a stolen document that lists the names of all known Allied spies. Told in a series of flashbacks from her debriefing in London, the film shows Broughton engaging with a host of other characters in Berlin, including MI6 station head David Percival (James McAvoy), rookie French agent Delphine Lasalle (Sofia Boutella), and Russian operative Aleksander Bremovych (Roland Moller) in a complex web of intersecting loyalties, betrayal, and violence.

Bridge of Spies and *Atomic Blonde* differ from each other in many ways and are set nearly thirty years apart, yet what is telling for us is how each film uses similar representations to evoke a strong sense of nostalgia for American exceptionalism. In a world defined by distrust, suspicion, and fear, both films offer audiences a comforting and alluring sense that the best Americans continue to stand up for our principles, that we can reclaim our place as the rightful leaders of the world, that we are powerful, clever, resourceful, and worthy of admiration.

American Identity as Exceptional

The question of what it means to be American is of crucial importance across twenty-first-century Cold War narratives. Part of what can make Cold War nostalgia narratives so compelling in the 2010s is a cultural sense that we have lost that clear identity—or at least lost a clear sense of being the "good guys." Jussi Hanhimäki notes that as we moved further away from the Cold War, "America's unique role as the global guardian of certain important values and freedoms—however self-appointed and contested that role may have been—became progressively less significant. In other words . . . 'being American' just does not mean what it used to mean."[43] Both *Bridge of Spies* and *Atomic Blonde* attempt to capture a sense of what being American used to mean—and thus also open up at least a hope of what it could mean again.

What is particularly interesting about the construction of American identity in *Bridge of Spies* is that it is most explicitly defined by the contrast between "good" and "bad" Americans rather than the contrast between Americans and Russians. Early in the film Donovan is followed and eventually cornered by Agent Hoffman (Scott Shepherd) of the CIA. As the two sit together, Hoffman asks Donovan what the Russian operative, Abel, has said in their defense meetings. Indignant, Donovan refuses to violate attorney-client privilege. Hoffman calls such protections "legal gamesmanship" and condescendingly tells Donovan, "Don't go Boy Scout on me. We don't have a rule book here."[44] Donovan responds by reflecting on their surnames, noting that Hoffman is German, Donovan is Irish. "But what makes us both Americans?" he asks. "Just one thing. One. Only one. The rule book. We call it the Constitution, and we agree to the rules, and that's what makes us Americans. That's all that makes us Americans. So don't tell me there's no rule book, and don't nod at me like that you son of a bitch."[45] Donovan then stands up and walks out, making it very clear that he wants no part of Hoffman's view of an America where the rules are situational and can be changed whenever we believe the circumstances warrant it.

Donovan's principled nature is further highlighted in a pivotal scene after Abel is initially convicted of spying. Abel says that Donovan reminds him of a friend of his father whom Abel met when he was young. At first, the man seemed unremarkable to the young Abel, but then their house was raided by guards who beat Abel's parents. The father's friend, who was present at the time, was also beaten by the guards. Abel explains that every time the guards knocked the man down, he stood back up, again and again. Eventually, Abel says, the beatings stopped in the face of this man's persistence. The guards called him *Stoikiy Muzhik*, which Abel says roughly translates to "Standing Man."[46] Donovan clearly exhibits the same determined qualities—the same sense of standing for his principles. Like the man in the story, Donovan has refused to be beaten down or to give in—even to those within his own country who try to get him to embrace expediency over moral conviction.

In a scene at the Supreme Court, Donovan makes another speech about the nature of American morality that is worth quoting here at length:

> Mister Chief Justice, and may it please the court, the Cold War is not just a phrase. It's not just a figure of speech. Truly, a battle is being fought between two competing views of the world. I contend that Rudolf Ivanovich Abel, Colonel Abel, as he was called even by the men who arrested him, is our foe in that battle. He was treated as a combatant in that war until it no longer suited our government to so treat him. Accordingly, he was not given the protections we give our own citizens. He was subjected to treatment that, however appropriate

for a suspected enemy, was not appropriate for a suspected criminal. I know this man. If the charge is true, he serves a foreign power, but he serves it faithfully. If he is a soldier in the opposing army, he is a good soldier. He has not fled the field of battle to save himself. He has refused to serve his captor. He has refused to betray his cause. He has refused to take the coward's way out. The coward must abandon his dignity before he abandons the field of battle. That, Rudolf Abel will never do. Shouldn't we, by giving him the full benefit of the rights that define our system of government, show this man what we are? Who we are? Is that not the greatest weapon we have in this Cold War? Will we stand by our cause less resolutely than he stands by his?[47]

While the speech begins with the contrast between America and the Soviet Union, it soon becomes clear that the speech is actually an indictment of failing Americans and another attempt to define what American identity should be. Abel is not the threat; his actions reflect honor in a way that should shame the American government and the courts, because he has stayed loyal and true to his cause. America fails not when we give in to competing ideologies but when we fail to faithfully uphold our own. We can think of many contemporary examples—CIA black sites, Guantanamo Bay, drone strikes, etc.—where Donovan's words seem equally applicable. His tone is explicitly chiding of both the court in the film and perhaps the world in 2015, but he also offers a simple way forward out of the moral morass. Uphold the ideals on which the country was founded, live by the principles we claim to hold so dear, and our American moral position is resecured.

As the film moves to Berlin, we see Donovan himself actualize that message in his negotiations with the Soviets and East Germans for the prisoner exchange. Upon learning that East Germany has captured and is holding an American graduate student, Frederic Pryor (Will Rogers), Donovan immediately resolves that the trade must include both the captured U-2 pilot (Powers) and the student. Despite repeated insistence by the CIA that "Powers is the whole ball game," Donovan refuses to back down, eventually issuing an ultimatum to the East Germans that the trade must include Pryor or it will not happen—and they will be responsible to the Soviet Union for the arrangement's failure.[48] Donovan's risky but moral stand pays off, and the trade takes place.

In *Atomic Blonde*, the links to American identity are, at first, less clear. The only character in the film initially identified as American is CIA agent Emmett Kurzfeld (John Goodman), whom Broughton dismisses with a sotto voce mutter of "cocksucker" in an early scene.[49] The characters we do meet, aside from our protagonist, Broughton, are portrayed as variously untrusting and untrustworthy. From the brutal Russian spy Bremovych to the naïve French agent Lasalle and the mercurial and violent British agent Percival, the world of *Atomic Blonde* is populated by a host of less-than-admirable characters. The presumed worst of the bunch is the Russian double agent Satchel, whose true identity is said to be revealed in the missing list of Allied agents that Broughton and Percival are charged with recovering.

Betrayal is the central theme of the story, as Broughton finds there is no one, either in Berlin or back in London, whom she can fully trust. Even the "good guys" are deeply compromised. For example, Percival, the British station head in Berlin, sets up Broughton from the beginning, leaving her to be met by Russian agents upon her arrival in Berlin, planting a bug in her coat to keep track of her conversations, and eventually even killing her lover, Lasalle. He also shoots the East German spy who has the list of agents as Broughton tries to get him into West Berlin. In the final confrontation between Broughton and Percival, Percival describes the work of a spy as "playing this crooked game in this crooked town filled with backstabbers and four-faced liars."[50] Broughton shoots him in the leg, and he reveals that he has seen the list and knows that she is the double agent, Satchel. After confirming that he was the one who betrayed her escape plan to the KGB, which nearly got her killed, Broughton refers to Percival as Satchel, kills him, and retrieves the list.

When next we see her, Broughton is with the Russian Bremovych, and he refers to her as "Comrade Satchel."[51] It is clear that the Russian is now suspicious of Broughton, however, and almost immediately he tries to have his men kill her. Broughton, fighting her way free, reveals that she has been feeding the Russian fake intelligence the entire time and is in fact an American triple agent. Lest anyone in the audience remain unsure after the fight that Broughton is in fact not a KGB double agent, she walks up to a mortally wounded Bremovych, declaring that she never worked for the KGB and that it was Bremovych, and the KGB, who were working for her and, by extension, for American interests: "Before you die I want you to get this through your thick, primitive skull. I never worked for you. You worked for me. Every false intel I gave you, a rip in the Iron Curtain. Every piece of intel you gave me, a bullet in my fucking gun."[52]

Unlike in *Bridge of Spies*, which foregrounds American exceptionalism from the start, *Atomic Blonde* makes us wait—reveling in the weaknesses and faults even of our supposed allies (the British, the French, etc.). The characters of *Atomic Blonde* thus seem to bear little resemblance to those of *Bridge of Spies*, but we argue that, like the nobly portrayed James Donovan, Broughton can function as another iteration of the American hero—a female version of "Standing Man." Given the sins committed by Broughton—for example, she sets up an allied agent as a traitor to protect her cover—it seems like she must be the polar opposite of the man who calls on us to be our better selves. Yet it is not Donovan's commitment to the law that reminds Abel of his friend's father. Rather it is Donovan's act of refusal—the refusal to submit to popular convictions—that leads Abel to characterize Donovan as "Standing Man." This same act of refusal defines Broughton's actions as a triple agent for the CIA. Despite the violence and abuse she suffers throughout the film, the setbacks and betrayals that threaten her mission and her life, Broughton never refuses to get back up and never betrays her true cause.

This idea is highlighted in the final sequence of the film. As Broughton walks across the tarmac toward the plane that will take her home, Queen's song "Under Pressure" plays loudly. The lyrics echo the message of the film: "It's the terror of knowing what the world is about, watching some good friends screaming 'Let me out!'"[53] We may be troubled by Broughton's violence and her acts of deception, but she is redeemed because she remains true to the higher purpose of American interests, battling back the terror to stand for American rightness. Through the actions of both Donovan and Broughton, Americans are firmly repositioned as winners whose steadfast refusal to be beaten—to be "Standing Men" instead—ensures victory over our enemies and superiority over those of our friends who fail to live up to our convictions.

East vs. West: The Berlin Wall

In both films, the backdrop of the Berlin Wall plays a significant role. In *Bridge of Spies*, we see the wall being constructed amid chaotic scenes of anxious German citizens, tanks, and soldiers. Briefing Donovan on the evolving situation, Agent Hoffman warns him to "stay away from the wall," explaining that the East Germans have cleared a line near the wall of buildings to create a "death line." Looking Donovan in the eyes, Hoffman says simply, "Cross it and you'll be shot."[54] On Donovan's initial train ride into the East, he looks out at the wall itself, topped by spirals of razor wire, the death line filled with floodlights, guard towers, and Czech hedgehogs to block vehicles. Snow and a gray sky make the scene almost monochromatic and add to the stark bleakness of the image.

In a particularly pivotal scene later in the film, Donovan is traveling by train back to the West at night, after having been detained by the East Germans. As he looks out at the wall, he sees several young people trying to flee. When they begin boosting one another over the barrier, the staccato sound of machine gun fire erupts and most of them fall dead, amid puffs of smoke and snow. The guards from the tower and on the ground continue firing into the bodies as Donovan and the other train passengers look on in horror. The scene is directly contrasted in the closing moments of the film. Back home in New

York City, Donovan is riding the train into work. Looking out on the streets with a slight smile, he notices a group of kids climbing over the chain-link fences separating the backyards of the small houses. His expression grows more pensive, and the audience is invited to reflect on the significance of that small moment. In America, we are reminded, climbing walls and fences may be mischievous, but it is not fatal.

Atomic Blonde opens with footage of President Ronald Reagan speaking the famous lines, "East and West do not mistrust each other because we are armed. We are armed because we mistrust each other. Mr. Gorbachev, tear down this wall!" The scene cuts to black, and text begins to appear, in the green Terminal font of 1980s computers: "In November 1989, after 28 years, the Berlin Wall came down and the Cold War ended." As the New Order song "Blue Monday" begins to play, a line of what looks like spray paint appears across the text, and red stenciled spray paint letters appear saying, "This is not that story."[55]

While the film is not in fact the story of the fall of the Berlin Wall, that story punctuates the larger spy narrative throughout the film in insistent ways. Whenever Broughton is near a television set in Berlin, the audience is treated to news footage and descriptions of the escalating tensions in Berlin. We are told of police "beating demonstrators with batons," informed that "it is not just new faces that are called for, but perhaps, a complete demolition of the wall," and hear the comment that "one has to ask how long the East German government can hold on."[56] The escalation of Broughton's quest to find the list is mirrored by the escalation of the tensions surrounding the wall.

At one point, Broughton is called to meet with CIA agent Emmett Kurzfeld. The meeting takes place on a small overlook on the Western side of the wall, now aged and covered in graffiti. A light blanket of snow sits atop the barriers and towers. As Broughton comes up to stand beside him, Kurzfeld gazes out at the death line and remarks, "That's quite a view: seventy miles of barbed wire, three hundred ten guard towers, sixty-five anti-vehicle trenches, forty thousand Soviet-trained, heavily armed frontier troops. All that and five thousand GDR citizens still had the brass balls to escape."[57] As in *Bridge of Spies*, the wall is presented here as that which brave and heroic individuals try to cross—it is not a security measure, but a literal barrier to the freedom and ideals of the Western world. The escaping East Germans are admirable from the American perspective: they are risking everything to gain what we already have.

The conception of the wall as the physical barrier between two disparate worlds is a familiar trope of the Cold War. The wall is the physical manifestation of the bipolar conception of the world, reducing the complexities to a simple ideological struggle between two "mutually exclusive ways of life."[58] The West is defined by its relative wealth and safety, while past the barriers and checkpoints, the East is defined by crumbling buildings, lawlessness, and dysfunction. These familiar distinctions are woven throughout both films: Bremovych beats an East German boy to death while the East German police stand guard, Vogel has Donovan detained overnight as a form of petty revenge for his negotiations with the Soviets, and so on.

Both films also use the distinctions between East and West to emphasize the centrality of culture to the Cold War. From family to music, fashion to food, the West is a space of openness, authenticity, and abundance, while the East is a stark place defined by deprivation and government control. Donovan's home life is depicted as a traditional 1950s vision of the warm and loving nuclear family. They are a stark contrast to the unconvincing actors hired to play the "family" of Abel in East Berlin during the negotiations. In his first few moments in East Berlin, Donovan's coat is stolen by a roving gang of East German youth as he tries to walk to his meeting at the embassy. When Schischkin, the KGB head that meets with Donovan at the embassy, comments on his lack of coat, Donovan angrily explains that it was stolen. With a bland look, Schischkin asks guilelessly, "Well, what did you expect? It was from Saks Fifth Avenue, wasn't it?"[59]

In one of the funnier scenes in the film, Donovan returns to West Berlin after spending the night in an East German cell. Instead of going back to the miserable safe house provided by the CIA, he instead goes to the Hilton—where the CIA agents have been staying during the entire operation. The dining room reflects the abundance of the West with white tablecloths, well-dressed clientele, and attentive waitstaff. The contrast is further emphasized when a hungry Donovan orders two large breakfasts—"the Hilton Combo" and "the American Breakfast"—and asks for them all to be brought out as quickly as possible. As he sips his coffee and waits for the food, Agent Hoffman enters. Surprised to see Donovan, Hoffman says he should not be there, and Donovan replies, "Well, sometimes in Germany, you just want a big American breakfast." After learning of a new development in the negotiations, Donovan leaves quickly, just as the waitress fills the table with plates of food. Donovan says to Hoffman, "Oh, I ordered. Enjoy your big American breakfast."[60] Hoffman looks nonplussed at the feast spread before him, a visual expression of wealth and plenty.

In *Atomic Blonde*, musical elements play a key role throughout the film and help highlight the ways that the culture industry is inextricably tied to our understandings of the Cold War. In the scene where Bremovych beats the East German to death, he begins by playing the cassette tape in the captured boy's boombox. The song "99 Luftballons," which tells of a war started by East German pilots firing on balloons that have floated across the Berlin Wall into the East, fills the scene as Bremovych orders the boy to dance. After the boy makes a few half-hearted attempts at breakdancing moves, Bremovych uses the boy's own skateboard to beat him to death. And the final battle against Bremovych and his men, when Broughton is revealed as an American agent, is set to Vladimir Vysotsky's "Capricious Horses," a song likely to be familiar to aficionados of Cold War cinema as it was also featured in a key scene in the 1985 film *White Nights*. Vysotsky's music, often critical of Soviet life, was never accepted by the Communist Party, but many of his songs became underground favorites in the 1970s throughout the Soviet Union. In *White Nights*, Mikhail Baryshnikov's character dances to the raw and emotional "Capricious Horses" as a way of demonstrating to his former girlfriend—whom he had left behind in Russia to defect to the United States—the power of cultural freedom. "You whisper his songs," he says to her accusingly. "I want to scream, like he does. I can't lie anymore."[61] His dance, or rather the cultural freedom it signifies, reduces her to tears.

The playing of "Capricious Horses" helps illustrate the centrality of culture and the culture industries to (re)generating and sustaining belief in the possibility for victory. In *White Nights* it is the stage (dance is the stage for showcasing and challenging the Soviet state), in *Bridge of Spies* it is the family (the harmony of Donovan's heteronormative nuclear family in contrast to Abel's dysfunctional family) and displays of abundance, while in *Atomic Blonde* it is popular music's ability to cross the death line and animate the people who will soon take to the streets to tear down the wall. As they present these homages to culture and the culture industry, *Bridge of Spies* and *Atomic Blonde* influence not just our conception of how the US achieved victory in the Cold War, but how it will achieve victory in the current moment. Since 9/11, global terrorism has been cast as an existential threat to the United States. Both films cast culture and the culture industries as key sites in that Manichean struggle. The struggle may be long and arduous, but we will come out the victor, as Americans have the ultimate weapon: our practices and ideas, which will inspire others, both at home and abroad.

Conclusion: Coming Home

In her analysis of *Saving Private Ryan*, another Steven Spielberg and Tom Hanks collaboration, A. Susan Owen notes that calls to return home to America's mythic past are often vexed by the trauma of Vietnam. When Americans have become disillusioned or turned cynical by political scandals, lies, and fraud, when faith in a unified national identity anchored in America's mythic past has been "so deeply shaken,"[62] how can they heed a call to return home? As the War on Terror has revealed its own moral quagmires and questionable tactics, and as Russia has re-emerged to threaten our elections and our security (as becomes clear from the 2019 Mueller Report), we again find ourselves in a moment of national trauma and uncertainty. Cold War nostalgia films offer audiences a way to return to a sense of home as a site of moral certainty by removing the complexity of global politics and giving us heroes whose idealism and exceptionalism can restore our faith in America. In other words, they offer us a nostalgic vision of home as both safe and victorious.

Indeed, going home is even featured in the films as the ultimate reward for both Donovan and Broughton. *Atomic Blonde* presents this idea simply and directly. As the film is ending, we see Broughton boarding a plane to meet CIA Agent Kurzfeld. As Broughton settles into her seat, the captain's voice comes over the intercom: "Estimated flight time to Langley, eleven hours, thirty-seven minutes. Cleared for takeoff." Kurzfeld says simply, "Let's go home." Broughton heaves a massive sigh of relief and closes her eyes briefly: "That sounds good."[63] And it is clear that there is nothing in the world that she wants more. After all the struggles, betrayals, and encounters that defined her journey from London to Berlin—from British agent, to traitor, to American operative—she is finally granted the opportunity to return to the home that her sacrifices have secured and protected. The home that we as the viewers now occupy.

Bridge of Spies also emphasizes the idea of returning home as the end point of a job well done. When negotiating with Soviet and East German representatives for the release of Pryor and Powers, Donovan is repeatedly characterized as impatient for trying to move the trade along swiftly. When asked why he is in such a hurry, he states wearily, "Because I have a cold, I don't live in Berlin, and I want to go home."[64] Amid chaotic, dreary, uncomfortable, and at times even lawless conditions, Donovan simply has one desire—the safety and comfort of home. Yet the desire to return home never becomes an excuse for not getting both Powers and Pryor. When the moment of exchange finally arrives, it is only Powers that is initially presented. The CIA operatives are willing to make the unilateral exchange, but Donovan insists that they wait until Pryor is freed as well. Hoffman urges Abel to cross the bridge and make the exchange, but Abel asks Donovan about his hesitation. Donovan explains that they are waiting to get word of another man's release and tells Hoffman, "We just have to stand here, show them we won't [give in]." Abel reiterates his designation of Donovan as *Stoikiy Muzhik* and declares that he will wait—will stand with Donovan until the job is done.[65] In a few moments, the call confirming Pryor's release comes through and Donovan watches as Abel crosses the bridge to rejoin his countrymen.

On the plane flying back to the US, the captured pilot, Powers, tries to explain to Donovan that he gave the Soviets no information. Donovan cuts him off and says simply, "It doesn't matter. It doesn't matter what people think. You know what you did."[66] The message is clear: Do what is right, because that is what it means to be American. When Donovan finally reaches his house, he pauses outside and his wife, Mary, comes out to greet him. After an embrace and a brief exchange, Donovan asks about his son. Mary replies, "He's home. Carol's home. Peggy's home. Everyone's home."[67] We are invited here to be part of the *everyone*—we can see ourselves at home again in a secure and desirable America.

These films offer audiences a way to reestablish a sense of themselves as righteous and strong and to fight back against the uncertainty and fear of the War on Terror and the new Cold War. In his review of *Bridge of Spies* for the film podcast *Blank Check*, Griffin Newman states passionately, "Now more than ever, we need movies like this. . . . I need movies about how good people can be."[68] Now, more than ever, that is, we need to know how good we as Americans can be. And for a brief moment as we watch these films our nostalgic longing for the surety that Americans are morally right and ultimately victorious is fulfilled, at least until the credits stop rolling.

Notes

1. Jacob Weisberg, "Bush in His Own Words," *The Guardian*, November 3, 2000, https://www.theguardian.com/world/2000/nov/04/uselections2000.usa5.

2. Josh Rogin, "Top Republicans Call for Return to Cold War," *The Daily Beast*, February 23, 2014, https://www.thedailybeast.com/top-republicans-call-for-return-to-cold-war.

3. Michael Pickering and Emily Keightley, "The Modalities of Nostalgia," *Current Sociology* 54, no. 6 (2006): 921.

4. Tom Engelhardt, *The End of Victory Culture: Cold War America and the Disillusioning of a Generation*, 2nd ed. (Amherst: University of Massachusetts Press, 2007).

5. Uri Friedman, "Trust Is Collapsing in America," *The Atlantic*, January 21, 2018, https://www.theatlantic.com/international/archive/2018/01/trust-trump-america-world/550964.

6. Cynthia Weber, *Imagining America at War: Morality, Politics, and Film* (New York: Routledge, 2006), 4.

7. Robert Elder, "Movie Theater Attendance Is Declining as Cord Cutting Becomes More Popular," *Business Insider*, September 7, 2016, https://www.businessinsider.com/movie-theater-attendance-is-declining-as-cord-cutting-becomes-more-popular-2016-9; Ian Westbrook, "Are We Falling Out of Love with the Cinema?," *BBC News*, September 6, 2017, https://www.bbc.com/news/business-41161056.

8. Klaus Dodds, "Review Article: Hollywood and the Popular Geopolitics of the War on Terror," *Third World Quarterly* 29, no. 8 (2008): 1621, https://www.jstor.org/stable/20455133.

9. Mark J. Lacy, "War, Cinema, and Moral Anxiety," *Alternatives: Global, Local, and Political* 28, no. 5 (2003): 614, https://www.jstor.org/stable/40645126.

10. Tony Shaw, *Hollywood's Cold War* (Edinburgh: Edinburgh University Press, 2007), 112.

11. Shaw, *Hollywood's Cold War*.

12. Engelhardt, *The End of Victory Culture*, 4.
13. Englehardt, *The End of Victory Culture*, 4.
14. Shaw, *Hollywood's Cold War*, 5.
15. Shaw, *Hollywood's Cold War*, 2.
16. Shaw, *Hollywood's Cold War*, 65.
17. George W. Bush, "Text: President Bush Addresses the Nation," *Washington Post*, September 20, 2001, http://www.washingtonpost.com/wp-srv/nation/specials/attacked/transcripts/bushaddress_092001.html.
18. David Ryan, "'Vietnam,' Victory Culture and Iraq: Struggling with Lessons, Constraints and Credibility from Saigon to Falluja," in *Vietnam in Iraq: Tactics Lessons, Legacies and Ghosts*, ed. John Dumbrell and David Ryan (New York: Routledge, 2007), 130.
19. Bush, "Text: President Bush Addresses the Nation."
20. Ryan, "'Vietnam,' Victory Culture and Iraq."
21. David W. Moore, "Support for War on Terrorism Rivals Support for WWII," Gallup, October 3, 2001, https://news.gallup.com/poll/4954/support-war-terrorism-rivals-support-wwii.aspx.
22. Baxter Oliphant, "After 17 Years of War in Afghanistan, More Say U.S. Has Failed than Succeeded in Achieving Its Goals," Pew Research Center, October 5, 2018, http://www.pewresearch.org/fact-tank/2018/10/05/after-17-years-of-war-in-afghanistan-more-say-u-s-has-failed-than-succeeded-in-achieving-its-goals/.
23. Oliphant, "After 17 Years of War in Afghanistan."
24. Donald J. Trump, "Remarks by President Trump on the Strategy in Afghanistan and South Asia," WhiteHouse.gov (website), August 21, 2017, https://www.whitehouse.gov/briefings-statements/remarks-president-trump-strategy-afghanistan-south-asia/.
25. Department of Defense, *Enhancing Security and Stability in Afghanistan*, June 2018, https://media.defense.gov/2018/Jul/03/2001938620/-1/-1/1/1225-REPORT-JUNE-2018-FINAL-UNCLASS-BASE.PDF/.
26. John Mueller and Mark G. Stewart, *Public Opinion and Counterterrorism Policy* (Washington, DC: CATO Institute, 2018).
27. Mueller and Stewart, *Public Opinion and Counterterrorism Policy*, 19.
28. Brian Michael Jenkins, Andrew Liepman, and Henry H. Willis, *Identifying Enemies among Us*, (Washington, DC: RAND Corporation, 2014), 3, https://www.rand.org/pubs/conf_proceedings/CF317.html.
29. Mueller and Stewart, *Public Opinion and Counterterrorism Policy*, 33.
30. Edward Lucas, *The New Cold War: Putin's Russia and the Threat to the West* (New York: Palgrave Macmillan, 2009); David E. McNabb, *Vladimir Putin and Russia's Imperial Revival* (Boca Raton, FL: CRC Press, 2016).
31. Stephen Cohen, *War with Russia? From Putin and Ukraine to Trump and Russiagate* (New York: Hot Books, 2019); Jeremy Kuzmarov and John Marciano, *The Russians Are Coming Again: The First Cold War as Tragedy, the Second as Farce* (New York: Month Review Press, 2018).
32. Lucas, *The New Cold War*, 2.
33. Lucas, *The New Cold War*, 6.
34. Mark Lasswell, "A Shelf of Standouts," *Wall Street Journal*, December 26, 2008, https://www.wsj.com/articles/SB123005247899530357.
35. Pickering and Keightley, "The Modalities of Nostalgia."
36. Kimberly K. Smith, "Mere Nostalgia: Notes on a Progressive Paratheory," *Rhetoric & Public Affairs* 3, no. 4 (Winter 2000): 509.

37. Janelle L. Wilson, *Nostalgia: Sanctuary of Meaning* (Minneapolis: University of Minnesota Press, 2014), 26, https://conservancy.umn.edu/bitstream/handle/11299/189216/Nostalgia_fulltext.pdf?sequence=1.

38. S. D. Chrostowska, "Consumed by Nostalgia?," *SubStance* 39, no. 2 (2010): 54.

39. Chrostowska, "Consumed by Nostalgia?," 54.

40. David Lowenthal, "Nostalgia Tells It Like It Wasn't," in *The Imagined Past: History and Nostalgia*, ed. M. Chase and C. Shaw (Manchester: Manchester University Press, 1989), 28.

41. Wilson, *Nostalgia*, 25.

42. Steven Spielberg, *Bridge of Spies* (Los Angeles: DreamWorks Pictures, 2015).

43. Jussi M. Hanhimäki, "The (Really) Good War? Cold War Nostalgia and American Foreign Policy," *Cold War History* 14, no. 4 (2014): 681.

44. Spielberg, *Bridge of Spies*.

45. Spielberg, *Bridge of Spies*.

46. Spielberg, *Bridge of Spies*.

47. Spielberg, *Bridge of Spies*.

48. Spielberg, *Bridge of Spies*.

49. David Leitch, *Atomic Blonde* (Los Angeles: Focus Features, 2017).

50. Leitch, *Atomic Blonde*.

51. Leitch, *Atomic Blonde*.

52. Leitch, *Atomic Blonde*.

53. Leitch, *Atomic Blonde*.

54. Spielberg, *Bridge of Spies*.

55. Leitch, *Atomic Blonde*.

56. Leitch, *Atomic Blonde*.

57. Leitch, *Atomic Blonde*.

58. Shaw, *Hollywood's Cold War*, 11.

59. Spielberg, *Bridge of Spies*.

60. Spielberg, *Bridge of Spies*.

61. Taylor Hackford, *White Nights* (Los Angeles: Columbia Pictures, 1985).

62. A. Susan Owen, "Memory, War, and American Identity: *Saving Private Ryan* as Cinematic Jeremiad," *Critical Studies in Media Communication* 19, no. 3 (2002): 250.

63. Leitch, *Atomic Blonde*.

64. Spielberg, *Bridge of Spies*.

65. Spielberg, *Bridge of Spies*.

66. Spielberg, *Bridge of Spies*.

67. Spielberg, *Bridge of Spies*.

68. Griffin Newman and David Sims, "*Bridge of Spies*," May, 13 2017, in *Blank Check with Griffin and David*, podcast, produced by Ben Hosley.

BIG REWARDS FOR THE SMALL SCREEN
The Man from U.N.C.L.E. during Both Cold Wars

Helena Goscilo

The only thing that will redeem mankind is cooperation.
—Bertrand Russell

I have no spy stories to tell, because I saw no spies. Nor did I understand, at that time, any opposition between American and Russian national interest.
—Elia Kazan

Shifting Cooperation from Space to Screen

In a speech at the UN General Assembly on September 30, 1963, President John F. Kennedy proposed that the US and the USSR adopt a joint expedition to the moon. "Why," he queried, "should man's first flight to the moon be a matter of national competition?"[1] This ostensibly affable overture, one should note, came two years after Yuri Gagarin's momentous journey into space (April 1961), a year after the Cuban Missile Crisis (October 1962), and just three months after Valentina Tereshkova's historic space flight (June 1963)—hardly insignificant considerations, though unspoken in his proposition. Kennedy was assassinated shortly afterward (November 22, 1963), and despite Soviet foreign minister Andrei Gromyko's praise for his speech, the space alliance never eventuated. But Kennedy's suggestion, marrying canniness with purported cordiality toward the Soviet Union, adumbrated the appearance of a highly successful, pioneering, and, for that time, venturesome American TV series that soon followed: NBC's *The Man from U.N.C.L.E.* (1964-68).[2]

The series' scenarios hinged on the cooperation of the two superpowers as an indomitable spy weapon against an endless barrage of international enemies. It featured covert operations that paired the cool, sophisticated American, Napoleon Solo (Robert Vaughn), with his enigmatic, intellectual Soviet counterpart, Illya Kuryakin (David McCallum). According to an interview with Vaughn, "the show was intended to be James Bond for television"—in its initial stages, too obviously so.[3] Transparently spawned by the first James Bond film, *Dr. No* (1962), the show bore unmistakable traces of Fleming's fingerprints and, after undergoing modification, became a part of the small-screen spy-mania of the sixties: *The Avengers* (1961-69), *The Saint* (1962-69), *I Spy* (1965-68), *Mission: Impossible* (1966-73), and *The Prisoner* (1967-68), all predated by *Danger Man* (1960-68), from which Bond's legendary self-introduction ("Bond, James Bond") is borrowed.[4] *The Avengers* (reprised as a film in 2012), *The Saint* (also rebooted for the big screen in 1997), *The Prisoner*, and *Danger Man* were British and starred, respectively, Patrick Macnee and Diana Rigg, Roger Moore (who inherited the role of James Bond from Sean Connery), and Patrick McGoohan (who was in both *The Prisoner* and *Danger Man*).[5] Their American analogues included *I Spy* (1965-68), which returned in 2002 as a pseudocomic movie with the same title; *Mission: Impossible* (1966-73), transformed into a glut of lucrative Tom Cruise films starting in 1996; and half a dozen less memorable and short-lived series, including the nerveless spinoff *The Girl from U.N.C.L.E.* (1966-67). Sixties TV series, not unlike comics, proved fertile ground for movies of the nineties and the twenty-first century—an era of fettered imagination and parasitical practices that mined the small screen's past triumphs in hopes of maximizing profit even as the second Cold War loomed and bloomed.[6] And *The Man from U.N.C.L.E.* participated in this trend.

Predictabilities and Surprises in the TV Version of *The Man from U.N.C.L.E.*

Unquestionably the most original aspect of the TV series *The Man from U.N.C.L.E.*—what one commentator called "a casting that went against Cold War expectations"[7]—was the audacious concept of an American and a Soviet as colleagues in an international, New York–based, secret counterespionage and law-enforcement agency who were entrusted with the globe-trotting task of repeatedly battling murderous enemies of nothing less than world peace.[8] Academic Cold War specialists such as Michael Kackman tend to ignore the bold originality of such a concept and its implications, but after the stridently anti-Soviet 1950s, producers Norman Felton and Sam Rolfe took considerable risk in selecting a Soviet agent as a member of such an organization.[9] Markedly departing from 1950s anticommunist propaganda films such as *My Son John* (1952), *Jet Pilot* (1957), and *Red Nightmare* (1957), the series differed in its attitude "toward the Soviet Union, the threat of domestic espionage, and the dangers of nuclear war," for the show "put style and process ahead of political harangue."[10] Whereas Sean Connery's Bond constantly came up against SPECTRE (SPecial Executive for Counterintelligence, Terrorism, Revenge and Extortion), the intrepid, gadget-blessed duo from U.N.C.L.E. (United Network Command for Law and Enforcement) combatted THRUSH, a hazily defined entity that shared SPECTRE's ambition for worldwide domination at any cost. Significantly, THRUSH was never specifically identified with the USSR or any other country, and its representatives spanned a broad range of vicious, unprincipled individuals across the globe.

To track the development of the series is instructive, for it illustrates the decisive influence of audiences on television programming. Originally the show focused exclusively on one protagonist—the American agent, extravagantly dubbed Napoleon Solo by Fleming and clearly conceived as a clone of Bond. Far from a common name, *Napoleon* ineluctably evokes the military hero who conquered most of Western Europe in the early nineteenth century, while the surname *Solo*, later borrowed for the protagonist in George Lucas's *Star Wars* (1977), suggests the singlehandedness of his fight against evildoers through derring-do. The subsequent decision to give Solo a partner bred certain illogicalities in the retention of his name and the actual title of the series, for now there were two men from U.N.C.L.E. Whereas choice of name obviously was intended to glamorize Solo's image, that of Illya Kuryakin for his Soviet partner carried no readily recognizable cultural associations—a consequence either of the early intention to subordinate him to Solo or of the executives' ignorance of Russian.[11]

Interestingly, contrary to many critics' misapprehension of Kuryakin as Russian, he was supposedly a Ukrainian raised in Kiev—a distinction of which the show's creators seemed unaware, for at that time the West automatically equated *Soviet* with *Russian*. In one of the several inconsistencies on the show, though identified as having spent his childhood in Kiev, Kuryakin replies in the affirmative when asked whether he is Russian ("The Shark Affair," series 1, episode 4).[12] Since McCallum's afterthought character was extremely sketchy at the outset, prompting him famously to limn his own persona, it is not impossible that the contradiction was intentional, calculated to emphasize his inscrutability—like that of Russia, famously defined by Winston Churchill in 1939 as "a riddle, wrapped in a mystery, inside an enigma."[13] Unknowability, of course, invites speculation, thereby making Kuryakin's personality endlessly alluring for American audiences.[14] Identifying the Slavic traits in his persona would present a challenge to anyone, however, for though "Russian" and therefore exotic, within the series he seemed little different from "one of us," to quote Joseph Conrad's Marlow. During one episode, upon watching a luxurious estate party with self-indulgent, rich guests, he remarks, "Suddenly I feel very Russian," but notably, the participants in that conclave are in collusion with the THRUSH villain ("The Love Affair," series 1, episode 26), so an average American viewer might have shared his alienation. By not endowing him with the clichéd Slavic traits of irrationalism, drunkenness, and unchecked passion, the series operated both sides of the street, sustaining an aura of mystery by withholding information or presenting contradictory facts about him while not stigmatizing him as a "typical Soviet."

Indeed, the text on the forty-one-disk DVD box set promotes the two young leads in revealing terms: Solo as "suave, seductive and trained to kill," Kuryakin as "mysterious, calculating and deadly efficient."[15] "Suave and seductive" translated in practice to knee-jerk promiscuous, while "mysterious and calculating" delineated a rational and dispassionate Soviet fully capable of keeping up with his American partner in their unlikely daredevil escapades. Intended to pique viewers' interest—perhaps especially that of young ones—the blurb notably omits the significant presence of their superior, the avuncular executive officer Alexander Waverly, played by Leo G. Carroll, an experienced British stage and screen actor recognized for his roles in two other series, six Hitchcock films, and numerous other movies. While lending the show gravitas, Carroll, in his seventies at the time of filming, would not attract a wide following, owing to his age and the brevity of his customarily nonaction appearances or his infrequent deus ex machina arrivals with armed agents at the conclusion of several episodes to rescue his two apparently favorite underlings.[16]

The Actor or the Action?

Viewers of the originally black-and-white series quickly proved beguiled less by Solo than by the polymath Kuryakin, or at least by McCallum in the role of the Soviet agent.[17] Doubtless, their response to the Scotsman's self-contained, largely unsmiling demeanor ("mysterious"), youthful looks, and blonde locks (which anticipated the mop-top haircut popularized by the Beatles), accounted for the series transforming his career from that of a relative unknown to a wildly popular turtlenecked sex symbol.[18] Reportedly, he "received more fan mail than any actor in the history of MGM, the studio that produced 'U.N.C.L.E.'"[19] The words of one ardent fan urging her friend to watch the show summarized a female teenager's reaction to McCallum in the role: "Ya gotta see this show, *The Man from U.N.C.L.E.* Especially Illya—he's so cute."[20] That perception apparently was shared by enthralled thousands. Even before the second season got underway, as both Vaughn and McCallum toured the country in an advertising blitz, the series was a spectacular success, "merchandised to the hilt. Toy U.N.C.L.E. guns and cars were big hits. There were U.N.C.L.E. dolls, board games, comic books, magazines, paperback novels, and record albums."[21] Tellingly, audience preference induced the series' creators to equalize the relationship between the two secret agents—as I discuss below.

According to a journalist who confessed to being addicted to the show in her teens, "Many U.N.C.L.E. fans developed an interest in Russian culture as a result of their exposure to the character of Illya Kuryakin and ended up studying Russian language and literature. One wonders what beneficial effect Kuryakin had in softening American attitudes towards people from the Soviet Union in the Cold War era."[22] One must continue to wonder, it seems, for no scholarship on that question exists. Unexpectedly for the show's masterminds, Vaughn as Solo elicited considerably less enthusiasm and, in some cases, even prompted reactions bordering on revulsion. At least one critic found him "lizardy and vaguely epicene," with "a slightly nasal voice and ever-present smirk. The overall effect," in his view, "was one of effete chilliness."[23] Once Kuryakin was elevated to co-star status, however, all commentators found the chemistry between the two actors a key selling point for the series. The program also benefited from its peppering of cultural allusions, usually emanating from Kuryakin, which probably led some viewers to suppose that they were part of an educated audience—indeed, college students proved effective advertisers of the series as it progressed.[24] As the more intellectual enforcement agent to Solo's lubricious action man, Kuryakin possessed recondite knowledge of various cultures and supposedly had an MA from the Sorbonne as well as a PhD in quantum physics from Cambridge University. The show featured not only cinematic intertextuality but also quotations from Shakespeare, Andrew Marvell, Robert Browning, and Mozart's *Don Giovanni*, as well as references to a famous chess gambit, classical music (Bach, for example),[25] the painters Perugini and Correggio, and other high-culture sources—hardly commonplace in 1960s (and subsequent) popular series. Though these references may have bypassed the majority of viewers, their inclusion in *The Man from U.N.C.L.E.* certainly sustained the impression of an "intelligent" spy series—thus a cut above average.[26] And the ironic tone of the program, which Rolfe, the mastermind behind the series, deemed inseparable from its overall identity, buttressed that impression and the aura of sophistication until the third season, when slapstick humor primitivized the show, ultimately resulting in its demise.[27]

The Soviet Buddy

The principle of contrast operates as the indispensable device not only of comedy duos but also of buddy films and TV programs, as demonstrated by Laurel and Hardy, Abbott and Costello, *Butch Cassidy and the Sundance Kid* (1969), *Thelma and Louise* (1991), *Route 66* (1998), *I Spy*, *Starsky and Hutch* (2004), and numerous other examples. Casting two physically and temperamentally dissimilar stars as antithetical personae promises dynamic dialogue and doubles the likelihood of attracting audiences. Unlike comedy, which opts for short and fat alongside tall and thin, the buddy genre juxtaposes blonde and brunette, cautious and impulsive, impassive and emotional, formal and casual, and so forth, with various degrees of competition and playfulness inflecting what is fundamentally a mutually supportive relationship. *The Man from U.N.C.L.E.* was no exception to this paradigm. From the outset the Nordic-looking Kuryakin was prudent, sober, and thoughtful, preferred informal clothing, and manifested indifference to women, not unlike his predecessor Danger Man. Dark-haired and dark-eyed Solo always seemed to enjoy a private joke, favored formal wear, smiled incessantly, leered at and bedded (off screen) practically every woman he met, including the ultraglamorous THRUSH agent Angelique ("The Deadly Game Affair," season 1, episode 5). Whereas Solo conducted sequential, consummated romances with countless women in the series, Kuryakin's fantasized romance was with the female members of the audience, many of whom reportedly lodged outraged protests when he actually kissed a woman ("The Bow Wow Affair," series 1, episode 20)—the sole instance of such an "unpardonable" act on his part, since alienating a sizable percentage of the audience made no financial sense.[28] Audience reaction thus functioned not only as a belated guarantee of Kuryakin's equal prominence in the series, but also as censorship of the Soviet agent's sexual conduct; and, fascinatingly, that censorship coincided with Soviet standards of on-screen morality for its own favorite secret agent, though for different reasons.[29] Kuryakin's lack of interest in women, however, proved insufficient to endear him or the series to the Soviet Union, which decried Kuryakin as "bloodthirsty" and condemned the program as capitalistic and materialistic.[30]

Contrary to political expectations in light of Soviet-American hostility during the sixties, the series had the two focal protagonists alternate in repeatedly rescuing each other and exchanging even-handed banter. Their jesting repartee and ironic closing words of thanks to nonexistent agencies, their amusing on-screen announcements of changes in scheduling within the series, and their apostrophes to the audience and other forms of fourth-wall elimination led some commentators to characterize the show as parodic or even campy. Such an opinion, however, while certainly applicable to the disastrous third season, must overlook the first two, in which humor was ironic and measured, but never tipped over into camp. Moreover, unlike in propagandistic films of the 1950s, American one-upmanship did not rear its antagonistic head. The show never directed criticism or suspicion at Kuryakin's Soviet identity, even when he was unexpectedly recalled to the Soviet Union to avert a potential agricultural disaster owing to a destructive missile ("The Neptune Affair," series 1, episode 11)—though Khrushchev's ill-judged initiative to cultivate corn in the Soviet Union during the fifties would have been an easy target of ridicule.[31] Tellingly, though the episode opens with a brief glimpse of Kuryakin in a military uniform in the fictitious town of Orbesk observing the effects of the deadly weapon, it is Solo who solves the problem (from California!), while his Russian counterpart disappears for much of the plot.

Secondly, McCallum's accent was neither overly strong nor geographically specific—hardly a handicap, for it did not project a disaffecting foreign identity, but a vague exoticism that demonstrably engaged at least the female contingent of viewers.[32] And Kuryakin's advanced education in France and England could account convincingly for the nature of that accent. Furthermore, his moral values may have appeared more admirable than Solo's, for whereas Solo teased Kuryakin randomly, the latter was more apt to voice criticism of his partner's fatuous, rampant pursuit of women (see, for example, his disgust at the conclusion of "The Ultimate Computer Affair," series 2, episode 3). In fact, some viewers likely shared Kuryakin's fastidious disapproval of Solo's lack of discrimination in affairs of the flesh. If the series cast Solo in the familiar Bond mode, Kuryakin had no predecessors—his image as a cool-headed, celibate, Soviet partner was sui generis, and the originality of his persona, no doubt, partially explained his popularity with viewers.

Anyone anticipating that an American series during the official Cold War would depict a Russian agent as inferior to his domestic counterpart would be disappointed by *The Man from U.N.C.L.E.* Very rarely and ambiguously did Kuryakin seem the lesser of the two professional partners. Whatever nation-based competition existed in the series was occasional and far from clear-cut. It is possible to read Kuryakin's more frequent absences from episodes than Solo's as a subtle indicator of Solo's supremacy only if one ignores the slightness of that discrepancy, which is concentrated in the initial narratives, for McCallum originally was issued only a partial contract.[33] Additionally, whereas Solo never lost his aura of smug superiority, Kuryakin's liking for food, about which Solo commented sardonically, was exaggerated for the sake of humor ("The Shark Affair," series 1, episode 4), but that taste could potentially win over some food enthusiasts in the audience, especially given McCallum's lean physique, which exempted him from "fat people" humor. What lent Kuryakin a special distinction, in fact, was his facility in donning sundry ethnic disguises that enabled him to infiltrate, undetected, an array of societies and organizations, masquerading as an Arab, a Balkan intelligence officer, a Mongolian warlord, and so forth—disguises that further minimized his Sovietness.[34] In short, mainly as a consequence of McCallum's vociferous fans, the show—intent on retaining the broadest possible viewership—proved surprisingly nonpartisan in its treatment of the dynamic duo, apart from the fact that in the early episodes Solo introduced himself to the viewer first, while Kuryakin followed before passing the baton to Waverly—a formula quickly abandoned.

Ultimately, the series elevated both Vaughn and McCallum to star status, and though McCallum never recaptured the hysterical adulation of Kuryakin, he became forever identified with that role. When in 1965 he hosted NBC's teen music variety show *Hullabaloo*, he did so as Illya Kuryakin, not David McCallum.[35] More remarkably, in 1966 the American government had McCallum (the program's Soviet spy!) endorse American savings bonds, complete with his photograph in the advertisement. Titled "A message from U.N.C.L.E. (UNCLE SAM, that is)," the ad labeled him the "enigmatic agent McCallum."[36] Even a half century later, audiences old enough to have watched *The Man from U.N.C.L.E.* have written fan messages inspired by his Kuryakin years to the now 85-year-old McCallum in the role of the coroner Dr. Donald "Ducky" Mallard in the police procedural *NCIS* (2003–). And in an extraordinary moment *NCIS* itself broke down the fourth wall by referencing his earlier incarnation as Illya Kuryakin.[37]

Live and Let Die: *The Return of the Man from U.N.C.L.E.: The Fifteen Years Later Affair*

Perhaps owing to the rose-tinted perspective of nostalgia, many years later everyone who had participated in the sixties TV series, from the two major actors to the professionals behind the scenes, unanimously recalled the experience with uncommon affection.[38] Such sunny recollections prompted a follow-up film titled *The Return of the Man from U.N.C.L.E.: The Fifteen Years Later Affair* (1983), which reunited Vaughn and McCallum. The eight *U.N.C.L.E.* feature films released during the 1960s simultaneously with the series simply had been expanded episodes of the TV show. In contrast, the new film, produced and scripted by Michael Sloan and directed by the British Ray Austin, opted for "originality." Without input from the original screenwriter, Sam Rolfe, whose fertile imagination had accounted for much of the show's popularity, it failed miserably on all fronts.

Indeed, the strengths of the series are notably absent: the plot is tedious and sluggish; the sets are cheap and unconvincing; the blocking borders on the amateurish; the dialogue is deficient in wit; the acting of secondary characters is feeble; and the interaction between the two agents, so crucial to the success of the original, is minimal, for after their reunion they essentially go their separate ways. Moreover, the retired duo's post–U.N.C.L.E. jobs—computer salesman for Solo and successful fashion designer for Kuryakin—are little short of ludicrous. Plus, the abrupt presence during a humdrum car chase in Las Vegas of the most embarrassingly inept Bond—a tuxedoed George Lazenby—in a car with the license plate JB, signals nothing less than desperation on the director's part. Above all, the competition of the two Bond big-screen films that year (1983), Roger Moore in John Glen's *Octopussy* and Sean Connery in Guy Hamilton's *Never Say Never Again*, which worldwide grossed $119.6 million and $138 million, respectively, simply buried Sloan's effort. Paul Mavis, who had praised the "charm," "sharp, amusing dialogue," and "witty, continental flair of the writing" in the first two seasons of the TV series,[39] justly deplored the remake as a "limp, unfocused comeback," with a "mediocre" script and production design.[40] Even the two actors' skill in resurrecting their younger personae, in tandem with the self-assured assumption of Leo G. Carroll's role by Patrick Macnee of *The Avengers* fame, could not salvage the film.

Failed Friendship and Evolving Enmity

The British Prime Minister Winston Churchill's memorable declaration in March 1946 that "an iron curtain has descended on Europe" officially acknowledged the start of the Cold War. Followed by the Truman Doctrine (1947–48) and the Marshall Plan (1948), the Berlin Blockade (1948–49), and the Soviet-enforced Warsaw Pact (1955), the ideological divide between West and East found its concrete geographical mise en abîme in Berlin, with the construction of the wall (August 1961), which split the city into democratic West Berlin and its communist East counterpart. In the ensuing decades the United States and its established allies and the Soviet Union and its satellites played out a variety of propagandistic and military scenarios as they struggled for geopolitical influence throughout the world. Espionage flourished in covert operations and on American and Soviet screens, as did competition in sports, space, and industrial production. Film and other cultural genres in the Soviet Union and the United States reflected the shifts in hostilities between the two superpowers. According to Thomas Doherty, the period from 1948 to 1954 alone witnessed the production of approximately forty anticommunist—or what he calls "Hollywood agit-prop"—films.[41] Such fare subsequently decreased, yet it persisted into the early 1980s, with television spy shows during the 1960s enjoying particular popularity in both Great Britain and the United States. And the James Bond franchise glamorized a fundamentally amoral profession spuriously legitimated by "righteous" Western values and the perceived imperative of crushing the "Red Peril."

The accession of Mikhail Gorbachev to the post of general secretary in 1985, the policy of *glasnost* and *perestroika* he introduced in 1987, and the fall of the Berlin Wall just two years later led to a provisionary rapprochement between the long-standing ideological foes that eventually culminated in the formal dissolution of both the Warsaw Pact and the USSR. With Boris Yeltsin at the helm during the volatile 1990s and a rocky transition to a market economy, political and financial chaos reigned, and crime proliferated—the latter phenomenon exploited by American directors gratified to expose Russia's literal and metaphorical bankruptcy in the face of American superiority. Formally, the Cold War was over, with the purported victors now condescendingly offering advice to their defeated enemy and the release of such triumphalist films as *The Hunt for Red October* (1990), *The Russia House* (1990), *Company Business* (1991), *Crimson Tide* (1995), *The Jackal* (1997), *The Saint* (1997), *Air Force One* (1997), and *Virus* (1999) capturing American complacency. As the nineties drew to a close, however, and the unexpected presidency of Vladimir Putin loomed on the horizon, disillusionment by both erstwhile enemies, who had transformed into so-called partners, was already heard, though tentatively, in comments about a new Cold War, signaled in Nikita Mikhalkov's costly, virulently anti-American *Barber of Siberia* (*Sibirskiy tsiryulnik*, 1998).[42] And films released in both countries during the first decade of the new millennium registered a renewed combative mistrust that gradually gathered momentum: *The Sum of All Fears* (2002), *Spinning Boris* (2003), *The Bourne Supremacy* (2004), and a mounting number of other cinematic narratives that responded to Putin's expanding efforts to restore Russia's status of empire in a world radically changed by advances in technology, the globalization of the financial sector, and unprecedented modes of communication.

Fundamental differences between the first and second Cold Wars—the latter currently at its height—include the international "star" status of Putin as the successful, aggressive, and enormously influential leader of a country that has reinstated many aspects of Sovietdom; Russia's ability to infiltrate countries in Europe, Africa, and Asia with the use of technology in order to disseminate disinformation and denigrate democracy and liberalism, which Putin explicitly decries as moribund; the role of finance in the new enmity, as America imposes politically based economic sanctions on Russia's wealthy elite; and, perhaps most insidiously, the unofficial nature of the Cold War, which has not been acknowledged formally by either side, though journalists and individuals within each government have referenced the term. The spate of assassinations and suspect deaths of various Russians (Anna Politkovskaya, Alexander Litvinenko, Sergei Magnitsky, Boris Nemtsov, and many others)[43] who have spoken out against the Kremlin and particularly Putin, deemed synonymous with the country he heads, have upped the ante since the first Cold War. Predictably, these new-old relations between Russia and the West have revived enthusiasm for cinematic spies on screen, who seem continuous with the reality that often surpasses them. After all, Putin, always "the strongman par excellence" in the news,[44] was a KGB agent until the Soviet Union imploded, and many of his ploys, such as the surreptitious spread of disinformation and the mysterious elimination of threats, constitute classic KGB maneuvers. Troucing or outclassing Russians on celluloid compensates in some small measure for American failure to contain Russia's combative stratagems in real life. Perhaps that accounts for the keen interest in the Jack Ryan, Bourne, and Bond series of films, as well as *Breach* (2007), *The November Man* (2014), *Bridge of Spies* (2015), *Atomic Blonde* (2017), and remakes of sixties TV offerings.

Reprising International Cooperation during the Second Cold War

With few exceptions, critics have compared big-screen versions of spy narratives unfavorably with their sixties TV originals, despite the huge financial success of, above all, the *Mission: Impossible* franchise, owned by Tom Cruise—what the critic Anthony Lane memorably called "the brand that will not die."[45] So, especially in light of the signal failure of *The Fifteen Years Later Affair*, one may ask what prompted the British director Guy Ritchie to revamp the 1960s *The Man from U.N.C.L.E.* series into a film in 2015, when relations between post-Soviet Russia and the US were (and remain) at a nadir. A steady stream of off-screen spy dramas involving poisonings, hackings, and efforts to undermine political processes in the West by such Russian secret service personnel as Lydia Guryeva, Anna Chapman, Anatoliy Chepiga, Alexander Mishkin, and most recently Maria Butina would seem to have rendered celluloid narratives about spies gratuitous. Whatever the reason for resuscitating the original Cold

War narrative, critics are virtually unanimous in judging Ritchie's film inferior to the series, while praising his visual re-creation of the 1960s.[46]

Reworking an established source that had spawned countless films and TV series, Ritchie's two moneymaking *Sherlock Holmes* movies, starring Robert Downey Jr. and Jude Law (2009, 2011), had featured a classic contrasting duo of male investigators—an experience on which the director's version of *The Man from U.N.C.L.E.* could build. Yet the notion of American-Russian cooperation at a time when the earlier attempt at a more amiable "reset" between Barack Obama and Vladimir Putin had yielded to overt enmity seemed downright wrongheaded. Relations between the two countries, however, have seesawed so drastically during Putin's prolonged presidency that predicting the political situation at the time of the film's shooting (2013) would have challenged even experts in American foreign policy, let alone a British filmmaker with an incomplete secondary-school education known primarily for his brief but profitable marriage to Madonna (2000–08).[47] Released in 2015, a year after Russia's annexation of Crimea, Putin's unambiguous efforts to seize control of other areas in Ukraine, and the repeated imposition of American sanctions, the film landed in theaters when media and government personnel no longer hesitated to mention a second Cold War. As illustrated by the period's numerous spy films focused on Russia, Ritchie was not alone in reviving secret-agent TV dramas on the big screen even as real-life events continued to overtake Hollywood scenarios. Only *The Man from U.N.C.L.E.*, however, required a sea change in the original conception of the Russian partner in espionage.

David vs. Goliath: The Small and the Big Screen

The intrinsic differences between a series and a film are substantial and ultimately leave the latter at a disadvantage. Like any TV series, by virtue of reappearing every week inside viewers' homes, the original *The Man from U.N.C.L.E.* bred not only loyalty among viewers, but also expectations regarding the familiar leads and the nature of their activities, rendering explanations superfluous. Sarah Ruth Kozloff's fruitful comparison of TV series with fairy tales, as mapped out according to functions by the structuralist Vladimir Propp, inventories the following features as constitutive of the genre:

> predictable, formulaic storylines; multiple storylines intertwined in complex patterns and frequently interconnecting; individualized, appealing characters fitting into standardized roles; emphasis on the interrelationships between these characters; endings of texts mark a return to the same state of affairs; settings

and scenery either very showy or merely functional; . . . voice-over narration or direct address often employed; . . . reliance on ellipsis and scene; . . . lengths cut to fit standardized time slots; and a tendency towards universality, away from topicality.[48]

The pertinence of these attributes to *The Man from U.N.C.L.E.* is immediately apparent to anyone who ever watched it. So, how does a series that finds favor with audiences overcome the genre's self-evident limitations while deriving benefits from its regular iterations?[49] *The Man from U.N.C.L.E.* provided some useful answers, not the least being the invaluable principle articulated long ago by a TV executive: Combine the safely familiar with the innovative ("totally new and just like X").[50]

First, each week *The Man from U.N.C.L.E.* boasted as guest stars some of Hollywood's best-known actors/actresses as well as an entire gallery of instantly recognizable, gifted TV regulars, usually playing innocent bystanders or evildoers: Joan Crawford, Eleanor Parker, Elsa Lanchester, George Sanders, Curt Jurgens (the villain to Roger Moore's Bond in the 1977 film *The Spy Who Loved Me*), Angela Lansbury, Anne Francis, Janet Leigh, Vincent Price, Jack Palance, Joan Collins, Herbert Lom, Leslie Nielsen, Martin Balsam, Rip Torn, Jill Ireland, Cher, Broderick Crawford, Telly Savalas, Robert Culp (later one of the leads in *I Spy*), Luciana Paluzzi (a sexy villain in the fourth Bond film, *Thunderball* [1965]), and many others. Their appearances guaranteed the pleasures of recognition as well as diversity. As one critic phrased it, series spotlighting the same regulars week after week "depend upon the guest villain, whose office is that of providing a fresh problem for a resident staff of heroes to solve."[51] That principle also held true for the various guests playing the innocent characters routinely allied with the daring duo. Owing to that combination, freshness comported with intimacy and continuity. By definition, film lacks that luxury unless it embraces an episodic structure, which Ritchie wisely forwent.

Second, 105 discrete episodes likewise ensured a wealth of impressively diverse plots (variations on a paradigm), while the fifty-minute constraint for each episode imposed rigorous editing that resulted in quick action sequences and a dynamic narrative line. Like any series, *The Man from U.N.C.L.E.* was inevitably formulaic, but within that formula it managed to vary stories, settings, issues, and characters to create the illusion of the spies' exciting, risk-laden life across continents, with the aid and the hindrance of a boundless array of individuals from all walks of life. It wasted none of its fifty minutes, fruitfully relying on audiences to fill in whatever gaps the speed of developments created. In that sense it corresponded to the mood of the sixties: "fast-paced, daring, different, irreverent, 'cool.'"[52] At the same time, the appeal of the two major stars, who reappeared each week and sustained a humorous, friendly professional bond, attracted ever-larger audiences. Quite simply, viewers found Solo and especially Kuryakin captivating, and the actors incarnating them charismatic, as attested by the fan mail inundating the studio.

In Ritchie's 116-minute-long film—roughly the equivalent of two TV episodes from the sixties—that rich diversity shrank to a single plot with a circumscribed set of characters and locations, though the latter, unlike in the series, are authentic and beguiling. Set in Berlin and Rome, the film traces a simple plot that fundamentally alters the nature of the TV series, for its spies' professional allegiances set the United States and the Soviet Union at loggerheads from the start. In 1963, CIA agent Solo (Henry Cavill) extracts Gaby Teller (Alicia Vikander), daughter of Dr. Udo Teller (Christian Berkel), an alleged Nazi scientist now collaborating with the United States, from East Berlin, despite strenuous efforts by KGB operative Illya Kuryakin (Armie Hammer) to thwart the American mission. Solo learns that Gaby's Uncle Rudi (Sylvester Groth), subsequently exposed as a Nazi war criminal, works in a shipping company owned by the ominously named Vinciguerras (Elizabeth Debicki and Luca Calvani)—affluent Nazi sympathizers intent on using Teller to manufacture their own private nuclear weapon and turn it over to some unidentified Nazis. Given the world-threatening dimensions of such a crisis, the CIA and KGB order Solo and Kuryakin to join forces, with the stipulation that each steal Teller's research for his own government. At the conclusion, Teller proves to be an agent hired by the British MI6 under Waverly (Hugh Grant), and after the triumvirate foil the Vinciguerra couple's intentions and kill both, Waverly announces that the three spies will form a team employed by—yes—U.N.C.L.E. In short, the film serves as a prequel or, as Peter Bradshaw grandly phrased it, "an origin myth" for the sixties' series.[53]

Superman, or What's in a Name?

From the outset the script triangulates the mutually inimical security agencies of the two superpowers and the British MI6, in addition to specifying not THRUSH but Nazis as the enemy. Such a move replaces the universality of the TV series with a pointedly political agenda. The early scenes establish the film's strategy of pitting the two agents against each other in a relationship of precisely the one-upmanship that the TV show eschewed. Competition rather than cooperation is the order of the day, enacted in one sequence after another. At film's end, with the enemy dead, that competition turns potentially lethal when Kuryakin, obeying orders, plans to kill Solo for the disk containing

Teller's nuclear data. Absurdly, he abandons that "national" task when Solo returns to him the watch that he had inherited from his father but lost to the Vinciguerras' henchmen.

Ostensibly demonstrating equitableness in the portrayal of the two agents, the film imitates the TV show by having Solo and Kuryakin take turns in rescuing and besting each other. For instance, though Solo ends up spiriting Gaby out of Berlin despite Kuryakin's violent obstructiveness, Kuryakin possesses better equipment when both set out to break into the warehouse at a shipping yard. He also saves Solo's life when the duplicitous Uncle Rudi is about to electrocute the American. Yet that sequence is brief and treated seriously, whereas Solo's rescue of him earlier in the film is embedded in a lengthy, supposedly comic scene that has Solo seated in a truck with a basket containing a cloth napkin, a bottle of red wine, and a sandwich, which he proceeds to consume while listening to an Italian pop song, and abandons reluctantly only when he notices Kuryakin about to drown. Here, as elsewhere, what humor the film possesses is juvenile and at the Russian's expense, diminishing his image while aggrandizing Solo's. The two agents adopt the nicknames "Cowboy" and "Peril" ("Red Peril"?) for each other, and initially Solo dehumanizes Kuryakin by referring to him as "it"—presumably because of his "Hulk" size and strength (Hammer stands 6'5"). A running gag, predictable after the first couple of times, shows Kuryakin besotted with Gaby, about to kiss her, but never achieving that teenage goal. By contrast, the film casts Solo as so irresistible that a hotel receptionist instantly succumbs to him, and the murderous, Nazi-allied Victoria Vinciguerra cannot forgo spending a night of lovemaking with him, loud enough to be heard next door by the frustrated couple, Gaby and Kuryakin.[54] Yet Cavill's robotic enactment of sexual attraction renders the film possibly "the first spy thriller in which the only person the secret agent hero really wants to sleep with is himself."[55]

The images of the two spies leave no doubt about Solo's intended superiority. Immaculate suits, unshakable self-possession, sexual prowess, and smoothness define the American, who at almost every turn puts his lesser Russian equivalent in the shade. By disadvantageous contrast, Kuryakin favors more proletarian attire (complete with Lenin-style flat cap) and is volatile, driven by passion, and inclined to wreck hotel rooms when angry. Viewers repeatedly see him clenching and unclenching his fists in efforts to control his seething emotions. Moreover, this is a KGB agent who in a Roman boutique protests, "You can't put a Paco Rabanne belt on a Patou"—the knowing reference supposed to replace the rich cultural intertextuality of its TV predecessor. Such a characterization is ridiculous even to those unaware of KGB training techniques, which school its agents to remain imperturbable under any circumstances rather than to become excited about fashion trends. After all, we have an exemplar of a KGB agent in Vladimir Putin, whose basilisk gaze and cold-bloodedness perfectly capture the external desiderata of the role. Whereas calm inscrutability defined the TV Kuryakin's demeanor, Ritchie subscribes to the stereotype of the irrational, no-holds-barred Russian. As reviewers observed, "Ritchie turns Kuryakin into a semi-psychotic,"[56] "a chess-obsessed strong man with rage and daddy issues."[57] Consequently, as the more percipient agent, Solo time and again has to instruct him—not to react violently to muggers, to curb his instincts, and so on. That strategy evokes America's condescension to just-desovietized Russia in the early 1990s, when so-called experts from the US paternalistically advised the humiliated former foe on how to administer the country. Little wonder, then, that by film's end audiences are unsurprised that it is Solo who devises the scheme to annihilate Victoria Vinciguerra, thereby saving the all-important disk with the crucial information about warheads, as well as Kuryakin's stolen watch. Indeed, the last sequences of the film, which relegate Kuryakin to the background, are unabashed imitations of Bond denouements.

Ultimately, the film's impact depends not only on the handling of the narrative—which suffers from longueurs owing to slack editing—but also (and perhaps more importantly) on the image of the two male leads and their interaction. And here casting is a major drawback. Unlike the relatively slight Vaughn and McCallum, the two lead actors are tall and beefy, but ineffective in roles that call for magnetism with at least a modicum of subtlety. Presumably cast as Solo because of his starring role as Superman in *Man of Steel* (2013), Cavill plays the American U.N.C.L.E. agent as a cardboard character straight from the comics that bred Superman, but in this case, capeless and poured into flaunted designer three-piece suits. Wooden and obliviously self-enclosed, his Solo utterly lacks charm and betrays few human tendencies. Summing up Cavill's portrayal, one critic remarked, "The Solo we have here is a clothes rack, not a protagonist."[58] And another quipped that "the line between phlegmatic suavity and downright dullness is rather more easily breached than the Berlin Wall."[59]

Playing Kuryakin "with a grumpy beefcake deadpan," Hammer exhibits none of the magnetism that two years later would prove his calling card in Luca Guadagnino's *Call Me by Your Name*.[60] At the same time, the puerile nature of his scripted role hardly conduces to complexity or seductiveness, for, like the narrative, personae are hollow and dull, the two spies endowed "with all the sexy danger of M&S men's underwear models."[61] If, as one film reviewer maintains, McCallum's Kuryakin "was a one-man precursor of détente,"[62] Hammer's version solidifies the Western Cold War cliché of the uncontrollable, mercurial Russian outshined by his American counterpart. Secondary characters do little to improve the sense that the film's personae were primitively conceived. As in

Ritchie's other offerings, Vikander's Gaby essentially functions as decoration, while the intelligence chief as played by Grant, who has made a career of British embarrassment, cannot save the film, which deservedly has been panned as "slow, lethargic, and utterly lacking in charm and undeserving of the Cold War setting that is its best trait."[63] "At times," a reviewer rightly contends, "*The Man from U.N.C.L.E.* works better as a fashion show than a movie, with a wardrobe . . . that expresses more about the era than anything in the script."[64] Indeed.

It is not difficult to extrapolate from the film a self-congratulatory Superman complex that celebrates Anglophone machismo, ingenuity, superior style, and serene confidence in its own rightness. Such a scenario relegates Russia to secondariness, arguing that it may boast of brute strength (in a fury, Kuryakin removes part of Solo's car with his bare hands), but should learn from the more civilized West if it wishes to move forward and retain the best from its historical past (symbolized by the watch of Kuryakin's father). Soviets, it seems, cannot even operate a slide projector correctly. Unlike its TV predecessor, which envisioned an alliance that contravened official international relations, the big-screen *The Man from U.N.C.L.E.* seems a throwback to Western attitudes of the early 1990s while concurrently tapping into today's renewed hostility between Russia and the West—a situation that has triggered not only mutual recriminations by politicians, but also a slew of cultural products. The most recent is a game invented by Mikhail Bober that, "out of exasperation at Western news reports of the crime," transforms Russian agents' attempted murder of Sergei Skripal and his daughter in the United Kingdom into entertainment.[65] The fate of Ritchie's lackluster foray into cinematic spy adventures, released the same year as the megaprofitable fifth installment in the succession of *Mission: Impossible* films with Tom Cruise (*Mission: Impossible—Rogue Nation* [2015]), suggests that belittling the enemy during the second Cold War holds little appeal for audiences, particularly if the director confines himself to stereotypes, sluggish pacing, and a shallow sense of both political antagonism and international partnership.[66]

Notes

My gratitude to Bożenka for her response to an earlier draft of this essay.

1. John F. Kennedy, "President Kennedy's Final Address to the United Nations General Assembly," September 20, 1963, C-SPAN.org, https://www.c-span.org/video/?315975-1/president-kennedys-final-address-united-nations-general-assembly. Kennedy's famous admission of enthusiasm for Fleming's Bond novels doubtless boosted both the books and the films based on them.

2. Practically all commentaries about the TV series claim that it appeared "at the height of the Cold War"—a view likely inspired by Soviet first secretary Nikita Khrushchev's melodramatic "We Will Bury You" speech addressing Western ambassadors at a reception at the Polish embassy in Moscow on November 18, 1956, followed by his fabled shoe thumping as premier

at the United Nations four years later. In fact, the series, conceived during Khrushchev's reign, hit the small screen after Kennedy's death and at the end of the domestic liberal period under Khrushchev, deposed and replaced in 1964 by Leonid Brezhnev, who curbed the freedoms introduced by his predecessor.

3. THR Staff, "'The Man from U.N.C.L.E.': THR's 1964 Review," *Hollywood Reporter*, August 11, 2015, https://www.hollywoodreporter.com/news/man-uncle-1964-tv-review-814603.

4. The formula would be echoed by Solo in the feeble film *The Return of the Man from U.N.C.L.E.* fifteen years later. That iteration alone betrayed the movie's lack of originality and conviction, as I discuss later in the essay.

5. An intellectual Irishman, McGoohan not only starred in *The Prisoner* but also produced it, wrote some of the scripts, and directed several episodes. He later remarked on viewers' frustration with the concluding episode, which conveys a psychological insight at odds with the formulaic Bond franchise and other narratives that titillate and entertain. See "Patrick McGoohan: 'The Prisoner Explained,'" accessed January 20, 2019, https://www.youtube.com/watch?v=-XQrcyGJajo.

6. For an analysis of symptoms of the Cold War in American cinema of those decades, see Helena Goscilo and Margaret B. Goscilo, *The Cold War Ex-Enemy in Russian and American Film, 1990–2005* (Washington, DC: New Academic Publishing, 2014).

7. THR Staff, "'The Man from U.N.C.L.E.': THR's 1964 Review."

8. Though New York and the wider world were emphasized, the bulk of the series was filmed on the MGM set in California.

9. Michael Kackman, *Citizen Spy: Television, Espionage, and Cold War Culture* (Minneapolis: University of Minnesota Press, 2005). With minimal and selective analysis of the show's episodes, Kackman forces the series into the Procrustean bed with which he begins his study, and consequently sees little difference between it and the purely comic *Get Smart* (2008), let alone among the various seasons of *The Man from U.N.C.L.E.*

10. Rick Worland, "The Cold War Mannerists: *The Man from U.N.C.L.E.* and TV Espionage in the 1960s," *Journal of Popular Film & Television* 21, no. 4 (Winter 1994): 152. Worland's analysis is one of the most perspicacious among many articles and books devoted to the series.

11. The grammar-resistant website MeTV claims that the name *Illya* "was taken from the lead character in Jules Dassin's 1960 film *Never on Sunday* . . . a carefree prostitute in Athens, Greece," but provides no support for this peculiar explanation of origins. See "11 Top Secret Facts about 'The Man from U.N.C.L.E.,'" MeTV, August 4, 2016, https://www.metv.com/lists/11-top-secret-facts-about-the-man-from-uncle.

12. Occasional carelessness regarding details marked the show, for instance, Kuryakin's wearing a wedding ring on his left hand (Soviets wore them on the right), though he presumably has no spouse. In the course of the second season, the ring moved to the right hand. See Kathleen Crighton, "*The Man from U.N.C.L.E.*: A Retrospective: Background and History," January 1994, at https://www.manfromuncle.org/kcretro4.htm.

13. Alan Cowell, "Churchill's Definition of Russia Still Rings True," *New York Times*, August 1, 2008, https://www.nytimes.com/2008/08/01/world/europe/01iht-letter.1.14939466.html.

14. For the series' determination to maintain Kuryakin's character as enigmatic, see Jon Heitland, *The Man from U.N.C.L.E. Book: The Behind-the-Scenes Story of a Television Classic* (New York: St. Martin's Press, 1987), 47. Heitland covers all aspects of the series in devastating detail.

15. All four seasons, with subtitles, include this "information" on the covers. See wbtvondvd.com, 1964, 1965, 1966–1967, 1968.

16. Reportedly, Carroll had trouble remembering his lines and, finding his role too sedentary, requested to leave his desk occasionally for involvement in the action. See Heitland, *The Man from U.N.C.L.E.*, 127, 114.

17. After the first season the series switched to color.

18. According to Heitland (*The Man from U.N.C.L.E. Book*, 48), the press called McCallum's hairstyle the "Beatle cut," which certainly augmented his popularity.

19. Mark Feeney, "In the Company of Spies," *Boston Globe*, November 2, 2008, http://archive.boston.com/ae/tv/articles/2008/11/01/in_the_company_of_spies/?page=2.

20. Crighton, "*The Man from U.N.C.L.E.*: A Retrospective."

21. Crighton, "*The Man from U.N.C.L.E.*: A Retrospective." For fascinating specifics about merchandizing the series, see Heitland, *The Man from U.N.C.L.E. Book*, 159–66.

22. Crighton, "*The Man from U.N.C.L.E.*: A Retrospective."

23. Feeney, "In the Company of Spies." An early review in the *Hollywood Reporter* focused on Solo and stated that "David McCallum, a newcomer, doesn't have much to ingratiate his audience with as a starter, but he will be more prominently in the forefront as the series grow[s] into one of those inevitable residual propositions." See THR Staff, "'The Man from U.N.C.L.E.': THR's 1964 Review."

24. Heitland, *The Man from U.N.C.L.E. Book*, 46, 58.

25. The son of two classical musicians, McCallum played various instruments on the show, including the flute, drum, and French horn (in the "Off-Broadway Affair," the sixty-ninth episode of the entire series), as well as singing with Nancy Sinatra in "The Take Me to Your Leader Affair," six episodes later (Heitland, *The Man Man from U.N.C.L.E. Book*, 87). These episodes belonged to the third season, when it became increasingly clear that the series had lost its way.

26. For a detailed list of situations, dialogues, and other aspects of the series, see "Series/*The Man from U.N.C.L.E.*," accessed January 19, 2019, https://tvtropes.org/pmwiki/pmwiki.php/Series/TheManFromUNCLE.

27. Laudatory epithets repeatedly applied to the show by both its creators and critics were "sophisticated" and "elegant." Unfortunately, despite the attempt to recapture that mode in the fourth season, the crassness of the third lost *The Man from U.N.C.L.E.* the huge audiences it had acquired by the middle of the second season.

28. Crighton, "*The Man from U.N.C.L.E.*: A Retrospective."

29. *Seventeen Moments of Spring* (*Semnadtsat mgnoveniy vesny*, 1973), the only Soviet TV series featuring a World War II Soviet spy—the iconic Shtirlitz (né Maksim Isaev)—showed him not only unwaveringly faithful to his wife, but never even tempted by another woman. Such a characterization subscribed to mandatory Soviet puritanism as regarded its heroes as well as what was permissible on screen.

30. Heitland, *The Man from U.N.C.L.E. Book*, 158. As Heitland notes, the show was telecast in over sixty countries and enjoyed enormous popularity in Great Britain and Japan (157–58).

31. For information on that campaign, see James von Geldern, "Corn Campaign," in *Seventeen Moments in Soviet History*, accessed January 12, 2019, http://soviethistory.msu.edu/1961-2/corn-campaign/.

32. McCallum, who believed that his accent *was* Russian, took pains to reduce it gradually as the series developed, on the logical grounds that spending years in the United States and interacting with Anglophones would erode a foreign accent.

33. For information about the comparative length of the two actors' appearance on screen in the various episodes and the reasons behind it, see Heitland, *The Man from U.N.C.L.E. Book*, 114.

34. On Kuryakin's disguises, see Heitland, *The Man from U.N.C.L.E. Book*, 141–42.

35. Heitland, *The Man from U.N.C.L.E. Book*, 53.

36. The ad appeared in sundry magazines, including *Boys' Life*, January 1967, 68; *Ebony*, September 1966, 133; and many others. Google search for "David McCallum and American Savings Bonds," accessed December 2, 2018.

37. Many of the 2018 messages by women (and some by men) greeting McCallum's Facebook announcement of his continued presence on *NCIS* with delight affirm that their affection for him dates from his role of Kuryakin more than fifty years ago. See https://www.facebook.com/DavidMcCallumWriter/photos/a.107091362972150/626260494388565/?type=3, accessed December 2, 2018. When one of the characters in *NCIS* asks the leader of the unit who the chief medical examiner was in his youth, the reply he receives is "Illya Kuryakin." See season 2, episode 13.

38. For the camaraderie among the entire collective, see Heitland, *The Man from U.N.C.L.E. Book*.

39. Paul Mavis, "*The Man from U.N.C.L.E.*: The Complete Series," DVD Talk (website), December 6, 2007, https://www.dvdtalk.com/reviews/31609/man-from-uncle-the-complete-series-the/.

40. Paul Mavis, "*Return of the Man from U.N.C.L.E.—The Fifteen Years Later Affair*," DVD Talk (website), March 3, 2009, https://www.dvdtalk.com/reviews/36838/return-of-the-man-from-uncle-the-fifteen-years-later-affair/.

41. Stephen Prince, *Visions of Empire: Political Imagery in Contemporary American Film* (New York: Praeger, 1992), 52.

42. On this phenomenon, see Helen and Margaret Goscilo, *Fade from Red: The Cold War Ex-Enemy in Russian and American Film, 1990–2005* (Washington, DC: New Academia Publishing, 2014).

43. For a fuller list, see David Filipov, "Here Are Ten Critics of Vladimir Putin Who Died Violently or in Suspicious Ways," *Washington Post*, March 23, 2017, https://www.washingtonpost.com/news/worldviews/wp/2017/03/23/here-are-ten-critics-of-vladimir-putin-who-died-violently-or-in-suspicious-ways/?utm_term=.6c51fc1cea05. Some of the homicide attempts have proved unsuccessful, such as the thwarted poisoning of Sergei Skripal and his daughter, and of Vladimir Kara-Murza.

44. See Christian Caryl, "How Vladimir Putin Became the World's Favorite Dictator," *Washington Post*, May 8, 2018, https://www.washingtonpost.com/news/democracy-post/wp/2018/05/08/how-vladimir-putin-became-the-worlds-favorite-dictator/?noredirect=on&utm_term=.9c6a667ea0c9.

45. Anthony Lane, "Odd Couples," *New Yorker*, August 24, 2015, https://www.newyorker.com/magazine/2015/08/24/odd-couples-the-current-cinema-anthony-lane.

46. Costing an estimated $75 million, the film made only $45,445,109 domestically, though the cumulative worldwide gross was $109,845,109. See IMDb's page for *The Man from U.N.C.L.E.*, accessed January 8, 2019, https://www.imdb.com/title/tt1638355/.

47. "Madonna Gives Guy £50m in Divorce," BBC News, December 15, 2008, http://news.bbc.co.uk/2/hi/entertainment/7784519.stm.

48. Sarah Ruth Kozloff, "Narrative Theory and Television," in *Channels of Discourse: Television and Contemporary Criticism*, ed. Robert C. Allen (London: Routledge, 1989), 70.

49. As one scholar justly noted, "Art always thrives on restraints and prohibitions." David Thorburn, "Television Melodrama," in *Television: The Critical View*, ed. Horace Newcomb (New York: Oxford University Press, 1979), 552.

50. For the phenomenon of combining novelty with familiarity, see Lorna Sage, "Kojak and Co.," in *Television: The Critical View*, 153. On TV's goal of selling the new, see Michael Novak, "Television Shapes the Soul," in *Television: The Critical View*, 311.

51. Fred E. H. Schroeder, "Video Aesthetics and Serial Art," *Television: The Critical View*, 417.

52. Heitland, *The Man from U.N.C.L.E. Book*, 206.

53. Peter Bradshaw, "*The Man from UNCLE* Review: Style Paired with Deathly Boring Substance," *The Guardian*, August 11, 2015, https://www.theguardian.com/film/2015/aug/11/the-man-from-uncle-review-style-paired-with-deathly-boring-substance.

54. Victoria Vinciguerra does not live up to her name, for she does not win the conflict, despite her designation as victor and her surname of battle-conqueror.

55. Robbie Collin, "Guy Richtie's Reboot of the Sixties TV Show Mixes International Intrigue with Escapist Fun," *The Telegraph*, August 11, 2015, https://www.telegraph.co.uk/film/the-man-from-uncle/review/.

56. Anthony Lane, "Odd Couples."

57. Glenn Kenny, "The Man from *U.N.C.L.E.*," RogerEbert.com, August 11, 2015, https://www.rogerebert.com/reviews/the-man-from-uncle-2015.

58. Michael Phillips, "'The Man from U.N.C.L.E.': Nice Suits; Dull Movie," *Chicago Tribune*, August 11, 2015, http://www.chicagotribune.com/entertainment/movies/ct-man-from-uncle-review-20150811-column.html.

59. Anthony Lane, "Odd Couples."

60. Bradshaw, "*The Man from UNCLE* Review."

61. Bradshaw, "*The Man from UNCLE* Review."

62. Feeney, "In the Company of Spies."

63. Joe Neumaier, "'The Man from U.N.C.L.E.' Review: 60s' Spying Ages Badly with Henry Cavill, Armie Hammer and Alicia Vikander," *New York Daily News*, August 13, 2015, http://www.nydailynews.com/entertainment/movies/man-u-n-e-review-60s-spying-ages-badly-article-1.2324597. A positive aspect of the film is its linguistic authenticity: Soviets speak genuine Russian, which rarely happens in Anglophone films.

64. Manohla Dargis, "'The Man from U.N.C.L.E.' Resurrects a Glossy, Action-Packed '60s," *New York Times*, August 13, 2015, https://www.nytimes.com/2015/08/14/movies/review-the-man-from-uncle-resurrects-a-glossy-action-packed-60s.html.

65. Ellen Barry, "Russian Flag Flies on Cathedral in English Town Where Ex-Spy Was Poisoned," *New York Times*, February 17, 2019, https://www.nytimes.com/2019/02/17/world/europe/russia-flag-salisbury-cathedral-uk.html.

66. *Mission: Impossible—Rogue Nation* more than recouped its budget of $150 million, with worldwide earnings of over $682 million and domestic receipts slightly over $195 million.

THE WESTERNIZATION OF STALIN
Late Hollywood Readings of Real-Existing Socialism

Lucian Țion

The fall of socialism did not usher in peaceful coexistence—to paraphrase a famous Khrushchev-era slogan—between the erstwhile ideological enemies of the Cold War, the East and the West: it merely moved that ideological animosity underground. As a result, the ensuing era of capitalist globalization that saw the East scrambling to copy the West (while being mainly swallowed up by it) merely transformed the onetime ideological differences into cultural ones. Once the political changes in the former Eastern Bloc took hold, these differences began to plague the renewed conflict between an eager-to-catch-up East and an increasingly affluent West, legitimizing therefore the very difference between the East and the West that distinguished the haves from the have-nots in the first place. This effectively turned the post–Cold War East into an Other for the West yet again—an "Eastern Other" that the West apparently needed as a backdrop for the performance of its own ideology.

If the Cold War did not manage to show a clear military or technological winner over the forty-odd years of its span, the parting of the Iron Curtain as a result of the 1989–91 revolutions and the alleged political egalitarianism fashioned in its aftermath clearly tipped the scales of power in the West's favor. While at its apogee the Cold War helped balance an otherwise disproportionate array of forces—which were also kept in check through mutual ignorance, suspicion, and second-guessing on behalf of the Soviet and Western governments—the unipolar world created in the aftermath of the Cold War in fact reinforced the position of the winner. Not only did it reinforce it: Feeling the need to demonstrate its superiority, the West also proceeded to *perform* its position as a winner. The result of this performance was that, instead of respecting or at least keeping its distance from the values of socialism over which it ultimately prevailed, the West found it necessary to belittle these values in order to augment its own to prominence.

My argument is therefore that the Cold War, which was once famous for dangerous military standoffs and aggressive tactics promoting mutually destructive policies, has been merely altered today to reconceptualize the extant cultural differences that continue to describe the Eastern/Western divide.

In this essay I analyze the above-referenced metamorphoses of ideological tropes into cultural ones, which, I argue, emerge in films discussing the memory of the Cold War in today's neoliberal world. What I will show is that the particular version of the Cold War that's increasingly being popularized as an accurate reading of history on the Western side of the former Iron Curtain is nothing but a reprisal of projections of Western ignorance about the East. This version of the Cold War therefore not only seeks to impose a Western reading of Eastern history, attempting to "sell" democratic liberalism as superior to any other political and economic system of governance, but also assumes that the cultural values birthed in liberal capitalism are the only values according to which the world and its history should be judged. Indeed, as we will see in the two works discussed in this essay, the us-and-them divide of the Cold War is currently making a comeback in films produced in the West as a form not only of legitimating but of performing the latter's superiority.

In *A Nation T(w/o)o: Chinese Cinema(s) and Nationhood(s)*, film scholar Chris Berry assigns post-Maoist war films to the category of "excess," arguing that their profligate abundance in contemporary Chinese cinema ultimately stems from late socialism's conservative need to relegitimize early communist history (Maoism included), even though this unfortunately demonstrates a lack of creativity that makes these films—in Berry's formulation—"hysterical."[1] As univocal as this may sound for the Chinese war film genre,[2] what is important to point out in Berry's criticism is that the Chinese unwillingness to abandon cinematic traditions built during Mao's time in power ultimately results in cultural stagnation, and consequently a drying up of the creative pool that inspired the otherwise strong war film genre of the early fifties.

Without scrutinizing too deeply Berry's claim, I would like to turn this statement on its head, somewhat, by applying it to the Western production of films treating the communist Other after the demise of communism in the Eastern Bloc in 1989. Simply put, the reversal may sound like this: In the same way that Chinese cinema's refusal to abandon the ideology of communism results in cultural stagnation, Hollywood's continuing demonization of the formerly communist East effectively imprisons the postsocialist Other in the ideological frame of totalitarianism dictated by Hollywood's newfound—for lack of a better word—democratic normativity.

This means that inasmuch as cinema is concerned, not only is there no practical dialogue within the purported (capitalist) fraternity of the new East and the West, but the Cold War on screen has not effectively ended, and judging from late Hollywood, it shows no signs of abating in the near future. Moreover, not only has Hollywood preserved its approach toward the former Red Other, but, because of a different type of excess—this time resulting from its own ideological victory over communism—the West has practically *increased* rather than diminished its condemnation, veering from a subtle form of polysemic satire, such as that used in the Western films of the fifties and sixties,[3] to the imposed reading of a monosemic interpretation of the East's past.

Communism as Scapegoat

In an article written twenty years after the revolutions of the "anno mirabilis" 1989, political scientist Jacques Rupnik—an authority on the Czech Republic and Poland writing from Paris—summarizes what went wrong with the transition from communism to capitalism in Eastern Europe as follows:

> In 1989, the democratic culture of Central and Eastern Europe, in the form of various dissident movements, rose up and overwhelmed the decaying political structures by means of which communist rulers had been straining to keep democracy in check. Yet once the "game" of ordinary parliamentary politics began, the onetime communists, with their superior levels of cohesion and experience, outplayed the more democratic but less well-organized former dissidents.[4]

Rupnik's point of view—popularized both in academia and the media at large since the early nineties—constructed a global view of postsocialist politics seeing communism as the immediate culprit for the failure of democracy to properly take root in Eastern Europe, a phenomenon which in the early 2010s was becoming readily apparent to Rupnik himself:

> With the state stepping back in to rescue capitalism, post-1989 market liberalism lay shattered. Local variations notwithstanding, Central and Eastern Europe's political and economic elites have all had to confront the reality that their chosen model was in crisis. The "liberal" moment within the larger process of transition has come to a close.[5]

Faced with the shameful defeat of a policy seen until then as infallible,[6] the liberal West had to create the myth of what Slavoj Žižek would call the saboteur, that is, a figure responsible for the derailment of the capitalist project in an Eastern Europe otherwise duly enamored of the West and its values. This saboteur—both Rupnik and public opinion in the West had it—was personified by none other than the undead figure of Bolshevism, whose Marxian specter continues to haunt Europe's accursed Eastern parts and keep Western bourgeois democracy at bay. Taking issue with the failed experiments of democracy in Hungary and Poland in the wake of the populist Orbán and the Kaczyński presidencies of the mid 2010s, Roger Cohen writes in a *New York Times* op-ed in 2018:

> Bolshevism, the cradle in which Orban and Kaczynski were rocked, was an ideology bent on force-marching society toward some higher ideal. In fact, the reality, as the Polish poet Zbigniew Herbert put it, was that it "poisons wells, destroys the structures of the mind, covers bread with mold." Something of this urge, it seems, remained in the two men. It was not enough for them to succumb to the permissiveness of the West. They needed a mission. They have decided to save Christendom, no less—and to heck with open societies.[7]

This organicist metaphor, according to which communism is coeval with mold, is thus corroborated with the picture painted by Rupnik, who sees the old communist *nomenklatura* (the higher echelons of the Communist Party, involved in administration and government) as responsible for most of the ills that plague Eastern democracy today. The complete picture generated is therefore one of an old evil—a vampiric imagery, ultimately—unwilling to die and returning to poison the minds of recurring generations of postsocialists with the dangers of tried-and-tested utopianism.

According to Rupnik, what the East needs to engage in today in order to root out this evil is a continuing commitment to washing clean the economic and political systems of the lingering effects of communism:

> The peaceful transition negotiated in 1989 between ex-dissidents and excommunists allowed the former to impose their liberal agenda of "procedural democracy" while the latter converted to capitalism and "free enterprise." This curious mix of a transition beset by "original sin" and of the "revolution betrayed" is most explicitly stated in the rhetoric of Poland's Kaczyński twins. . . . The result, according to this view, is moral, political, and economic corruption. Hence the dual focus of the campaign against the transition-era elites: decommunization and anticorruption.[8]

While Rupnik has enough common sense to notice that these two pillars of "democratizing" society, decommunization and anti-corruption, have in fact brought to power the Orbán/Kaczyński authoritarian forms of government in whose names a purge of ex-communists only helped cement the populists' authorities, Rupnik's vision of the transition period in postsocialist economies remains Manichean, therefore limited and unconstructive.

Moreover, what we fail to note in Rupnik's argument (along with the entire Western capitalist consensus on the postsocialist development of Eastern Europe) is the taking for granted of the organicist metaphor that communism equals mold/poison. As stated above, Rupnik himself agrees that we are seeing the instrumentalization of the decommunization paradigm to strengthen the power of both the nationalist and the capitalist elites. Yet neither he nor others dare to go so far as to blame liberalism for what Rupnik calls "democracy fatigue." Instead of highlighting the crisis of a liberalism that's been adopted lock, stock, and barrel by the East, Rupnik prefers to focus on the reformation of the transition society, while communism remains understood in scientific language as a metonymy for failure, destruction, and crime. This, of course, has the effect of not only not weakening the anti-communist stance of the West, but of strengthening liberalism, Western democracy, and capitalism, and of blaming communism, the past, and "the East" en masse for their inability to correctly implement the otherwise blemishless values of the West in the East.

The Short Historical Context

From a socio-anthropological perspective, it is no surprise to anyone today that, aside from deepening the rift between two modern ideologies, the Cold War helped significantly increase the already extant ethnic, racial, and (post)colonial differences that originally helped divide the world along ethno-racial as well as ideological lines. As we learn from Larry Wolff, Eastern Europe and Russia were not created by Winston Churchill's emblematic speech in Fulton, Missouri, but in the philosophical and geographical imagination of the Enlightenment.[9] It is therefore imperative to think of the East today, in a postcolonial, postsocialist context, as not only the ideological Other of capitalism but also the Other in the sense that Edward Said, Franz Fanon, and Gayatri Spivak have used the term in the field of postcolonial and subaltern studies.[10] The failure of the post-1989 moment to "democratize" this Eastern Other, as Rupnik posits, should therefore be seen as a failure to bridge the ethno-racial and historical divide *as well as* the ideological one.

Put differently, if the Western consensus imagines an East that is stubbornly maintaining its totalitarian course, this equally reinforces (and re-creates) the centuries-old differences that allegedly divide a democracy-loving West from the tyranny-bound Eastern Other who was—as Wang Hui puts it—equated with despotism since at least the time of the Ottoman Empire.[11] In other words, it is not only communism that helps feed the organic metaphor of mold/poison in the Western imaginary, but also the ingrained love of despotism and authoritarianism that the East has allegedly been nursed on that makes it difficult for postsocialist regimes to implement change (read "Western systems").

It is this conviction (as old at least as Voltaire, according to Wolff) that gives the West authority to preach democracy to the East. And it is equally this conviction that seeps into the West's new representation of the East in film and literature. What this effectively leaves us with in the age of purported postcolonial rapprochement between the East and the West is that popular fiction is nothing but window dressing used by Western ideology not only to indoctrinate the East or the West, but to force the Other to continue to occupy his or her subaltern position in relation to the superior one of the Western Self.

If it is true that socialist and postsocialist Chinese war films generate their own excess from their overzealous conscription to Maoist propaganda, Western productions taking as their subject recent socialist history are produced in countries that fall squarely outside the former perimeter of an "authoritarian government," be that the one of contemporary China or Russia. This doesn't stop Western film on and about the East, however, despite its subscription to the (newfound) goals of liberalism and democracy, from generating at least the same excess as Chinese war films, and from being ultimately informed by the principles of at least as much authoritarianism as its Eastern counterpart.

Satirizing History

It is interesting that 2017 is the year that witnessed (almost three decades after the collapse of communism) the almost simultaneous release of two satirical productions that address the memories of this political system: one a semi-obscure Amazon-produced six-episode series ridiculing the leadership of late-communist Romania—*Comrade Detective*; the other a British satire turned international blockbuster featuring the crème de la crème of Hollywood and British cinema and directed by the uncrowned king of contemporary political satire, Armando Iannucci: *The Death of Stalin*.[12]

The production of *Comrade Detective* was apparently motivated by the infringement by communist regimes on what Joseph Gordon-Levitt—one of the voice-dubbing stars of the series—calls the "values I hold dear: freedom of speech, press, and religion, the right to privacy, a fair trial, and I could go on," values which the "brutal, tyrannical dictatorships" of "the Communist regimes of the Cold War" "completely shat on."[13] This gives license to the series creators, Brian Gatewood and Alex Tanaka—in Gordon-Levitt's view—to make fun of these regimes, "and then some."[14]

The result is a present-day fictional reshoot of an alleged (albeit equally fictional) communist propaganda film produced in Romania in the eighties. However, this is not the eighties socialist Romania of the anti-capitalist film: it is a communist Romania created through the cliché of a buddy detective seriocomedy set not on the streets of Miami but those of Bucharest, where the American Ford cop car is replaced for authenticity with the sluggish symbol of communist industrial proprietorship, the Romanian-made Dacia. Moreover, in this version of the Stalinist eighties, the American-transplanted communist cops do not only carry guns, but they also fire them against representatives of organized crime, such as a ring of cocaine dealers (unheard of in any socialist country at the time) or black-marketeers smuggling blue jeans and selling them from the back of a truck to disgruntled inhabitants of capitalism-starved Bucharest. Finally, in this version of socialism, capitalist thugs, when attacked by the communist police, respond by firing machine guns on their attackers, thereby initiating veritable street battles of the like Bucharest wouldn't even see during the bloody 1989 Romanian revolution.

This is, of course, fiction, and our criticism of Gatewood and Tanaka should not call them out on their free use of imagination in an otherwise satirical creative effort. The apple of discord is that the series' creators insist on allegedly basing their satire on a real propaganda film produced by the Romanian government, while, of course, neither the propaganda film from the eighties, nor the type of socialist reality *Comrade Detective* purports to depict actually exists.[15] This ultimately shows, as it is symptomatic of excess, that real-existing socialism had failed to speak out in defense of itself, and after ceding its rights of representation to the American authors, it allowed them to project American realities and values onto Romanian socialism. The result is a fantastic version of communism that exists solely in the creators' imagination—an imagination, beyond the clichéd portrayals of communism as criminal and oppressive, replete with the upmost markers of capitalist values, including consumerism and the law, battling for survival on the streets of Bucharest.

Condemning Propaganda

As Gatewood himself states in an interview (also quoting his star, Channing Tatum), if *Red Dawn* (1984) and *Rocky IV* (1985) represented a type of Western propaganda that Americans were unknowingly consuming in the eighties, "showing the reverse . . . is both 'hilarious and really poignant right now.'"[16] Satirizing communist propaganda, the producers reason, is therefore educational because timely satire is supposed to make us aware of the changing power of political indoctrination and the subtler implications of propaganda today in a society in which populism is seeping into our lives more insidiously than ever before in the guise of either Trumpism or Orbánism.

The only problem with the producers' goals of universally treating propaganda as dangerous in a post–Cold War context is its historical decontextualization and interpretation solely from the American point of view. For it is not *their own* propaganda the creators are satirizing, but precisely that of the Other. And while parodying a genre in itself can indeed be both progressive and educational (the creators' effort resonates with early parodic instances such as Woody Allen's *What's Up, Tiger Lily?* (1966) by way of resignification of an original message), their undertaking also reminds one of Foucault and his pronouncement that "truth is an additional force, and it can be deployed only on the basis of a relationship of force."[17] In other words, for a culture to use an artifact created by another culture and sell it as truth, the ideological scales need to be favorably tilted toward the more powerful culture.

In these circumstances, it turns out that the otherwise noble gesture of Gatewood and Tanaka, namely that of equating the West with the East in the name of condemning both of their succumbing—at one time—to the production of what is by today's standards useless and shameful propaganda, is actually a gesture of obliteration. In this gesture, the East is being erased and exchanged for a version thereof that the West has created for it, with the effect of equally erasing in the process the historical conditions that birthed communist propaganda in the first place, namely anti-colonialism and anti-imperialism.[18]

Ben Travers of *IndieWire* states that the series's "intent is not to mock the mind control measures employed by America's Cold War foes, but to point out the commonalities between the countries' tactics,"[19] while Tatum and Gordon-Levitt press the point that the American anti-Red propaganda of the eighties was a mirror image of the communist-produced anti-American propaganda of the Eastern Bloc.[20] For Tatum, *Comrade Detective* is therefore supposed to redress an imbalance by offering a view of "ourselves" from "the other side." Of course, Tatum's naïve insistence on correcting the imbalances of the American propagandistic past has the effect of not only replicating them in the present but de facto redoubling them by projecting the American version of the Cold War onto the past of America's erstwhile enemies. In their efforts to eliminate othering, the producers reinforce it, for othering cannot be eliminated without replacing it with a version of the Other invented by the Self.

Finally, in an interview that plays as a performative continuum to the series, Gatewood and Tanaka explain in an introduction (and at the same time extranarrative prolongation supplementing the series proper) that their (fictional) decision for making the series was the replacing of the alleged anti-Western propaganda of the Bucharest government with one that can be re-created for purposes that would induce us to revaluate the old series from the wiser position afforded us by hindsight. What this effectively accomplishes, however, is a true mutation from contents to context: The signified, as in Roland Barthes's semiology, retreats to give way to the signifier, which becomes merely an index in Charles Sanders Peirce's sense. Barthes puts this very well in the opening vignette of his classic *Mythologies*, "The World of Wrestling," when he states that in the hyped-up image of the fierce combatants, "what the public wants is *the image* of passion, not passion itself."[21] As in Barthes's reading of this "ignoble sport," communism and capitalism become actors, indeed wrestlers involved in a performative fight. What matters is not their history but their significance—to be more precise, their *roles*. And since history is written by the victors, it is the *role* of the ethically wrong ideology that communism plays in the American interpretation of the East that takes precedence over historical reality. "This emptying out of interiority to the benefit of its exterior signs," Barthes continues, is also pantomimic: the sign by itself commandeers meaning.[22] Applied to our case, this means that history has lost its content (it doesn't matter what actually happened *in* history as long as it belongs to the conceptual "past"), and the mere referencing of an indexical sign—the invocation of communism—will suggest not only the association of the East's past with evilness and crime, but the (re)othering of the Other, who continues—with the help of this semiology—to be made coeval with the organism prohibited from regenerating because of its having ingested the poison of communism.

Thus, it is not (only) socialism that is being condemned in *Comrade Detective* but the idea of difference, which is something that runs against the very intention of its producers. Moreover, difference is condemned here not through opposing ideologies, a point the series obsessively insists on, but through the more vulgar end-of-the-Cold-War contrast between haves and have-nots. Thus, in the person of the communist detectives roughing up cocaine dealers who claim to the cops' faces that they want the implementation of market capitalism in their country, we have an incarnation of (excessive) democracy talking down to poverty, à l'américaine, which is *not* evidence of a superior ethical system trumping an inferior one but rather the reinforcement of a point of view that forces the East to be "read" through the filter of poverty and subalterity, a reading that is itself indebted to the colonial-era paradigm of the *mission civilisatrice*. If there is, therefore, any vampirism involved in our transition from communism to liberalism it is not that of Bolshevism returning to haunt freedom but that of permanentizing an Enlightenment-era discourse which posits the fear of the Eastern Other as integral to the identity of the Western subconscious.

Put succinctly, the colonial racist discourse of the victorious West returns in the guise of the terror of returning communism. In a preemptive move, *Comrade Detective* projects therefore the Western fear of the underprivileged Eastern Other qua difference of ideology, thus reinstating the only schism between the new East and the West that could keep the potentially hazardous ghosts of otherness at bay.

Finally, to take things one step further, what we see in current Western representation of the East with *Comrade Detective* is the anxiety caused by (a potential) revolt carried out by the underprivileged postcolonial class against American hegemony. Such an instantiation would eventually lead not only to a revamping of class struggle in perfect accord with Marxist dialectics—a struggle this time played out between the West and the subaltern Other—but also to a questioning of the eternal American obsession with communism, which is in fact an obsession with the perceived loss of America's privileged status in the world.

A Couple of Interventions in Cinematic Satire

What *Comrade Detective* makes clear is that Rupnik's affected call for continuing decommunization and democratization of the East is not necessarily a subterfuge through which the postsocialist state seeks to strengthen its former power but a scapegoat for the recolonization of the East by the West. As such, in *Comrade Detective* we saw how a conflict that was historically ethno-racial, postcolonial, and economic *as well as* ideological was reduced, through the a posteriori repositioning of the Cold War and the literal staging of the battle between consumerism and paucity qua ideology, to a condition that is only apparently ideological. What we in fact watch in *Comrade Detective* is not so much a clash of ideologies as the rewriting of Eastern history by Western narratives of neocolonial/neoliberal power masquerading as democracy.

In *The Death of Stalin* we witness not only an instantiation of a Western power rewriting Eastern history, but a case of replacing one theatrical and cinematic genre—in this case satire—with another: propaganda, coated in the appearance of what is otherwise thought of as inoffensive popular fiction. In other words, we are witnessing a case of using fiction to "sell" politics (or a politicization of fiction qua entertainment) in a way that is as undetectable as Gatewood's alleged neo-propaganda subtly infiltrating the media in the age of populism.

To assess the revolutionary change that occurred in the genre of satire between mid-century and late Hollywood, I need to briefly point out the evolution of the style from Joan Littlewood's use of satire in Richard Attenborough's 1969 adaptation of *Oh! What a Lovely War* to Armando Iannucci's 2017 purported use of satire as a weapon against totalitarianism in *The Death of Stalin*. Although it is not a treatment of the communist East proper, I position Littlewood's theatrical production as a counterpart to *The Death of Stalin* because, on the one hand, both films satirize the atrocities resulting from political fallout in the twentieth century, and on the other, because Littlewood's play arguably represents a high point of satirical writing that greatly influenced the use of satire in the West to advocate political change thereafter. Finally, I use Littlewood's film because both her production and Iannucci's belong unmistakably to the realm of British satirical writing, a style that has evolved to become part of the Western canon and, implicitly, Hollywood.

A farcical view of the useless slaughter that claimed at least sixteen million lives due to the corrupt politics of bourgeois governments in Europe, *Oh! What a Lovely War* is quintessential satire, as Nadine Holdsworth posits, in that it ridicules "the capitalist imperatives, powerbrokering, class relations and devastating human consequences of the Great War, a 'War To End All Wars,' re-interpreted in the long shadow of the Second World War and the widespread political fall-out of the very present Cold War."[23] Inspired by Littlewood's involvement in the Theatre Workshop, a leftist theater group advocating social change, with roots in the agitprop and epic theater of Brecht and Piscador that emerged in Britain after WWII, *Oh! What a Lovely War* uses the theatricals of satire and the style of musical theater to condemn the mismanagement of international policies not only by early twentieth-century governments but by those of the director's own 1960s, in which the film was produced. As such, in a fashion reverberating Gatewood's intentions avant la lettre, Littlewood satirizes not only the Great War but, as Holdsworth rightly points out, the ridiculousness of both Western and Eastern policies, and in that sense the film serves as a possible reference for Stanley Kubrick's landmark satire *Dr. Strangelove*, released in 1964, only a year after Littlewood's stage production went up.

As British theater critic Ronald Hayman claims, it is difficult to gauge the effect of Littlewood's play at the time it was written:

The preposterousness of the stylistic mixture [in *Oh! What a Lovely War*] has been imitated so often since 1963 that it is hard to recall the impact it made then, but style was inseparable from substance in the resultant exposure of historical falsifications. Ruthlessness, mindlessness, and inefficiency had been disguised as recklessness, patriotism, and courageous disregard for actualities.[24]

Of course, satire has been used to criticize politics and mores ever since Aristophanes and Juvenal, and in Britain it had a particularly strong tradition, as shown by the caricatural works of the nineteenth-century political satirists gathered around *Punch* magazine, the rich tradition of pantomime, and finally, the theatrical works of Bernard Shaw and even the fiction of George Orwell or Aldous Huxley. However, as Hayman argues, Littlewood's play, unlike the satire of previous British playwrights, "represents a turning point in the history of English theatre" in that, as British theater theorist Derek Paget puts it, it represents Littlewood's acceptance of "a European, anti-naturalistic political theatre to infiltrate the British scene."[25] Indeed, what makes Littlewood anti-naturalistic, and her expression a development from the previous use of satire and pantomime in the British tradition, is the particular Brechtian and agitprop heritage, and therefore the valorization of a new way of integrating the *Verfremdungseffekt* (alienation effect) into satire. It is therefore to this type of early communist propaganda—the same that Brentwood and Tanaka wish to abolish—that we owe such humorous language as that of Monty Python, or the later television series *Yes, Prime Minister* (1986–87), which we regard as representative for the style of British satire in general.

Why is this important? Because I claim that Armando Iannucci's 2017 production, while paying due homage to these influential predecessors in earlier works like *In the Loop* (2009) and *The Thick of It* (2005–12), takes an abrupt turn to the right, and with *The Death of Stalin* starts engaging in a populist condemnation of non-Western politics using an originally leftist discourse as shield against criticism. That is, it engages precisely in what both Rupnik and Gatewood preach that today's society should be vehemently against: populism.

Purporting to delve into the chaos following Stalin's death in 1953, Iannucci paints a farcical portrait of the power struggle that befell Stalin's epigones, who not only had to contend with the dictator's bloody heritage but also use this heritage in order to further their own political goals. The resultant image is that of a society temporarily ruled by contingency, fear, and violence, from which it would appear there'd be no escape if it weren't for Khrushchev's normalizing, if vulgar, presence to sow some reason into the heads of an unruly political entourage otherwise steadily approaching entropic doom.

In Iannucci's numerous interviews with large media conglomerates—although the film was completed before Trump's election as president—he is happy to press the point that his project was timely in that it almost prefigured through an inspired choice of subject the turbulence that was about to hit Western democracies following such unfortunate events as the cropping up of the Orbán-style nationalisms that Rupnik warned about. Furthermore, in an interview with *Time*, Iannucci stated:

> I was already thinking . . . of looking at a fictional dictator. . . . There were unusual things happening in Europe . . . strong leaders emerging, and nationalist movements and disruption. Then I got sent [the book on which the film is based]. . . . I thought, "Why come up with a fiction when it's all true?"[26]

The media took this statement and ran with it, interpreting the film afterward solely in the key provided by Iannucci, therefore as an alarm signal against contemporaneous totalitarianism in the West.

However, the final consensus of the mass media didn't stop here. Going beyond pointing the finger at the newly dictatorial West alone, as Iannucci indicated, Zaid Jilani of *The Intercept*, in the paper's self-titled "adversarial journalism" style, declares that the film should become a global warning against non-Western un-democracy:

> Remember that four times as many people are governed by the rising Chinese government than live in the United States. And of all the countries in the world, China may be second only to North Korea in embodying Stalin's vision of an all-powerful state governed by an all-powerful few.[27]

In a fashion eerily mirroring that of the Western consensus on Eastern politics propagated by the likes of Rupnik, what gradually became implicit for Western journalists through statements similar to that of Jilani's was that it was the East—through its unkosher political machinations—that was becoming a bad influence for an otherwise (or at least erstwhile) incorruptible West, and therefore that references to the far more totalitarian East should take the form of monosemic and vituperous condemnation.

Satire as Propaganda?

In gauging the reaction to *The Death of Stalin*, film critics didn't depart too widely from the consensus of the mass media. As such, *Sight & Sound* sees *The

Death of Stalin as a culmination of the satirical trend that enabled Iannucci to paint such devastating portraits of the corruption and complacency of Western political power in *Veep* or *The Thick of It* or *Veep* (2012–19).[28] We can anticipate academia underscoring the same connections, and it is therefore constructive to read closely Laura Basu's analysis of *The Thick of It*, as it may bear indirectly on *The Death of Stalin*. While discussing the former film as part of Iannucci's previous oeuvres, Basu somewhat dryly sums up that *The Thick of It* "is hilarious but the picture it paints is actually very bleak,"[29] a verdict we can almost transmute to apply to the corruption and authoritarianism of Iannucci's last film.

Simplistic as this may sound, Basu justifies her statement by otherwise correctly arguing that Iannucci's earlier satire of the British political system "gives us no normative term and no gold standard against which to judge its targets,"[30] as classical works of political satire did in the nineteenth century, for example. What makes *The Thick of It* outrageous in fact, Basu contends, is not that the entire political leadership of a democracy like Britain's seems to have been overtaken by corruption, but that "where we might assume an opposition, *none in fact exists.*"[31]

The release of *The Death of Stalin* makes it apparent that the gold standard that Basu references as absent in the director's earlier work returns in Iannucci's last film, and that the missing standard is undoubtedly the Eastern Other, communism, and totalitarianism. And if we concede Iannucci the right to satirize Western authoritarianism in *The Death of Stalin*, we have to equally admit that this satire is only made possible through the employment of another old Barthian paradigm.

In another essay in Barthes's *Mythologies*, "Operation Margarine," the French philosopher contends that "a little 'confessed' evil saves one from acknowledging a lot of hidden evil."[32] The reference Barthes makes is to critiques of public institutions such as the army or the clergy, which—public opinion has it, according to Barthes—everybody knows are corrupt (who, in fact, isn't?) but are still necessary for our survival. Or, as Barthes puts it within the frame of his metaphor: "What does it matter, after all, if margarine is just fat, when it goes further than butter, and costs less?"[33] Doesn't Iannucci similarly teach us with his satire on Stalin that even if Western democracy is flawed—and this is evident from *The Thick of It*—it is vastly superior to any form of nondemocratic government, and we should therefore consider ourselves fortunate that we do not live in a totalitarian society?

The opposition to corruption that Basu claims she cannot find in *The Thick of It* therefore makes a sumptuous comeback in *The Death of Stalin*; indeed, it is clearly in our face. In previous satires, in the opinion of theorist Robert Paulson, "the satirist . . . demands decisions of his reader, not mere feelings";

he "wishes to arouse [the reader's] energy to action, not purge it in vicarious experience."[34] And as Laura Basu also writes, the purpose of classical satire indeed "is to inspire action."[35] But if that is really the case, *The Death of Stalin* is not a reversion to a more classical style of satire: it is not really satire at all. What Iannucci's film appears to be is mere propaganda parading as satire.

Samuel Johnson would also probably agree, as he calls satire "a poem in which wickedness or folly is censured,"[36] meaning—as in Mikhail Bakhtin—that satire should be allusive, polysemic, carnivalesque.[37] By referencing history, or rather reenacting it as a projection of Western ethnocentrism (often enough the quibbling over power between Khrushchev and the politburo is reminiscent of the confused haranguing of the ministerial staff in *The Thick of It*), Iannucci defeats the purpose of any action in the spectator, except that directed toward relishing the present, a present that forces this spectator to automatically equate the actions of Stalin with those of Eastern totalitarianism today, which is precisely the reading favored by the mass media, as we have seen from Jilani's writing. In other words, far from inspiring action, Iannucci invites us to enjoy the status quo; however, not any status quo, but that of the corrupt yet noncriminal one of Western democracy.

If, on the one hand, it may appear that Iannucci universalizes the existence of corruption in his previous work, in his new work he also seems to say that as long as corruption is not totalitarian, as long as it does not lead to mass murder, it is acceptable. By creating the "bad standard" of Stalinism, Iannucci in fact exonerates his own previous work from the very condemnation he implicitly raised against it. With the incorporation of Stalin into the world system of evilness, Western democracy becomes a farce, but Eastern totalitarianism is doomed to remain a tragedy.

The Entertainment-ization of Politics

No one disputes the fact that Iannucci's earlier work is satirical. But, as Laura Basu points out, "the trouble is that satire, even relatively radical satire like *The Thick of It*, has been so incorporated [in media representations thereof] that it does not lead to a disengagement from bad politics."[38] What we can infer from this statement is that Iannucci's earlier cinema actually integrates consent in the form of apparent dissent. As such, one wonders if Noam Chomsky's marginalization of dissent in the American media by filtering out what is "inappropriate" should even be pointed out today, as cinema itself censors dissent by universalizing the corruption of Western politics, or, as Basu contends, by making politics more bearable.[39] In other words, by integrating satire into the very media system it satirizes, cinema, to paraphrase an Adornian warning, leads to an entertainment-*ization* of politics.

What we witness in the transition from Iannucci's earlier works to *The Death of Stalin* is therefore a shift from incorporating dissent into the system to actually propping up the system. Rather than a rebellion against the autarchic tendencies of Western democracies (or rather than being "about Trump," as Iannucci repeatedly insists), Iannucci's last work appears to represent the defense of the Western system on the sole grounds that this system allows the voicing of dissent—a dissent, however, that expresses itself solely as legitimization of Western democracy and as anti-communism, which, according to Chomsky's plastic formulation has become "a national religion and control mechanism."[40] In this context, it is hard not to see *The Death of Stalin* as a metaphor condemning totalitarianism—as indeed it should—but a totalitarianism of a particular *Eastern* type infiltrating the democratic West, à la Rupnik. And only following this rationalization does totalitarianism in general regain its significance as a universal marker for evilness threatening the hard-gained fruits of democracy; only after this, indeed, does totalitarianism motivate the birthing of dissent. This, of course, has the effect not only of echoing Rupnik's professed fear of the failure of decommunization, but also of reinforcing Wang Hui's understanding of "Asiatic despotism," according to which the East never faltered from its proclivity for authoritarianism ever since—in the European mind—the Ottoman Empire embodied this undemocratic form of government.

This problematic view of the Eastern Other forces us to question the nature of satire in postsocialism. If Gatewood and Tanaka's intent was to uniformize and demonize propaganda *en gros* regardless of historical context, and if it is true that beyond the universalizing of evil in fact lies the fear of Eastern danger, this is highly problematic for satire because, as Ruben Quintero rightly claims, if nothing else, satire "requires the inclusion, not the exclusion, of human failing."[41] Thus, "in political rhetoric," Quintero tells us, "when one national leader demonizes another, calling him a Hitler or a devil, satire ends and propaganda begins."[42] He is quite right to isolate this paradigm to politics and to distance it from fiction. For if that is indeed true, what becomes apparent is that what we have on our hands with *The Death of Stalin* is a political rather than a fictional artifact. Under the apparent deception that it reverts to classical satire, therefore, Iannucci's film in fact departs from the canonized laws of satirical writing altogether to simply offer a cohesive reading of history that makes sense for the anxiety of the West, a history that results, in exact replica to what Chris Berry indicts post-Maoist cinema of doing, from excess. What we witness here is the simple turn of history into reality, that is, the affirmation—through a simple (yet wannabe satirical, that is, parodic) reenactment of the past—that the farcical monstrosity of what happened in the Stalinist purges was altogether real.

However, this reality doesn't educate, nor does it—in typical Andersonian fashion—preclude a future massacre on the basis of negative memorialization.[43] As Žižek claims, the invocation of totalitarianism, primarily of fascistic—but also of communist type, as apparent with Iannucci—is a stopgap for critical thinking.[44] In Iannucci, communism carries an invocation of fear, a paralyzing warning that any other writing of communist history aside from the one condoned by the West makes possible the spread of disorder and contingency.

Without recurring to Theodor W. Adorno's questioning the possibility of poetry in the aftermath of tragedy, what we are left with, inasmuch as cinema is concerned, is the fact that Western narrative discourse, and ultimately Hollywood style itself, *becomes* reality. With that the erstwhile credited power of satire to stir the imagination is lost in the detriment of purported historical truth obtained through a return to an essentially realistic mode of representation. If credit for satire should go to somebody in *The Death of Stalin*, this is not Iannucci, but historical Stalin himself. All Iannucci has to do is point the camera to the East, and to the East's past, and reveal it—an interpretation also warranted by his own statement: "Why come up with a fiction when it's all true?"

But this also means that what we are witnessing is both the politicization and (re)geographization of the Eastern Other and the Other's history. In Iannucci, satire doesn't rely anymore on characterizations based on reality as in Littlewood, or even as in Gatewood's *Comrade Detective*, where characters are purportedly *inspired* by real life. The satirist here is no more a "cautionary prophet or an idealistic visionary,"[45] as Quintero describes him, despite what Iannucci styles himself as, but a simple interpreter of history, a mere documentarian who, in the age of orgiastic reenactment,[46] abandons the very function of satire previously used to ridicule in order to correct, to enact change. While serving no ulterior purpose but visual pleasure alone, the "pleasure" of—as any History Channel documentary would put it—bringing the past back to life, reality is re-created for its own sake; it becomes entertainment, in the same way that the satirized subject in *The Thick of It*, as Basu puts it, enjoys its own satirized image.

Quintero warns that "such confusions between literal fact and the truth of art remind us that satirists must ultimately rely on audiences to share a common ground of reason and, as far as literary satire is concerned, of belief."[47] And indeed, this is exactly what is shared between the public and the satirist in *The Death of Stalin*, only the common denominator is the ethnocentric Western reading of world history in the key of late capitalism.

Iannucci's film, as opposed to Littlewood's satire, does not let the spectator indulge in the satirical spectating act of imagining, or detaching himself in Brechtian fashion from the action: it is purely Hollywoodesque in that it involves the spectator completely in the action; it asks him to identify with a satirist who doesn't have an object of castigation but an object of *condemnation*. In *The Death of Stalin* the dialectical character of satire as claimed by Shaw is lost in favor of emitting direct judgments, not of pointing the way without going there, as the same director adroitly managed to do in his previous works.

Erasing Communist History in the Name of Democracy

Just as Chinese obsession with the anti-Japanese war originating in excess ultimately produces cultural stagnation in Chinese cinematic representations of the past, as Chris Berry argues it does, Hollywood's insistence on portraying Russia and the former communist East as the Other of the liberal West enforces the popularization and acceptance of a unilinear reading of history. In this reading, communism is the Manichean Other representing the culmination of centuries of despotism and barbarism of Eastern imperial type, which on the map of the newly globalized neoliberal world stands for horror and abjection. This monovalent interpretation of communism is both exaggerated and inappropriate, as it stems from the neoliberal persistence to overpower the history of the Eastern Other.

The implications of this action are twofold. First, if the Eastern Other is portrayed in recent history as the "unhappy" counterpart to Western democracy, the West can legitimate—through mere invocation of a gruesome past—further capitalist penetration of the East, ultimately leading to real political encroachment of one "side" by the other. Second, if communism is used à la Žižek by Western rhetoric, that is, if it is brought up in the style of totalitarianism—which when invoked it precludes further critical thinking about the past—this has the successful effect of endorsing a monovalent reading of Eastern history as a mere bleak antipode of the thriving Western civilization, an act which in a close reading will prove to be but a reiteration of the Enlightenment and the ensuing colonial moments (rather than the much-despised Bolshevik one). In other words, what both examples discussed in this essay, *The Death of Stalin* and *Comrade Detective*, do is reaffirm the legitimacy of the West to culturally claim ownership of a new East that is not only economically resurgent, but that, if disengaged with, would be on the brink of rediscovering a personal, unique, different version of history completely unaligned with the one that the West is trying to impose.

What is by now rather obvious is that—in the inverse formulation of Jilani—it is not only authoritarian rulers that create totalitarianism but also excess that (re)creates self-promoting propaganda. Just as Iannucci's reason for making *The Death of Stalin* was not Western populism but Western anxiety, the audiences who were laughing did so not at the risible misconduct of Easterners channeling through alter egos the corrupt Westerners, but at the very Easterners Iannucci's film virulently condemns and warns against as carrying the potential of corruptibility for the West. Although Iannucci repeatedly states in his interviews that what happened to the people of the Soviet Union under Stalinism was no laughing matter, satirical laughter is apparently the very response Iannucci wanted to elicit with *The Death of Stalin*, albeit with a twist: If in works criticizing Western democracies there was escape in what Basu calls the power of those satires to make life more bearable, in *The Death of Stalin* there is no such escape for the Eastern Other except, of course, into the arms of Western democracy, a move which replays the typical, older Cold War–style scenario.

Friedrich Nietzsche spoke of humanity as continuously re-creating the past so as to give itself a nobler, higher pedigree. In the same fashion, we, the postsocialists, cannot be the same persons who existed in our pasts. The series and the film seem to teach us that there should be no continuity between us and our former selves—both Eastern and Western. We should be smarter, more knowledgeable and well refined, and superior both to our former selves and to others—the socialists, the unconverted colonials, the Soviet nostalgics, and finally, the geographical peripherals that refuse to acknowledge the benefits and wisdom of progress.

What both *Comrade Detective* and *The Death of Stalin* perform is the ultimate othering necessary to legitimate these identitary delusions of grandeur by delimiting the West (and whoever wants to belong to it, as long as it is on "our" terms) from the Other and the Other's past. Judging by their choice of subject and geography (communism in 1950s Russia and 1980s Romania, respectively), these productions' settings are ideal for blowing the whistle on a resurgent Eastern "totalitarianism" seen as a possible cause for such slippages of the West as personified by both Brexit and Trump. By writing a plea for tolerance with one hand and an execution order with the other—to use one of Iannucci's obsessive images—the West betrays its own anxiety and xenophobia for an East it neither knows nor understands. And by resorting to the unilateral condemnation of this East's past, what becomes evident with both *The Death of Stalin* as well as *Comrade Detective* is that Hollywood (and the West in general) is gradually becoming as totalitarian and as propagandistic in expression as the very Stalinism and totalitarianism it wants to condemn.

Notes

1. Chris Berry, *A Nation T(w/o)o: Chinese Cinema(s) and Nationhood(s)*, in *Colonialism and Nationalism in Asian Cinema*, ed. Wimal Dissanayake (Bloomington: Indiana University Press, 1994). Chris Berry refers to the post-Mao-era war films, which sprang up in Chinese cinema as early as the 1990s. Themselves a continuation of the fifties and sixties tradition of revolutionary cinema, which emerged as a dominant style after the establishment of communist China in 1949, war films from the nineties and the first two decades of the twenty-first century continue to paint the liberation war as a valid marker of the post–Cultural Revolution/post–Tiananmen political landscape, therefore preserving their ideological colors intact despite the sociopolitical shifts brought about by these otherwise momentous events. Berry's implication in my reading is that these films' fixation on the erstwhile ideological goals of socialism, a fixation that stubbornly continues to characterize the Chinese transition to market economy despite the country's apparent embrace of Western cinematic means of expression, contributes to this "hysteria."
2. Of course, Berry only references here the war film genre that continued after the death of Mao, and *not* the fifth- and sixth-generation "new wave" cinema that equally appeared in the late eighties and early nineties and adopted a more critical stance toward the values of Maoist socialism.
3. I refer here to satires in the style of *Dr. Strangelove*, which, in their turn, I consider as having been influenced by Hollywood's somewhat ambivalent heritage of representing the Red East on screen. One of the most famous examples of this (earlier) heritage is, of course, Ernst Lubitsch's *Ninotchka* (1939). This discrepancy between Hollywood's mid-century use of satire and the present is detailed in the second part of this essay when discussing *The Death of Stalin*.
4. Jacques Rupnik, "In Search of a New Model," *Journal of Democracy* 21, no. 1 (2010): 108.
5. Rupnik, "In Search of a New Model," 110.
6. Such as Jeffery Sachs's "shock policy," which was unilaterally applied in both the former Soviet Union and Central/Eastern Europe in the early nineties as jump-starter for quick and necessary reforms that would transition these economies to a capitalist market-based system.
7. Roger Cohen, "How Democracy Became the Enemy," *New York Times*, April 6, 2018, https://www.nytimes.com/2018/04/06/opinion/sunday/orban-hungary-kaczynski-poland.html.
8. Jacques Rupnik, "From Democracy Fatigue to Populist Backlash," *Journal of Democracy* 18, no. 4 (2007): 21. Rupnik was advocating this point in 2007, after almost twenty years of transition and despite what he calls in this article "democracy fatigue." Judging by his most recent work, in articles such as "The Crisis of Liberalism," his take on the normative trajectory of liberalization in Eastern Europe hasn't changed. While Rupnik continues to identify populism, "culture wars," and nationalism in 2018 as the main evils of postsocialism, his solution for fixing this "democratic backsliding" continues to be a recoupling of the unfortunate separation between "democracy" and "liberalism," as well as a strengthening of civil society and the influence of the European Union. This undoubtedly means more liberalism and a more lawful implementation of capitalist reforms in Eastern Europe.
9. Larry Wolff, *Inventing Eastern Europe: The Map of Civilization on the Mind of the Enlightenment* (Redwood City, CA: Stanford University Press, 1994).
10. Edward Said, *Orientalism*, (New York: Vintage, 1979); Franz Fanon, *Black Skin, White Masks* (New York: Grove Press, 2008); Gayatri Chakravorty Spivak, "Can the Subaltern Speak?," in *Can the Subaltern Speak? Reflections on the History of an Idea*, ed. Rosalind Morris (New York: Columbia University Press, 2010), 21–78.

11. Wang Hui, *China from Empire to Nation-State* (Cambridge, MA: Harvard University Press, 2014). In his monumental study of Chinese modernity, *The Rise of Modern Chinese Thought*, and particularly in his English-translated introduction to this study, *China from Empire to Nation State*, Wang Hui identifies the paradigm according to which Europeans have understood "despotism" to have been shaped by their perception of the Ottoman Empire, with which Europeans had closer contact—a paradigm Westerners later freely projected onto the rest of the Asian peoples and implemented to demonize all Asiatic forms of government.

12. *The Death of Stalin* stars, among others, such American-British screen icons as Steve Buscemi and Michael Palin. For this reason, as well as Iannucci's frequent work on both sides of the Atlantic, and as also evident from the later discussion of satire in this essay, my argument is that this otherwise eminently British film is conflatable with the conventions and style of Hollywood at large, for which reason I treat the two as similar.

13. Joseph Gordon-Levitt, "Amazon's 'Comrade Detective' Doesn't Belong to the Right, or the Left—Exclusive," *IndieWire*, August 11, 2017, https://www.indiewire.com/2017/08/joseph-gordon-levitt-comrade-detective-controversy-exclusive-1201865653/. Gordon-Levitt wrote his own article on *Comrade Detective* in *IndieWire*, showing therefore at least some degree of old-style political engagement going beyond his mere implication in the series as dubbing talent. Although the miniseries stars Romanian actors Florin Piersic Jr. and Corneliu Ulici, they are dubbed in English by Gordon-Levitt and Channing Tatum.

14. Joseph Gordon-Levitt, "Amazon's 'Comrade Detective' Doesn't Belong to the Right, or the Left."

15. The producers do have a particular "film" in mind, the Czechoslovak series *Thirty Cases of Major Zeman* (*Třicet případů majora Zemana*), which aired between 1975 and 1980. However, while *Zeman* may constitute a point of conceptual inspiration, it is far from serving as a model for *Comrade Detective*, which appears indisputably more similar in tone and style to a TV series like *Miami Vice* (1984–89).

16. Chloe Schildhause, "What the Hell Is 'Comrade Detective'?," *Vanity Fair*, August 4, 2017, https://www.vanityfair.com/hollywood/2017/08/comrade-detective-amazon-channing-tatum-communist-propaganda.

17. Michel Foucault, *Society Must Be Defended* (New York: Picador, 1997), 53.

18. It is equally symptomatic in this respect that the voices of the Romanian actors—whose accented English could have been preserved to give the show a tinge of extra authenticity—have been replaced by those of the American actors.

19. Ben Travers, "'Comrade Detective' Review: Channing Tatum's New Cop Drama Is Not What It Seems—It's Better," *IndieWire*, August 4, 2017, https://www.indiewire.com/2017/08/comrade-detective-review-channing-tatum-cast-amazon-series-1201863535/.

20. Tatum and Gordon-Levitt make this point in an interview with Marah Eakin, a senior editor of A.V. Club. It can be watched at https://www.youtube.com/watch?v=PIWyAgSSAv4.

21. Roland Barthes, *Mythologies* (New York: Noonday Press, 1991), 16, italics mine.

22. Barthes, *Mythologies*, 16.

23. Nadine Holdsworth, *Joan Littlewood* (New York: Routledge, 2006), 32.

24. Holdsworth, *Joan Littlewood*, 82.

25. Holdsworth, *Joan Littlewood*, 111.

26. Lily Rothman, "Armando Iannucci on *The Death of Stalin* and Making a Funny Movie About Real Historical Trauma," *Time*, March 5, 2018, http://time.com/5179752/armando-iannucci-death-of-stalin/.

27. Zaid Jilani, "The Hilarious, Terrifying, British "Death of Stalin" Shows How American Comedy's Gone Wrong," *The Intercept*, March 17, 2018, https://theintercept.com/2018/03/17/the-hilarious-terrifying-british-death-of-stalin-shows-how-american-comedys-gone-wrong/.

28. Ben Walters, "Room at the Top," *Sight & Sound*, November 2017.

29. Laura Basu, "British Satire in 'The Thick of It,'" *Popular Communication* 12, no. 2 (2014): 92.

30. Basu, "British Satire in 'The Thick of It,'" 92.

31. Basu, "British Satire in 'The Thick of It,'" 92, italics in original.

32. Barthes, *Mythologies*, 41.

33. Barthes, *Mythologies*, 41.

34. Ruben Quintero, introduction to *A Companion to Satire* (Malden, MA: Blackwell Publishing, 2007), 3.

35. Basu, "British Satire in 'The Thick of It,'" 97.

36. Quintero, introduction to *A Companion to Satire*, 5.

37. M. M. Bakhtin, *The Dialogic Imagination* (Austin: University of Texas Press, 1981).

38. Basu, "British Satire in 'The Thick of It,'" 99.

39. Basu, "British Satire in 'The Thick of It,'" 101.

40. Noam Chomsky and Edward S. Herman, *Manufacturing Consent: The Political Economy of the Mass Media* (New York: Pantheon Books, 1988): 2.

41. Quintero, introduction to *A Companion to Satire*, 2.

42. Quintero, introduction to *A Companion to Satire*, 2.

43. Benedict Anderson, *Imagined Communities: Reflections on the Origin and Spread of Nationalism* (London: Verso, 1983). In his emblematic work on nationalism, Anderson claims that the American Civil War and the St. Bartholomew's Day massacre are held up as acts of negative memorialization accomplished by historiography's up-front focusing on tragedies for the purpose of not repeating these tragedies in the future.

44. Slavoj Žižek, *Did Somebody Say Totalitarianism? Five Interventions in the (Mis)Use of a Notion* (London: Verso, 2001).

45. Quintero, introduction to *A Companion to Satire*, 2.

46. Jean Baudrillard, *The Transparency of Evil: Essays of Extreme Phenomena* (London: Verso, 1993).

47. Quintero, introduction to *A Companion to Satire*, 5.

PART II
NEW AESTHETICS OF THE OLD PAST

THE COLDEST CITY
Berlin and the Remapping of Cold War Movie Aesthetics

Ian Scott

"The Cold War Never Ended"

In *Red Sparrow*, Francis Lawrence's 2018 adaptation of the Jason Matthews novel, Charlotte Rampling's Matron reminds her Russian Intelligence Service (SVR) protégés in training, including former ballerina Dominika (Jennifer Lawrence), that the Cold War is alive and well. It is an entreaty that Hollywood movies took increasingly to heart in the course of the 2010s. In addition to reviving traditional Cold War narratives, movies and television were busy initiating a whole set of new storylines about infiltration and subterfuge, typified by Matthews's book and Lawrence's cinematic realization. This restoration was predicated upon a wider twenty-first-century reevaluation of the old East/West rivalries, conceived out of the mass technological extension of spying and surveillance that had allowed for a perpetuation of observation well beyond the confines of the previous Cold War. That surveillance and infiltration were made alarmingly real by revelations about Russian interference in the 2016 US presidential election and the capabilities of Russian hackers especially for wider online systems meddling. And the result of that election produced the wildly quixotic relationship between celebrity businessman turned president Donald Trump and arguably the most dominant leader of Russia since the days of Leonid Brezhnev, Vladimir Putin.

Red Sparrow is a movie that hints at these contemporary geopolitical intricacies—the book even includes Putin in its storyline—not least through a plot that is willfully convoluted at times. Dominika, a former ballet dancer trained in the ways of *kompromat* (compromising or damaging information about an individual), is sent on a mission that involves locating a mole inside the Russian secret service and where she ends up as a double agent—in the pay of CIA operative Nate Nash (Joel Edgerton)—playing both sides against each other. If the film's narrative conceits reflect on contemporary Russian and American détente, its aesthetic presentation is more neatly locked into traditional Cold War imagery. Russia remains a typically gray, regimented society full of decaying housing blocks and regressive everyday clothing, a place where long crane shots follow lonely vehicles making their way to rural, secretive training schools designed in the Palladian style. Even the classified material that Dominika acquires from the Americans while secretly working for them is in the form of floppy disks rather than anything as sophisticated as a memory stick.

And while the film's soundtrack shies away from the use of Russian composers as diegetic accompaniment to these visual regressions, the adoption of Grieg's Piano Concerto, as well as incidental music composed by James Newton Howard that gives a nod to Mozart and Stravinsky, connects the tone of the movie with a professed and serious Russian classicism. The film bends toward grand nationalist traditions where the preservation of high culture is woven into the fabric of the nation's being.

Red Sparrow's Cold War is therefore neatly inverted between twenty-first-century superpower suspicions and old-style visual and aural signifiers. And it's not alone, as this essay argues. From Checkpoint Charlie to Hansa Studios, from Red Square to Gorky Park, from the Friedrichstrasse to Berlin Station, Cold War aesthetics became part of a historical reappropriation of time and place in movies and TV of the 2010s. But this exercise in reminiscence is also a cultural outlier signaling the re-emergence of Cold War–era Russian-American relations once thought consigned to history that are escalating again toward mistrust and accusation. That at least is one reading of Putin-led Russia, one that had clear enough antagonisms directed at the Bush and Obama administrations. One that had a clear schematic associated with it then, until the moment Donald Trump arrived on the US political scene.

This essay traces the history of the movie aesthetic that has grown up around the fraught relationship Russia has had with the West. It also accounts for the ways in which 2010s movie culture explicated the Cold War revival, first via iconic homage and associative locations, most especially in Tomas Alfredson's updating of John le Carré's classic *Tinker Tailor Soldier Spy* (2011), and then through an intricate profusion of style and influence aggregated around up-to-date concerns and relations, in David Leitch's *Atomic Blonde* (2017). In a new

Cold War era where traditional bipolar rules of engagement no longer seem to apply, the aesthetic convergence of a host of signifiers in Leitch's movie points toward this bewildering state of East/West relations, as well as political culture more generally, in the Trump/Putin world where things are not what they seem.

Acute aesthetic sensibilities are nothing new in Cold War thrillers of course. Visual convergences were a mainstay of the genre in the United States, Britain, and further afield for over forty years. Some were more attentive than others to the visual dynamics that historical setting and events offered, but the recognition of symbol and metaphor occurred almost immediately at the point at which Cold War politics and culture took a grip after 1945. That hold was apparent in cinematic uses of certain central European locations—Vienna, Budapest—as well as postwar London; but its real gravitational force occurred at the centripetal point of Cold War collisions, Berlin, and never really left.

Soon after the end of the war, for example, there emerged the so-called Berlin rubble films, including documentaries such as *Germany, Year Zero* as well as noir-ish spectacles like *A Foreign Affair* and *Berlin Express* (all 1948), each accentuating personal grief and national loss marked by the profusion of debris across the shattered city. From *The Spy Who Came in from the Cold* (1965) to *Funeral in Berlin* (1966), and from *The Man Between* (1953) to *Torn Curtain* (1966) and *A Dandy in Aspic* (1968), a bipolar conveyance of mood and atmosphere—in films that offered the divided city as a fulcrum for such feelings—was sometimes as important as plot and political verisimilitude. In Tony Shaw's words, "Berlin was *the* prominent symbol of the Cold War and the divided nature of Europe."[1]

This locational influence in "classic" Cold War cinema is no better realized than in Carol Reed's *The Man Between* from 1953. As Rob White observes, Reed was one of the "great directors of the city-experience," able to locate his protagonists among urban landscapes where they were both hunter and hunted. Operating climatically as a place of "evidence and surveillance," the city is the ultimate hiding place and the loneliest prison, as Reed masterfully displays with his rendering of postwar Vienna in his tour de force, *The Third Man* (1949).[2]

That White gleefully reports that nothing came of Oliver Stone's attempts to update that story to modern Berlin back in the 1990s does nothing to dispel the pervasive power of the Cold War imagery that Reed gave such vent to. The affinity of Stone and other directors of his generation toward the verisimilitude of Reed and cinematographer Robert Krasker's display of Cold War chiaroscuro was clearly felt, driven as Reed's cinema was by European cities literally subdivided through power, politics, and ideology.[3]

In *The Man Between*, Susanne Mallinson (Claire Bloom) visits her brother, a military doctor in Berlin treating victims of war and its aftermath at the end of the 1940s. Martin (Geoffrey Toone) is married to a German, Bettina (Hildegard Knef), and their house affords a view across the bombed-out wasteland toward the pitted and discolored Brandenburg Gate, which marks the border between the Allied and Russian sectors. Bettina agrees to show Susanne around the city, including a trip to the Eastern side, already strewn with propaganda posters of Lenin and Stalin. Here they meet Ivo Kern (James Mason), a shady character of no discernible abode in either the East or the West. Bettina's relationship to him—they were previously married—only seeps through gradually, while Susanne falls for the charming yet illusive Ivo, with disastrous consequences when she is mistakenly kidnapped.

While their relationship forms the bond that crosses the divides of the city, the film's (non)handling of increasingly complex motivations and maneuvers infecting Berlin as the Cold War hardens—the elite of Berlin society contrasted against the disenfranchised and disowned is repeatedly seen but never considered—has been an enduring criticism of a production that was persistently marred by problems.[4] In addition, the actions of the Western powers on one side of Berlin's divide—who are intent on "rescuing" people from the East's increasing repression—set against the trigger-happy communist forces on the other, become a simplified cat-and-mouse chase at the climax amid newly constructed offices and houses. While Kern turns out to be a human trafficker shuffling people from the Eastern to the Western sectors, like Harry Lime before him, he is anything but a predictable cipher for the ethics that swirl round the city's legitimate as well as illegal activities.

Regardless of the film's wider sociopolitical dilemmas, critics were united on its foundational visual language, the location shooting of which helped perpetuate what the director took to be the city's pervasively "jittery feeling."[5] The rubble takes on an aesthetic of its own, one that would soon dissipate as Berlin continued its reconstruction. And yet Reed's film seems to capture an enduring permanence to the devastation—in wintry scenes full of snow, the mounds of dirt and detritus convey an almost brutalist immovability—that is as illusory as the thousand-year Reich but as real as the battle of ideological wills going on in the streets adjacent to the gate, symbol of a global descent into capitalist and communist division.

Reed's film oozed magnetic manipulation of people battling for survival then, and showed a city in hock to an ideological war it couldn't stop from happening. Filmed in black and white and on a shoestring budget, the picture helped define the real and metaphorically desolate landscape the Cold War was creating. So it's instructive that some twelve years later, Martin Ritt's adaptation of up-and-coming novelist John le Carré's *The Spy Who Came in from the Cold* should also be in black and white. Ritt's direction further reinforced the cancerous dogma of separation spreading through Reed's picture and solidified le Carré's dictum that the Cold War had by now become a "condition of human illness."[6]

Le Carré's world, in this only his third novel, gravitates toward Douglas McNaughton's description of spies and spying as a quotidian affair, bound up in bureaucracy, a world where ambivalent morals and even more hesitant motivations abound.[7] The film, released two years after the publication of the book, employs Richard Burton's laconic style to create the cynical MI6 Berlin station chief Alec Leamas. Leamas is a spy who's gotten lost in the tangled idealistic configuration of the world he's trying to promote or save—he no longer seems to know which. With the action beginning in London soon after Leamas has been brought "in from cold," the Berlin he is eventually thrust back into—masquerading as a disaffected double agent—is one of familiarly austere tension and dissonance. His attitude to the task is offset by his scorn about the whole "Circus," a reference to the controlling office in London but also a play on the intelligence histrionics characteristic of the Cold War in the early 1960s. As Stephen J. Whitfield underlines, while the East is aesthetically "bleak and drab"—an echo of its reactionary social policies—the West as represented by Leamas has a "spiritual hollowness and nagging conscience" eating away at it. Whitfield identifies this pessimistic equivalency between competing systems as a challenge to the real political and intelligence establishment of the time, who felt threatened by the popularity of such films, which were seen to be undermining the "ideological intensity" of the conflict at hand.[8]

Shaw reinforces the point in *Hollywood's Cold War*. The history of American cinema's documentation of the Soviet-American clashes of the postwar era tells of a conflict fought more often than not within the realms of propaganda. Movies were indexically linked into battles for supremacy by virtue of their cultural projection of a set of mandated values and ideals designed to vanquish communist foes and conspiratorial plots. Indeed Shaw suggests that while propaganda relayed through film has conventionally been viewed as an adjunct to the more serious planks of Cold War rivalry—politics, economics, military superiority—the evidence points in fact to "propaganda and ideology [going] hand in hand, reinforcing one another" in a psychological battle for hearts and minds.[9]

Along with this belief in culture's more direct role in the Cold War conflict as histories of artistic production from both the West and the East have surfaced is, however, the intrinsic acceptance that cinema was engaged in a fight to document the "real"—that is to say, politically messy—Cold War. From a British cinematic perspective, there is no better example of this than *The Spy Who Came in from the Cold*, with its morally ambivalent, adversative characters of dubious persuasion—even on the same side—and refusal to neatly tie up narrative strands for redemptive, goodly reason. Here were history, people, conflicts, and events polished within a cinematic frame so as to reflect starkly upon real ideological battlegrounds and on authentic philosophical and psychological deconstructions of capitalist and communist mentalities. By way of contrast, Shaw emphasizes how a series of paradigmatic movies around the same time defined Hollywood's Cold War contribution in a somewhat different vein, notably *On the Beach* (1959) and *The Manchurian Candidate* (1962).[10] And through genres like science fiction and even biblical epics, as much as through storylines of assailants on the trail of spies or subversives from behind the Iron Curtain, the American cinematic mise-en-scène instead privileged the ideological necessities and melodramatic certainties behind communist aggression.

But the iconographic touchstones representing the Cold War remained similar on both sides of the Atlantic and indeed became locked in place by the 1970s. Like Berlin, "Cold War Eastern Europe had a stable cultural identity [by] the time of [the BBC's production of *Tinker Tailor Soldier Spy*]," a follow-up to the Leamas story from le Carré, who by now had become the master of the opaque espionage thriller. The semiotic core of the series, like this genre of fiction, had begun to revolve around shorthand optics like checkpoints, watchtowers, Trabant cars, pine forests, and urban wastelands. For McNaughton, "these liminal boundary sites reflected the Cold War's border crossings and moral ambiguities." This place discourse could be traced back to *The Spy Who Came in from the Cold* and might be termed the apogee of "the Iron Curtain discursive unconscious."[11] But then the wall fell and the Cold War concluded.

"All That Matters Is That We Won. And Who Cares What the Game Was Anyway?"

The end of the Cold War brought a marked turn in the liminality of Cold War imagery, for Hollywood at least. Bryn Upton remarks upon the disparity between the extended postwar movie era and the one commencing in the 1990s. Alternative tendencies in the cultural and political plotting of new enemies emerged: from Bond to Bourne, from impending nuclear Armageddon to postapocalyptic landscapes, and almost every other style in between. Hollywood reinvented all-consuming battles for good and evil through revised binary collisions between ideology and identity. It searched for, and found, new enemies in the post–Cold War era with new designs on takeover. This is most obviously realized in the all-conquering Marvel/DC superhero universes that began expanding in the 2000s into a seemingly never-ending selection of franchises. "In the post-Cold War era, superheroes have come to represent a new American identity," thinks Upton. "One in which the nation has had to learn the responsibilities that come with power and re-evaluate what leadership in the world means."[12]

European cinema, meanwhile, remained closer to traditional Cold War landscapes, notably in films like *Good Bye Lenin!* (2003), *The Lives of Others* (2006), and *The Tunnel* (2012), all of which glanced behind the wall and projected the splayed lives of East Germans coping with the final dissolute years of the GDR and its collapsing systems of labyrinthine surveillance and control. Each had some influence upon the popular *Deutschland 83* TV series, a German-American coproduction from 2015 whose 2018 follow-up, *Deutschland 86*, was a spy thriller that continued to follow the lives of people staring at the end of a divided Germany as the decade races toward its conclusion.

The Western equivalent of these texts offered a similar aesthetic pretension that called attention to visual landmarks and detail, which became the calling card of stories seeking to rekindle the look and feel of those times. This is most apparent in Alfredson's updated *Tinker Tailor Soldier Spy* (2011), in which a sepia-soaked Britain positively reeks of 1970s decay and deindustrialization. As McNaughton recounts of the novel: "[It] reflects a sense of national decline" while acting as "an elegy for empire."[13] And in that vein Alfredson's visual signifiers, courtesy of cinematographer Hoyte van Hoytema, are all centered on a chromatic pitch of brown and gray decorating dingy offices and covering bare streets that speak of metaphorical rust and national retreat. London is glanced at from underneath railway arches and out of dingy hotel rooms; St. Paul's Cathedral is spotted in one early scene, its lead dome weather-beaten and dirty, as though a remnant of the Blitz that had remained untouched ever since. Cars of the day like Morris Marinas and Rover P6s blend in to dark and mustard-colored exteriors. It's a picture of decay Eric Morgan spots as "evok[ing] that analog world via saturated colors of grey, brown, and burnt orange, all designed to capture the depressed nature of the 1970s. The British Empire is depicted as literally rusting."[14]

The atmosphere matches the arch–spy catcher George Smiley's reluctant demeanor too. Smiley (Gary Oldman) is a Cold War warrior of the old school, clinging to the last vestiges of decorum and propriety in a graceless world as he investigates the infiltration of the Circus by a plant orchestrated by his archnemesis in Moscow Centre, Karla. The secrets of British intelligence often lie in the shadowy corners of living rooms and safe houses in Alfredson's film, where the dim light from stained lampshades cannot reach into the impenetrable darkness.

Amidst this gloomy, brooding mise-en-scène, Mark Fisher senses the film occasionally indulging in a somewhat hyperreal "1970s theme park" atmosphere, with "branded goods (Trebor mints, Ajax household cleaner) pushed to the foreground of our attention" aimed at reproducing prevailing popular homilies of the decade's aesthetic.[15] This discursive unconscious—the reduction of personal items and geographical space down to their most persuasive and recognizable signifiers—retains similar focus on acute staging and regalia in Steven Spielberg's *Bridge of Spies* (2015) too. An early 1960s excursion into Berlin historically accounting for the repatriation of shot-down U-2 pilot Gary Powers, Spielberg's movie is at pains to realize the Cold War appearance—long trench coats, snow-covered streets, the initial stages of the wall's construction—as one deeply researched and precisely rendered, if not quite as cynically presented as in *The Spy Who Came in from the Cold*.

So historical totems become important in these films as both signifier and signified: a metaphoric reminder of what might be around the corner for East/West relations and a precise historicization of the Iron Curtain discursive unconscious. Indeed films like *Red Sparrow* and TV shows such as *Berlin Station* (2015–19) see the contemporaneity of their stories periodically giving way to revived Cold War ritual and metonymic presentation as the discursive unconscious routines break through and audiences are reminded of the indicative space. *Red Sparrow*'s aestheticizing of a Russian society that is dour, snow-covered, and populated by weathered people enjoying timeless high cultural pursuits (like the Bolshoi Ballet, for example) is a persistent and recognizable refrain. *Berlin Station*, by comparison, is a show about the lives and deceptions of CIA agents working within the titular unit that is firmly located among the vistas of modern-day Berlin. Yet it still returns its audience to the classic Cold War dividing points along Friedrichstrasse and Potsdamer Platz, at times placing them virtually underneath the now fractured and broken old wall, a memento of times past. All of this is played out to the soundtrack of David Bowie's 1990s catalog (the "I'm Afraid of Americans" theme song used in the credits) framed as a rejoinder to and updating of his *"Heroes"/Low*-era recordings of the late 1970s. Bowie lived during that time in the Schöneberg district of Berlin and used the city's status as a political crossroads for his musical inspiration.[16] This is most apparent on the title track of the 1977 *"Heroes"* album, which was recorded at the legendary Hansa Studios, taking its inspiration from a location that was literally, as the lyrics confirm, "standing by the wall."[17]

Bowie's fascination with the Berlin aesthetic continued throughout his career and was famously resurrected for his 2013 comeback single, "Where Are We Now?" A touristic gaze across the urban landscape he once scoured for ideas, the lyrics suggest how he never knew you could get a train from Potsdamer Platz across the divide, perhaps? Mention of this central arc of the city that was left desolate and subdivided during the Cold War seems significant, and it prompts further recollections of trademark East/West cultural collisions in the song, not least Nürnberger Strasse and its well-known nightclub, The Jungle, as well as the Bösebrücke Bridge. This last location was the site of the Bornholmer Strasse border crossing on November 18, 1989, which prompted the abandonment of checks and restrictions for East Berliners coming to the West and the beginning of the end of the wall and the East German state.

Bowie's song might be no more than an elegiac refrain for the site of past glories being visited one more time during his inspirational late-period work. But the cover of the album from whence "Where Are We Now?" is taken, *The Next Day*, pinpoints the source of this retrospective allusion that other artistic forms are adhering to by shrewdly layering a plain white box on top of Masayoshi Sukita's famous *"Heroes"* photo and crossing out that previous title.

Berlin Station's own "white box" layering of past and present is apparent in post-2016 films where musical signifiers like Bowie are surrounded by all sorts of ironic pastiches that result less in the discursive unconscious than perhaps a mindful recursivity. The Cold War, I want to suggest, is now increasingly being filtered through the lens of nostalgic pop-culture referents. The locations are not simply backdrops but active signifiers, the characters less archetypes than reassembled studies in past cinematic cutouts or RPGs, the soundtracks no longer a somber diegesis but rather a mixtape of your favorite songs of the era. While *Red Sparrow* provides some evidence of this assembly, it is in *Atomic Blonde* where such aesthetic conceits collide in a bombardment of graphic novel vignettes punctuated by ironic contemporary dialogue and lashings of violence and sexuality.

As if channeling Bowie's own playful sense of the way iconography can be both reinforced and discarded, sometimes at one and the same time, *Atomic Blonde*'s own mindful recursivity starts before the opening credits have arrived. The film, set in the days surrounding the fall of the wall, begins with stock footage of Ronald Reagan's June 1987 speech at the Brandenburg Gate in which he invites Russian general secretary Mikhail Gorbachev to "tear down this wall" as a way to quicken the forging *perestroika* Gorbachev had begun enacting. We switch to a snow-covered Berlin darkly blue in tone and an assassination by the Spree, within sight of the iconic Fernsehturm television tower constructed by the GDR in the late 1960s, which dominates the skyline. The accompaniment to this sharp opening action is "Blue Monday" by New Order. Almost immediately we cut to MI6 agent Lorraine Broughton (Charlize Theron) still in an azure light immersing herself in an ice bath while overlooking Whitehall and Big Ben, the epitome of establishment power in London. As she seeks to repair her apparently bruised and broken body, the second track of the film is, unsurprisingly, by Bowie. "Cat People" from 1982—written for Paul Schrader's thriller of the same name, itself a loose interpretation of Jacques Tourneur's 1942 classic—then plays over the introductory credits as Broughton, like many before her, also "comes in from the cold" and reports to headquarters on the mission that seems to have nearly cost her life.

As Lorraine recalls the events of the previous days, the camera cuts back and forth between the interrogation room and Berlin, where recurrent symbols like concrete blockhouses and garish graffiti form the backdrop to an appointment at the wall with a Stasi informant codenamed Spyglass for James McAvoy's Berlin station chief, David Percival. Lorraine had been sent to Berlin to find out who has "the list," a microfilm collection of agents working on either side of the political as well as physical wall. As she relates to her handlers—Emmett Kurzfeld (John Goodman) and Toby Jones as the appropriately named Eric Grey, a nod to his turn as Percy Alleline in *Tinker Tailor*—immediately on arriving at Tempelhof Airport, Lorraine gets picked up in a car by two KGB agents sent to intercept her. Realizing her predicament, she attacks the agents before deliberately crashing the car. Percival, who has been tracking these events, pulls her from the wreckage and sets out to navigate the sights of Berlin in his Porsche, pointing out each landmark to Lorraine—Brandenburg, Checkpoint Charlie—until she arrives at her garish neon hotel room. The film's knowingly scripted use of its iconic urban landscape is reinforced by the recurrent after-dark time-lapse photography accelerating the action, optically presenting the city in light trails, and helping collapse the historical timeframe around the characters as the wall's downfall gets ever nearer. This visual exhibitionism is courtesy of Jonathan Sela's striking cinematography. A veteran of visually stylish comic book adaptations—*Max Payne* (2008), *John Wick* (2014)—with an ability to parade monochromatic palettes with precise color grading, Sela's photography blends the 1980s setting with a lingua franca of the past matching a dystopian future/present look.

Documenting the past as it happens, so to speak, is thus *Atomic Blonde*'s aesthetic conceit. The music is of the time, but not of the moment—the songs are more often from the early eighties trend for electronica; the clothes loosely reflect the decade's influences, but rarely endorse the fashions of 1989 specifically—Lorraine's dress sense is near enough contemporary. In other words the film fastens onto the truths of the Cold War endgame but peddles the fakery of the post–Cold War—and more accurately post-2016—moment, and that much more forcefully. The populace's tearing down of the wall only ever happens on TV in the film, even while the characters are residing nearby. But, rather like the aestheticization of wider politics for the later 2010s, attendant reality is not the same thing as assertive re-creation.

Therefore, *Atomic Blonde* is filled with pop-culture ephemera that hint toward knowing irony even while the plot suggests operatives playing both sides against each other in a more or less faithful Cold War narrative reenactment. Lorraine's oversized T-shirt with the word *BOY* plastered on it smacks of Katharine Hamnett's 1980s designs, particularly her famous "Choose Life" shirts for Wham!, George Michael's band. Michael's own solo work then features in the apartment-complex scene that ends in violent confrontation with several Stasi officers. "Father Figure" plays on an iconic Nakamichi Dragon cassette deck so as to signal the technology of the era. In the early interview scenes, Lorraine is asked for her impressions of David and sagely remarks that he was good-looking, but with a "disastrous Sinead O'Connor haircut."[18] The bisexual subplot between Lorraine and French agent Delphine (Sofia Boutella) as well as the cool music are all a way to, in director Leitch's words, "reinvent the stuffy Cold War spy movie."[19]

That relationship, which conceivably genders the traditional spy-game milieu's hypermasculine environment, posits the Cold War as a site of female empowerment, not simply one of patriarchal mind games. But it's neither a new nor an untroubled concept. Movies like *Salt* (2010) starring Angelina Jolie as a CIA agent in an exhaustive conspiratorial deception game hinting a decade beforehand at a new era of Russian interference, as well as 1990s pictures such as Luc Besson's *Nikita* (1990) and *The Long Kiss Goodnight* (1996) with Geena Davis, mined the same impulses. But objectification and what one critic describes as the "discomforting gaze" in *Atomic Blonde* and *Red Sparrow* especially remain closer to the foreground than transformative sexual politics.[20] It's sometimes as if a movie imprint is simply being rehashed, one that stretches back into the depths of the Cold War itself to recall the arch-villainess Rosa Klebb tackling Bond in *From Russia with Love* (1963).[21] Ironically enough, only *Tinker Tailor*'s arcane 1970s world challenges in a small way the objectification of women that infects its male characters—with a piece of graffiti on a wall near the safe house where Bill Haydon (Colin Firth) has been handing over the service's secrets. It reads pointedly, "the future is female."

Atomic Blonde's cinematic allusion also resides in layers of supposition and meaning. As Lorraine makes her way into the East in search of the list, the modernist theater she finds herself in is showing Andrei Tarkovsky's 1979 postapocalypse film, *Stalker*, about a mythic search for a place known only as "the room." The aesthetic composition of rooms and their ransacking in the search for meaning—just like in *Tinker Tailor*—therefore takes on a dual import, both for the characters looking for clues that will unravel the plot and the audience seeking out signification there on screen. In the club where Lorraine meets Delphine, the axiom "everything you've ever wanted is on the other side of fear" blazes in neon from high up on a wall. A reference to self-help guru George Addair, the phrase becomes a running metaphor—for the protagonists, the city, and the future.

And as the events of the movie are wound up and the bluff and double bluff that have been carried out by numerous protagonists is slowly unknotted, the film finishes as it began, with Bowie, this time performing "Under Pressure" with Queen. In a contemporary gesture toward the modern East/West dichotomy that the film's tangled cultural orbits of music, fashion, and fads scoop up, the overall aesthetic conceivably begins to match the political expediency echoed in Trump's chaotic presidency, as well as gesturing to the more traditional Cold War posturing embodied within Putin's regime.

Conclusion: "It Was an Aesthetic Choice as Much as a Moral One"

At the close of *Tinker Tailor Soldier Spy*, Smiley visits Haydon in the detention center where he resides before being traded to the Russians as a consequence of his traitorous actions. "I had to pick a side, George," he explains. "It was an aesthetic choice as much as a moral one. The West has become so very . . . ugly."[22] Haydon implies mental as well as physical deterioration, and it is a conclusion the new Cold War movies pick at with abandon. Aesthetics over morals, boorish populist catchphrases over high-minded statecraft, the previous certainties of secrets and deceptions against the current artificiality of post-truths and fake news: the retrospective Cold War narrative of the 2010s not only asserts the East/West ideological conflagration as one not easily separated by good and evil, but presses the case for the very tenets of that battle as all part of a wider cultural tapestry. Contemporary Realpolitik and down-at-heel movie parlance help *Atomic Blonde* bring together the past and present; a readable subtext of shorthand Cold War theory meets realigned geopolitical diplomacy.

Catherine Kodat, in examining what she calls the metapolitics of Cold War culture, maintains that artwork is still regarded in many quarters as a subordinated form when considering its impact upon society at large. But there is a view nevertheless that sees cultural products as "manifestations of deep social forces."[23] Art, as the unconscious face of politics (as Jacques Rancière would suggest), acts as a break with traditional (Marxist) theoretical forms, which saw the underclass as but guided and brainwashed by art as a form of social and political control. For Rancière there must be some understanding of art's independent potential to break free of privilege and domination by the elite, to not simply be a form that is contained by the leading interrogators' vision of art, or fixed in place for the appropriation of the state.[24]

So for Rancière, as Margus Vihalem expresses it, the interest is not only in aesthetics as practice (and therefore what the inherent value is in art) but also its function within a wider democratic base. Rancière's "democratic paradox" is precisely the way art informs the workings of society. Politics is problematic because it questions not only what is of democratic value in the functioning of government but also what is at stake in the democratization of life, and these two projections are difficult to reconcile. As Vihalem reports, countries of the Warsaw Pact under Soviet control attempted to stimulate democracy, or at the very least convince the populace of democratic principles during the Cold War, by information and assertion, the very mode of which contradicts democratic functionality by bringing attention to the fact that the masses are in fact being subordinated or brainwashed by an insistence on the presence of democracy within their midst."[25]

The signified tropes that inhabit movies such as *Red Sparrow* and *Atomic Blonde* may not be new concepts for the thriller genre therefore. But these and other aesthetics in the modern context have been reframed in order to underpin a revised conceptual overview of the Cold War itself that tests the state of Rancière's paradox. They are cultural rejoinders, in other words, to the emergence of the unlikely Trump-Putin worldview inhabited in the late 2010s. More important than ever in that world, where the moorings of traditional geopolitical relations are untethered, is the way these aesthetics reflect on the new normal in a political culture that takes pastiche, cliché, fakery, and the contrived to be acting as discourse, authority, and philosophy. We live in a surface age, but more critically a surface age adopted by many leaders—not just Trump—that is repeatedly perceived to be reality, a superficiality, we are assured, that does have depth and meaning, but only on these leaders' say-so.

"When reality is ignored or re-characterized in ways that defy logical thinking and mute rational rebuttal, then 'new normal' becomes, drip by drip, just another category of current events." *Washington Post* columnist Kathleen Parker's remarks here reflect the thoughts of many commentators in the midst of Donald Trump's presidency and were preceded by a headline that pleaded for society's rational consideration of its direction: "The New Normal Isn't Normal at All."[26]

"New Normalism" presents a picture of democratization and a rhetoric that allude to commonality of purpose while—allegedly—attacking the elitism upon which this vision of normality was forged. The trend-spotting and visual panache employed in *Red Sparrow* and *Atomic Blonde* is surface-level appropriation conceived of as New Normalism. One is located in the modern day but reconstitutes a vision of Russia thought to have been relegated to the history books, while the other is set in 1989 but smacks of contemporary attitudes towards the "new" Cold War. In other words, both movies are imbibed with designs on fusing past Cold War themes and theory with the present: that once upon a time Hollywood and the real Cold War aesthetically mimicked each other, aware of the respective hold both had over the public's imagination and fears, but they are now perhaps engaged in a different kind of imitation for entirely different purposes. That Cold War dialogue of old did have layers of brooding philosophizing punctuated by an associated language that must be learned—the "invented nomenclature," as Fisher calls it—and a set of rules that were deliberately impenetrable. This vocabulary became an accepted if clichéd mantra of the habits of the times.[27]

As these new films stress, le Carré's world, the *Tinker Tailor* universe of the Circus, control, and Karla, may have been acutely sensitive to the actual diplomatic and intelligence maneuvering being done during the Cold War, but the films are also exposing their belief in the cinema's core rationale: how spy-thriller-ish the scenarios of deception and double bluff all were. How in train with the fears and perceptions of the Cold War purveyors they became. How much, despite the fears of the establishment that Whitfield describes, the films were in fact *reinforcing* the dominant view of the Cold War's potent and ongoing threat.

A clash of ideals and history that continues to separate America/the West and Russia/ the East at the Cold War's traditional frontier, Berlin, is the message of these new films' verisimilitude, reread as readily as the events since 2016 have ended up dismissing all previously conventional norms. That in the twenty-first century a claim as incendiary as the presumptive president of the United States being in the pocket of the Russian leader, an admirer, a secret ally in Putin's consolidation of power and influence, seems no longer as fabricated as, well, as a Hollywood movie would have us all believe. Trump repeatedly stated a liking for Putin, conducted meetings off the record with him, and failed to fully endorse the intelligence agencies' summation that Russian hackers had been behind the break-in to the Democratic National Committee computers during 2016. There was, as Luke Harding puts it, "a strange fealty at work. Trump didn't praise any other leader in quite the same way. Or as often. His obeisance to Putin would continue even as he ascended to office."[28]

Just as the "first" Cold War dealt in anxiety about the prospect of the world ending, so one sees in this modern crop of films existentialist cinematic tendencies toward throwing the metaphorical kitchen sink at the screen, almost as if the profusion of perceptive imagery were designed to confuse and discombobulate the superpowers into conflict as a matter of course. And in so doing, *Atomic Blonde* and others reach into the contemporary world's wary understanding of how and why conventional diplomacy and Realpolitik have been hemorrhaging in the current era. Where once coded language and posture defined diplomatic business, brash bravado and trash talk are now the twenty-first century's weapons of choice.

Donald Trump's record in this rhetorical arms race is unprecedented of course. From inauguration crowds and an immigration crisis of huge proportions gathered at the US-Mexico border to Trump's relationship with Putin, we see that history, the facts, and diplomatic niceties are never allowed to get in the way of his loquacious commentary. The issue then is that the "new" Cold War may or may not be fact, and the US/West-Russia diplomatic breakdown and growing tension may be real, or it may be a figment of lawmakers' imagination, or entirely antithetical indeed to a much more covert and profitable relationship that some sources understand has been cultivated between Trump and Putin. A return to what was once rooted in the discourse of language, behavior, and adherence to national and international affairs pre-Trump is what film critics have readily picked up in these movies too. As Robbie Collin expressed it: "Here is a boost for those of us who were getting disillusioned by the idea that all Russian spies did these days was sit in a warehouse in St. Petersburg for 12 hours at a time and tweet about Donald Trump. Per *Red Sparrow*, the latest film to star Jennifer Lawrence, far sexier things are afoot, with pliant young patriots like Dominika primed to seduce and destroy enemies of the state."[29] The certainties of the old Cold War, in other words, no longer apply, and the issues are perhaps confined to films, appearing to appropriate past imagery and ideology mixed with modern genre tropes and mythical pretensions, out to gainsay some predetermined present and future now no longer as assured as it once felt.

Since Donald Trump, in other words, the reinvention of the Cold War in the twenty-first century has seen a daringly new disjunctive form of presentation that rifles the old-style Cold War hot-button signifiers and mashes them up into an alternately crazed dish. As this essay has examined, the new Cold War films are less about sending up previous pretense than they are about hyperextending the milieu to the point of confusion. Rather in the vein of TV series such as *The Americans* (2013–18) and *Deutschland 83/86*, the rehabilitation of the era is on one level a poetics of catalogued and randomly distributed tick-box arrogations of memory and feeling, from cars and clothes to toys and tableau, via music and mementoes. But, as this essay has argued, the course of the Cold War on film in the 2010s, from *Tinker Tailor* to *Atomic Blonde*, has seen reminiscence move from Iron Curtain discursive rendering to a jumble of ideological contradictions earmarked as a disorderly Cold War 2.0. This is less recuperation than reinvestment then: in the disorganized Trump-era moment amid the disbanding of traditional Western liberal elite rhetoric and reflection in favor of braggadocio and bravado. The Cold War may never have ended, but it will also never be the same again.

Notes

1. Tony Shaw, *British Cinema and the Cold War: The State, Propaganda and Consensus*, (London: I. B. Tauris, 2006), 70.
2. Rob White, *The Third Man*, (London: BFI Publishing, 2003), 46–49.
3. White, *The Third Man*, 71.
4. Peter William Evans, *Carol Reed* (Manchester: Manchester University Press, 2005), 128.
5. Shaw, *British Cinema and the Cold War*, 72.
6. Shaw, *British Cinema and the Cold War*, 60.
7. Douglas McNaughton, "Cold War Spaces: *Tinker Tailor Soldier Spy* in Television and Cinema," *Journal of British Cinema and Television* 15, no. 3 (2018): 395.
8. Stephen J. Whitfield, *The Culture of the Cold War* (Baltimore: Johns Hopkins University Press, 1991), 208.
9. Tony Shaw, *Hollywood's Cold War* (Edinburgh: Edinburgh University Press, 2007), 3.
10. Shaw, *Hollywood's Cold War*, 5.
11. McNaughton, "Cold War Spaces," 383–84.
12. Bryn Upton, *Hollywood and the End of the Cold War* (London: Rowman & Littlefield, 2014), 174.
13. McNaughton, "Cold War Spaces," 377.
14. McNaughton, "Cold War Spaces," 382. See also E. J. Morgan, "Whores and Angels of Our Striving Selves: The Cold War Films of John le Carré, Then and Now," *Historical Journal of Film, Radio and Television* 36, no. 1 (2016): 88–103.
15. Mark Fisher, "The Smiley Factor," *Film Quarterly* 65, no. 2 (2011): 41.
16. Dylan Jones, *David Bowie: A Life* (London: Windmill Books, 2018), 264–66.
17. David Bowie, "Heroes," Track 3 on *Heroes*, RCA, 1977, compact disc.
18. David Leitch, *Atomic Blonde* (Los Angeles: Focus Features, 2017).
19. Alenya, "*Atomic Blonde* Goes Nuclear," *The Silver Screen Show*, August 5, 2017, https://thesilverscreenshow.com/2017/08/05/atomic-blonde-goes-nuclear/.
20. Stephanie Merry, "'Red Sparrow' Is a Spy Thriller with an Identity Crisis," *Washington Post*, February 27, 2018, https://www.washingtonpost.com/goingoutguide/movies/red-sparrow-is-a-spy-thriller-with-an-identity-crisis/2018/02/27/b5635e52-174e-11e8-b681-2d4d462a1921_story.html?utm_term=.f97e9af4da41.
21. Anna Smith, "Violent Femmes: *Atomic Blonde* and Hollywood's New Wave of Killer Women," *The Guardian*, July 27, 2017, https://www.theguardian.com/film/2017/jul/27/violent-femmes-atomic-blonde-and-hollywoods-new-wave-of-killer-women.
22. Tomas Alfredson, *Tinker Tailor Soldier Spy* (London: StudioCanal/Focus Features, 2011).
23. Catherine Kodat, *Don't Act, Just Dance: The Metapolitics of Cold War Culture* (New Brunswick, NJ: Rutgers University Press, 2015), 35.
24. Kodat, *Don't Act, Just Dance*, 37–38.
25. Margus Vihalem, "Everyday Aesthetics and Jacques Rancière: Reconfiguring the Common Field of Aesthetics and Politics," *Journal of Aesthetics & Culture* 10, no. 1 (2018): 3–4.

26. Kathleen Parker, "The New Normal Isn't Normal at All," *Washington Post*, November 20, 2018, https://www.washingtonpost.com/opinions/the-new-normal-isnt-normal-at-all/2018/11/20/a3907cc8-ecff-11e8-96d4-0d23f2aaad09_story.html?noredirect=on&utm_term=.261bf125f591.

27. Fisher, "The Smiley Factor," 41.

28. Luke Harding, *Collusion: How Russia Helped Trump Win the White House* (London: Guardian Books, 2017), 8.

29. Robbie Collin, "*Red Sparrow* Review: Jennifer Lawrence Plays Tinker Tailor Soldier Sexpot in a Suspense-Free Spy Caper," *The Telegraph*, March 1, 2018, https://www.telegraph.co.uk/films/0/red-sparrow-review-jennifer-lawrence-playstinker-tailor-soldier/.

"YOUR BODY BELONGS TO THE STATE"
The Mobilization of the Action Heroine in Service of the State in *Red Sparrow* and *Atomic Blonde*

Dan Ward

A key theme of Cold War cinema historically in the US has been the projection of difference between Russians and Americans. Films of this era acted as a vehicle for particular politicized archetypes, not only in terms of projecting an idealized image of capitalist America but also in establishing its antithesis in the shape of communists and, by extension, Russians. These antagonists were not just ideologically dissident, but fundamentally *other*: identified allegorically with aliens by their "lack of feelings" or "the absence of individual characteristics,"[1] and associated with the twin themes of corruption and possession,[2] a malign, invasive force. As well as demonizing Russia, this representational strategy was premised on building an image of America as its antithesis: for instance, Matthew S. Hirschberg discussed how *Rocky IV*'s (1985) main plotline pits "the striving American spirit" against "the regimented, controlled Soviet regime."[3] Russia serves in such films to help define America by what it is not.

While the Cold War and the rise of the Soviet Union provided the framing device for such representations, in reality this is only one epoch within the much longer tradition of unsympathetic portrayals of Russia in Western (and particularly American) media. As pointed out by James Chapman, the frequent portrayal of Russia as "a geopolitical threat to the West" predates the Cold War, and as such it is questionable whether the contemporary cycle of Russian antagonists currently prominent in Hollywood constitutes a resurgence of negative depictions or is simply the latest phase in this representational tendency.⁴ As well as individuals, institutions are at the heart of these polarized representations. My focus in this essay will be on the contrasting representations of the Russian and American security services in two recent exemplars of the genre: *Atomic Blonde* and *Red Sparrow*. Underpinning this analysis is the centrality of the female protagonist in each film to the framing of these agencies, building on broader trends within both the entertainment industry and news media. It is my contention that the films co-opt the ostensibly progressive figure of the self-reliant, resourceful female action hero in the rehabilitation of institutions such as the CIA, while also mobilizing issues of gender to demarcate the familiar perception of difference from Russia and its own institutions.

A Market Empire

The relationship between the state and the culture industry cannot be ignored in considering how particular representations of institutions and organs, or even systems, of government are shaped. Tony Shaw has pointed out that Washington has historically regarded Hollywood as "an indispensable means of projecting what it saw as the superiority of capitalism within and beyond its own immediate sphere of influence."⁵ Mutual interests and cooperation between the two stretch back to the early part of the twentieth century, and the State Department has been identified as taking a turn toward a more proactive involvement with the movie industry from its release in 1944 of a memorandum entitled "American Motion Pictures in the Post-War World."⁶ The industry itself also quickly recognized the political potential of its output in promoting the interests of the US government abroad, with producer Walter Wagner referring to Hollywood movies at the outbreak of World War II as "120,000 American ambassadors."⁷ Referring to information contained within a tranche of cables released by WikiLeaks in November 2010, Paul Moody has identified an "increasingly interventionist," though overwhelmingly clandestine, approach from around the middle of the previous decade by the State Department and US embassies to manage perceptions of America globally, with the film industry central to this.⁸ This has included political and economic interventions into the industry, such as providing support for the expansion of Hollywood production and distribution into strategically important markets like Eastern Europe. The importance of market forces and commercial productions sometimes distinct from the direct hand of the state is also acknowledged as significant in Westernization processes in countries such as Saudi Arabia, with ideological and economic motivations often appearing fairly fluid, in line with Victoria de Grazia's characterization of America's postwar soft power as part of a "market empire."[9]

Along with this more general state involvement in the film industry, there has also been acknowledgement of extensive direct Pentagon influence within the entertainment industry, as detailed by David Robb, Tricia Jenkins, and Matthew Alford and Tom Secker.[10] Alford and Secker identify over eight hundred films, and one thousand television productions between 1911 and 2017 that received direct Department of Defense support, the more overt examples of this including assisting with script development in Michael Bay's *Transformers* films (2007–17), in order to use the franchise as an "opportunity to showcase the bravery and values of our soldiers and the excellent technology of today's Army to a global audience," in the words of a US Army ELO report from 2010.[11] This allusion to the "global" audience of course chimes with the aforementioned tendency to view films as "ambassadors" for America worldwide. In more recent years, it is not only the muscular jingoism associated with traditional promotion of the US military and security services that has been privileged, but a more contemporary emphasis on representations that seek to identify these institutions as progressive and enlightened, while nonetheless powerful or effective. The way in which women in service are represented is a cornerstone of this strategy.

It is necessary to consider the cultural and political context in which these particular gendered representations arise. Following the 2018 US midterm elections, a not insignificant section of media coverage was allotted to the gains made by new female candidates within the Democratic Party. While the focus on identity politics as a barometer of supposed progressiveness within contemporary political spin is nothing new, what is striking is the rhetoric that accompanied this coverage. Much of it centered around discourses of toughness, the focal point being the group dubbing themselves "the Badasses": a set of five female Democrats with backgrounds in the military or national security establishment. *USA Today* reported approvingly that "DC is about to get an influx of tough, battle-tested women,"[12] while Reuters stated that some Democrats perceive "a woman with national security experience" as the best hope to unseat President Donald Trump. An article in *The Atlantic* suggested that these women "could be the start of a redefined party that's more closely associated with national security,"[13] and CNN admiringly reeled off the achievements of women described as "pretty badass as individuals . . . Army and Air Force veterans, a military pilot, a former CIA agent, and a former CIA analyst."[14] There is little in the way of cautionary notes within these reports (all from outlets that position themselves as either nonpartisan or nominally left-leaning) regarding the potential tensions between the activities of the American military and security services and the ostensible values of liberal-minded voters. Rather, first-hand experience within the military/security establishment is framed as a guarantor of a female politician's strength, a necessary bulwark in the face of potential accusations of weakness from political opponents. The mobilization of such women in conspicuous opposition to the totemic figure of Trump also confers an implicitly progressive veneer: Jeremy Teigen, a political scientist cited in the aforementioned Reuters article, calls female military veterans "the antidote to a guy who is a potential draft dodger and misogynist."[15] It is telling in this framing that Trump's nonparticipation in a conflict as polarizing as Vietnam is positioned as equally toxic to his misogyny, and speaks to the uncritical attitude toward the US military and security services within such coverage (that he "questioned the findings of US intelligence agencies" is another mark against Trump for Teigen).

In these discourses, the female political hopefuls and the national security state enjoy a symbiotic relationship: their service confers on them the stamp of "toughness" and acts as a political shield against opponents who would typically call such qualities into question in a female Democrat. In the Reuters piece, pollster Celinda Lake suggests that Democrats often face a problem "not just in being perceived as liberal, but that liberal often ends up being perceived as weak. But you can't run weak against these women—they're tougher than nails."[16] For the military and intelligence organizations themselves, it feeds into a wider narrative of such institutions as increasingly progressive, particularly where gender is concerned. On January 9, 2019, NowThis, a news site that claims an audience comprised more than two-thirds by millennials,[17] tweeted that "the CIA's highest level positions are now all held by women—another stride towards progress."[18] This echoes official material promoted on the CIA's own website, which proclaims that the 2013 recommendations made by the CIA director's Advisory Group on Women in Leadership have resulted in women comprising 43 percent of officers promoted to senior ranks in 2018, as well as 36 percent of the Senior Intelligence Service.[19]

Again, there seems to be some cohesion between the agency's image-management talking points, at least where gender politics are concerned, and the relatively sympathetic manner of its coverage in many ostensibly liberal media outlets. Jordy Cummings, writing for *Jacobin*, suggests that the CIA's "rebranding" in the public consciousness has its roots in the near aftermath of the 9/11 terrorist attacks and the so-called War on Terror, when the agency was able to position itself as a comparatively liberal cadre working within the reactionary government of the George W. Bush administration. Cummings sees as central to this the example of the Joseph Wilson–Valerie Plame affair, which involved the outing of a CIA agent by a conservative journalist in retribution for public challenges the agent's diplomat husband made about government narratives on Iraq.[20] For Cummings, instances such as this "allowed the CIA to cultivate an image of itself as a liberal and rational technocracy." What is perhaps most significant about Cummings's observations in relation to the concerns of this essay is how this "rebranding" embedded itself within popular media representations. Referencing examples like the independent, individualist protagonists of texts like Kathryn Bigelow's *Zero Dark Thirty* (2012), Stephen Gaghan's *Syriana* (2005), and the CIA-focused TV series *Homeland* (2011–20), he argues that such depictions have become so prevalent in popular culture, irrespective of direct agency influence on the industry, because "it has become common sense that CIA agents are cool, liberal, and cautious, but ready to fight the terrorists to the last drop."[21] This dichotomy positioning the CIA as a necessary, steadfast check against abuses of power by reactionary administrations has undoubtedly come to the fore once again since the election of President Trump in 2016 and the aspersions regularly cast on the legitimacy of that election in the months and years following. Moreover, the narrative has continued to be bolstered by popular culture, particularly evident in a text like the aforementioned *Homeland*; despite Carrie Mathison's (Claire Danes) turbulent and often fractious relationship with her employers, her loyalty to the agency as ultimately a force for good endures. This is most evident in the show's seventh and most recent season, featuring a plotline in which Carrie battles to secure the release of hundreds of intelligence operatives placed under arrest by a paranoid president. Predictably (and of relevance to the themes of this essay), the divisions between the president and her well-meaning intelligence community are ultimately shown to be the result of deliberate meddling by malign foreign operatives—specifically Russian ones.

"Am I Your Bitch Now?"

Atomic Blonde takes the form of a period piece set in the near past and situated within the geopolitical hinterland of Berlin in the days preceding the collapse of the Soviet Union. As a genre, costume or period drama has often been identified as a strategic vehicle for representing contemporary issues or anxieties through an aesthetic lens that hearkens back to another time.[22] The rationale behind this may be as pragmatic as it is artistic, for instance in sneaking potentially radical themes past zealous censors, in much the same way that the more politically subversive science fiction writers have utilized the opportunities afforded by that genre in the past to critique governments or other influential elements within society. Given the tone of the film's representation and the present geopolitical hostilities, such a motivation seems unlikely in this case, as there certainly seems to be little reluctance on the part of either Western governments or the culture industry to use the media to fan the flames of tensions with Russia. Indeed, the film is one of several recent examples to invoke period aesthetics in playing to these attitudes: it has become an especially popular device in television drama in recent years, with notable examples including *The Americans* (2013–18) and *Deutschland 83* (2015), a collaborative German-American production. Both of the aforementioned productions, like *Atomic Blonde*, are set in the final decade of the Soviet Union's existence, underscoring the sense of inevitability of the triumph of capitalism alluded to in much of the revisionist rhetoric especially popular in the immediate post-Reagan years. This does, of course, raise questions about the intrigue this specific period of the Cold War seems to hold for contemporary Western media producers.

In *Atomic Blonde*'s case, its central conceit is the immediate proximity of the film's setting to the demolition of the Berlin Wall and the collapse of the German Democratic Republic. Its main plotline is labyrinthine, following the interagency machinations and betrayals brought about by the loss of a secret list containing the names of every espionage operative active in the city during the period. Charlize Theron takes the starring role as Lorraine Broughton, ostensibly an MI6 agent sent to Berlin to retrieve the strategically crucial information. What follows is a chaotic battle across the turbulent terrain of the city, involving a mass of British, Russian, German, French, and American agents, all with clandestine motivations and conflicting loyalties. The Berlin portrayed in David Leitch's film is characterized primarily by chaos, with the instability inherent in the period immediately preceding the transition to capitalism and liberal democracy mirrored in the physical turmoil experienced by Lorraine and her peers through the film's many fast-paced, visceral action sequences. The violence is graphic and brutal, but heavily stylized, and almost fantastical in regard to the sheer volume of physical punishment Lorraine in particular is able to endure, dispatching scores of interchangeable enemies in close-quarters combat as she traverses the city.

The portrayal of Broughton's almost superhuman fighting skills and resilience feeds in not only to the contemporary discourse on "badass" women in the military and intelligence services, but also broader trends within popular culture giving increasing prominence to representations of strong, battle-hardened female protagonists. The initial emergence of this tendency was highlighted by Sherri Inness in 2004, noting "an explosion of tough women in popular media."[23] Inness cites examples from a range of media products, including video game characters like Lara Croft, television characters like Xena the Warrior Princess and Buffy the Vampire Slayer, and wrestlers such as Chyna. As is made clear by the title of Inness's book, *Action Chicks*, the major commonality among the majority of the case studies featured is that the women are physically active, unafraid to use violence, and more often than not more proficient at it than their male counterparts. For Inness and the authors featured in her collection, the figure of the action heroine and her increasing prominence in popular culture is bound up directly with the destabilization of gender norms and assumptions about behaviors and roles that are "natural" for women. Though not unproblematically, the figure of the action heroine has thus been for the most part received by critics as a generally progressive one, with its popularity continuing to grow in recent years. Increasingly over the past few decades, the roles of action heroine and CIA agent have intersected within popular culture, with notable examples including films like *Salt* (2010) and television shows like *Alias* (2001–6). The latter is a particularly notable example of how the agency has attempted to co-opt the positive associations of the action heroine, much like it has mobilized the narrative of feminist progress within the CIA in service of its "rebranding." Not only did the agency provide direct assistance to the production of the series, in the form of on-set technical advice from official liaison Chase Brandon,[24] but it also enlisted the star of *Alias*, Jennifer Garner, to film a recruitment video. The press release that accompanied the advert stated that

> the video emphasizes the CIA's mission, and its need for people with diverse backgrounds and foreign language skills. Ms. Garner was excited to participate in the video after being asked by the Office for Public Affairs. The CIA's Film Industry Liaison worked with the writers of "Alias" during the first season to educate them on fundamental tradecraft. Although the show "Alias" is fictional, the character Jennifer Garner plays embodies the integrity, patriotism and intelligence the CIA looks for in its officers.[25]

It is this kind of background that makes it impossible to examine *Atomic Blonde*'s depiction of a tough, independent CIA officer without also considering both the cultural context it emerges from and its implicit ideological underpinnings. Like *Red Sparrow*, the film is an adaptation from literature, in this case Antony Johnson's graphic novel *The Coldest City* (2012). Along with screenwriter Kurt Johnstad and director David Leitch, who had previously been an uncredited codirector on another fast-paced action thriller featuring disposable Russian antagonists, *John Wick* (2014), Charlize Theron took an active role in the production of the film through her company, Denver and Delilah Productions.

One aspect of *Atomic Blonde*'s narrative that is absent from its source material is the characterization of Lorraine as bisexual. The film's somewhat offhand treatment of her relationship with French spy Delphine (Sofia Boutella) seems to have been a deliberate creative choice on the part of Theron, born in part from her "frustration of how that community is represented in cinema"—or not represented—as well as her desire to avoid what she sees as the cinematic trope obliging the depiction of a sexually active woman falling in love. Theron describes the development of the character's sexual identity as "one of my proudest parts of the development, when we came up with that." For her, the portrayal of Lorraine's sexuality is about empowerment rather than male titillation. In the same interview, Theron also makes extensive reference to the gender politics of the film industry, alluding to the gender pay gap revealed through the Sony hacks and the rise of female action stars.[26] Such emphases in the promotional campaign for *Atomic Blonde* underline the centrality of the identity politics underpinning Theron's apparent vision of her character, and by extension the film itself, as progressive (in spite of the prolific male-on-female violence featured within, along with the decision to violently kill off the film's only openly gay character).

The liberal individualism embodied in the character of Lorraine is contrasted with the film's characterization of Russians, or perhaps more accurately the lack thereof. The majority of the enemies Lorraine comes into conflict with over the course of the film are positioned as physical obstacles for her to overcome, stations on the manic obstacle course that is Leitch's Berlin, rather than fully developed characters with identifiable human motivations. Aside from the hedonistic rogue British agent Percival (James McAvoy), the film's main antagonist, the only potential exemption to this tendency is Aleksander Bremovych (Rolland Moller), a senior Russian intelligence officer in Germany. Although he appears infrequently within the film, Bremovych is totemic of *Atomic Blonde*'s debt to the broader trends within contemporary media with regard to representing Russians. A hulking, brutish figure, he is first seen interrogating a group of young street punks who claim to have seen the potential defector known as Spyglass. The fashion stylings and apparent cultural tastes of the punks identify them clearly with the Westernization of Berlin, and Bremovych torments one of them by forcing him to breakdance as Nena's Cold War pop anthem "99 Luftballons" plays from a boom box. When the display is ended, he beats the young man to a pulp with his own skateboard. The scene functions as a means of associating Russia, through Bremovych, crudely with the past, oppressive and cruel and standing in violent opposition to anything symbolizing resistance or change.

Outside of Bremovych, the USSR is represented mainly by proxy, through scores of East German Stasi henchmen. The only one of these presented as any kind of consistent threat to Lorraine is a resilient, sadistic bleached-blonde assassin who, when he appears to have subdued Lorraine in a fight, calls her a bitch. She eventually turns the tables on him, and before she kills him reminds him of the insult with the pointed rebuke, "Am I your bitch now?"[27] This is, of course, another way to underscore the gender politics of the film, and the way it transposes them onto geopolitics. The East is presented as rooted firmly in the past, misogynist, regressive, and violently resistant to progress. The West (and specifically America) is its antithesis, the inevitable tide of market liberalism, pop culture, and sexuality, American hard and soft power embodied in the seductive yet lethal figure of the action heroine. The old-versus-new dichotomy is underlined in the film's final scenes, when Lorraine is revealed to be an American CIA agent who has been playing both the Russians (who believed she was a double agent) and British (who believed she was their agent) all along. Dropping her British accent before she kills Bremovych, she tells him, "I want you to get this through your thick, primitive skull—I never worked for you. You worked for me."[28] The exchange again posits Bremovych as an anachronism, and Lorraine as insistently independent. Her pretense dropped, she is seen at the end of the film joining her real boss, CIA agent Emmett Kurzfeld (John Goodman), on a plane back to America. As the old order collapses in Berlin, the film's conclusion shows the dying empires of the old world unable to keep pace with the savvy adaptability of America's market empire.

"The Cold War Did Not End —It Merely Shattered into a Thousand Pieces"

Red Sparrow tells the story of Dominika (Jennifer Lawrence), a Russian ballerina forced into premature retirement after suffering a career-ending injury during a performance. After being coerced into working for the SVR by her uncle Ivan (Matthias Schoenaerts), the deputy director of the organization, Dominika is trained as a "Sparrow," an operative who employs sexual seduction as the cornerstone of their espionage activities. Over the course of her assignments during the film, she comes into contact with CIA agent Nate Nash (Joel Edgerton), and, having become increasingly disillusioned and desperate as a result of the abuse she endures from her employers and the state more generally, begins to see Nash and the CIA as a possible way out of her predicament.

While it is unclear whether the production of *Red Sparrow* featured direct input from Washington and the Pentagon, the film does have its origins in a novel written by a former CIA operative, Jason Matthews. In an interview with the *Hollywood Reporter*, Matthews reveals some salient facts about both the novel's conception and some of the ideological underpinnings of its representations. First, the novel itself was checked and approved for publication by a CIA review board, ostensibly to ensure that the book would not inadvertently reveal real sources; second, Matthews himself acted as a technical advisor for the film's script, to "correct or suggest ways to make the tradecraft and even the dialogue sometimes and the action more authentically CIA." Again, it is not yet evident whether the Pentagon provided direct assistance in an official capacity on the production of the film in the typical manner identified by Jenkins, Alford, and Secker, but, through the processes noted above, the agency certainly seems to have been involved by proxy. Matthews's support for official NATO and State Department narratives prevalent in the Second Cold War discourse is also obvious in the interview, as he states his belief that Vladimir Putin's goals are "to weaken the United States, to weaken NATO and the Atlantic alliance." Matthews also reaffirms this essay's position on what is intentionally conveyed through the film's gender representations: Downplaying suggestions that sexual harassment may be an issue in the intelligence community, he acknowledges that "in the early days of the agency, I don't think it was as enlightened" (as he presumably believes it is now), but as a counterpoint uses the example of his own wife's career progress within the agency to reiterate its implicit fairness and commitment to equality. Tellingly, he also makes a point of contrasting that with women in the Russian secret service, who "probably have a big challenge ahead" of them to achieve similar career development. As a point of note, Matthews admits that he never worked or lived in Russia during his thirty-three years with the CIA.[29]

Familiar tropes about Russia are evident throughout the film. In a scene where the Sparrows undergo their training, Dominika and her fellow trainees are instructed to take off their clothes. Noting her surprise and hesitation, the older, female instructor turns to Dominika and explains: "Your body belongs to the state. Since your birth, the state nourished it, now the state asks something in return. You must learn to sacrifice for a higher purpose, to push yourself beyond all limitation and forget the sentimental morality with which you were raised."[30] Here, the body is conceived as a weapon or piece of industrial machinery that the state has invested in. The implicit discourse sees that investment as a proprietary one, and hence the "request" being made by the state is framed as a matter of duty and obligation rather than personal choice. In line with familiar Cold War propaganda directed against socialism more generally, the rights and agency of the individual are disavowed in deference to the "higher purpose," reducing them effectively to cogs in the machine whose duty is to conform. Perhaps ironically within the identity-focused representational framework discussed elsewhere in the essay, the fact that Dominika's trainer (who also instructs young male Sparrows at the school) is a female officer who has obviously risen through the ranks of Russian intelligence might plausibly be read as a surprisingly progressive representation of the SVR's employment practices. Within the broader context of the scene and the film's plot, though, it is more clearly framed as an example of the sacrifices women must make to have such opportunities in Russian intelligence, the older officer doubtless having had to give her body over to these practices in the past, and now co-opted into coercing other young officers into surrendering to similar sexual exploitation themselves. Charlotte Rampling, who plays the officer in charge of training the Sparrows, states in a promotional interview that "the point is to break down these girls."[31] This underscores the message that initiation into the service of the Russian state is not about empowerment, but rather the removal of autonomy. Tellingly, the only name given to Rampling's character is Matron: her status comes at the expense of the erasure of any semblance of individuality, even a name.

In line with the temporal manipulation employed in feeding contemporary anxieties about Russia through the lens of the Cold War in the period texts previously discussed, *Red Sparrow* also has its own take on this motif. The Sparrow program that is the film's central conceit has been discussed by Jason Matthews in a CNBC interview promoting the film. He claims to have based the story's portrayal of the program on anecdotes and rumors from Russian sources about "a state school where women trained in these arts." Tellingly, he also admits his belief that this school has "long since closed," speculating that "honey trap" seduction of foreign diplomats and businessmen is likely outsourced to "independent contractors" such as sex workers in the modern day. Nevertheless, *Red Sparrow*'s representations of modern Russia and its institutions seem satisfied to conflate the alleged practices of the Soviet past with today's society, with all the ideological and geopolitical implications that entails; the Matron at Sparrow school tells her charges that "the Cold War did not end, it merely shattered into a thousand pieces," and the aforementioned article itself describes the film's themes as "a throwback" and "seemingly anachronistic."[32] Significantly for the contentions of this essay, the same cannot be said of the film's treatment of the CIA.

The Russian state's coldness and brutality toward its "assets" is directly contrasted with the CIA, embodied in Joel Edgerton's portrayal of agent Nate Nash. In February of 2018, prior to the film's release, Jason Matthews participated in a live question and answer session on the popular discussion site Reddit. In response to a question asking him what fictionalized media texts about the CIA most often "get wrong," he responded that the "CIA in movies and television is usually portrayed as a ruthless organization which thinks nothing of betraying its employees. There is nothing farther from the truth."³³ It is clear that Matthews seeks to redress this alleged inaccuracy in *Red Sparrow*, instead projecting this ruthless disregard for human assets onto Russia and the SVR, with the CIA framed as humane and compassionate by comparison. Rather than accomplishing this by creating a heroic savior caricature in Nash, it is through the agent's banality and weaknesses that the organization is humanized. Edgerton describes his character as "this lonely, hapless, slightly alcoholic loser." Though this assessment seems far from flattering, in context it is important in establishing a distinction between the flawed but human CIA agents and the familiar trope of the cold, robotically efficient Russian. Edgerton goes on to qualify his analysis: "Because he opened a space in his life for trusting people, being a CIA operative meant that that was sort of a weakness, and because he formed these connections with his mole, and was willing to protect that person, he kind of got suspended from his job." Given Matthews's description of what popular culture gets wrong about the CIA, the function of Nash's characterization seems to be to highlight the ultimate humanity of the agency. When Nash allows his personal attachment to his asset to compromise his professionalism, he is, to quote Edgerton, "kind of suspended from his job."³⁴ This relatively lenient disciplinary approach is, again, another means by which the US intelligence services are distinguished from their Russian counterparts: when things go wrong in Dominika's assignments, she is blackmailed into sexual subjugation under pain of death and subjected to brutal physical torture.

This reaches its apex in the film when Dominika is suspected of working with the Americans: taken to a cold, dull cell, she is stripped, doused with water, and beaten methodically with a club. The banal aesthetics of the cell are reflected in the stoicism of her interrogators and the steady, deliberate build of the torture, with very precise targeting of strategic points of the body, and the jarring thumps and cracks of the club's impact, coupled with Dominika's screams, providing an uneasy juxtaposition with the empty silence of the room. Again, the disturbing representation here of the violent interrogation of a suspected traitor is another means by which the ruthlessness of the Russian state is contrasted with its American equivalent. The contrast here is achieved by way of omission: we simply are not shown in the film how the CIA deals with such situations. Despite public revelations of the CIA's pioneering of "enhanced interrogation" techniques including "waterboarding, mock executions, 'rectal feeding,' sleep deprivation, stress positions and other cruel, inhuman and degrading treatment of detainees,"³⁵ this is not apparently the story that Matthews or the producers of *Red Sparrow* want to tell. Of note here is the fact that Gina Haspel, whose promotion to the position of CIA director is one of the examples of the agency's "progress" touted by identity-focused media discourse like the aforementioned NowThis tweet, has been personally implicated in the direct supervision of such torture.[36]

The history of the CIA reveals connections and policies far removed from the liberal branding implicit in these representations. A set of previously classified documents released due to the 1998 Nazi War Crimes Disclosure Act confirmed CIA recruitment of networks of Nazi war criminals throughout Eastern Europe, whose purpose was to act as spies and provocateurs within the Soviet Bloc. Former congresswoman Elizabeth Holtzman, a member of the panel examining the files, opined that the documents could not be written off as "dry historical documents," but rather that they held implications for the conduct of American foreign policy and the origins of the Cold War.[37] Holtzman's conclusion has been supported in the years following by continued US financial and strategic support for neo-Nazi groups such as Ukraine's Azov Battalion, reaffirmed by a 2016 funding bill alleged by House Speaker Paul Ryan to provide for "European countries facing Russian aggression," and which effectively removed a 2015 amendment by Congressman John Conyers that placed restrictions on "arms, training, and other assistance to the neo-Nazi Ukrainian militia, the Azov Battalion," based on the erroneous claim that such limitations would already be covered by the existing Leahy Law.[38] Similar controversy has surrounded CIA arming and training in recent years of "rebel" groups in Syria, with US-provided weapons often finding their way into the hands of explicitly Islamist jihadist groups such as the al-Qaeda–affiliated al-Nusra Front, who often fought alongside the CIA-backed militants.[39] Much as the roots of support for groups like Azov Battalion can be traced back to the CIA's postwar machinations in Eastern Europe, so too connections to jihadist groups in conflict zones like Syria and Libya[40] can be seen as a continuation of the policies enacted during the Soviet-Afghan War, during which the CIA provided arms and training to mujahideen such as the Hezb-i-Islami group.[41] None of this is to suggest that the CIA is remarkable or distinctively amoral in comparison to any other geopolitical power's intelligence services, but rather precisely to underscore that it is not. A commonality in the examples listed here is proxy enmity with Russia, and this seems to confirm that the agency's instinct when faced with an apparently revanchist or aggressive Moscow is almost always to lurch right, to combat what it sees as reactionary activity with greater reaction. Moreover, that the continuing pattern of collusion with profoundly illiberal elements across the globe suggests that the current popular narrative—promoted through official materials and reaffirmed through a range of media representations—framing the agency and the US security apparatus more broadly as "progressive" through an emphasis on gendered identity politics amounts to little more than an ideological fig leaf.

Conclusion

This essay's title has dual meaning. Its case studies are two films that feature female protagonists working within rival security agencies, ostensibly in service of two enemy states. However, my underlying analytical focus is the means by which both films mobilize the female protagonist in ideological terms in service of American soft power and in support of broader narratives promoting the alleged liberal and progressive nature of the American state's clandestine services.

The implications of the representations in these films are clear: work in the security services for American women is associated with empowerment and independence. For Russian women, it is characterized by exploitation and sexual abuse. In both films, the body is conceived as a weapon, to be wielded in service of the state. However, it is the way in which that weapon is employed, and the degree of autonomy afforded it, that reveals the ideology underpinning the texts. Charlize Theron's characterization of Lorraine Broughton as a tough, empowered, sexually independent woman who happens to be in service to the CIA reflects contemporary media discourse about the "badass women" of the military and security services currently making waves in American politics, and particularly the disavowal of any contradiction between involvement with these institutions and the liberal, progressive politics the women supposedly embody. In *Red Sparrow*, the ostensible heroine of the story is not in the direct employ of the CIA, but it is through the agency's help that she is able to find some degree of personal relief and redemption from her troubled and abusive past. These representations work as part of an ongoing campaign to rehabilitate the image of the CIA in public perception, in spite of the decidedly illiberal history of the institution and the ongoing collusion between the national security state and reactionary groups across the globe.

The way notions of time are employed is an important element of these functions. In the case studies, as in many of the recent texts dealing with Cold War II themes, Russia is associated firmly with the past. A common motif for representing Russia and Russians in contemporary media is through the form of period drama, invoking the established generic technique of transposing present-day themes onto the aesthetics of another period in time, and in this case projecting the ideological polarization of the Cold War onto current geopolitical tensions. *Atomic Blonde*'s application of the period format contrasts the pragmatic flexibility of America's market empire, embodied in the film in its institutions and their savvy agents, with the self-destructive amorality of the dying empires it is pitted against. In *Red Sparrow*, a different approach is taken to the strategic blurring of past and present: here, the conflation of the

Soviet-era USSR with the modern neoliberal capitalist Russian state is more overt, with the plot focused around a covert Cold War training program that the story's original creator admits is a thing of the distant past. The regressive gender politics apparent in such a program are another means by which Russia is associated firmly with the past, and though there are male trainees among Dominika's classmates, we do not see them exposed to the brutal sexual coercion and abuse that Dominika undergoes on her initiation into the service. This is directly contrasted with the film's depiction of the CIA, which is imagined as a relatively modern, progressive organization by comparison. As in the typical representational strategies of more traditional Cold War films, the portrayal of Russia and its institutions is framed primarily in terms of presenting a clear antithesis to America: again, America defined by what it is not.

The representation of Russians in these films is marked primarily by conformity: hearkening back to the alien-invasion films that denied Russian-coded characters any individual characteristics, here they are portrayed either as homogenous, disposable sadists or subjugated automatons cowed into surrendering their autonomy in service of a cold, brutalist state that does not reciprocate their loyalty. The exception, of course, is Russian characters whose own resilience, independence, and innate sense of justice lead them to transfer their loyalties to the one state where such qualities might be nurtured and rewarded: the United States of America. In their affirmation of ultimately hackneyed narratives furnished with an identity politics veneer and coupled with a remarkably uncritical portrayal of the American security services, the conformity that the films finally reveal most acutely is their own.

Notes

1. Mark Jancovich, *Rational Fears: American Horror in the 1950s* (Manchester: Manchester University Press, 1996), 26.

2. Ronnie D. Lipschutz, *Cold War Fantasies: Film, Fiction & Foreign Policy* (Lanham, MD: Rowman & Littlefield, 2001), 36.

3. Matthew S. Hirshberg, *Perpetuating Patriotic Perceptions: The Cognitive Function of the Cold War* (Westport, CT: Praeger, 1993), 104; Sylvester Stallone, *Rocky IV* (Hollywood: United Artists, 1985).

4. Quoted in Tom Brook, "Hollywood Stereotypes: Why Are Russians the Bad Guys?," BBC Online, November 5, 2014, http://www.bbc.com/culture/story/20141106-why-are-russians-always-bad-guys.

5. Tony Shaw, *Hollywood's Cold War* (Edinburgh: Edinburgh University Press, 2007), 4.

6. Ian Jarvie, "The Postwar Economic Foreign Policy of the American Film Industry: Europe 1945–1950," *Film History* 4 (1990): 277–88.

7. Paul Moody, "Embassy Cinema: What Wikileaks Reveals about US State Support for Hollywood," *Media, Culture & Society* 39, no.7 (2017): 1063–77.

8. Moody, "Embassy Cinema."

9. Victoria de Grazia, *Irresistible Empire: America's Advance through Twentieth-Century Europe* (Cambridge, MA: Harvard University Press, 2005).

10. David Robb, *Operation Hollywood: How the Pentagon Shapes and Censors the Movies* (Amherst, NY: Prometheus Books); Tricia Jenkins, *The CIA in Hollywood: How the Agency Shapes Film and Television* (Austin: University of Texas Press, 2012); Matthew Alford and Tom Secker, *National Security Cinema: The Shocking New Evidence of Government Control in Hollywood* (Scotts Valley, CA: Createspace Independent Publishing Platform, 2017).

11. Alford and Secker, *National Security Cinema*, 8.

12. Lindsay Schnell, "Tough Talk, Tough Women: New House Members Come Together to Form 'the Badasses,'" *USA Today*, November 14, 2018, https://eu.usatoday.com/story/news/politics/elections/2018/11/13/election-2018-new-female-u-s-house-members-form-badasses/1981743002/.

13. Priscilla Alvarez, "What a New Crop of Veteran-Lawmakers Means for Democrats," *The Atlantic*, November 18, 2018, https://www.theatlantic.com/politics/archive/2018/11/female-veterans-usher-change-democratic-party/576076/.

14. Stephanie Coontz, "The 'Year of the Badass Woman' Holds a Message GOP Needs to Hear," CNN, December 18, 2018, https://edition.cnn.com/2018/12/17/opinions/gop-worry-badass-women-coontz/index.html.

15. Amanda Becker, "'Badass' National Security Women Offer Democrats a Trump Antidote," Reuters, December 5, 2018, https://www.reuters.com/article/us-usa-politics-women/badass-national-security-women-offer-democrats-a-trump-antidote-idUSKBN1O419I.

16. Becker, "'Badass' National Security Women Offer Democrats a Trump Antidote."

17. Anthony Ha, "Video News Startup NowThis Raises $16.2M Led by Axel Springer," *TechCrunch*, December 8, 2015, https://techcrunch.com/2015/12/08/nowthis-series-d/.

18. NowThis (@nowthisnews), Twitter, January 9, 2019, 11:33 a.m., https://twitter.com/nowthisnews.

19. "CIA Makes Progress on Women in Leadership," Central Intelligence Agency News & Information, July 11, 2018, https://www.cia.gov/news-information/featured-story-archive/2018-featured-story-archive/cia-makes-progress-on-women-in-leadership.html.

20. "Timeline: The Valerie Plame Affair," *The Guardian*, October 28, 2005, https://www.jacobinmag.com/2016/12/cia-russia-wikileaks-podesta-trump-clinton-obama.

21. Jordy Cummings, "The CIA Is Not Your Friend," *Jacobin*, December 21, 2016, https://www.jacobinmag.com/2016/12/cia-russia-wikileaks-podesta-trump-clinton-obama.

22. Paul Coates, *Cinema, Religion & the Romantic Legacy* (Abingdon, UK: Routledge, 2017), 108.

23. Sherri A. Inness, ed., *Action Chicks: New Images of Tough Women in Popular Culture* (New York: Palgrave Macmillan, 2004), 1.

24. Nicholas Schlou, "How the CIA Hoodwinked Hollywood," *The Atlantic*, July 14, 2016, https://www.theatlantic.com/entertainment/archive/2016/07/operation-tinseltown-how-the-cia-manipulates-hollywood/491138/.

25. "New Recruitment Video on the CIA Careers Site," Central Intelligence Agency News & Information, June 17, 2008, https://www.cia.gov/news-information/press-releases-statements/press-release-archive-2004/pr03082004.html.

26. "Charlize Theron on *Atomic Blonde* and Female Action Stars," *Variety*, July 11, 2017, https://feature.variety.com/charlize-theron-atomic-blonde/.

27. David Leitch, *Atomic Blonde* (Los Angeles: Denver and Delilah Productions, 2017).

28. Leitch, *Atomic Blonde*.

29. Katie Kilkenny, "How *Red Sparrow* Author Made the Film More 'Authentically CIA,'" *Hollywood Reporter*, March 1, 2018.

30. Francis Lawrence, *Red Sparrow* (New York: TSG Entertainment, 2018).

31. Movieclips Coming Soon, "*Red Sparrow* Featurette—Story," March 2, 2018, YouTube video, 2:34, https://www.youtube.com/watch?v=wRk8URix-v8.

32. Javier E. David, "'Red Sparrow' Used to Be an Actual Phenomenon during the Cold War, and in Some Ways Still Is: Author," CNBC, March 4, 2018, https://www.cnbc.com/2018/03/03/red-sparrow-used-to-be-an-actual-phenomenon-during-the-cold-war.html.

33. Jason Matthews, "Hi there! I'm Jason Matthews, former CIA officer and author of Red Sparrow, soon to be a major motion picture. Ask Me Anything!," Reddit, February 19, 2018, https://www.reddit.com/r/books/comments/7yq3oo/hi_there_im_jason_matthews_former_cia_officer_and/duift72/.

34. HeyUGuys, "Joel Edgerton Talks *Red Sparrow* & Working with Jennifer Lawrence," February 26, 2018, YouTube video, 4:53, https://www.youtube.com/watch?v=F4dVPnkrxhc.

35. Amnesty International, "Exposed: Torture and the CIA," *Amnesty International UK*, January 12, 2018, https://www.amnesty.org.uk/exposed-torture-and-cia.

36. Jeremy Scahill, "U.S. Navy Reserve Doctor on Gina Haspel Torture Victim: 'One of the Most Severely Traumatized Individuals I Have Ever Seen.'" *The Intercept*, May 17, 2018, https://theintercept.com/2018/05/17/gina-haspel-cia-director-torture/.

37. Martin A. Lee, "The CIA's Worst-Kept Secret: Newly Declassified Files Confirm United States Collaboration with Nazis," *Institute for Policy Studies*, May 1, 2001, https://ips-dc.org/the_cias_worst-kept_secret_newly_declassified_files_confirm_united_states_collaboration_with_nazis/.

38. James Carden, "Congress Has Removed a Ban on Funding Neo-Nazis from Its Year-End Spending Bill," *The Nation*, January 14, 2016, https://www.thenation.com/article/congress-has-removed-a-ban-on-funding-neo-nazis-from-its-year-end-spending-bill/.

39. Mark Mazzetti, Adam Goldman, and Michael S. Schmidt, "Behind the Sudden Death of a $1 Billion Secret CIA War in Syria," *New York Times*, August 2, 2017, https://www.nytimes.com/2017/08/02/world/middleeast/cia-syria-rebel-arm-train-trump.html.

40. James Risen, Mark Mazzetti, and Michael S. Schmidt, "US-Approved Arms for Libya Rebels Fell into Jihadis' Hands," *New York Times*, December 5, 2012, https://www.nytimes.com/2012/12/06/world/africa/weapons-sent-to-libyan-rebels-with-us-approval-fell-into-islamist-hands.html.

41. Jason Burke, "Frankenstein the CIA Created," *The Guardian*, January 17, 1999, https://www.theguardian.com/world/1999/jan/17/yemen.islam.

THE SHAPE OF WATER AND THE COLD WAR REVISITED

Cyndy Hendershot

Guillermo del Toro's *The Shape of Water* (2017) reimagines classic Cold War science fiction film for a twenty-first-century audience. The Oscar-winning film is part of a recent trend in American cinema, with such films as *Bridge of Spies* (2015), *Hail, Caesar!* (2016), and *Atomic Blonde* (2017) using a Cold War setting to try to make sense of the vexed relationship between America and Russia. The film also breaks with stereotypes in the classic Cold War genre by creating characters that would have been impossible in 1950s and 1960s American cinema.

Del Toro has maintained that the film is rooted in his admiration for the classic B movie *Creature from the Black Lagoon* (1954). As a six-year-old, del Toro was taken by "seeing the Gill-man swimming underneath Julie Adams and falling in love with him falling in love with her."[1] In that film Julie Adams is a traditional 1950s beauty with whom the Creature falls in love. In del Toro's retelling of the story, Elisa Esposito (Sally Hawkins) is a unique beauty, a mute janitor at a military facility where she encounters the Creature (Doug Jones), known as "the Asset" in the film, and forms a strong bond with him. Both the original Creature and del Toro's originate in the Amazon, but del Toro's Creature is gentle and kind, while the Creature from the Black Lagoon is violent but made sympathetic because of his deep love for the woman. In *The Seven Year Itch* (1955), the Girl (Marilyn Monroe) and Richard Sherman (Tom Ewell) go to the movies to see *Lagoon*. Afterward, in the iconic steam-vent scene, the Girl says that she "just felt so sorry for the Creature."[2] She recognizes the Creature's loneliness, while Richard is baffled by her reaction. Del Toro has maintained that he felt a strong desire for the Creature and the woman to end up together.

He approached film executives with an idea for a remake of *Creature from the Black Lagoon* with the stipulation that the Creature and the woman end up together, but was turned down.³ While the Creature is killed in *Lagoon*, del Toro allows for an ending in which the Creature and Elisa end up together in the water, as it is revealed that Elisa's neck wounds are in fact gills.

Gay Men in the Kennedy Era

Del Toro's film, however, is not just an exercise in nostalgia for the Cold War and its classic cinema. He maintains about nostalgia "that we think it was all good in the past, and it wasn't. We had the same problems then that we have now."⁴ There are several aspects of the film that make it very much a reflection of the twenty-first century. The issue of homosexuality, which could not have been addressed directly in classic Cold War cinema, is explored in two main characters in the film. Elisa's neighbor and best friend, Giles (Richard Jenkins), struggles with his attempt to live a full life as a gay man in early 1960s America. Giles frequents a diner, Dixie Doug's, that specializes in pies. He orders the pie, which is inedible, in order to be close to a worker there, Pie Guy (Morgan Kelly), on whom he has a crush. When he finally gets the courage to express his desires to Pie Guy by touching him on the hand, Pie Guy bans him from the restaurant. Pie Guy pretends to be from the South but is really from Iowa. However, his attitude toward homosexuals and African Americans is a stereotypically Southern, 1960s reaction to difference, but also a problem in our world. President Trump's cabinet has been peopled with a number of homophobic individuals, including former attorney general Jeff Sessions, "whose actions include a vote against the LGBT inclusive hate crimes law that President Obama signed in 2009 and which the Justice Department is charged with implementing."⁵ Thus, the Trump administration oddly mirrors Putin's "gay propaganda law" passed in 2013.⁶

Giles feels a strong connection with the Creature, who serves in the film as a signifier of difference. When Giles first sees the Creature, he says, "He's so beautiful."⁷ Like Elisa, he sees a beautiful creature, not a monster. While the Creature is surviving in Elisa's bathtub, Giles talks to him. As he sketches the Creature, he asks him, "Have you always been alone?" He concludes, "Maybe we're both just relics."⁸ The loneliness of the creature mirrors Giles's own loneliness as a gay man stuck in a society that will not accept him. Due to his isolation, Giles lives vicariously through old movies. We see him watching *The Little Colonel* (1935), with its iconic and taboo-breaking tap dance on the stairs with Shirley Temple and Bill Robinson.⁹

Giles watches other films and television shows that both point to his penchant for escapism and reference the interspecies love story. We see him watching Betty Grable dance with a human dressed as a horse in *Coney Island* (1943), and he is watching *Mister Ed* (1958–66), a show about a talking horse, as the Creature emerges from Elisa's bathtub. At one point, Giles refuses to watch civil rights protests on television, indicating his desire to insulate himself from the contemporary world, in which he does not fit. He loses his job as an ad man because he draws red Jell-O instead of green in a layout for his boss. The boss tells him that "the future is green."[10]

While Giles is a sympathetic character struggling with his sexuality in a prejudiced society, the other gay character in the film represents a darker side of Kennedy-era homophobia. Commenting upon the character of Richard Strickland (Michael Shannon), del Toro says that he wanted to make him the true monster of the story and emphasize his homosexuality.[11] As the film's narrator, Giles calls Strickland "the monster who tried to destroy it all."[12] When Elisa and her coworker, Zelda Fuller (Octavia Spencer), first meet Strickland, he barges into the men's room while they are cleaning. He urinates in front of them and puts his cattle prod, which he calls an "Alabama howdy-do," down on the sink, then tells them that a proper man washes his hands before urinating.[13] The cattle prod, which he uses to torture the Creature, symbolizes his violent desire to be a "real" man. It serves as a phallic symbol and as a signifier for the devices often used against civil rights protestors. A. O. Scott comments that Strickland's cattle prod "links him to the Southern sheriffs occasionally shown terrorizing Civil Rights demonstrators on television."[14] Whereas Giles avoids the demonstrations on television, Strickland embraces the violent masculinity associated with oppressors. He hurls racist comments at Elisa and Zelda, treating them as unintelligent inferiors.

Strickland's relationship with the Creature is the opposite of Giles's reaction to him. Strickland calls the Creature "an affront," while espousing fundamentalist Christian ideas. He calls the creature "ugly as sin."[15] He relentlessly tortures the Creature, using the cattle prod on him and keeping him in shackles. Finally, his cruelty results in him losing two of his own fingers. The Creature heals Giles's wounds and cures his baldness, but he also poisons Strickland. As Strickland's fingers get more and more infected, he swaps his candy for painkillers and begins to spiral out of control.

Strickland tries in many ways to affirm his "normal" masculinity. When he has sex with his wife, he covers her face, and the act is one of hatred, not love. He reads *The Power of Positive Thinking* and purchases a Cadillac, both indicators of normative masculinity in the Kennedy era. African Americans in the 1960s were not allowed to purchase Cadillacs from dealerships—they were forced to buy them used from white owners.[16] Thus, Strickland's desire for a Cadillac can be seen as indicative of his desire for white heterosexual power and privilege. *The Power of Positive Thinking*, published in 1952, has remained a popular work for those attempting to gain success. President Donald Trump, for example, has called the book's author, Norman Vincent Peale, "his pastor."[17] In Strickland's case, however, the positive thinking does not help him at all. He is constantly angry and abusive, wielding his power over those who are powerless, like the Creature and Elisa. Ultimately, Strickland loses everything, including his life. When he discovers that he has been outwitted by Giles, Elisa, and Zelda, he is infuriated, raging that he was fooled by "fucking help . . . shit cleaners . . . piss wipers."[18] When he is dressed down by his superior, General Hoyt, for losing the Asset, he asks him, "When is a man, sir, done proving himself?"[19] Before the Creature kills Strickland, he realizes that the Creature is a god after witnessing him healing himself. Strickland reverses the classic Cold War trope of the heroic American battling threats: he is a repressed, cruel, and ultimately pitiable example of failed masculinity.

A "Good" Spy

Another reversal from the classic Cold War narrative is evident in the character of Dr. Robert Hoffstetler (Michael Stuhlbarg). "Bob" is really Dimitri, a Soviet scientist and spy sent to discover the power of the Creature for Cold War power. Unlike in classic Cold War films, however, he is a sympathetic character, joining the group of outsiders to help save the Creature. Representations of Russians in American film have been varied, and early American film was drawn to the tragic story of the Romanovs, dramatized in such films as *Rasputin and the Empress* (1932). In these narratives the ushering in of communism after the Bolshevik Revolution displaced the "good" Russians, replacing them with ideological monsters. World War II changed the narrative, as the US was allied with Russia. Films such as *Song of Russia* (1944) portrayed a happy, idyllic Soviet Union. After the war, however, the image of the Russian as unequivocally evil emerged in films such as *The Red Menace* (1949) and *Jet Pilot* (1957). Harlow Robinson argues that in postwar America, "Russia was our chief ideological and military enemy, with vast and terrifying resources—by the middle of the century capable and allegedly desirous of blowing us all off the planet."[20] The 1960s saw films that indicated that Russians are people like us, such as *The Russians Are Coming! The Russians are Coming!* (1966). Reagan-era America saw a revival of anti-communism and depictions of Russians as pure evil in such films as *Red Dawn* (1984) and

Rambo III (1988). More recently, films such as *Eastern Promises* (2007) have portrayed Russians as criminals involved in human trafficking.

The Shape of Water revives the notion of an evil Soviet state, but with the character of Dimitri illustrates that Russian scientists could be victims of the extreme nationalism of the Soviet Union. When Dimitri sees Elisa communicating with the Creature, teaching him sign language and bringing him boiled eggs, his view of the Creature is changed. He meets with his Soviet superiors and praises the Creature's intelligence and communication skills. He no longer sees the Creature as an asset, but as a sentient being. Dimitri tries to convince the general and Strickland of the potential that the Creature holds for the Cold War, especially regarding the space race. Strickland wants to dissect the creature, and Dimitri tries to persuade the general to reconsider this action, but to no avail. Dimitri's superiors order him to kill the Creature, giving him an "Israeli popper" to create a diversion. Dimitri balks at this. His superior says, "We don't need to learn. We need the Americans not to learn."[21] Dimitri is caught in a world where the sheer politics of the Cold War outweigh learning and scientific discovery, a world in which he and the Creature are mere pawns in ideological warfare.

Ultimately, Dimitri joins the band of outsiders who want to save the Creature. He helps Giles, Elisa, and Zelda abduct the Creature so he will not be killed by either Soviet or American power brokers. Dimitri is shot by his Soviet contact, and Strickland finds him dying. He uses the cattle prod on him, asking for the names of the Soviet spies who have abducted the Creature. As he is dying, Dimitri reveals that it was "the help" that pulled off this feat. Dimitri gives his life to save the Creature: he is a fully developed character, not a crude caricature of the Russian scientist. Caught in an impossible situation, he must follow his conscience rather than the Soviet party line.

African Americans in the Kennedy Era

The character of Zelda also defies the stereotypes of classic Cold War film. Neda Atanasoski argues that the dominant Cold War approach to representations of African Americans was "a fantasy of racial inclusion to oppose US freedom with Communist unfreedom."[22] Zelda, however, encompasses racial tension while also being a fully developed character. At first, she seems to be a comic relief figure, but she soon emerges as a developed character. Zelda is very protective of Elisa. She punches Elisa's work card for her despite some coworkers' unhappiness. When Elisa asks about Zelda's husband, she describes him as being "silent as the grave." Communication, or lack thereof, is central to the film. Zelda works a hard job, and her husband does not support her emotionally or financially. She becomes part of the outsider group that helps the Creature escape. When Strickland comes to her home, her husband betrays her by telling him where Elisa lives. Zelda's skepticism of men comes from her experience as an African American woman who is the breadwinner. She does not have time or energy to engage in politics. She shows her immense strength as she refuses, after being slammed against the wall, to give in to Strickland's sadism.

The Shape of Water also reimagines the Cold War B movie genre by creating a very detailed and beautiful film. Del Toro was not constrained by the low-budget world of classic Cold War cinema. For example, the cinematography, created by Dan Lausten, uses the color green in extremely effective ways. Near the beginning of the film, Elisa is seen in her green bathtub, pleasuring herself. Later she will have her first sexual encounter in the same bathtub with the Creature. The beautiful and positive green of her apartment is contrasted with the toxic green of the facility where she works and the teal green of Strickland's Cadillac. Also toxic are the green key lime pies of the diner where Giles is rebuffed by Pie Guy.

Del Toro's *The Shape of Water* is both a love letter to the Kennedy era and an exposure of the problems that beset those years—problems that we still deal with in twenty-first-century society. A love story, an espionage film, a social commentary, and more, the film both entertains and elucidates. So many of the motifs found throughout the film are drawn directly from the Cold War—spies, mistrust of Russians, personal ambition wrapped in the cloak of patriotism, and the second-class status of those who fail to embody the "right stuff"—and are a too-familiar part of America's wider historical landscape.

Cold War II, or the New McCarthyism

As those themes are brought forth on screen in *The Shape of Water*, it should not surprise the viewer to find more than a few correlations with the current epoch. After the McCarthy era, tearing down the wall was a signature triumph of America's Hollywood-pedigreed President Reagan, and to many it seemed to signal an end point for the Cold War. A closer look at twenty-first-century developments, however, reads very much like the beginning of a sequel.

Although some of the names and faces have changed over time, today we see many familiar memes and scenarios filling newspaper headlines, media commentary, and the thoughts of the American public. Will we return to fixing furniture between ourselves and the fantasied rain of commie missiles with nuclear warheads? Will there be censorship or even blacklists among our progressive and creative classes again? Are loyalty oaths in the offing? Does anyone feel a draft coming on? If so, it might not be simply a random coincidence. If there were such a thing as "architects" of the Cold War, could we make a logical assumption that the forces which shaped those players would act with strikingly similar force on later generations? Many of those who made the headlines in the Cold War era, such as Joseph McCarthy and John Edgar Hoover (and some that stayed in a more shadowy corner), are of course long gone. But did a new generation of American manipulators spring up like the dragon's teeth of Cadmus to create the political reality of today?

Of the two major players in the Cold War, the USSR has nominally vanished, while the USA is still basically the same geopolitical entity. The aforementioned wall that President Reagan opposed is long gone, Germany is united, and the former Soviet Bloc nations are free. That this is a good thing is a staple of Republican legend. But perhaps we should ask a less adulatory question: Who was it really good for? If we consider that the Berlin Wall not only kept people in thrall but also kept the post-WWII economic growth of the West out, then it should surprise no one to see that after its removal, Russia was relieved of the financial burden of keeping the satellite nations afloat economically. As a stand-alone country, Russia is now in possession of a dramatically modernized military, a markedly improved standard of living, and a renewed sense of political will.[23]

And while the headlines in America no longer trumpet "Red Scare," not a day goes by that some journalist does not find a way to work "Russian collusion" into their writing. Instead of the Rosenbergs and espionage, we find ourselves wondering where the latest investigation into Russian money and American recipients will lead.

Divisiveness, Again

More specifically aligned with the tableau of *The Shape of Water* is a renewed internal divisiveness between conservatives and those citizens that were once known as fellow travelers, or perhaps even more telling, as outside agitators. Congress has fired up their chambers, and the news once again shows grim-faced elected officials wielding verbal swords of outrage and suspicion. Fingers are pointed, tables are pounded, and files and dossiers are kept on citizens for transgressions purported to threaten the safety and security of our most sacred Union.

In del Toro's cinematic world, the work of keeping America safe from the Red Menace falls on the seemingly sturdy shoulders of square-jawed, clean-cut men of resolve and drive: military men such as General Hoyt, agency men such as Strickland. Even the scientists who serve their country and follow orders are represented as exceptionally American. Arrayed against them are the disabled, the racial minorities, the outliers of sexuality and creativity, the Enemy in the guise of a Russian operative, and a potentially harmful Nature, which the Creature certainly represents.

The nonfictional cast of characters today includes not only military veterans holding elected office but a parade of generals in and out of positions in the federal government. And just as "Tail Gunner Joe" McCarthy in the Cold War era turned out to be exaggerating his combat experience (a "resume enhancement" that also afflicted President Lyndon Johnson's apparently self-awarded Silver Star), today we find "Stolen Valor" to be a politicized smear that has been attached to the White House and some of its prominent supporters, such as high-profile "man of God" Pat Robertson. The supporting cast of federal agents, subpoena servers, and investigators remains as vital to the cause as it did in the 1950s and 1960s.

And who are the American people being protected from? The Other today includes immigrants who do not look anything like the president, or his men and women. While the courts have granted legal protection to racial and sexual minorities (as well as women), those rulings are regularly cited by conservative politicians and followers as one of the insidious threats against America. Rhetoric and actual attacks against gay and transgender people are prevalent. Creativity, be it in the form of a play about Alexander Hamilton or spoofs of the president on *Saturday Night Live*, is excoriated with polemical rants, threats of punitive legislation, and lawsuits. And Nature remains a favorite enemy, with those who oppose oil pipelines and draw attention to global warming finding themselves cast in as anti-American a light as any gill-bearing denizen of the Amazonian waters.

At this point, if we find ourselves distressed by the perception that history might be repeating itself, perhaps we should not adopt the willing suspension of disbelief of the moviegoer and simply let the scenes before us play themselves out. Finding a way back from the déjà vu of our contemporary circumstances is most certainly going to depend greatly on making the best choices—now and in the immediate future. And the more informed those choices are, the better. But of course we are now well into the Information Age, and like in a certain classic book by George Orwell, language has become an unreliable narrator, and misinformation can be power. How to avoid becoming a sequel to our own history, then? Maybe it is time to learn from history and, for once, refuse to repeat it.

Rather than simply lay out the assertion that things are in a Cold War–redux state of decline, perhaps we should briefly take a look at some of the factors and commonalities in play. I will bring up a few and leave it to the reader to see if they want to uncover others.

A prominent figure during the Cold War was Senator Joseph McCarthy. His rise and fall are well documented in many sources. What is more often a footnote, however, is the supporting cast who helped him do the damage he did but who did not suffer long-term loss of power. One of those became a household name, Richard M. Nixon—not only because he became president, but because of his behavior in office and the manner in which he was forced out of it. Paranoia and impeachment are the bookends of his legacy. Less often in the forefront of public scrutiny was the attorney Roy Cohn. A standard-bearer for all things moral and patriotic, Cohn's personal life may have run counter to his proclaimed values. But his effectiveness in political machinations was unrivaled. Like the character of Strickland in *The Shape of Water*, his outward dedication to mainstream values seems to have masked an internal conflict that included traits—such as sadism—that he himself would have labeled as deviant.[24]

That deviance in the form of sadism is another part of the Cold War legacy. A "real" patriot is not supposed to be squeamish about how they defend the American way of life, are they? "By any means" was a core part of the raison d'être for undermining various governments in parts of the world that might have tipped toward communism or simply toward independence.

In the immediate aftermath of WWII, while the Dulles brothers were ignoring pleas from Vietnam to help them remain free of forcible recolonization by the French, and while the Bay of Pigs was rolling inexorably toward crisis, the carte blanche of "fighting the spread of communism" led to the establishment of the infamous School of the Americas (SOA). It immediately became well known for providing technical assistance to the elite forces of nations run by brutal regimes on such matters as the proper way to wire electrical generators to various body parts. Although rebranded in 2001 as the less sinister-sounding Western Hemisphere Institute for Security Cooperation (WHINSEC), their clientele and mission remained essentially the same, leaving America presumably safer with the introduction of waterboarding, extraordinary rendition, and of course, the ever-popular transfer from gamer culture known as targeted precision strikes.[25] One is free to wonder if Strickland would have been student or faculty in such a place, given his cattle prod expertise.

It is not so difficult to discern these lineal transitions from politician to politician, and from patriot to patriot. And there are of course other fundamental links between the very real Cold War past, del Toro's cinematic depiction, and business as usual in today's American shadow world of agencies and assets. Axioms such as Lord Acton's observation about the corruption of power still prove themselves, psychological studies from Stanford and elsewhere still hold a mirror to the "Creature" inside of us, and another chapter remains to be written on the always-human trait of othering that *The Shape of Water* has laid out against its beautiful backdrop of love and tragedy.

Notes

1. Ryan Lamble, "Guillermo del Toro Interview: *The Shape of Water*, Shame and Perversity," *Den of Geek*, February 13, 2018, https://www.denofgeek.com/uk/movies/guillermo-del-toro/55247/guillermo-del-toro-interview-the-shape-of-water-shame-and-perversity.

2. Guillermo del Toro, *The Shape of Water* (Century City, CA: Fox Searchlight Pictures, 2017).

3. Garth Franklin, "Del Toro Talks Black Lagoon Influence on 'Shape,'" *Dark Horizons*, November 5, 2017, https://www.darkhorizons.com/del-toro-talks-black-lagoon-influence-on-shape/.

4. Lamble, "Guillermo del Toro Interview."

5. Michelangelo Signorile, "Trump's Cabinet: A Who's Who of Homophobia," *Boston Globe*, December 15, 2016, https://www.bostonglobe.com/opinion/2016/12/15/trump-cabinet-who-who-homophobia/9UDr8MnXIQAxjO369qzToJ/story.html.

6. Miriam Elder, "Russia Passes Law Banning Gay 'Propaganda,'" *The Guardian*, June 11, 2013, https://www.theguardian.com/world/2013/jun/11/russia-law-banning-gay-propaganda.

7. Del Toro, *The Shape of Water*.

8. Del Toro, *The Shape of Water*.

9. Constance Valis Hill comments that "she took his hand and learned his steps, and they danced their way into cinema history as the first interracial tap-dancing couple, albeit a six-year-old white girl and a fifty-seven-year-old black man." "Shall We Dance? Shirley Temple and Bill Robinson: Hollywood's First Interracial Couple," *Huffington Post*, May 30, 2012, https://www.huffpost.com/entry/shirley-temple-bill-robinson_b_1554517.

10. Del Toro, *The Shape of Water*.

11. Lamble, "Guillermo del Toro Interview."

12. Del Toro, *The Shape of Water*.

13. Del Toro, *The Shape of Water*.

14. A. O. Scott, "*The Shape of Water* Is Altogether Wonderful," *New York Times*, November 30, 2017, https://www.nytimes.com/2017/11/30/movies/the-shape-of-water-review-guillermo-del-toro.html.

15. Del Toro, *The Shape of Water*.

16. Warren Brown, "Cadillac's Cultural Turn," *Washington Post*, December 24, 1995, https://www.washingtonpost.com/archive/business/1995/12/24/cadillacs-cultural-turn/7374f4c7-b78f-4007-9938-51ab24bf3522/.

17. Gwenda Blair, "How Norman Vincent Peale Taught Donald Trump to Worship Himself," *Politico Magazine*, April 4, 2018, https://www.politico.com/magazine/story/2015/10/donald-trump-2016-norman-vincent-peale-213220.

18. Del Toro, *The Shape of Water*.

19. Del Toro, *The Shape of Water*.

20. Harlow Robinson, "Russians in American Movies: Imagining the Enemy," *Russian Life*, November 1, 2008, https://www.russianlife.com/magazine/nov-dec-2008/imagining-the-enemy/.

21. Del Toro, *The Shape of Water*.

22. Neda Atanasoski, "Cold War Carmen in US Racial Modernity," *Cinema Journal* 54, no. 1 (Fall 2014): 88–111.

23. David Rudge, "Russia's Huge Military Build Up—A Modern Military for the 21st Century," *Russia Insider*, May 29, 2015, https://russia-insider.com/en/military/russias-huge-military-build-modern-military-twenty-first-century/ri7529.

24. Marcus Baram, "Eavesdropping on Roy Cohn and Donald Trump," *New Yorker*, April 14, 2017, https://www.newyorker.com/news/news-desk/eavesdropping-on-roy-cohn-and-donald-trump.

25. Jake Hess, "Infamous US Military School Still Draws Fire," Al Jazeera, December 9, 2014, https://www.aljazeera.com/indepth/features/2014/12/infamous-us-military-school-still-draws-fire-201412521041105726.html.

LAUGHING AT THE EARLY COLD WAR
Communism, the USSR, and the Comedy of *Hail, Caesar!* and *The Death of Stalin*

Lori Maguire

Although a deadly serious conflict that threatened the existence of the entire world, the Cold War found some of its most memorable commentary in American and British film comedy. Soviet citizens, usually identified as Russians, very often played an important role. This genre peaked in the 1960s and then again in the 1980s. With a few exceptions, primarily related to Germany, like 2003's *Good Bye Lenin!* (Wolfgang Becker), the genre effectively died out when the USSR dissolved. It thus can be seen as a matter of some importance when it re-emerged in the 2010s as part of a general reappearance of Cold War–themed movies. Certainly this revival did not occur in a vacuum but rather in an atmosphere of worsening relations between Western nations and Moscow: the 2006 murder of Alexander Litvinenko in Britain; the 2008 conflict between Russia and Georgia over South Ossetia; the 2014 takeover of the Crimea in Ukraine; disputes over Syria; and Russian support for extremist groups, cyberattacks, and disinformation campaigns in Western nations. All of this took place against a worsening climate of dictatorship in Russia itself that included the jailing and murder of political opponents, growing censorship of the press with the murder of journalists, and even the jailing of a punk band, Pussy Riot, in 2012.

All of these events and more compounded to make Russia look like a renewed threat to European and world peace. In such an atmosphere it was almost inevitable that this new conflict would be perceived in terms of the previous one, and so it is hardly surprising to find the return of the Cold War film. In particular, it gives filmmakers the possibility of commenting on today's events without directly referring to the current regime in the Kremlin. Instead, one can find ways of suggesting that the situation has not really changed very much (except perhaps for the worse) since the fall of communism.

This essay considers two films, one American and one British, made a year apart: *Hail, Caesar!* (Joel and Ethan Coen, 2016) and *The Death of Stalin* (Armando Iannucci, 2017). Both are set in the early 1950s, one of the tensest periods of the entire conflict, although each takes place in a different superpower. Both use humor to examine very serious events. The first takes place during the second Red Scare in the United States, also known as McCarthyism, and the infamous investigation by the House Un-American Activities Committee (HUAC) into Hollywood, which would result in the industry imposing its own blacklist of suspected communists. The second looks at the violence and instability of the USSR under Stalin, examining the power struggle that followed his death and would result in the rise of Nikita Khrushchev. Both are thus based on real occurrences and include among their characters real people or, at least, characters based on real people. Both have appearances by Russians (although, admittedly, they have little screen time in *Hail, Caesar!*). Furthermore, although at first glance their tone may appear to differ greatly, with one seemingly bathed in nostalgia for the Hollywood Golden Age while the other treats with especially black humor the brutality of Stalinism and its aftermath, both satirize their subject, both contain "evil Russians," and both look at the image each superpower sought to convey as well as the reality behind it. These two Cold War II comedies break with the genre in important ways, and these differences are particularly revealing about current attitudes toward the Russia of Vladimir Putin. For this reason, this essay will begin with an analysis of the Cold War comedy before turning to examine each of the films under study in detail in order to highlight the similarities and the differences with earlier examples.

The Cold War Comedy

Often neglected by critics (with the notable exception of *Dr. Strangelove*), the Cold War comedy turns to ridicule, scorn, and laughter certain major aspects of that conflict, such as the superpower rivalry, the arms race, the space race, spying, invasion fears, and the excesses all of these could lead to. Paradoxically, the genre began before the actual Cold War with Ernst Lubitsch's 1939 film, *Ninotchka*, which compared a bright and alluring Paris to the drabness and shortages of the Stalinist Soviet Union. In the end, the beautiful Ninotchka (Greta Garbo), the convinced communist, and her friends cannot resist the attractions of the West and return to Paris. This dreary vision of the USSR persisted. But in the 1950s, few in Hollywood or elsewhere seemed to think that the Cold War, with its threat of universal destruction, could be laughed at. Admittedly, Tony Shaw and Denise Youngblood have taken a much broader view of what constitutes a Cold War film, arguing that, like their Soviet equivalent, Hollywood comedies, by showing the "benefits" of the American way of life, did have a propaganda effect.[1] They use the example of William Wyler's *Roman Holiday* (1953) to show that "Hollywood ... promoted capitalism indirectly and largely unwittingly, by portraying it in lifestyle terms."[2] Their point is a valid one.

This essay will only consider those comedies in which a specific Cold War trope figured prominently. Here the British led the way, focusing, in particular, on mockery of the secret services on both sides of the Iron Curtain, but especially their own. In *Top Secret* (Mario Zambi, 1952), a plumber (George Cole) unwittingly gets hold of plans for a new atomic weapon and is pursued by both British and Soviet intelligence. A similar theme appears in the film of Graham Greene's novel *Our Man in Havana* (Carol Reed, 1959), set at the time of the Cuban Revolution, which tells the story of James Wormold (Alec Guinness), a vacuum cleaner salesman recruited by MI6. In order to get more money, he begins to invent agents (based on real people he does not know personally) and secret plans (based on his vacuum cleaners). When the other side intercepts some of his messages, things get hotter and his so-called agents begin to be assassinated. Wormold's deception is revealed to MI6, who immediately cover it up, reward him with honors, and appoint him to teach intelligence. Subjects for mockery expanded after the Americans got into the act. In 1961's *One, Two, Three* by Billy Wilder (who incidentally also coauthored *Ninotchka*), both capitalism and communism and their supporters come in for ridicule. In Berlin before the wall, the daughter of a Coca-Cola salesman (Pamela Tiffin) marries an East German communist (Horst Buchholz) and originally plans to head east, prompting this comment on living conditions there: "They've assigned us a magnificent apartment, just a short walk from the bathroom!" However, the husband eventually embraces his wife's family and becomes the head of Coke's operations in Europe.[3] Satire, however, reached its scathing zenith with *Dr. Strangelove or: How I Learned to Stop Worrying and Love the Bomb* (Stanley Kubrick, 1964), which, while set in America and striking specifically at its military-industrial complex, does not neglect to mock the Soviets who have, without announcing it, invented and deployed a Doomsday Machine capable of destroying the world. If comedy is traditionally supposed to have a happy ending, this film certainly does not since it finishes with an atomic Armageddon. But even when faced with the end of the world, the two sides continue their petty quarrels, with the Soviet ambassador Alexi de Sadesky (Peter Bull) and the American General "Buck" Turgidson (George C. Scott) literally fighting each other.

All of these films treated Cold War rivalries, whether in the military, the intelligence services, or in the ideological debate itself, with derision—themes that had often earlier, especially in the US, been treated with seriousness, and with American characters portrayed as heroes. Other comedies, however, while critical of the Cold War, showed less contempt. In *Romanoff and Juliet* (Peter Ustinov, 1961), which, as its title suggests, is a comic version of Shakespeare, the children of the US and Soviet ambassadors fall in love. In *The Russians Are Coming! The Russians Are Coming!* (Norman Jewison, 1966) a Soviet submarine runs aground on a New England island. Far from invading, the Soviets simply want to repair their submarine and leave: both sides are terrified of each other at first but finally become friends. These two films are more gentle, pleading for understanding and trying to show that, while both sides can be criticized, they are not really that different.

The second period of Cold War comedies came in the 1980s, which saw a time of heightened tensions after the Soviet invasion of Afghanistan and Ronald Reagan's election to the American presidency. In the early part of the decade, Hollywood gave voice to a renewed hostility toward the USSR, most famously with *Rambo: First Blood Part II* (George P. Cosmatos, 1985)—although it must be said that in the film the United States comes in for even more criticism for "betraying" its veterans.[4] Another famous example is *Rocky IV* (Sylvester Stallone, 1985), in which the Soviet boxer Ivan Drago (Dolph Lundgren) challenges, defeats, and kills Apollo Creed (Carl Weathers) only to be vanquished himself by Rocky (Sylvester Stallone).[5]

In general, however, comedy continued to take a more nuanced approach. Incompetence on both sides continued to be a major theme, as did the negative portrayal of the Eastern Bloc. As before, the military and the intelligence services came in for the greatest mockery. Among the examples are *Stripes* (Ivan Reitman, 1981), which has two future Ghostbusters (Bill Murray and Harold Ramis) as devil-may-care US soldiers improbably rescuing their platoon from the Soviets (thus suggesting that the Red Army was even more incompetent); *Top Secret* (David Zucker, Jim Abrahams, and Jerry Zucker, 1984), in which yet another innocent outsider (in this case a rock star) muddles into both an East German plot to cripple NATO and the resistance to that nation's government; *Jumpin' Jack Flash* (Penny Marshall, 1986), which concerns a British spy trapped in the Eastern Bloc who is saved by another outsider, this time a bank employee (Whoopi Goldberg); and *Spies Like Us* (John Landis, 1985), in which some remarkably ineffectual American spies stumble into a Soviet military base and, believing they have started a nuclear war, pair up for sex with their Soviet counterparts. The very assertion that naïve outsiders and incompetent, brazen semi-insiders can succeed better than the professionals of both blocs is, in and of itself, a sarcastic statement on the entire Cold War rivalry and the military-industrial complex it generated.

Not surprisingly, the tone changes after Mikhail Gorbachev's rise to power in the USSR in 1985. For example, *Red Heat* (Walter Hill, 1988) has Arnold Schwarzenegger as a Soviet police officer paired with Chicago detective James Belushi to capture a Georgian drug lord who has fled to the US. A buddy film, it shows the two leads as having much in common, but unlike Ninotchka, Schwarzenegger's character chooses to return to Russia.[6] The film suggests the end of the USSR and a new Russia that will become more like America.

What these examples show is that comedy tended to mock both sides, with the Americans and the British generally coming in for more sarcasm because people from those nations made the films—although the assessment of living conditions in the Eastern Bloc remained negative. However, depending on the picture, people on both sides shared the same fears, the same wishes, or the same stupidity, pettiness, and hunger for power. It may come as a surprise then to realize that the recent examples of the Cold War comedy under study here break this mold. Any obvious equation between the two sides has disappeared.

Hail, Caesar!

Written and directed by the Coen brothers, *Hail, Caesar!* coincided with their coauthorship (with Matt Charman) of *Bridge of Spies* (Steven Spielberg, 2015).[7] The two films are set only a few years apart, and both concern the classic theme of communist infiltration. Unlike the Spielberg film, *Hail, Caesar!* takes place at the time of the notorious attack on Hollywood by the House Un-American Activities Committee (HUAC) and the industry's response with the infamous blacklist. It details the life of Eddie Mannix (Josh Brolin), a "fixer" (a term for someone who "cleans up" scandals) for the fictional Capitol Pictures (which also appears in *Barton Fink* [1991] another film about writers in Hollywood) who shares the name of the very real fixer for MGM who lived at the same time.[8]

The title of the Coen brothers' film comes from that of the most important feature being made at Capitol Pictures, *Hail, Caesar! A Tale of the Christ*, whose absurd name contains a clear reference to *Ben-Hur* (William Wyler, 1959) since they share the same subtitle. The basic plot concerns the kidnapping of the picture's star, Baird Whitlock (George Clooney), by a communist cell calling itself "the Future" and consisting predominantly of scriptwriters. However, in the course of little more than twenty-four hours, Eddie Mannix's day concerns much more: He must deal with an unmarried, pregnant star of aquamusicals (obviously based on Esther Williams and played by Scarlett Johansson), a Gene Kelly–like song-and-dance man named Burt Gurney (Channing Tatum) who turns out to be a communist agent, and an unexpectedly shrewd Western star (Alden Ehrenreich) grotesquely miscast in a comedy of manners. Along the way he encounters the rival twin gossip columnists Thora and Thessaly Thacker (Tilda Swinton) while being courted for a job at Lockheed.

Religiosity infuses *Hail, Caesar!*: it begins and practically ends in a confessional and includes a theological discussion between a rabbi, a Protestant minister, and a Catholic priest (assembled by Mannix to make sure that nothing in the big-budget Bible movie can offend anyone). This is clearly in keeping with the spirit of the early 1950s that saw religion triumph in politics, with the addition in 1954 of the words *under God* to the Pledge of Allegiance; in television, with Archbishop Fulton Sheen's highly successful series *Life Is Worth Living* (DuMont, 1952–55, and ABC, 1955–57); and, of course, in film. *Hail, Caesar!*, the film within the film, as in *Ben Hur*, makes a rather obvious equation between the oppression of Rome and that of the Soviet Union, as the narrator tells us: "As oppressed people everywhere writhe under the Roman lash, freeman and vassal are united in one compulsory worship."[9] This fits neatly with the American Cold War rhetoric that portrayed the USSR as oppressors who forced everyone to worship at the altar of communism. Mannix clearly is in a moral dilemma over his efforts at covering over Hollywood scandals since they involve lying, forced marriages, and occasional violence (he does not hesitate to slap stars if he feels they have gone too far). The point is clear: Hollywood is about image; the reality does not matter so much, as long as it is kept hidden from view.

Indeed, the difference between the real Mannix and the movie character shows exactly this dichotomy: The real Mannix, although a Catholic who refused divorce because of his religion, was a womanizer, was rumored to have Mafia associations, and was linked to the mystery around the death of actor George Reeves (subject of the film *Hollywoodland* [Allen Coulter, 2006]). He was far from the conscience-plagued, happily married father of *Hail, Caesar!*: a man who exhausts his priest with his compulsive confessions—leading the latter to insist with a sigh, "You're not that bad."[10] The film does to Eddie Mannix what Mannix did to the stars—it whitewashes him to create a more wholesome image, more in keeping with the spirit (or possibly hypocrisy) of his times.

Interestingly enough, one of the plot points is that Mannix is being sought after by Lockheed, which offers him an executive position. Their recruiter,

Mr. Cuddahy (Ian Blackman), emphasizes that Mannix would receive a significantly higher salary, but he also stresses their seriousness of purpose. The Lockheed recruiter is extremely dismissive of the cinema industry, which he calls "frivolous" and "make-believe." Instead, he brags about the real power of Lockheed, insisting that, if he worked there, Mannix would be part of "the future."[11] This future turns out to be the hydrogen bomb, and Cuddahy brags about Lockheed's role in its creation—although Mannix suggests that this future looks more like the end of all things, like Armageddon.[12] Here we see a debate over which is the more powerful, hard power or soft power. The hydrogen bomb of course destroys, but it cannot remake the world in its own image as Hollywood can. In the end, Lockheed fails to convince Mannix, who, after having his conscience eased by a priest, turns down the offer, preferring Tinseltown, Hollywood, the dream factory. The suggestion is that America won the Cold War not through weapons but through its ability to entertain by creating enticing dreams. Furthermore, the fact that Lockheed sees itself as "the future" and that the communist writers' group calls itself "the Future" points to the ideological battle between the two superpowers, both of whom claimed to be the way of the future.[13]

Although presenting a conscience-stricken figure at its center, the movie is oddly lacking in criticism of one of the great scandals of Hollywood: the industry's blacklist of writers and performers because of suspected communist sympathies. Far from presenting them as victims, *Hail, Caesar!* shows the group of screenwriters as nursing a grudge because they feel exploited and underpaid. They meet in the palatial Malibu residence of actor Burt Gurney, where they have a "study group" led by another figure based on a real person, Dr. Marcuse (John Bluthal), who obviously refers to the German American philosopher Herbert Marcuse. Once again reality is askew for, although influenced by Marx and a critic of capitalism, the real Marcuse was not a communist. They kidnap and hold for ransom star Baird Whitlock in an attempt to get back some of the money they feel the studio owes them. They even make a temporary convert of Whitlock.

Communists, of course, had long considered films as important vehicles for their ideas. Lenin had asserted that "of all arts, cinema for us is the most important."[14] For Stalin, the key figures were writers, whom he saw as "engineers of human souls." This led him to officially impose, in 1934, socialist realism, the idea that the arts should promote a true socialist society.[15] Communists argued that the application of their doctrine in a society would lead to the creation of a new man, and in the USSR this person became known as the "new Soviet man," who would be strong, disciplined, intellectual, and selfless. This figure would become a staple of Soviet cinema[16] and finds its echo in *Hail, Caesar!*

Professor Marcuse tells Whitlock that they are working for "the creation of the new man," and the narrator tells us later that Whitlock has become committed "to the quest to hasten an end to history and bring on the new man" (although this is illustrated with an absurd story about shaving the back of the American comedian Danny Kaye). Later, one of the writers salutes Gurney with the words, "You are going to Moscow to become Soviet man."[17] Paradoxically, the new Soviet man will be an American dancer.

At first glance, the Russians play only a tiny role in *Hail, Caesar!* There are in fact only two Russian characters, neither of whom even has dialogue. The first, Mr. Smitrovich (Alex Karpovsky) is part of the "study group" and spends most of his time on screen scowling and taking photos of Whitlock, presumably in case it may be necessary to blackmail him.

The second, although we see him for only a few seconds, is far more significant, for he is the commander of a Soviet submarine that surfaces off the coast of Malibu. Unlike in nightmare scenarios of the 1950s, he does not come to attack America, nor, as in *The Hunt for Red October* (John McTiernan, 1990), is he trying to defect, nor, as in *The Russians Are Coming! The Russians Are Coming!*, is he looking for materials to repair a damaged ship. Rather, he has come to pick up Hollywood star Burt Gurney. Obviously based on Gene Kelly, whose first wife was suspected of being a communist sympathizer and who was himself a member of the Committee for the First Amendment, Gurney goes much further than left wing Democrat Kelly. He hosts the "study group"; he takes the ransom money to its members; he has a dog named Engels; he even bears a resemblance to Yuri Gagarin. As Alex von Tunzelmann pointed out in *The Guardian*, the filming of his defection resembles socialist realism, but it also copies a lot of the movements he made earlier in the big dance number, notably jumping on a ladder.[18] His position and facial expression after making the jump are thoroughly posed, suggesting that this is just one more performance. The members of "the Future," who have rowed him to his rendezvous, decide that they should give Gurney the ransom money for the "cause." As he waits on the ladder, they toss him the briefcase, which he catches once again in a theatrical fashion. But as he is about to climb into the submarine, his dog, Engels, who cannot bear to be parted from him, jumps into his arms. In catching the dog, Gurney drops the money into the sea, where it sinks. Gurney then boards the submarine and leaves.

But the submarine commander is the big surprise, being a cameo by Dolph Lundgren. Lundgren, of course, has played numerous Russian villains, such as a KGB thug in the James Bond film *A View to A Kill* (John Glen, 1985), another Soviet operative in *Red Scorpion* (Joseph Zito, 1988), and, as I have already noted, Ivan Drago in *Rocky IV*. His brief presence here is no accident, for he represents Hollywood's vision of the evil Russian. But in this case, the evil Russian is only interested in a Hollywood singer and dancer—a star of one of the least serious and the least realistic of genres. The Russians are not seeking the new Soviet man but an American actor. Hollywood has a magic so great that the Soviets seek to steal it. Things we may dismiss as pure entertainment are more powerful than we realize.

One of the most interesting features of the film is its soundtrack, most of which was composed by Carter Burwell in imitation of actual music from movies of the time. As the submarine scene approaches, the music moves from imitating Hollywood to imitating Soviet cinema. Burwell composed a track entitled "The Hands of Communists" that appears significantly after Burt Gurney's big number. Burwell has two other similar contributions, "In Pursuit of the Future" and "Soviet Man," but at key moments he also uses traditional Eastern European revolutionary songs performed by the Red Army Choir. As "the Future" is rowing Burt Gurney out to the submarine, we hear "Slavery and Suffering," a popular revolutionary song that was used in Soviet films. During the submarine scene, we can hear "Varchavianka," often translated as "Whirlwinds of Danger" or "March Song of the Workers," originally a Polish workers' anthem adopted by the Russians and also heard in Soviet films. At the end, during the credits, another socialist revolutionary melody is heard, "Echelon's Song," written in the 1930s about the Russian Civil War (1917–22). The use of such music in a film about Hollywood, in combination with the arrest of the members of "the Future" and the defection of Gurney, suggests that there might have been some truth behind HUAC's investigation into the film industry. Communists, and more particularly Russians, do seem to be lurking in the background—much as they lurked behind the scenes in social media in the 2010s. By giving credit to Soviet subversion in the 1950s, the Coens may actually be referring to issues of our own time and Russian attempts to subvert Western media. In the end, *Hail, Caesar!* states that soft power is much greater than hard power and that Hollywood, for all its silliness, is the finest expression of the American Dream—to such an extent that even the Russians are ready to send their hard power to get a bit of American soft power.

The Death of Stalin

The Death of Stalin is a British film, but one that has important links with the United States. To begin with, two of its stars are American, Steve Buscemi and Jeffrey Tambor. Furthermore, its Scottish director, Armando Iannucci, is renowned for his political satire, first mocking British politics with the television series *The Thick of It* (BBC, 2005–12) and the film *In the Loop* (2009) and then turning his attention to the United States with another series, *Veep* (2012–19), on HBO, which has won a number of awards. Iannucci has become famous for deriding politicians as egotistical, petty, frequently incompetent, often amoral, and more interested in reaching the top of the greasy pole than in improving the world. With *The Death of Stalin*, Iannucci leaves the realm of democratic politics and turns his attention to that of dictatorship and the particularly violent one of Stalin's USSR. To show the depth of that regime's evil, Iannucci surpasses even *Dr. Strangelove* in black humor, combining slapstick and horror as he shows viewers the nightmare of life in the USSR. Set at the same time as *Hail, Caesar!*, this movie presents a profoundly different and much darker world where fear governs existence. Based on a two-part French graphic novel by Thierry Robin and Fabien Nury,[19] the film concerns the events on the evening of Stalin's death and during the following days.

The film has been criticized for being historically inaccurate, but this primarily concerns the chronology, with events that took place over a much longer period of time being compressed into a few days. As the historian Richard Overy pointed out in his review of the film, Molotov had not been foreign minister since 1949, Zhukov was not at the time commander of the Red Army, and Beria was only executed in December—nine months after Stalin's death instead of a few days.[20] Beria was indeed arrested by the Presidium, although he did have a trial before the Supreme Court of the USSR—without any defense lawyer or possibility of appeal.[21] But focusing on these historical inaccuracies misses the point because it denies the film the right to any form of dramatic license. The essential facts are true although they may not have taken place when, where, or exactly how they are portrayed in the film. Furthermore, this is in keeping with Stalin's Soviet Union, where "facts" were continually being revised and people were often erased from photographs (something that is actually shown in the closing credits).

For a film that contains so much ugliness, the first sounds are surprisingly beautiful, being from Mozart's Twenty-Third Piano Concerto. But the music is interrupted by a telephone ringing. When it is discovered that the caller is Stalin (Adrian McLoughlin), the staff panics and we begin to get an idea of how widespread fear is in this country. The scene then switches to Stalin's dacha, where the great leader himself sits behind his desk, listening to the concerto and smiling as he discusses a new list of arrests and assassinations with Lavrentiy Beria (Simon Russell Beale). Nearby are Vyacheslav Molotov (Michael Palin) and Georgy Malenkov (Jeffrey Tambor), who listen as Nikita Khrushchev (Steve Buscemi) recounts what he (and Stalin) consider a funny anecdote: how he threw a live grenade among prisoners at Stalingrad. Beria then takes out the list to waiting officers, instructing them to "shoot her before him, but make sure he sees it. . . . Kill him, take him to his church, dump him in the pulpit."[22] We then see the raids as people are hustled out of their apartments in the night. Later, Beria will tell Khrushchev and Malenkov that Molotov is on the list as everyone waves goodbye to him. The point is clear: This is a regime that rules by fear, and its leaders, especially the man at the top, are evil—although their evil is remarkably nonchalant and banal. In this atmosphere everyone is ready to do anything to survive, most notably to denounce one another.

The first casualty of fear is truth. When Stalin is alive, the members of the Presidium of the Supreme Soviet, in theory the highest state authority, do everything to ingratiate themselves to him. The elderly, overweight members act like buffoons for his amusement. In this world, everyone must watch what they say, hiding what they really think, for even the most offhand comments can get them sent to the Gulag. This has become such a part of their lives that Malenkov remarks at one point, "I can't remember who's alive and who isn't."[23] As the members of the Presidium carry Stalin's inert form into his bedroom, Nikolai Bulganin (Paul Chahidi) complains how heavy he is. This causes Beria to comment menacingly that Bulganin thinks Stalin is heavy. Panicked, Bulganin can only respond idiotically that Stalin is heavy like gold. Later, when Stalin briefly recovers and gestures toward the wall, they all outdo each other in interpreting what he means according to the tenets of socialist realism.

Needless to say, when Malenkov seeks to become the new leader, he tries to cast himself within the framework of imagery that Stalin created. The brutal dictator had loved presenting himself as the father of his people. Malenkov becomes comically obsessed with replicating a famous picture of Stalin with a little girl. He sends the security forces to find the girl, and when they cannot, he rejects all their suggested replacements. When she is eventually found, he rejects her too since she has grown into a gawky adolescent. He finally chooses another little girl, but when he appears on the balcony with her—his great statement of continuity with Stalin—she is so tiny that only the top of head can be seen. Indeed, Malenkov becomes so obsessed with his looks that he dyes his hair, puts on a girdle, and dresses in white.

The essence of the film is the jockeying for power as everyone begins plotting against one another. As Stalin lies unconscious on his bed, the group splits into pairs, discussing the succession. When Stalin's popular daughter, Svetlana, arrives, they literally race to be the first to greet her with one member asking, "How can you run and plot at the same time?"[24] The humor here is pure slapstick, like their buffoonery earlier for Stalin. After Stalin's death, the plotting picks up in earnest. Molotov invites Khrushchev and Lazar Kaganovich

(Dermot Crowley) into his car and gets his dog to start barking, explaining that he does not want the drivers outside to overhear them. In the cacophony that ensues, Kaganovich comments, "I've had nightmares that made more sense than this."[25] Later, all the leaders get in their cars and block each other since no one wants to let the other go first. At other moments, they flatter each other as they plot each other's downfall. Beria is the worst here, pardoning prisoners to gain popularity while blackmailing the people around him.

The tone changes in the last part of the film as the others turn against Beria and engineer his death. It becomes more serious, although the dark humor continues—Beria is arrested by Zhukov and some of his officers and is taken, with the members of the Presidium, to the men's toilet, where he is chained to the urinals. Once the army has seized control of the Kremlin from the NKVD, they truss him up like a pig and take him into a storehouse for his so-called trial. While all this is going on, Molotov exclaims gleefully, "Stalin would be loving this." After Beria is killed, Khrushchev states, "I wish the old man could have seen this." The implication is clear: Stalin may be dead, but the system he created lives on. This is brought home as the scene continues. Khrushchev tells Kaganovich, "Now we can turn the corner," to which the latter replies, "Yes, put all that bloodshed behind us."[26] But Khrushchev's very next words show that this will not happen since he states that he is worried about Malenkov. They will continue to claw for power, denouncing any who stand in their way or even any they fear may stand in their way. The point is hammered home in the last scene, where we return in effect to the beginning. The same pianist is playing the same Mozart concerto while the same radio staff broadcasts it. Only this time Khrushchev's photo has replaced Stalin. We are told that a few years later he demoted Molotov and Malenkov and became ruler of the USSR only to be deposed in his turn by Leonid Brezhnev in 1964. The last image of the film is of a young Brezhnev, sitting behind Khrushchev and staring at him. The suggestion is that the USSR is in a cycle in which its leaders devour each other. And the existence of this cycle suggests that *The Death of Stalin* reaches beyond 1953 to make a comment on contemporary Russia.

Certainly, many critics understood it as making such a comment. Overy, for example, wrote, "It mocks by implication the Russia of today, a country still shaped in some ways by the legacy of Stalin's modernisation drives and the operation of the Stalinist state."[27] Another reviewer noted, "the Russian government quite likes to be feared; what it can't bear is to be treated as a joke."[28] That the Russian government saw the film as a criticism is shown by the fact that they banned it. Vladimir Medinsky, the minister of culture, justified this by arguing that "many people of the older generation, and not only, will regard it as an insulting mockery of all the Soviet past, of the country that defeated fascism and of ordinary people, and what's even worse, even of the victims of Stalinism."²⁹ Very few people, however, seem to have believed that explanation. Indeed, the same article quotes criticism made by the deputy head of the culture committee in the State Duma, whose comments point toward the Kremlin seeing contemporary implications in the film: "It's an effort to breed bad blood into the social harmony that has been reached in Russian society."³⁰ Dictatorships are not renowned for appreciating mockery, and one can certainly interpret Malenkov's absurd preoccupation with his appearance as a commentary on Vladimir Putin's own obvious cosmetic surgery and penchant for posing shirtless. Furthermore, Vladimir Putin has created a cult of memory around the Second World War or, as it is called in Russia, the Great Patriotic War, moving, for example, the honor guard that used to be around Lenin's tomb to the tomb of the unknown soldier.³¹ A side effect of this has been a certain rehabilitation of Stalin. Numerous books on Stalin and his period have been published, and Khrushchev's granddaughter notes that most of these "treat Joseph Stalin with kid gloves and are filled with unabashed nostalgia for a great but vanished past, for a time when the Soviet Union was feared, admired, even respected."³² The personality cult around Putin has also been widely noted.³³

The evil Russian of *The Death of Stalin* is, of course, Stalin himself, the spider who initially spun the web of deceit and terror. The members of his government act like buffoons to keep in his good graces while plotting, not admittedly against him, but against one another, using the security forces and the army to torment the population. In this darkest of dark comedies, the humor, rather than making light of serious events, actually increases the horror. The Keystone Cops–type chase scenes are those of people running hopelessly from security forces who have orders to kill them. The film presents us with a sad, sick society whose malady is self-perpetuating.

Conclusion

Although belonging to the genre of the Cold War comedy, these two films may seem profoundly different, and yet both use their setting in the early 1950s to make a commentary on the contemporary situation with regard to Russia. At first glance, this question may appear to be of little importance in *Hail, Caesar!*, which seeks to pay tribute to the end of Hollywood's Golden Age. And yet the main plot of the film concerns the kidnapping of Baird Whitlock by communist film writers who admit to trying to influence people through their scripts. The Coen brothers here appear to suggest that there was some truth to HUAC's accusations. Certainly those two filmmakers are renowned for their subversive interpretations of the past, and yet throughout the film characters based on actual people differ profoundly from the reality. We may wonder if the Coen brothers are truly rewriting the history of Hollywood or simply making a comment on the situation of today, when Russia does seem to be attacking America in a number of ways, notably through its subversion of social media, and when, all too often, Americans seem to be helping them.

The contemporary implications of *The Death of Stalin*, on the other hand, were understood immediately and led to the film being banned in Russia. This black comedy suggests that violence was ingrained in the Soviet system and that its leaders actually took a cruel delight in it. By portraying this behavior as part of a cycle, Iannucci insinuates that it continued after the breakup of the USSR and that the current Russian regime is still a part of it. Certainly, while the US has experienced more subtle forms of subversion, the UK has seen a number of high-profile crimes committed in its territory, notably the dramatic murder of Alexander Litvinenko, which may in part account for its darker vision. And of course the UK is much closer geographically to Russia, which may make it feel more threatened.

The return of tensions between Western nations and Russia under Putin has found a reflection in the world of popular culture, notably in cinema, and has led to a new interest in the period of the Cold War. This includes the reappearance of the stereotyped evil Russian, notably in a category in which it had been largely absent during the real Cold War: comedy. During the actual Cold War, this genre had usually ridiculed both sides, insisting that they both had defects and often pleading for understanding between them. It thus tended to create a kind of equivalence between the two blocs, even during the heightened tensions of the early 1980s. However, in the recent rebirth of the genre, this equation has been largely dropped. The two most recent examples, *Hail, Caesar!* and *The Death of Stalin*, are distinctly one-sided, especially the latter. The tensest period of the entire Cold War conflict was certainly in the last years of Stalin's rule, which was, perhaps not surprisingly, a time when comedies about the Cold War did not exist. The genre only began to appear some years after his death, during the period of the thaw under Khrushchev. The fact that both of these films are set in the early 1950s suggest that their creators feel that current relations may be nearly as strained as in that time.

Notes

1. See Tony Shaw and Denise Youngblood, *Cinematic Cold War: The American and Soviet Struggle for Hearts and Minds* (Lawrence: University of Kansas Press, 2010), in particular pages

98–112, which analyze *Roman Holiday*. Certainly, that seems very close to the Coen brothers' argument in *Hail, Caesar!*

2. Shaw and Youngblood, *Cinematic Cold War*, 98.

3. Billy Wilder, *One, Two, Three* (Culver City, CA: MGM, 1961). For an in-depth analysis of this film, see Massimo Olivero, "La vision critique de Billy Wilder sur la Guerre froide," in *Cinéma et Guerre froide: L'imaginaire au pouvoir, CinémAction*, ed. Lori Maguire and Cyril Buffet (Condé-en-Normandie: Éditions Charles Corlet, 2014), 150.

4. There have been a number of analyses of the *Rambo* films, especially in the decade after their appearance. There is not the space here to list them all, but here is small sample: Carl Boggs and Tom Pollard, "The Imperial Warrior in Hollywood: Rambo and Beyond, *New Political Science* 30, no. 4 (2008): 565–78; Susan Jeffords, *Hollywood Masculinity in the Reagan Era* (New Brunswick, NJ: Rutgers University Press, 1994); Jerry Lembcke, *The Spitting Image: Myth, Memory and the Legacy of Vietnam* (New York: New York University Press, 1998; Gaylyn Studlar and David Desser, "Never Having to Say You're Sorry: Rambo's Rewriting of the Vietnam War," in *From Hanoi to Hollywood: The Vietnam War in American Film*, ed. Linda Dittmar and Gene Michaud (New Brunswick, NJ: Rutgers University Press, 1990); Frank Sweeney, "'What Means Expendable?' Myth, Ideology and Meaning in *First Blood* and *Rambo*," *Journal of American Culture* 22, no. 3 (Fall 1999): 63–69; Adi Wimmer, "Rambo: American Adam, Anarchist and Archetypal Frontier Hero," in *Vietnam Images: War and Representation*, ed. Jeffrey Walsh and James Aulich (Basingstoke, UK: Palgrave Macmillan, 1989) 184–95; Shaw and Youngblood also discuss this film.

5. Stephen C. Le Sueur and Dean Rehberger, "*Rocky IV, Rambo II* and the Place of the Individual in American Society," *Journal of American Culture* 11, no. 2 (Summer 1988): 25–33, examines both films.

6. Tony Shaw, *Hollywood's Cold War* (Edinburgh: Edinburgh University Press, 2007), makes the point that there is no need for Schwarzenegger's character to consider defecting because "his younger, less regimented generation is going to benefit from Russia's Westernisation" and because he is "a proud Russian nationalist" not "a devout communist who needs to be converted to capitalism," 290.

7. There is a certain similarity between the two films, notably their nostalgia. This theme in *Bridge of Spies* is discussed in the essay in this book by Vesta Silva and Jon Wiebel, "The Warm Glow of Cold War Nostalgia," which could also serve as a title for a discussion of *Hail, Caesar!*

8. A number of other things link the two films, including the appearance of a Wallace Beery Conference Room in *Hail, Caesar!*

9. Joel and Ethan Coen, *Hail, Caesar!* (Universal City, CA: Universal Pictures, 2016).

10. Joel and Ethan Coen, *Hail, Caesar!*

11. Joel and Ethan Coen, *Hail, Caesar!*

12. He shows Mannix a photo of the testing at the Bikini Atoll, which would date the film as taking place in 1954. However, the date of 1951 can be seen in a film's credits. The Coen brothers are clearly playing with history here and making it impossible to accurately date the movie. The year 1951 is significant because that was the high point of McCarthyism.

13. M. Keith Booker develops this point in *The Coen Brothers' America* (Lanham, MD: Rowman & Littlefield, 2019), 97–100.

14. Birgit Beumers, *A History of Russian Cinema* (Oxford: Berg, 2009), 38.

15. See Cécile Vaissié, *Les ingénieurs des âmes en chef: Littérature et politique en URSS (1944–1986)* (Paris: Belin, 2008). See also Vladislav Zubok, *A Failed Empire: The Soviet Union in the Cold War from Stalin to Gorbachev*, 2nd ed. (Chapel Hill: University of North Carolina

Press, 2009), 165; Lenin had already imposed it on literature in 1905: Vladimir Lenin, "Party Organization and Party Literature," *Novaya Zhizn* no. 12, November 13, 1905, https://www.marxists.org/archive/lenin/works/1905/nov/13.htm.

16. For more on this see John Haynes, *New Soviet Man: Gender and Masculinity in Stalinist Soviet Cinema* (Manchester, UK: Manchester University Press, 2003).

17. Joel and Ethan Coen, *Hail, Caesar!*

18. Alex von Tunzelmann, "*Hail, Caesar!* It's Screwball Comedy—Who Cares What Really Happened?," *The Guardian*, March 11, 2016, https://www.theguardian.com/film/2016/mar/11/hail-caesar-coen-brothers-eddie-mannix-reel-history-josh-brolin-george-clooney.

19. Thierry Robin and Fabien Nury, *La mort de Staline*, 2 vols. (Paris: Daqrgaud, 2010 and 2012).

20. Richard Overy, "Carry On up the Kremlin: How *The Death of Stalin* Plays Russian Roulette with the Truth," *The Guardian*, October 18, 2017, https://www.theguardian.com/film/2017/oct/18/death-of-stalin-russian-roulette-with-truth-armando-iannucci.

21. For a more detailed study see Amy Knight, *Beria: Stalin's First Lieutenant* (Princeton: Princeton University Press, 1993).

22. Armando Iannucci, *The Death of Stalin* (Toronto: Entertainment One, 2017).

23. Iannucci, *The Death of Stalin*.

24. Iannucci, *The Death of Stalin*.

25. Iannucci, *The Death of Stalin*.

26. All quotes in this paragraph are from *The Death of Stalin*.

27. Overy, "Carry On up the Kremlin."

28. Sophie Pinkham, "The Provocative Brilliance of *The Death of Stalin*: Why Is Armando Iannucci's New Film Effectively Banned in Russia?," *New Republic*, March 29, 2018, https://newrepublic.com/article/147691/provocative-brilliance-death-stalin.

29. Denis Pinchuk and Andrew Osborn, "Russia Cancels Release of 'Insulting' Film about Stalin's Death," Reuters, January 23, 2018, https://www.reuters.com/article/us-russia-film-stalin/russia-cancels-release-of-insulting-film-about-stalins-death-idUSKBN1FC1X6.

30. Pinchuk and Osborn, "Russia Cancels Release of 'Insulting' Film about Stalin's Death."

31. Seth Bernstein, "Remembering War, Remaining Soviet: Digital Commemoration of World War II in Putin's Russia," *Memory Studies* 9, no. 4 (2016): 422–36, argues that state and society have been interacting with regard to creating and re-creating the memory of that conflict.

32. Nina Khrushcheva, "'Rehabilitating' Stalin," *World Policy Journal* 22, no. 2 (Summer 2005): 67–73.

33. See, for example, Julie A. Cassiday and Emily D. Johnson, "Putin, Putiana and the Question of a Post-Soviet Cult of Personality," *Slavonic and East European Review* 88, no. 4 (October 2010): 681–707.

PART III
OF PATRIOTISM, CORRUPTION, AND OTHERNESS

OF MOTHERS AND MOTHERLANDS
Figurations of Parenting and Patriotism in *The Americans*

David LaRocca

As we are looking back to the Cold War, thinking about it anew in the light of present-day politics, popular culture, and the specter of a second Cold War, we draw in Joe Weisberg, creator of *The Americans* (2013–18), and his project to depict the life and times of a clandestine network of Russian agents in 1980s America. When Weisberg, a former CIA officer, came to decide on the temporal setting of his show, he chose a time when he himself was a teenager (he graduated from Yale in 1987). Moreover, in the moment that he was transitioning from college student to professional, his motivation to join the CIA was clear: "I wanted a job where I could be a cold warrior."[1] It may come as a shock to some readers, but there were in fact Russian spies infiltrating Washington, DC, in the early eighties—and so we might say that the show should not be described as based on a true story but rather a true premise. In the films, television shows, and popular narratives of that era, Russia-as-enemy, Reagan's "evil empire," and similar paranoia-driven (and thus distorting) sentiments fueled a confidence in moral binaries. There was a sense among purveyors of mainstream American culture then, as in the 1940s, that the good guys were identifiable (on one side—ours) and the bad guys expendable (and on the other side—theirs). Looking back to the 1980s, then, as Weisberg and his team of writers, producers, and actors have done (the show concluded in 2018 after running for seventy-five episodes over six seasons), we are provided with an invitation to think about the characterization of Russian spies. If the show had held to well-hewed traditions and habits of cinema and television during the

Cold War, the Russians would have been depicted as villainous, duplicitous, immoral, hateful—in short, worthy of our contempt. The show might simply have been called *The Russians*. Yet, from Weisberg's vantage, writing nearly forty years out from the show's temporal setting, it is precisely in the contests that defined the Cold War as it was experienced in those late days of the Soviet Union that the more compelling questions would entail thinking instead about the Russians as *The Americans*.

Moreover, Weisberg's treatment of Russians would proceed through deeply sympathetic portraits of specific human beings caught up in the generic, impersonal flow of history, struggling with their own radically intimate sense of agency and identity: Who were these Russians in America? Is being Russian an ontological state, whereas being an American is a performative one (a put-on identity like so many wigs and mustaches)? What does the experience of being a secret agent do to one's inner and outer lives? What does it look like to be loyal to one's child, to one's spouse, to one's profession, to an ideology, to a country? And how might those loyalties—including conflicting ones—impact one's ability to parent? Replies to these questions form the crux of what I aim to illuminate as one of the striking, original, and unsettling provocations of the show: to see it, among other things, as an extended meditation on the struggle to parent well—a meditation conducted by Russians (all of them portrayed, "figured" in the language of fiction and literary criticism, by adults who, like Weisberg, would have been children or teens during the years covered by the series and are, in the show, all shown to be parents: principally, Keri Russell, Matthew Rhys, Noah Emmerich, and Costa Ronin). To be sure, the show is *also* a distinctly compelling melodrama of marriage (including the importance of self-knowledge and knowledge of others), something I address in detail elsewhere.[2] On this occasion, though, we observe the ways in which parenting arises on a continual and thus extended basis: how to care for these children; how to develop and care for *their* agency.[3] The earlier questions, then, are extended and focused in the light of parenting—specifically, about what it entails under these conditions.[4] For example, do children get a say in what their parents believe in and do in response to those beliefs? Should children be told about their parents' work and cultivated as assets for the cause, or should they be shielded from the realities of the family business? What happens when the family business one might apprentice in turns out not to be travel brokering but international spycraft?[5] What is the nature of loyalty—to parents, to country (or countries)—when children are raised in the circumstances that Elizabeth (Keri Russell) and Philip (Matthew Rhys) chose? Or, how do loyalties evolve for these characters, given that *they too were children* when they signed up for service? Elizabeth and Philip themselves may have been parented poorly—not just by their parents but also their nation and its institutions. While Weisberg's series overlaps with the emergence of a newly prominent and politically revitalized Russia, Vladimir Putin's ascendancy, and the tumult of American politics circa 2016, it does not (even in the last couple of seasons, when it had the chance) become a direct, self-conscious commentary on present-day political topics. Rather, it hews closely to two fundamental, even classical themes—parenting and patriotism—and in so doing, it provides us one of the most profound depictions of Russians, Cold War or otherwise, that we have ever been privy to. (Indeed, there is a telling etymological consanguinity to be noted and enjoyed: that the Greek *patrios*, "of one's fathers," and the Latin *patria*, "fatherland," place parenting and patriotism in symbolic identity and thus symbiotic resonance.) Needless to say, in what follows, I aim to join Weisberg and his writers, producers, and actors in reflecting further on the particular lessons this televisual meditation has to offer on these intertwined topics.

As part of these prefatory notes, I wish to glance briefly at the question of the show's reception by the critics and the public alike. While *The Americans* is increasingly considered a critical darling, this esteem was not always the case. In fact, over the course of its six seasons on FX, though it was regularly nominated at the Emmys for outstanding drama (eighteen nods in all), it more often lost or was simply snubbed. Only very late in its life, indeed, in its last season, did it achieve a commanding presence at the prestigious television awards gathering when Matthew Rhys won the award for Outstanding Lead Actor in a Drama Series. Perhaps *The Americans*' slow-burning intensity as a show was matched by a very long period of courtship with Emmy voters, who only at the very end of the show's run feted it with top honors: Joe Weisberg also won for Outstanding Writing for a Drama Series. As we are taking this digression into cultural reception, we might also marvel at *The Americans*' success, despite the aforementioned notes. For example, consider how one television series takes off and another falters, a common enough quandary (*Firefly* [2002–3], for example, or Charlie Kaufman's *How and Why* [2014], which was commissioned but never picked up). Hence we might ask why *The Americans* prevailed while a similar show, *Allegiance* (2015), failed—the latter described as a show in which "a rookie CIA analyst doesn't know that members of his family are part of a Russian sleeper cell."[6] Too close? Maybe too late, appearing as it does a couple years into *The Americans*' tenure? Both of these cases—the Emmys' evolving regard for *The Americans* and the cancellation of *Allegiance*—remind us how significant *reception* (by critics and the general public) is for our understanding of film, television, and media.

In the spirit of reflection on *Allegiance*'s failure to catch on with critics and captivate audiences, and given the mandate of the present volume, it is worth dwelling on how *The Americans* provides a commentary (or not) on our contemporary moment—call it a "new" Cold War. Since the diegetic time of the show (namely, the "old" Cold War, or more specifically, the *end* of the old Cold War) stands in parallel to our time, we should take seriously the creative decision to avoid *direct* commentary on, or criticism of, the prevailing winds in the revitalized chill between the global nation-states that figure so dominantly in the show. In various interviews, Weisberg did acknowledge that he was still writing episodes of *The Americans* when Donald J. Trump was elected president of the United States and did consider featuring Trump "in his own time" (i.e., as a real estate tycoon of 1980s New York), but Weisberg decided against it. He noted, "When we started this show, the Soviet Union was gone. We were not in any kind of serious conflict with Russia. And it seemed like a good time to tell a story about those old bygone days."[7] And Weisberg kept to that original orientation and ethos for the entire show; he did not turn it, in its last few seasons, into a platform for direct (or even oblique) political critique on our current state of affairs. Some may claim this lack of political engagement as a fault or failure—a missed opportunity. Yet, I would counter that the relationship between art and politics is a contested one with a fraught history. As history appears to show, and enduring art repeatedly attests, it seems preferable that critics and scholars—such as those gathered in this collection—are the ones who should make comparisons of the sort Weisberg avoided. Indeed, Weisberg provides a clear and compelling example of the divided labors of art and of criticism, a division we should want to retain with some tenacity. We would not want the art of *The Americans* to be marred by satire or shtick by turning beloved characters into mouthpieces for trenchant political speech and the like. Weisberg's decision illustrates a sober instinct for art's domain, and for that reason the show he helped create is a better piece of art—indeed, it is worthy of our extended attention.

Unlike a feature film that might have a running time of a couple of hours, *The Americans* runs to about seventy-five hours, which amounts to a little over three and a half consecutive days. As with other fine series, plot points and story arcs that appear in an episode are added to the shape of a given season, and then seasons added together reveal yet another shape. There are many global comments about parenting and patriotism that can be made at this distance, and when covering this much ground, especially now that the show is complete, but I would prefer to study more closely a handful of representative vignettes—scenes or sequences that reveal something special and striking about the particular ways in which *The Americans* handles the interrelationship between parenting and spycraft during the first Cold War, the nature of living a double life (especially when one is also a parent), and the techniques by which the creators reveal their commentaries (and questions) about the values and virtues that underwrite the respective projects of these two competing empires (motherlands or fatherlands, depending on your preference). To help support a reading in relation to the chronology of the series, I will take up my analysis of episodes in the order they appeared.

The Son

As the episode title promises, in "New Car" (season 2, episode 8), Philip and his son, Henry (Keidrich Sellati), make their way to a Chevrolet dealership, where they encounter a white Chevy Camaro Z28. In his quick, elegant pitch, the salesman skips pricing and reason and goes straight for emotion: "And that is the beauty of the Z28. Chevy wants you to have the same experience as the professional. Why shouldn't you feel all that speed and power and freedom? . . . Buying a car is about feel. How does it make you feel?"[8] Soon enough Philip and Henry arrive home in the new car, where Elizabeth looks on incredulously and silently—an outsider, once again, to her potential maternal intimacy with Henry.

Father and son bonding over cars and music is later displaced, however, when it is reported that Henry has been breaking in (with a key) to a neighbor's house in order to play the coveted Intellivision, a then state-of-the-art video game system.[9] At the end of the episode, his parents enter his room to call him on his transgression, but he needs no prompting, and they remain silent for the duration of his remarkable, heartfelt soliloquy:

> You don't have to tell me. I know what you're gonna say. It's not like I haven't been thinking about it nonstop. I have. Makes me sick. Feel like I'm gonna throw up, but . . . I didn't take anything. I wouldn't do that, and I didn't hurt anybody. I know the difference between right and wrong. You know that, right? . . . I do, I do! It just seemed like no one would even know. And they weren't there. You guys weren't here. Once I did it, it seemed so easy to keep doing it. I know it was wrong. I'm not gonna do it again. I feel horrible. But they think I'm some kind of criminal, which I'm not. I hate that they think that and I hate them. And I hate that *you* think it. It's not true. . . . I'm a good person, I swear. You know that. You know that. I'm good. I am. I'm a good person. I swear, I'm good. I'm a good person. I swear, I'm good. I'm not gonna do it again. I swear, I'm good.[10]

On its surface, Henry's confession and self-assessment are mature and accurate, and for that admirable, but Elizabeth and Philip's faces call us to hear the lines through their ears. Henry's admission, and more pointedly his plea, is *theirs*.

They are good people. They know better. And yet they also know that "once I did it, it seemed so easy to keep doing it." They too do not feel like "some kind of criminal." Indeed, Henry's "crime" and the intensity of his guilt and regret are comically imbalanced when compared with his parents' exploits—a fact he, of course, is ignorant of, but we, as viewers, are invited to consider.

It is a measure of the development of Henry's conscience that he can be so self-aware—to discern the contours of right and wrong and also assess why those contours can be so easily skirted. Elizabeth and Philip remain silent, as priests might be in another context, and share knowing looks, for if their son is racked by the pain of guilt and regret by his infraction, we are invited to consider their own agonies in the wake of their actions (the lying, the murdering, the tactical sexual exploits, etc.). I reproduce this long speech because it also serves to outline why Henry will forever remain in the dark about his parents' true identity and actual behavior. Henry's goodness—here discovered so early (in his life and in the show) and so intensely—becomes a kind of shield: he is not the kind of person who could live a double life, who could lie without severe mental distress. Partly, Elizabeth and Philip hear his present moment (i.e., that Henry calls them out for not being around, in effect, for not parenting him) as their own present moment: that they share his wish for redemption. But they also hear the future, a future in which Henry cannot join them. He is already lost, on the other side of their life: he is an American. Since we know of Elizabeth's troubled intimacy with Henry, so familiar to the later seasons (where Philip seems to parent him nearly alone), her maternal caresses for her sobbing, anguished son are that much more devastating.[11]

The Daughter

A season later, in "Stingers," (season 3, episode 10), Elizabeth and Philip at last decide to tell Paige (Holly Taylor) that they are in fact not suburban parents working long hours as travel agents but instead spies for the Soviet Union. But, as usual, the episode is artfully framed to get us to think on multiple levels and with nuance. Pastor Tim (Kelly AuCoin) stops by the travel agency to book tickets for his summer mission to Kenya. He suggests that the whole Jennings family join Paige—to which Philip pauses to reply: "Now is not the right time, to be honest."[12] Pastor Tim sees a chance to sermonize: "I think it's *always* a good time for parents and children to get closer. . . . Yeah, teenagers can be challenging, right? But that's not always a bad thing. A kid like Paige really needs to be treated more like an adult than a child." Stifling his irritation at the unwanted advice, Philip calmly (or is it with underlying menace?) turns the questioning back to Pastor Tim.

> PHILIP: Do you have kids?
> PASTOR TIM: I have a flock.
> PHILIP: It's not the same.
> PASTOR TIM: No. No, it's not.
> PHILIP: Let's look at some dates.

As the earlier scene with Henry was structured as a silent confession to two judges—the child pleading for absolution from parents who are, or can be, in a position to grant such states of being—the new one, with Philip and Pastor Tim, reveals an iteration of the interventionist mode, where a childless man offers parenting advice to a parent, and a parent turns the questioning back to the "father" of the church and the "flock" he is said to guide. We are left to wonder, then, about the authority that animates good parental advice: Must it only derive from people who are parents themselves? As Henry revealed, sometimes even *children* may parent their parents and be a source of wise counsel. Pastor Tim, then, is meant to show that with parental advice, tone and intention matter.

A little later in the episode, when Paige makes an unexpected visit to the travel agency, Elizabeth and Philip greet her warmly (though not with a hug). Philip invites Paige to do a little work, to which she replies, "Trying turn me into a travel agent?"[13] We are not sure if Elizabeth's laughter is genuine or nervous, but the notion that parents (generally speaking) turn us into things is, we could say, a leitmotif of the entire enterprise. If this is what parents are for, then what they turn us toward or away from—and why—draws us closer to Elizabeth and Philip's particular parental crisis.

Children are perpetually being groomed by elders, not just parents. Stan Beeman (Noah Emmerich) takes an interest in Henry, and in the midst of his own divorce, Stan begins a slow-burn worry about his young neighbor, even as he is no longer sure if his own son, Matthew (Danny Flaherty), will continue to live with him.[14] Indeed, at the very end of the series, it is Stan's preoccupation with Henry, in particular his parental observation of how unaccompanied (or perhaps unparented) Henry is, that leads to the denouement that confirms Elizabeth and Philip as Soviet spies. Or, along a different plotline, consider how Philip (in character as Jim) cares for Kimmy (Julia Garner) but also manipulates her in their May–December flirtation—and in one of the most painfully taboo, morally transgressive scenes of the show, sleeps with her. Surrogacy, it turns out, is also part of parenting and being parented: we seek compensation as both child *and* adult. And in these proxy relationships (e.g., where Henry provides a son's company to a confounded father, and Stan attends to a son whose father is often absentee), we are reminded again that the source of parenting is not always a parent.

In this episode, at just about the midpoint in the entire series, Elizabeth and Philip arrive home in the middle of the night after meeting with Gabriel (Frank Langella) and find Paige, alone, in the kitchen.[15] As parents of teenagers are wont to do, they ask why she is up so late and whether everything is okay. Paige demurs. Everything is not okay. Playing to her own cliché, Paige asks her parents if they love her, to which they reply in kind, with the first parent saying, "Of course we do," and the second adding, "More than anything." So far, the encounter holds parents and children to type. But then Paige increases the stakes of the otherwise pro forma encounter: "Then tell me the truth." Elizabeth and Philip look at one another quizzically, as if to say, "What's she talking about?"

> PAIGE: Stop, don't do that. I'm right here. Just please look at me. I'm not stupid. I know there's something going on. You're out in the middle of the night. The phone rings and you're gone. We have no family here—no aunts, no uncles, no cousins, no nothing.

Elizabeth tries to reassure her by (parentally) saying her name, but Paige continues:

> This isn't normal. I felt it for a long time now and I thought it was me. I thought I was crazy. But it's not me, it's you. And I talked to Pastor Tim, and he agrees. I need to know the truth. I don't care what it is, but if you love me, if you really love me, then just please tell me. [*Beat*] What, are you in the witness protection program? Did you kill somebody? Are you guys drug dealers like your friend Gregory? Am I adopted? Are we aliens? What?! [*Beat, walking away*] You're just gonna keep lying to me.

The charges are, indeed, elevated—and beyond anything Elizabeth and Philip have yet fielded from their own children. The three of them gather at the family dining table to continue talking. Elizabeth and Philip confess, at last:

> ELIZABETH: Paige, your father and I . . . we . . .
> PHILIP: . . . We were born in a different country . . .
> PAIGE: What? Where?

ELIZABETH: The Soviet Union.
PHILIP: We came here before you were born.
PAIGE: I don't understand.
ELIZABETH: We're here to help our people. Most of what you hear about the Soviet Union isn't true. Everything we've told you about being activists, about wanting to make the world a better place . . .
PAIGE: So, you're . . .
PHILIP: We work for our country. Getting information. Information that they couldn't get in other ways.
PAIGE: You're spies?
ELIZABETH: We serve our country. But we also serve the cause of peace around the world. We fight for people who can't fight for themselves.
PAIGE: Stop.
ELIZABETH: Paige, we've wanted to tell you this for such a long time.
PAIGE: But you didn't.
PHILIP: No. No, you're right. We didn't.
ELIZABETH: We know how much this hurts, and we know it's upsetting.
PAIGE: Don't. I'm going upstairs.
ELIZABETH: Paige, knowing this comes with a lot of responsibility.
PHILIP: Paige, you can't tell anyone—not now, not ever. Not Pastor Tim. And not Henry.
ELIZABETH: No matter how much you trust someone or think that you trust them, you can't tell them.
PHILIP: This may seem obvious, but you're taking so much in tonight. So just in case you're not thinking quite clearly enough, we're gonna have to say this. If you do tell anyone, we will go to jail—for good.

After Paige retreats upstairs, and Philip (always mindful of human nature and spycraft best practices to counter it) pulls the phone from its carriage, the parents standing side by side in the kitchen, taking stock:[16]

PHILIP: You okay?
ELIZABETH: I don't know.

She does *not* ask Philip, like Paige, "Do you love me?"—but instead:

ELIZABETH: I don't know. Do you hate me?
PHILIP: No. I remember when you thought them finding out would kill them.
ELIZABETH: But things change, Philip. They changed.
PHILIP: I know. I know.

There are more than a few lines to dwell upon in this crucial, series-defining extended scene—one that lies at the intersection of parenting and patriotism. Out of order, we could begin with Elizabeth's claim that "most of what you hear about the Soviet Union isn't true." This feels like one of those comments that echoes in the present moment as we wonder what we do and do not know about Russia, or for that matter about the relationship between Russia and America. What is the state of that fraught affair, which is neither a marriage nor a divorce? And what could we, the children of these superpower parents, even hope to know about what goes on behind closed doors, when our leaders speak to one another frankly but privately and off the record? But back in the early 1980s, in the kitchen with the Jennings family, we have to wonder if Elizabeth's earnest claim should apply to her and Philip (as well as Paige): Do they—the active agents in the field—really know what is true about their motherland? One of the recurrent competitions between Elizabeth and Philip is the quality of their memory of Russia, especially as it is coupled with the inklings they might have about its current conditions. Have things gotten better or worse there? Are their severe, sustained sacrifices really helping "serve the cause of peace around the world" or just sustaining the perpetual threat of nuclear war? In the scene, Elizabeth's statement that "most of what you hear about the Soviet Union isn't true" is of course aimed at Paige, but as viewers, we also see how it is aimed at Elizabeth and Philip. And if we are really canny, we might also think it applies to us as well.

Such a volatile scene—full of charged accusation as well as measured candor—brings us to the question of the "normal" family, which Paige now decisively knows she is not a part of. In the midst of that particularly intense reality-distortion zone known as puberty, Paige may be having a bit of a nervous breakdown—feeling and fearing that she is, in fact, the paranoid culprit of her fantastical conjectures (drug dealers? adopted? aliens?). So it might come as a relief, in effect, to know the truth. And to get there—to become a counterintelligence agent and extract the information from her tight-lipped, secretive parents—Paige appeals to love, which is itself a form of loyalty. When her mom asks, "Honey, what's wrong?" Paige doesn't demand in reply, "Tell me the truth about who you are." She asks, instead, "Do you love me?" To which Elizabeth and Philip reply as loyal, loving parents: "Of course we love you. More than anything." Paige's difficult task to turn her parents, to make *them* confess, has begun, and it is predicated on the explicit statement of their committed, superlative love for her. This is Paige's conditional: "If you love me, if you really love me, then just please tell me." If love, then truth. Now it seems that the only way to prove their parental love—to confirm it—is to tell her the truth, which she so desperately desires.

The truth—that they are, in fact, Soviet spies—may explain things a bit, but it will not resolve the underlying condition. First, in telling Paige the truth, Elizabeth and Philip effectively confirm that their family is not normal. Second, they introduce an extrafamilial and higher loyalty, namely, to country (or to the "cause of peace," if you wish). Aside from the obvious, hurtful fact that Paige has been lied to all these years—all her life—by her parents, there is this added imposition: that their love also ties them to a nation, an ideology, and a set of clandestine methodologies that have come to define their lives.[17] They cannot abandon this love in order to love Paige; it is too late. Or rather, as Philip said, "We came here before you were born," which is to say: We fell in love with the country's cause and gave our hearts, minds, and bodies to it before there was a Paige to love. While parental love here feels genuine, it is also outflanked and outranked by love of country.

Now that Paige knows these truths, she cannot tell anyone, not even her brother, Henry. And so with truth comes "responsibility," a commitment to an extended purgatory of isolation from the world at large (including her brother, her friends, her neighbors, and what she might have hoped was an extended family, for example, with Pastor Tim and his family and the church he leads). And yet, in this apocalypse of truth, there is a new, unexpected realm of company and companionship: her parents. In Elizabeth and Philip's breach of privacy (for the sake of their love for their only daughter), they have also invited her into their secrecy, their intimacy. The party of two is now the party of three, and in time, Paige will also meet Gabriel and Claudia (Margo Martindale), among others in the cell, and be drawn into active training and, subsequently, active operations. The final note of advice Elizabeth offers (on the nature of Paige's newly bestowed responsibility) may seem like an admonition for the outside world (that is, the world beyond her parents), and yet we, like Paige, must also hear that it is a warning that applies inside the home: "No matter how much you trust someone or think that you trust them, you can't tell them." While love yielded truth, it is not clear how to navigate trust.

Parenting Paige

In the next episode, "One Day in the Life of Anton Baklanov" (season 3, episode 11), Elizabeth and Philip continue to navigate the implications of their revelation to Paige. In the privacy of the family sedan, parked in the garage, Elizabeth tells Paige that she understands that "there are certain things you missed out on. I know that."[18] And then, Elizabeth opens up—shares something of her personal history, which confirms that Elizabeth has missed out on even more: that her father was killed in the war when she was two, and that she was raised by her mother.[19] "You should've seen the way I grew up," Elizabeth laughs in embarrassment: "It was just me and her . . . and three other families in a single apartment." And then Elizabeth tries to link Paige to her grandmother, to broach the distance in time and space—and secrecy—that has separated them, lamenting that her extended family is one of the things they both "missed out on." Of her mother, Elizabeth says, "She had a real spirit, like yours. I haven't seen her since I came here." The moment of attempted pathos is undermined by Paige's reasonable skepticism: "How can I believe anything you say?" The truth she learned is the very sort of thing that makes trust so difficult, indeed, that makes it so difficult for her to get a handle on other (possible) truths. Elizabeth has no answer for her daughter.

Paige's knowledge of her parents' true identity becomes a central part of the plot for the rest of the series. We, like Paige, are forced to come to terms with the way this new knowledge—this truth—affects her life (just as the secret had its effect on her). And we also see other characters comment on the complexities of caring for the young, as when Pastor Tim drops by (in the following season, "Dinner for Seven," [season 4, episode 11]) to apologize for his wife's reaction to his disappearance in Ethiopia by saying, sincerely, "When I got lost, through my own stupidity, I was terrified that no one would ever find me. That I'd never see Alice again. See my baby born, grow up. I thought about you two and Paige: all the things that being a parent can mean. Anyway, sorry for what happened. That's it. That's what I came to say."[20] Pastor Tim's generous, accepting remark applies to Elizabeth and Philip, of course, but it also radiates out to the various parents and proxies that populate the entire world they inhabit—to Pastor Tim, of course, but also to Gabriel and Claudia, to Stan, to Oleg (Costa Ronin), and to all the parents featured in the scenes taking place in Russia, past and present.

Parents commiserate and question together and share their appreciation for support in trying to raise their children, as when Elizabeth stops in at Pastor Tim's office: "Honestly, I can only thank you for everything you've done for Paige. When she first started coming here, to church, I felt threatened. I was . . . I was afraid I was going to lose her." "To God?" asks Pastor Tim. "And to you. But it didn't happen. In fact, we've gotten closer and things have been better. And there's nothing that I did or Philip. It was you." In kind, Pastor Tim offers a self-deprecating, generous reply: "You took a risk. You opened yourself up to her. That took faith . . . in Paige."[21] They are both right, but not entirely for the reasons they think they are acknowledging. This scene can serve as an emblem of the artful way the show navigates pretext and subtext, since there is regularly a state of knowledge asymmetry (e.g., people *think* they know things; people are under the wrong impression; people are simply ignorant of facts, etc.). Still, the scene achieves a further explication of the interrelatedness of parent-child love, loyalty, truth, and trust.

An Education in Loyalty

If seasons three and four addressed the immediate effects of Elizabeth and Philip's unplanned, much-delayed admission to Paige about the truth of their identities, season five goes straight to the question Philip feared all along—the question that made him want to permanently keep the secret from her: having told Paige who they are, should they now groom her for service to the Centre?[22] We might ask, more generally: Should parents ever willingly "turn" a child into an asset of the state (a state that is the enemy of her own)? Aside from the comically superficial observation that they might violate child labor laws, we can look to the deeper issue of what it means for a parent to protect a child. If there are, in fact, many ways to parent—and with that an acknowledgment of all the things that being a parent can mean—is one of those ways a program of training and indoctrination in the clandestine services? To begin, how can Paige be loyal to a country that is not her own? Isn't any move toward the Centre an act of treason? But then can loyalty to parents—wanting to work with them, work for them, make them proud of you, etc.—be a loyalty a child might choose to uphold in the face of any real or perceived allegiance to a country (the child's own or another's)? Have Elizabeth and Philip chosen loyalty to country over loyalty to child, while Paige is asked to choose the inverse, namely, loyalty to parents over loyalty to country (i.e., the country of her birth, which she has known as her own)?

In the second half of the penultimate season, we begin to see how Elizabeth, Philip, and Paige handle these questions—along with their handlers. In "The Committee on Human Rights" (season 5, episode 7), the Jennings family (sans Henry) visits Gabriel for Paige's first meeting with him. Paige begins frankly: "Are you a spy?" Gabriel replies without pretense, "Yes."[23] By way of explanation, Gabriel tells Paige about her parents' bravery, their sacrifices, and their dedication to the cause of improving human welfare. Then Gabriel praises Paige for *her* courage, a courage revealed in her demand for the truth from her parents. After the meeting, when the Jennings family walks together, they speak of Gabriel as they might a parent or grandparent. Paige concludes: "He's like your family." "Yeah, he is," Philip says.[24] And we call to mind Philip's sad remark to Elizabeth in the previous episode: "I don't know anything. My own parents, I don't know anything at all."[25] Gabriel is yet another surrogate parent—an advisor, a guardian, a father figure who expresses love and care. But he is also a Soviet agent.

When Elizabeth returns alone to visit Gabriel, he says, "I've been thinking about Paige. You did well. She doesn't think the world owes her happiness, which is no small accomplishment growing up in this country."[26] Elizabeth replies, "Sometimes I think that we've put too much pressure on her." Gabriel dismisses the notion: "No, she has a big heart. She's not a quitter. She'll find her way." But when Philip makes a solo visit to Gabriel, a final visit, it turns out, Gabriel's tone and advice shift dramatically, perhaps because this is a goodbye: "I doubt we'll ever see each other again," Gabriel begins.[27] And in their last minutes together, in his parting words, Gabriel says: "You were right about Paige."[28] Philip furrows his brow, not sure what Gabriel means. "She should be kept out of all this," Gabriel concludes—his final words to his charge—and Philip is devastated. He and Elizabeth should have kept the secret, should have spared Paige the truth. Gabriel's advice at this fraught, terminal moment in their relationship is that Elizabeth and Philip have made the wrong parenting decision about their daughter.[29]

In the following episode ("Immersion," season 5, episode 8), Philip returns home late, where he finds Elizabeth in bed reading, and they discuss Gabriel as they would a parent—in particular, as children who are hurt or confused by a parent's behavior. And again, we can hear Elizabeth and Philip's own parenting decisions mapped artfully into the subtext of their remarks; and we may wonder further if they are not also ventriloquizing their own feelings under the guise of their reflections on Gabriel:

ELIZABETH: How'd it go with Gabriel?
PHILIP: I don't know....
ELIZABETH: I can't believe we're never going to see him again.
PHILIP: I'm glad.
ELIZABETH: Come on.
PHILIP: I am. All those years by our side.... I just think he was doing his job.
ELIZABETH: He can do his job and still care about us.
PHILIP: Yeah, he could. I just think when it comes down to things, us, or ... I don't know.
ELIZABETH: He's the one who wanted us to go home. He's a good person.
PHILIP: I think he got tired of this.
ELIZABETH: He did it a long time.
PHILIP: He's worried about Paige. He told me that she shouldn't do it. This.
ELIZABETH: He told you?
PHILIP: Yeah. It just came up.
ELIZABETH: Hmm. Wouldn't it be a nice world if nobody had to do this?[30]

Elizabeth's defense of Gabriel is part of her own defense of her work and of her parenting: she can do her job and still care about—still love—her children. And we hear echoes of Henry's earlier, plaintive plea—"I'm a good person"—projected onto Gabriel here: he is a good person too. And by the logic of transitivity, we are *all* good people, good people just doing our jobs.

If Paige is going to be properly trained for this job—cast in the mindset of her parents, that is, to be a good person doing a good job (i.e., loyal, moral, effective)—her parents will have to *continue* to divulge secrets. In "Dinner for Seven" (season 4, episode 11), discussed earlier, there is a scene in which Elizabeth and Paige are mugged. Elizabeth does not take the attack as a civilian, but immediately transforms into a lethal counterforce—and kills the man. Paige looks on in shock and horror. Though unplanned, this is still a radical disclosure. And it explains a lot to Paige about her mom even as it raises new questions (How many times has Elizabeth killed? Who is she killing? Do these attackers deserve to die? Will I have to kill?). Another kind of disclosure—also involving an attack—comes up in "Immersion" (season 5, episode 8). Elizabeth is training Paige in hand-to-hand combat, in the family garage, when mom decides to narrate how she came to her own pronounced physical training.

> PAIGE: I'm sick of being scared.
> ELIZABETH: I know. I know how hard it is. I was scared like that for a long time. When I was eighteen, a man . . . I was raped. And I couldn't stop thinking about it. And I didn't tell anyone about it for a very long time.
> PAIGE: Mom.
> ELIZABETH: No, no, no. Paige. No, listen to me. The thing is: I trained as hard as I could every day. I imagined that man's face every time I fought, and the more I fought the better I felt, until one day I knew no one was gonna hurt me like that again. And I'm okay. I'm not afraid anymore. And you're not going to be either. Okay?[31]

With this stark, brutal truth we face anew the question of what a child may or may not learn from a parent. Is this how a parent protects her child? Can the trauma a parent suffered—and in some sense overcame—be used productively by the next generation as a guide or a gird? Can Paige be motivated to protect herself through an awareness of her mother's assault and subsequent training against future attacks? Like Paige, we learn something of Elizabeth's often murky backstory (kept that way with a reticence and obscurity befitting a spy), and also, as the series comes to a conclusion, something telling about different understandings of sex and sexuality.

Among other points of disagreement in the relationship between Paige and her parents, we find an ongoing debate about the use of sex as a tool, as a weapon of spycraft. The series has from its earliest episodes offered us a frank, unsentimental glimpse of how spies use sex and sexuality to ply their trade; because of the tactical effectiveness of sex (since people are often so receptive to seduction), there regularly appears to be a kind of bracketing or even evacuation of moral judgment in the way Elizabeth and Philip handle their respective operations: in short, they return to the marriage bed (sometimes shaken or haunted, but almost always ready to resume duty—and genuine, mutual affection—within the structure of their suburban, American marriage).

A season later, in "Jennings, Elizabeth" (season 6, episode 9), two episodes from the series finale, Paige stops by the family house, finding Elizabeth in the kitchen.[32] Paige has a line of questioning motivated by moral outrage and moralizing about sex, which at first seems justified—and also shows that Paige herself has become a capable member of the team: she sees through her mom's guise, her mom's attempted dissimulation. But then, countering Paige's indignation and threats—and thus chastening the viewer, like Paige, for our affront—Elizabeth has her say, and her daughter is left speechless and leaves the house.

Elizabeth is surprised by Paige's visit. "Here I am," says Paige flatly, then says her friend Brian visited last night. "Brian who?" might be Elizabeth's reply, but Paige adds sharply: "The intern you thought I slept with to get"—and she is interrupted again by Elizabeth's parental, admonishing statement of her name. Paige continues undaunted to recall events of the previous evening, when Brian was at a party where a fellow intern got drunk: "And this kid is falling all over himself, sick, and crying, and he starts talking about how he slept with this older woman. He felt like she tricked him or something. He said she ruined his life. Now he's quitting and going home. He works for Sam Nunn. This happens right in the middle of the Summit. Was it you?" Elizabeth retorts sharply: "Don't be ridiculous." Paige persists: "Was it?" Elizabeth says sternly, "No." Her unequivocal and confident denial doesn't assuage Paige's suspicion, and she presses on to set new terms:

> PAIGE: If you lie to me now, after everything, I will never forgive you.
> ELIZABETH: Paige, I swear to you I'm not.
> PAIGE: Looking back, I've always known, mom. Every time, every lie, my whole life. And I know now.
> ELIZABETH: I had nothing to do with that boy.
> PAIGE: No wonder dad can't stand to be in the same room with you.
> ELIZABETH: Excuse me?
> PAIGE: You lie about everything.

ELIZABETH: Paige.
PAIGE: How many times? How many men? Were you doing this when I was a baby? You're a whore. Does dad know he married a whore?
ELIZABETH: Stop it.
PAIGE: Why? You don't want to know the truth. The truth is: that moment you told me who you really are, I should have done what Henry did—get as far away from you as possible.
ELIZABETH: That's enough! It doesn't mean anything to me. I wasn't brought up like you were. I had to fight. Always. For everything. People were killed, they died, all around me. If I had to give everything so that my country would survive, so that it would never happen again, I would do it gladly. We were proud to do whatever we could. Sex? What was sex? Nobody cared. Including your father.

As Philip Roth so ably diagnosed the moral and sexual panic of 1990s America in *The Human Stain* (2000)—for instance, exposing widespread hypocrisy motivated by a hidden, deep-seated puritanical fervor around the time of the impeachment of President Bill Clinton—so *The Americans* dramatizes a series of kindred debates, adding layers of nuance to them. We are, for example, not merely caught up in a quarrel between mother and daughter (e.g., about what should be sexually permissible for a married woman, etc.) but also a contest between the terms of clandestine operations (for instance, whether sex is fair game), and lastly, a comparison between what might be called Russian sentiments versus American sentimentality about sex. Paige's accusation "You're a whore" lands on Elizabeth on all three fronts—as a mom, as a spy, as a Russian. And her sober, righteous reply is a rebuke to her daughter's Americanness: "I wasn't brought up like you. . . . Sex? What was sex? Nobody cared." In effect, who has the time and energy for moral outrage about sex—what it is, what it might be used for—when people are starving, dying, and the country itself might not survive? For Elizabeth these are rhetorical questions; for Paige, they highlight the differences, indeed the divide, that will forever, tragically, separate her from her mother.

Concluding Lessons

Part of what is compelling about Elizabeth and Philip for us as viewers is that we want them to succeed, even though we know they are Russian spies (unlike others, even their intimates, such as Stan, who remains in the dark until the very end). But unlike the antiheroes familiar to Cold War films and television shows—and now, we might say, in Cold War II depictions of enemy spies, Russians, Soviet agents, etc.—the most significant amplification of the pathos in our affection for *these* antiheroes is predicated on our awareness that they are not just spies but also parents—in short, that they need to take care of their children. Moreover, they are children to their parent country, their motherland, which they so fiercely wish to honor, make proud, and be loyal to. So, when there is an operation—that is, a contest between Russian and American agents—we find ourselves rooting for them to survive, to prevail, to escape, to return to safety, to evade detection or imprisonment and, of course, to avoid death. And when we gain further insight into the Russian experience (e.g., with Oleg and his parents, and myriad other figures from the remembered past and in the muddled green-gray light of present-day Russia), there are additional valences of emotive effect. It is not too much to say that in *The Americans* the Russians are depicted with tremendous sympathy; even the cases that seem to suggest Russian cruelty or indifference (e.g., Gabriel's calm operational deliberateness) are just as often balanced with tenderness, loss, confusion, suffering, and sadness.

Now that *The Americans* is complete as a work of art—running from 2013, during the second Obama administration, to 2018, into the first Trump administration—we will watch and rewatch it for its particular contribution to the history we are living through and our rethinking the era in which the show took place. The transformative effects of art, of course, place *The Americans* at a great distance from being a chronicle of an era, much less a portrait of actual persons (however pronounced the resonances may be). But it is precisely the *separation* (between art and history) that provides the occasion for insight on the sense of repetition we are now experiencing in the ongoing, complicated relationship between the United States and Russia. If this is a second Cold War, for example, how would a representation of the first Cold War help? Precisely by enabling a double register of experience where we can undergo the unfolding of the second Cold War in the unrehearsed coursings of history while at the same time watching artful images of the first Cold War. We should not imagine that such a double consciousness will guard against making the same mistakes twice, but it will provide the conditions—call this *The Americans* as text worthy of close analysis—for readings of the nature and happenstance of being human, the sound and savvy interpretation of which is perennially in need. For this reason, *The Americans* is likely to survive, better than most serials, the current season of heightened tensions between classic national rivals, since it is not beholden to the first Cold War so much as it is committed to enduring problems of human existence: vocational and moral discernment, marriage, parenting, friendship, self-deception and the deception of others, lies and truth, authenticity and conformity, personal and national pride, loyalty, the costs of violence, and related vital interests that exceed the bounds even of the fraught moments in geopolitical life known as the Cold War and its latter iterations. At this point, we may wonder if the Cold War—then *and* now—is especially fecund in its revelations of these core human issues. Even if the second Cold War thaws to a moderate level, we can be sure that *The Americans* will continue to inform our approach to the problems that matter most. If the show, over time, becomes more abstract, less tied to history, its power as allegory will abide and may even intensify.

As an illustration of these claims, consider "The World Council of Churches" (season 5, episode 12), in which Elizabeth and Philip carry out a hit that has her asking to "get out"—that is, to return home to Russia. Meanwhile, as Elizabeth joins Philip in his already well-worn career crisis, the Centre has arranged for Pastor Tim to receive an offer he can't refuse from a church in Buenos Aires. And, as part of a farewell, Elizabeth and Philip visit Pastor Tim in his office, where they, of all things, seek parenting advice, and in particular ask what Pastor Tim thinks about the Jennings family's notion of moving (back) to Russia.[33] Pastor Tim goes from a note on the immediate decision to a more expansive reflection on parenting as such—what it is, what it entails, and what it doesn't:

> ELIZABETH: We don't know if they would ever really adjust to life there.
> PHILIP: But with the situation here, and everything, most of which you know about, and really, everything that goes along with it—it's not much better either.
> PASTOR TIM: Does Henry know anything? I think you'll have trouble either way. It's hard to imagine all the problems that two American kids will have adjusting to life over there. But there's a lot about life here that's not so great. You can't predict what a person's life will be. And you can't deny them the challenges that will shape them. Does Paige know you're thinking about this?
> PHILIP: Not yet.
> ELIZABETH: No. We will talk to her soon. We're just . . .
> PASTOR TIM: The temptation is to put off making hard decisions, but then that becomes its own sort of decision. Paige and Henry are teenagers. At this age, the transition would be a very difficult one for them, but in a few years, it won't be your decision to make anymore. I wish I could tell you what you should do, but I don't know.

With each new season of the show, the overt elements of the plot—America versus Russia versus America, the FBI versus the KGB, operations and events in Russia, extramarital relationships, neighborhood friendships, etc.—nearly all seem to reflect back upon central questions of parenting and being parented, perhaps especially as those questions refract strongly held patriotic convictions. As viewers, we are tormented by the competing loyalties that recurrently present themselves: to lie or reveal, to remain faithful to a mission or a marriage, to trust in others who may expose one's secrets, and perhaps most direly, from episode to episode, from season to season—how best to raise and protect one's children.

Now that the show has concluded, we might ask: What can parents learn from Elizabeth and Philip? And what can children learn from Paige? For Elizabeth and Philip, we might cite their poise and patience, their capacity to listen and to let silence do some work. Paige, on one hand, while often handling family secrets with discretion, is herself a reminder that *all* children arrive into families they do not choose, into circumstances that exceed their power and comprehension (they are, indeed, aliens—as their parents were before them). Likewise, it is tempting to judge Elizabeth and Philip for their decision to have children—could their choice be a species of human rights violation?—but then, they too provide a portrait of the predicament all parents face: being given children who are variable and who respond to circumstances in unpredictable ways. Even as we viewers are caught up in the specifics of the Jennings family—the status, actions, and decisions it faces—we are tacitly presented with an image of family life that should be recognizable. Not, of course, because we are spies or assassins, but because we are all children, have all been parented in some fashion (either by our parents, or through their neglect, or by those who are not our own parents), and, moreover, may now ourselves also be parents.

In the series finale of *The Americans* ("Start," season 6, episode 10), we find ourselves in what may be the last minutes of the Cold War—as peace talks are underway and treaties are being meted out (hence the double entendre of the episode title). Yet for all the revelations and resolutions, the most pressing is the one that has percolated steadily for seventy-five episodes: What happens to the children? And the finale, at last, depicts the logic we suspected all along: being exposed as spies will lead to a forced decision about whether the children stay or go. For Henry, the question seemed settled long ago—he's not in the family business and will have to be left behind; Stan's early and ongoing care for him provides solace and confirmation of a potentially meaningful parental surrogacy. But the real charge lies with Paige's fate. So, after all the near misses give the three of them safe passage on a train, Paige's stepping off—which is to say, back onto the platform of America—is the ultimate parental denouement.

Having arrived back in Russia, overlooking cold, blue Moscow in the depth of night, Elizabeth and Philip imagine an alternate history—where they never left their homeland. She worked in a factory, they met on a bus. There is no mention of the success or failure of their years as spies, no sense of regret or judgment about all their actions or sacrifices. Like all things in *The Americans*, in these last minutes of the show, the subject returns to the show's ultimate, central concern: the lives of parents and children.

> ELIZABETH: They'll be okay.
> PHILIP: They'll remember us. And, they're not kids anymore. We raised them.
> ELIZABETH: Yes.
> PHILIP: Feels strange.
> ELIZABETH: [*in Russian*] We'll get used to it.[34]

In the end, the entire show is a lie, a ruse. *The Americans* has tricked us into rooting for the Russians. We have been seduced by Elizabeth and Philip, like so many of their marks, and have unwittingly given them a glimpse of our own credulousness, our trust and affection. Despite knowing all that we know about them and having known it all along—the murders, executions, and dismemberments; the fakes and frauds; the many ways they harmed Americans, compromised the country, etc.—they still come out, in the end, as creatures worthy of our interest, and even love, profound love. These flawed human beings have been revealed to us by turns as neglected and wounded children, as capable, loyal patriots to their appointed cause, but perhaps most importantly and saliently, as worried parents. What an achievement of the show that, as we adults live with the Cold War in living memory and our children are raised in an era fraught with the threat or even the reality of a second Cold War, we have (despite all intentions and preconceived notions, all habits of thought, all prejudices, all well-worn cultural clichés) fallen in love with these devious Russians, Elizabeth and Philip, and want them to live on and live well. The Americans have, at last, become the Russians once again and faded into the arctic night of the motherland, their futures obscured from our view. Like them, we'll get used it.

Notes

1. Laura M. Holson, "The Dark Stuff, Distilled," *New York Times*, March 29, 2013, https://www.nytimes.com/2013/03/31/fashion/joseph-weisberg-uses-his-cia-time-in-the-americans.html.

2. David LaRocca, "'You Must Change Your Life': *The Americans*, (Concepts and Cults of) Authenticity, and EST," in *The Americans and Philosophy: Reds in the Bed*, ed. Robert Arp and Kevin Guilfoy (Chicago: Open Court, 2018). See also, Jessica Smock, "Why FX's *The Americans* is TV's Best Show about Parenting and Marriage," *School of Smock*, https://www.schoolofsmock.com/2013/02/why-fxs-the-americans-is-tvs-best-show-about-parenting-and-marriage/.

3. On Elizabeth and Philip's decision to have children, see Kevin Meeker, "Decisions that Change Who We Are," in *The Americans and Philosophy*.

4. See also Anna Nordberg, "What does *The Americans* Tell Us about Parenting? Everything," *Washington Post*, May 22, 2018, https://www.washingtonpost.com/news/parenting/wp/2018/05/22/what-does-a-show-about-soviet-spies-living-in-america-tell-us-about-parenting-everything/.

5. See Joshua Rothman, "The Cruel Irony of *The Americans*," *New Yorker*, March 16, 2016, https://www.newyorker.com/culture/culture-desk/the-cruel-irony-of-the-americans.

6. See IMDb's page for *Allegiance*, https://www.imdb.com/title/tt3581654/?ref_=nv_sr_1.

7. "*The Americans*' Showrunners on Writing Cold-War Era Drama amid New Russian Relations," *All Things Considered*, February 25, 2017, https://www.npr.org/2017/02/25/517262429/the-americans-showrunners-talk-writing-cold-war-era-drama-amid-new-u-s-russian-r.

8. 00:02:42. *The Americans*, the complete series, is available on DVD.

9. See also Evan McGarvey, "Familiar Miracles: On *The Americans*' Graceful Approach to the Parent-Child Bond," *Paste Magazine*, April 24, 2017, https://www.pastemagazine.com/articles/2017/04/the-americans-parenting-children.html; and earlier: Raef Harrison, "The Russians Love Their Children Too: The Americans Are Finally Learning to Parent," *Screener*, March 14, 2017, https://newmoviereleasesdvd.loginby.com/the-russians-love-their-children-too-the-americans-are-finally-learning-to-pare/; and Robert Blanco, "*The Americans* Faces a Treacherous Parent Trap," *USA Today*, February 25, 2014, https://www.usatoday.com/story/life/tv/2014/02/25/the-americans-review/5813823/.

10. 00:46:08.

11. See also Carole Avalon, "Henry and Problem Parenting in *The Americans*," *People's World*, May 7, 2018, https://www.peoplesworld.org/article/henry-and-problem-parenting-in-the-americans/.

12. 00:02:14.

13. 00:14:36.

14. 00:19:56.

15. 00:24:12.

16. 00:34:04.

17. For more on the role of lying in parenting, see Daniel P. Malloy, "Yes, Paige, There Is a Santa Claus," in *The Americans and Philosophy*. And for remarks on denial, see Rob Luzecky and Charlene Elsby, "How to Keep On Denying and Love Being a Spy," in *The Americans and Philosophy*.

18. 00:16:30.

19. See Jane Greenway Carr, "*The Americans* Made Motherhood the Ultimate Disguise," *CNN*, June 2, 2018, https://www.cnn.com/2018/06/02/opinions/americans-series-finale-elizabeth-jennings-maternal-instinct-carr-opinion/index.html.

20. 00:02:30.

21. Season 4, episode 11, 00:30:04.

22. See also Mary McNamara, "The Overlooked Victims in *The Americans*: The Kids," *Los Angeles Times*, February 26, 2014, https://www.latimes.com/entertainment/tv/showtracker/la-et-st-americans-review-20140226-story.html.

23. 00:01:50.

24. 00:04:26.

25. Season 5, episode 6.

26. 00:28:52.

27. 00:39:24.

28. 00:43:09.

29. See also Andrea Zanin, "We're Only What We Remember," in *The Americans and Philosophy*; and Frauke Albersmeier, "Better Never to Have Been?" in *The Americans and Philosophy*.
30. 00:02:01.
31. 00:25:05.
32. 00:41:26.
33. 00:26:13.
34. 01:06:40.

CONSERVATIVE UNDERSTANDING AND NATIONALIST EXCLUSION
Moral Equivalency as Contested Concept in *Bridge of Spies* and *Tinker Tailor Soldier Spy*

Christian Jimenez

The depiction of Russia by Americans has been a strong part of cinematic history since the first films began to appear. By far, the peak of this interest occurred during the Cold War, from 1945 to 1989.[1] On the Russian side, there has been a similar fascination, with Lenin believing that "of all the kinds of arts, the most important for us is cinema."[2] This essay focuses in particular on how "the Russian spy" as a construct has been so persistently a source of fear. Indeed, this can be noticed in numerous examples: from children's programs such as *The Bullwinkle Show* (1959–63), featuring the villainous Boris Badenov, to the recent TV show *The Americans* (2013–18), which tells the story of an attractive young couple masquerading as Russian spies.

This essay studies the neoconservative appropriation of the term *moral equivalence* via two post–Cold War, post-2001 films: Steven Spielberg's *Bridge of Spies* (2015) and Tomas Alfredson's *Tinker Tailor Soldier Spy* (2011). After their release, both films were attacked by some conservatives as being covertly pro-Russian.[3] I will show that while the concept of moral equivalence has some plausibility, it has been mainly used as a rhetorical and political instrument. It also serves a crucial purpose, moving beyond the Russians-are-devils framework of the 1950s and 1960s. Films of that period were satisfied with picturing Russia as an almost satanic threat. In recent decades, filmmakers have sought to retain this older understanding of good versus evil and not be as rigidly or dogmatically binary as in the past.

The explicit nature of equivalence as a concept came up, ironically, when then Fox News commentator Bill O'Reilly, in a February 2017 interview with Donald Trump, labeled Vladimir Putin a "killer." Trump merely responded, "There are a lot of killers. You think our country's so innocent?"[4] What is interesting here is the assumption O'Reilly thinks Trump must share: that there is not, nor can there ever be, anything that would make the US comparably immoral to Russia.

That the US and Russia must exist on two different theological planes is simply taken for granted by American commentators. America may err, but it is by definition noble and angelic. Russia, in contrast, is forever in some kind of dark hell. Whatever it does that is wrong is wrong in a specifically demonic way. Even sober analyses try to reach for some rhetorical way of underlining this difference. The journalist Steven Lee Myers, for instance, calls his book *The New Tsar: The Rise and Reign of Vladimir Putin* (2014).[5] Russia, presumably, has "czars," tyrants, but the US has no kings or czars to speak of.

The films that I focus on here, ironically, draw upon similar theological assumptions about good and evil. However, the directors are less explicit in condemning Russia, leading right wing critics to (wrongly) see both as guilty of moral equivalence. Both films do criticize US policies, but they do that from a highly patriotic and conservative perspective. Though both films have received some scholarly treatment, the discussions have been rather modest.[6]

The importance of this survey is based on two interrelated facts. One is how often tales of subversion are used to narrate the US-Russia relationship. Over and over again, American films, from *Invasion U.S.A.* (1985) to *The Hunt for Red October* (1990), depict nefarious KGB agents threatening America. A second fact is that while there is indeed a long history of Russia using spies in the US, the actual record is less exciting than in the films that have portrayed these efforts.

First, I examine the background of how moral equivalency arose and how it was defined by prominent conservatives. Then, I turn to the two films. Finally, I explore why fears about Russia still resonate, as well as how true or imaginary these fears are.

Hostility in Context

Russian and American animosities have been present for centuries, but they reached a fever pitch with the Bolshevik Revolution.[7] American troops joined a multinational effort to unseat the Bolsheviks, creating great suspicion between both camps. With the mutual need to fight Hitler, there was a brief period of friendly relations.

The Cold War reignited old fears, with many American elites seeing communist expansion by Stalin aiming at global revolution. In the 1940s and 1950s, the dominant, traditionalist analysis of US-Russia relations was to see the source of the conflict as the USSR being a totalitarian state with a wide gulf between its values and those of America.[8] This interpretation came under challenge by revisionists, who saw the bombing of Hiroshima, American aid to the right wing government in Greece, and the Berlin Blockade as part of a historic pattern of US imperialism.[9]

These schools of thought led to a third position: post-revisionism. Post-revisionists essentially took a middling position, that the Cold War may have been started by the US. In an exhaustive survey of the early Cold War, Melvyn Leffler concluded that all the evidence points to the indisputable fact that for the most part "Soviet actions were reactive."[10] Access granted to documents from the Stalin era, albeit limited, confirmed Leffler's interpretation.

Post-revisionists, liberal and conservative, argued that even if Russian imperialism, like American imperialism, were real, it was also true that a variety of motives (misperception, realism, religious identity) guided leaders in both countries.[11] But post-revisionists were forced to concede two major points to the revisionist side. First, the moral position of the US was not one of absolute good; selfish motives guided US leaders sometimes. Second, the positing of a Russian conspiracy, even if sincerely believed by some US politicians, has no confirming evidence. Some even repudiated the Cold War completely, with Robert McNamara admitting, "We [policymakers] were horribly wrong."[12]

The antiwar activism over Vietnam radicalized several American Catholic and Jewish liberal intellectuals, who began calling themselves neoconservatives.[13] By the late 1970s and early 1980s, parts of the public that were easily mobilized into supporting Cold War initiatives had become increasingly skeptical of US interventionism. The religious narrative of exceptional American goodness and satanic Russian evil was harder to maintain. Conservative intellectuals responded by reframing their ideology.

Neoconservatives, like post-revisionists, did not share the imperialist interpretation of US policy. But unlike many post-revisionists, neoconservatives were not scholars of a given subject but simply assumed that they could, authoritatively, make pronouncements on the Cold War as a whole, using mostly polemical journalism and short opinion pieces rather than peer-reviewed articles or dry, even-handed research books.[14]

Though there is no canonical formulation of equivalence, an essay by Jeane Kirkpatrick is referred to repeatedly as the best expression of how moral equivalence is understood by both right wing and left wing analysts.[15] Kirkpatrick begins her essay by arguing that moral equivalence is used mainly by communists and Marxists. To communists and Marxists, moral equivalence means that "practices are measured by abstract, absolute standards, practices are always found wanting. The communists who criticize liberal democratic societies measure our practices by our standards."[16] Kirkpatrick offers up the example of Grenada. She does not deny that the US invaded Grenada or even that it violated international law. Rather, she argues that the US has consistently used force to uphold the norm of independence and thus that the cases of Soviet interventionism like Afghanistan are not comparable. But the evidence for this claim is, at best, unclear.[17]

Another case cited also begs several questions. Kirkpatrick notes that guerillas in Central America are given tacit support by human rights organizations. No evidence is cited. But she notes that "national liberation movements," in the eyes of their supporters, do not "violate human rights."[18] No actual person or organization is cited maintaining this. She then notes that the Soviet occupation of Afghanistan was not universally denounced like the US invasion of Grenada. In that case, "American support for resistance forces" is condemned by Soviet officials like Andrei Gromyko.[19] Kirkpatrick is right that Gromyko's criticisms that the US was interfering in the internal affairs of a country can be rejected because the person is a bureaucrat employed by the Russian government. The problem is that Kirkpatrick takes an identical position, and she provides no scholarly sources to verify why US imperialist support for the Afghan rebels differs at all from Soviet support of their own rebels.

It would appear that her position is simply self-contradictory and based on little to no evidence. Kirkpatrick could simply argue that different countries pursue different interests, as realists argue occurs in international affairs. However, Kirkpatrick also rejects realism, making it unclear what she is arguing for. If countries can be judged morally, then the US will indeed be found faulty in various ways. She thus leans on a strong assumption that "totalitarianism" distinguishes US from Russian imperialism. One form of imperialism is against totalitarianism, and the other supports it.

The moral equivalence argument thus turns on the argument about totalitarianism. This pushes us back a step to ask if totalitarianism is a workable concept. Masha Gessen frames a book on Russia using totalitarianism with explicit reference to Hannah Arendt.[20] But this only creates further problems, as she admits.

A totalitarian society like Nazi Germany or the Soviet Union is defined by having a centralized state, a conspiratorial view seeing enemies everywhere, a charismatic leadership, and a need to constantly glorify its past. While this sounds plausible, much evidence has cast doubt upon the totalitarian concept.[21] Putin has used much propaganda, yet he has used terror more sparingly than

Stalin. Moreover, people have had some limited freedom to disagree or not care about official propaganda in Russia, even in the 1960s to the present.

Gleeson admits there is much empirically problematic, but the term *totalitarianism* ought to still be used.[22] However, if the bulk of evidence finds totalitarianism problematic then, at best, the moral equivalence argument needs refinement—or it is not being used analytically. When we turn and analyze both the Spielberg and Alfredson films, we shall see that reactions are often based on questionable uses of the moral equivalence argument. Like Kirkpatrick, these critics use dubious logic and minimal evidence to sustain interpretations.

Spielberg's War

If moral equivalence does not guide these films, what does? I argue that *Bridge of Spies* and *Tinker Tailor Soldier Spy* affirm a religious and patriotic nationalism as an alternative. Both films find Russian communism evil, but in ways that render both British and American imperialism as complicit in Soviet crimes. None of the states depicted are ethical. Another unifying theme is the concentration on white male pain. While women appear in both films, their role is less important than the theme of how middle-class, middle-aged men with political views either resist cynicism (Tom Hanks) or give in to it but try to preserve some sense of meaning (Gary Oldman).

Ethnicity rooted in nationalism grounds the actions of the characters. The most prominent British agents—all elderly white men—just take for granted that Britain is worth fighting for as a nation. Similarly, as an American Jew, Spielberg makes various allusions to Jewishness in America and Germany. While white men can be confident in American nationalism, minorities in America are more jaded about being loyal to American patriotism.

The film constantly gives reminders—most especially the case of the Rosenbergs—that American toleration has real limits and that those who violate those limits can be lethally disposed of. Thus *Tinker Tailor* frames its characters as cynical but patriotic. *Bridge of Spies* frames its characters as both cynical and idealistic; the dilemma of ethnic difference makes full affirmation of America a difficult matter. Nevertheless, in their totality, both films do affirm highly patriotic, conservative themes.

Bridge of Spies begins with Rudolf Abel (Mark Rylance) being (illegally) caught by the FBI. He is detained as an "illegal alien" (not a spy), so a legal case needs to be mounted. Initially, James Donovan (Tom Hanks) resists when he is chosen to defend Abel. He begins with the assumption that the government is sincere in wanting to convict Abel fairly. But he soon finds out that they chose him because he is not qualified at all and they merely want a nominal lawyer to pretend to defend Abel. They want him to lose to justify executing him.

Rylance plays Abel as an effective, deadly, and highly competent spy but also a fundamentally decent man.[23] In court, Donovan fails. What is essentially a show trial does render a guilty verdict, but Spielberg throws one of many misdirecting twists. Initially, an extremely patriotic judge refuses to hear Donovan's prudent plea that they may need Abel alive in the future. But when the sentence is delivered, the judge agrees, outraging a group of white Americans, who insist that Abel be killed.

The story moves several years into the future. The wall in East Germany is being built, and an American student, Frederic Pryor (Will Rogers), is captured because he is thought to be a spy. Another spy is also captured: Gary Powers (Austin Stowell), manning a secret spy plane (the U-2), is shot at and forced to land. He is taken by the Russians.

The story now shifts to Donovan being Abel's courier as well as saving the two Americans. The CIA sees an opportunity to get back Powers by trading Abel. Pryor is seen as unimportant. Initially, Donovan—unaware of Pryor—is thrilled. His constitutionalism is vindicated. Sparing Abel has allowed both sides to make a mutual exchange that will be mutually beneficial. But Spielberg implies that even after the shocking shooting of his home (which never occurred in reality) Donovan remains a naïve operative.

Abel is given a letter, which he is told is from his wife in Russia. Donovan is instructed by CIA director Allen Dulles to meet a man called Vogel (Sebastian Koch) to help get back Powers. When he arrives at the Russian embassy in East Germany, however, Donovan meets Abel's "wife," his "daughter," and a man—all of whom are clearly either actors or spies trained to fool him.[24] Puzzled, Donovan is then introduced to someone who is essentially a Soviet spymaster.

After all this, Donovan is shocked to find that Vogel is indeed a real person representing the East Germans. According to the GDR apparatchik (Burghart Klaussner), the Russians want a trade for Abel and Powers only—to make themselves look good. They have no interest in Pryor. But the East Germans want to trade Pryor and insert themselves into the bargain. Powers is treated brusquely by the Russians, as they need any little information he has before they release him. In reality, Powers was treated rather humanely—far better than Abel. While his trial is as fictive as Abel's, the Russians intend to parade him as a symbol of mercy.

The Soviets knew that Dwight D. Eisenhower was aware of their weaknesses. The film seems to take the revisionist side, that the Cold War was about powerful and cynical elites facing off against one another. Nevertheless, good people did exist and should be remembered. But the film in its totality wants to affirm a conservative post-revisionism that America was essentially good, even if some of its institutions (such as the CIA) were not.

An early scene frames this explicitly. A CIA agent, Hoffman (Scott Shepherd), tries to get Donovan to be an informal spy for the agency. He asks Donovan to share any information Abel might have offered as a client. Outraged, Donovan says, "We're not having this conversation," with Hoffman responding with a smile, "Of course not." "No, I mean we really are not having it," Donovan says. "You're asking me to violate attorney-client privilege." Hoffman continues to mock Donovan, saying, "Come on, counselor." Exasperated, Donovan angrily retorts, "I really wish *people like you* would quit saying, 'counselor.' I didn't like it the first time it happened today. A judge said it to me twice, and the more I hear it, the more I don't like it." Hoffman criticizes Donovan: "Don't go Boy Scout on me. We don't have a rule book here." Donovan appears to have lost, but reformulates his argument. He brings up patriotism. Questioning Hoffman, he notes that his name implies that he is of "German extraction." Hoffman is puzzled; "Yeah, so?" Donovan then gives a monologue:

> I'm Irish; you're German. But what makes us both Americans? Just one thing. One. Only one. The rule book. We call it the Constitution, and we agree to the rules, and that's what makes us Americans. That's all that makes us Americans. So don't tell me there's no rule book, and don't nod at me like that you son of a bitch.[25]

Ethnicity does matter. The coda Donovan gives is more sophisticated, more cynical than reviewers have let on. It is undeniable that the main interlocutors in this drama are white men. But Spielberg is hinting that he is not as naïve as is usually assumed. Racism is real, as Spielberg knows from his own experience. He personally experienced it as a teenager.[26] Self-interest and prejudice allow the government to violate the Constitution at will. But Spielberg holds onto a faith that the Constitution can provide *some protection* (including for minorities like Jews) even during wartime.[27]

While Spielberg shows both sides acting brutally, he never depicts either Eisenhower or Khrushchev. In essence, he simply ducks the issue of responsibility. Could the US have avoided raising tensions? The issue is not really addressed. There is no segment on the early Cold War. The viewer is just dropped into the late 1950s, the era that was dominated by the fear of the nuclear war.

To be sure, the portraits are fairly scathing. Overall, the CIA is shown to be composed of brave and powerful men. But these men are also cynical and manipulative; their main goal is to win. This is a broadly accurate representation. Robert Gates confirms much of this, admitting that clandestine service is much like "a priesthood. That's the positive side." But he also admits that it is "a closed fraternity [whose] attitude toward outsiders" is hostile. After all, "They start out in Third World hellholes.... They have a strong sense that almost no one understands them... they feel defensive and misunderstood."[28] The film reflects on this paranoia and hatred of outsiders. Because Donovan is not a spy, Hoffman hates him.

The flaw, however, is not in American nationalism per se. Spielberg is consistent in portraying Russian spies as no less competent—or cynical. Donovan tells "Secretary" Ivan Schischkin (Mikhail Gorevoy) after meeting Abel's alleged family that Abel acted honorably, giving up no secrets. Schischkin claims to be a diplomat, but Donovan, even without admitting it, can clearly see that he is a spy. Hence whereas Russia under the communists allowed virtually no space for individualism, even America during its McCarthy period did allow some limited freedom for people to not be forced into the Cold War.

The argument Spielberg makes is precisely that even in low points American ideals were compromised but not entirely abandoned. When the film concludes with Donovan cleverly having the East Germans and Russians agree to free both Pryor and Powers, the lesson is obvious: The CIA methods would have led to a dead Russian but also possibly other dead Americans and perhaps even outright war. But a good American really believing in his country's values saved his fellow citizens, not only in Germany but also in Cuba—a concluding crawl recounts Donovan's success in negotiating prisoners caught during the invasion of Cuba in the 1960s.

Despite the film's obvious attempt at evenhandedness, conservatives still see the film as being overly sympathetic to the Soviets. One reviewer, Brian Godawa, admitted that the moral equivalence thesis was illogical because the film had

> qualifying elements... [that] countered the moral equivalency of the story.... First, there is an eerie moment near the end where Hanks is riding a train in East Berlin (The Communist side). He sees a group of people running to the Berlin Wall and trying to climb over to the West Side to freedom. He sees them all get shot by East Berlin guards. Then at the very end, when Donovan is home in America, he's riding a train again. This time he sees a bunch of kids running to a fence and climbing it in their backyard. A brilliant counter image of freedom versus the captivity of Communism. So there IS a difference between the two worlds. They are not ultimately equivalent.[29]

Another conservative critic, Scott Holleran, also enjoyed this scene, alluding to it when he writes of the "expression on Donovan's face when he witnesses an act of Communism in practice—matched by a contrasting expression of his awakening to an act of liberty in practice—makes [it] . . . thought-provoking."[30] In other words, pro-American propaganda is thought-provoking.

In the liberal British magazine *The Guardian*, Peter Bradshaw praised Spielberg highly. For him, the film was "a true-life cold war spy-swap drama. . . . Those brought up on John le Carré might perhaps expect from this moral equivalence, shabby compromise and exhausted futility."[31] Thankfully, this is not the case with Spielberg, who uncovers "moral decency . . . amidst all the *Realpolitik*."[32] Conservative columnist Seth Lipsky did not see the film as celebratory as Bradshaw did, and he faults Spielberg.

To Lipsky, the Spielberg film had "hints" of moral equivalence. He was thankful that "all the gray [moral] tones were there, but they didn't ruin the story. The FBI, the CIA, the judge, Powers—they all came out looking better than the Communists."[33] Lipsky offers a rather odd interpretation, since certain scenes clearly show that the Americans do come off worse. Ironically, the fact that Lipsky did not pick up on this refutes the charge being made by conservatives and neoconservatives of a hidden left wing bias. That even when Spielberg was being critical he was not critical enough to merit notice suggests that the film treated US imperialism rather mildly, as indeed it did.

Other conservative critics were less kind because Spielberg still failed to show the enemy as wholly evil. But he did show their evil to a degree, and thus for these critics the film is still good. Holleran writes that Spielberg's film "is another carefully plotted exercise in moral equivalence and equivocation."[34] Yet, paradoxically, these critics were willing to that concede the film did work, but only when it depicted the evils of Russian communism. What clinches the argument that these perceptions are biased is that these critics were apparently unaware that the scenes they cite were completely made up. Donovan never witnessed Russian guards shooting children who rushed the Berlin Wall. This scene, however, vividly confirms the conservative Manichean view of Russian barbarity.

But critics even went further. They also misinterpreted what the film actually showed even when it fit their perceptions. For instance, Godawa applauds Spielberg for not portraying "the treatment of the American prisoner Gary Powers in Cuba [?] . . . as equivalent to the treatment of the Russian spy in America."[35] To his credit, Godawa writes, "Spielberg did show Powers being manhandled for information (child's play compared to today), while the Russian was questioned humanely in America. [Therefore] . . . I'll grant it's a somewhat nuanced moral equivalency."[36] Again, there was no torture of Powers—and the Russians did not ship him to Cuba for torture. It is questionable even in the film's own (false) timeline that Russian and Cuban relations had reached the point where they would do such a thing. Again, the historic record does not matter. What matters is only the evidence that affirms one ideology.

On the contrary, Powers was treated humanely—if only for propaganda purposes—and it was Abel who was treated brusquely. But when American evil is shown, however, Godawa, Kyle Smith, and others claim that the historical record is being manipulated. In reality, Spielberg's criticism of the CIA is mixed with affirming its positive virtues. Donovan's horse trading would not have worked unless the CIA had captured Abel.

Donovan, being a moralistic man, refuses to give up Abel unless he can free Pryor as well. The film therefore turns to how well Donovan can navigate the extremes in both countries. This essay is about *Bridges of Spies*, not *Munich* (2005), but there too Spielberg was accused of moral equivalence. Israeli assassins and the Palestinian assassins were depicted as being the same. Spielberg defended himself, noting that those who say the film is rooted in

> moral equivalence are some of the same people who say diplomacy itself is an exercise in moral equivalence, and that war is the only answer. . . . I believe every act of terrorism requires a strong response, but we must also pay attention to the causes. . . . Understanding does not require approval. . . . Israel had to respond [in 1972] . . . I agree with Golda Meir's response. . . . [But] this film is no more anti-Israel than a similar film which offered criticism of America is anti-American. Criticism is a form of love. I love America, and I'm critical of this administration. . . . Those who ask no questions may not be a country's best friends.[37]

We can see an obvious parallel. *Bridge of Spies* is critical of certain American tendencies—mob justice, cynical bureaucratism, and demonizing the Other for political gain. But these American tendencies are balanced by other, admittedly weak tendencies—arguing for mercy, prudence, and faith in constitutionalism and humanism.

Smith angrily writes in the neoconservative journal *Commentary* that Spielberg has made a leftist film. Assuming he can know Spielberg's intentions, he interprets the film as follows: "We spied on them, they spied on us, what's the difference?"[38] Spying is normalized as simply an activity that both countries do. Yet to Smith, American spying was (by definition) heroic and hence noble. Russian spying was, in contrast, inherently evil. Because the film fails to make this binary distinction between an angelic America and an evil Soviet Russia in a clear-cut manner, Smith believes that it has created a fantasy and that

> Spielberg, like virtually all of Hollywood, either thought Communists in America were a phantom threat (they weren't), were idealists (not true) or, at worst,

that there was little to no moral difference between the Soviet Union and the United States in the Cold War.... Murderers and their executioners are both guilty of killing, after all.[39]

Repeatedly, Soviet agents and East Germans are shown to be moved by either their duty or bureaucratic jockeying for power. Nowhere is idealism explicitly given to them, with the exception of Abel, who is portrayed with empathy and shown to be, like Donovan, a good man in a bad system.

Holleran frames comparison as not even being possible because "the accused aims to aid the enemy in gaining a capacity to destroy New York City."[40] There is overwhelming evidence that the opposite is true—Soviet capabilities were rather weak.[41] There is no evidence the Soviets had any such attack planned, nor is there any evidence Abel was materially aiding the Russians to destroy New York. The author is apparently ignorant that Abel was mainly based in New Jersey. Holleran also refers to "Mark Charmin" as an author; the real name is Mark *Charman*. Yet Holleran, while he admits his ignorance in key places, still affirms he is qualified to write on these issues.

The oddity is that Charman and Spielberg as well as Alfredson do assume that a basic difference exists between states during this period in terms of their records of repression and international aggression.[42] But the difference is small, because they simply see the US side as flawed and corrupt, yet still better. It is unclear if this stance can be maintained, but it is one the film commits to—and yet the critics keep seeing criticisms of the US where there are none.

Redemption and Pragmatism

Tinker Tailor Soldier Spy is based on the popular novel of the same name by John le Carré, who was himself in British intelligence before he became a full-time writer. *Tinker Tailor* focuses on middle-aged British spy George Smiley (Gary Oldman), who is tasked with finding a Russian mole within British intelligence. *Tinker Tailor* had previously been adapted to television for the BBC. That version was deliberately patriotic in tone and veered away from the novel's amoralism. Le Carré, however, approved of that version, despite how it differs from the novel.

For the 2011 film version, both le Carré and director Tomas Alfredson agreed that the tone should be close to the original. Le Carré noted, "When you come to make this movie [in 2011], [the need for patriotic affirmation] isn't there anymore. The ethic and affections have all shifted. This has to be a much tougher thing, with a great deal less sentiment."[43] Smiley, who has been retired, accepts the role of Control's (John Hurt) helper in finding the mole.

Bridge of Spies deliberately mythologizes past episodes, but those events did happen. *Tinker Tailor*, although wholly fictional, does allude to real events. Le Carré has in mind the so-called Cambridge spy ring featuring Kim Philby and Anthony Blunt, who were discovered to have been working for the Soviets for years. As in real life, Smiley has narrowed the search to five suspects.

The plot itself is thick and features dizzying back-and-forth movements to try condense material the television miniseries took longer to explore. For our purposes, however, the plot is less important than what Smiley symbolizes. Whereas the *James Bond* films feature a fantasy version of the spy life with adventure, wine, and women, *Tinker Tailor* depicts the day-to-day operation of spying as tiresome and unrewarding. Smiley is unsure if there is any reason to continue fighting.

As Mark Riebling notes, Richard Helms, who headed the CIA, "hated" le Carré's novels precisely because he accurately depicted the amoralism of spies in the West.[44] There is no great moral purpose driving Smiley. He knows that the ostensive propaganda justification—saving the Free World, stopping totalitarianism—is not true. The British are allied with the Americans against another state with opposing interests. The game is simply one of different actors with different interests.

Like Spielberg, Alfredson did not make the film to equate Soviet behavior with that of the British or the Americans. The equation could be made, but he avoids it. Alfredson admitted, "I read many of John le Carré's books. I thought [*Tinker Tailor Soldier Spy*] was a very moving piece about loyalty and friendship and the human cost that the soldiers of the cold war had to pay."[45] This admission is shocking. The sympathy is not for the countless millions of lives in the Third World.[46] The primary focus of the film is transmitting sympathy for the spies (the "soldiers").

Alfredson tries to reproduce this dreary, grim view through dark lighting and characters who cynically lose themselves in excesses of drinking and fornication. Even the architecture is depicted as being in a state of decay. "The British Empire is depicted as literally . . . collapsing on itself. The decade's economic woes are prevalent throughout the film, with the Circus's civilian overseers admonishing the spy organization for keeping an expensive safe house for a secret operation."[47] Corruption is explicitly verbalized by the characters.

In a meeting with Percy Alleline (Toby Jones) and Roy Bland (Ciaran Hinds), two members of the Circus's inner sanctum—one of whom also may be the Soviet mole—Oliver Lacon (Simon McBurney), the civilian overseer of the Circus, comments the meeting is "very unaccountable." Bland retorts, "So where do you propose we meet? In a café?" But Lacon notes, "The rents and rates on this house have doubled." Bland answers cynically: "We spent millions on nuclear warheads. We're asking for a few thousand for a house. I wonder if Karla [a Soviet agent] has the same problem with the treasury at the Kremlin."[48]

This is the argument of the film in a nutshell. The US and the USSR are simply two amoral animals pitted against each other. The slogans may differ but the result is the same—especially from the British perspective. The two countries are formally allies, but in reality the British serve the Americans. Blunt just accepts this, yet Alfredson presents this view and does not necessarily endorse it.

But there is an added layer to the dialogue. Bland, as the name hints, is merely giving a robotic answer. If the house seems to cost so much, it is rather minor compared to the money spent on warheads. In other words, perhaps British spies are stealing money. But, comparatively, the theft is small. Then comes the closing argument—the Soviet spies have no such issue. They can get whatever they please. In essence, anything evil or amoral done by the British or Americans can always be justified by turning to the Russians.

Not surprisingly, the Russians themselves do not really appear in the film. This is both the paradox and dilemma Smiley faces. The Russian influence is there—Alfredson does not argue that Russian spies are not operating in Britain—yet the real enemy is internal. It is not the Russians who made Bland or others in the Circus corrupt; that decision is one the British spy establishment and Britain as a whole have made—and made consciously.

Smiley finds the mole. But there is not much evidence that it matters. When Smiley confronts Karla, he is unable to offer a strong rebuttal as to why the British should fight: "Look, we've both spent our lives looking for the weaknesses in one another's systems. Don't you think it's time to recognize there is as little worth on your side as there is on mine?"[49] The interaction with Smiley has a double meaning. He is admitting that the British record is a hard one to defend and suggesting that it is sensible to let the Russians maintain their empire while the British maintain theirs: a live-and-let-live pragmatism.

Moral equivalence is not an issue. If the world depicted is really so brutally governed by realism, then moral critiques are pointless. But Alfredson does have a moral critique: it is just weaker than the revisionists being outraged over the coups and even genocides the West has committed. This is to embrace a strong universalism, whereas the film offers a pragmatic patriotism as a lesser evil.

In one scene, Smiley visits Connie Sachs (Kathy Burke), a former colleague at the Circus. As they speak, both reminisce about how the Circus once had morality. As Connie notes, the spies of the 1960s and 1970s began their work during World War II. "That was a good time, George," Connie says, with Smiley responding, "It was the war, Connie." Connie then says that World War II was "[a] real war. Englishmen could be proud then."[50]

This last bit of dialogue needs to be emphasized because it criticizes not only the US but also England itself. World War II was a *"real* war. *Englishmen* could be proud then." As Smiley's use of the word *then* indicates, World War II is metaphysically distinguished from the Cold War. The danger and extremism of Hitler and the Nazis were real and undeniable. The Russians posed no similar threat. As Smiley says, without feeling, "The Americans have had [Karla] tortured. No fingernails."[51] American torture is horrific to the point that it cannot be shown.

But there is no outrage. Nothing is outrageous because the Cold War has normalized all forms of brutality. The film rejects the pretext of the Cold War, and some blame is given to the Americans. However, as Connie's interesting gendering of the word *Englishmen* indicates, the disgust that she and Smiley share is only partially due to their aiding American nationalism: they are also disgusted that British (male) nationalism is tainted.

The conclusion of the film, then, does not lead to nihilism. Rather, like Spielberg, Alfredson wants to affirm le Carré's belief that British patriotism can be redeemed. "We cannot," le Carré explicitly argued, "judge our society by the quality of our secret services. That's absolutely absurd and dangerous." For le Carré, "You've got to have spies, but the important thing is that you're not enchanted by them. Use them and don't let them use you."[52]

However, unlike Spielberg's film, which offers Donovan as a rare moral saint, *Tinker Tailor* has no spectacular event signaling reawakening or reform. When Smiley finally confronts the mole, Bill Haydon (Colin Firth), Haydon justifies his act, saying, "I had to pick a side, George . . . the West has become . . . so ugly, don't you think?"[53] Unlike much of the dialogue, it is unclear here what Haydon means. He could be a nihilist. But the dominant tone suggests that Haydon's betrayal originates in wanting to believe in a true faith, and the Russians, at least, are sincere in their duplicity.

Supposedly, the Russians know that they are not for justice or democracy, that they are just fighting for power. Unfortunately, Alfredson implies that American policymakers responded with a fight-fire-with-fire approach. Instead of pure evil on the Russian side and pure goodness in the West, the film shows how

> Control and the Circus violated the basic tenets of Western democratic society. . . . For le Carré and these directors, the Cold War was a dangerous and ultimately unnecessary conflict that led to the degradation of essential Western principles of democracy and accountability, eroding the very souls of Great Britain and the USA in the process.[54]

The use of "souls" here is interesting and demonstrates the problem with applying ethical judgments to these films. Alfredson is less overt, but like Spielberg he wants to affirm that there was a spiritual issue separating the West and Russia. Admittedly, both sides were evil, but one side was still more evil. The Americans and the British, at least, felt guilty in staining their spiritual purity.

Even when reframing the Cold War as an amoral fight, Europe can still be proud. Like the East Germans, Britain and other NATO allies were pawns being manipulated by more powerful parties. Far from embracing moral equivalence, Alfredson rejects it. America acted badly due to a flawed fanaticism. In principle, though, the West can temper this tendency toward fanaticism and strike a balance between security and nationalist pride.

Conservatives, however, saw Alfredson only capitulating to political correctness. Peter Wilson mocks "what [le Carré and] the left call 'moral complexity,' and what the rest of us call 'moral equivalence.'... Le Carré flirts with a moral equivalence between the democracies of the West and murderous Communist dictatorships."[55] Andrew Roberts also saw that an "inevitable despicable moral equivalency" was in the film.[56]

But no comparison is acceptable—none—even if the actions are identical. The West is just metaphysically different from Russia. As Wilson argues, the comparison fails because the Russian side featured "decades of terror, targeted famine, gulags, bread lines, [and] corruption.... In the balance, Britain had ... crummy Vauxhall cars."[57] The long record of UK imperialism, which very much included gulags in Kenya and other nations under British control, is waved away.[58] Similarly, Roberts argues that the film has a "moral complexity ... [that] morphs into an attempt to portray western democracy as being as morally compromised as Soviet Communism."[59]

Either Wilson is not aware of contradictory evidence or insists that even if Britain sometimes starved opponents (the Irish, the Indians), they remained morally pure. While Wilson is willing to be harsh when Alfredson shows UK imperialism badly, Russian imperialism being shown harshly is applauded. We see

> Russians brutally murder people and torture one of the British intelligence agents. The British never resort to skulduggery [sic] and ... are portrayed as flawed but decent blokes fighting for Queen and country. They defeat the Russians with cunning and hard work; Smiley pulls all-nighters. ... The plot revolves around a traitor, and there's never a suggestion of sympathy for a rat who would betray his country.[60]

In essence, the parts of the story affirming nationalism are true. Those suggesting that the British or Americans were not morally pure are treated with severe skepticism or outright denial. Reacting to the statement by Smiley that the Russian "system" might have some favorable aspects, Roberts writes that the dialogue is "repulsive" because one cannot agree that

> the democratic West in the Cold War, with all its faults but with its free press and representative institutions and rule of law, was in some way the moral equivalent of the totalitarian USSR, with its gulags, censorship, satellite slave-states and its cowed and oppressed populace.[61]

On one hand, this statement slyly admits that the one side is not pure, but no examples are given of this impurity. In contrast, the Russian side is filled with faults.

This position is demonstrably false: let two examples suffice. Roberts states that one side clearly had a "free press and representative institutions and rule of law" and the other featured "censorship" and an "oppressed populace." Nevertheless, censorship was rife in Britain and America during the Cold War, and one could find easily an "oppressed populace" (blacks, Hispanics, Asians) in both countries.[62] Either Roberts is genuinely ignorant or sees no basis for comparison. Similarly, he asserts that only one side had "satellite slave-states" and the US and the UK had no equivalent. But there is overwhelming evidence that both the US and the UK had their own satellite slave-states, whether in Cuba, Haiti, Iran, Guiana, or Kenya.[63] Either Andrews really does not know this literature, or he is simply making a bald assertion with no evidence.

However, in fairness, some conservative critics did not simply see ideology at work in the film. James Bowman thought part of the problem came from the genre. In the film,

> not only Cold War spies but spies in general are seen as inhabiting that famously "twilit" world invented by Mr Le Carré to express his own conviction of moral ambiguity and, in consequence, a near moral equivalence between Communist slave states and what used to be called "the West."[64]

Bowman admits Alfredson is making a general criticism. But he still insists that alleged slave-states were simply worse. Yet he offers no documentation for this claim. Presumably, the reader just must accept this distinction as true.

What is interesting is how much both British and American critics impose a Christian notion of sin upon the films. Resisting Russian communism is both politically and spiritually necessary. Anything detracting from this supposedly spiritual duty is evil. Yet the conservatives do not see that Alfredson accepts this view to some degree.

When he catches the mole, Smiley says, "That's when I knew he could be beaten. He was a fanatic, and the fanatic is always concealing a secret doubt."[65] While this dialogue can be read in a purely secular manner, the wording suggests that Smiley, like a good priest, is able to find a sinner. He knows that the world of spying requires skepticism. A person who is too devoted makes himself suspicious in Smiley's eyes.

The Right in America and Britain hated this interpretation of Smiley. For them, a British spy should be a religious fanatic. That spy for them represents a good civilization (the West), whereas Russia is a symbol of barbarism and lack of civilization. The frustration is over Smiley having any doubts that what he is doing is always good. Fighting Russians is just assumed to be what any good person should do.

Conclusion

It would be easy to dismiss Spielberg's and Alfredson's critics as simply uninformed. They do not claim to be specialists on international politics or cinematic history. Major and minor mistakes of facts repeatedly occur in their writing, with scenes, timelines, and dialogue being mistakenly identified—making their findings all the more dubious.

Kirkpatrick, writing for print media, at least tries to make an argument, however faulty. The online critics are almost all dogmatic. Those tied to traditional media like newspapers are somewhat more moderate. Overall, however, conservative critics have become less and less careful with evidence.

Yet as has been shown, the criticisms are aimed at questionable targets, where the films are tagged as "leftist." In fact, the films work well within the mainstream in using religious symbols to attract a mass audience. Spielberg and Alfredson differ in how intensely they depict the West being more spiritual than Russia, but this spiritualized narrative shows up in both films.

The moral equivalence argument applied by conservatives is largely a myth. However, let us conclude by assuming that the right wing critics are correct. From this standpoint, the election of Putin to power in Russia is alarming. As is well known, Putin was for many years a KGB agent. According to one estimate, Russia employed *a half million* KGB agents during the Cold War.[66] For conservative critics, the West has for decades been blissfully blind to a man using cyberterror, online robots, and outright assassins and spies to delegitimize the West.

It is notoriously difficult to try to verify how extensive spying by someone is. It might be the case that Putin and former KGB agents have intervened in the 2016 elections, assassinated former spies in various countries, invaded and occupied whole countries, and flooded the US and other Western nations with covert propaganda. Some of these fears are real, as shown by a Russian spy ring captured in 2010. However, for the most part, these incredible accusations exist in shadowy space. And the films that discuss the relationship between the two countries operate in between empirical fact and myth, genuine history and fiction.

It would be wrong to believe that all these critics are either wrong or simply fearful of Russia alone. There have been a number of films in recent years on outside, subversive forces emanating from North Korea (*Red Dawn* [2012], *The Interview* [2014]) to the Middle East (*The Kingdom* [2007]) and Mexico (*Sicario* [2015], *Sicario: Day of the Soldado* [2018]). The panic over (alleged) Russian influence is simply part of a greater if lamentable tendency in Hollywood cinema to see enemies everywhere and divide them into simple categories of heroes capable of redemption (the Western heroes) and monsters beyond the pale who can only be seen in shadows (the anti-Western Russians). *Bridge of Spies* and *Tinker Tailor Soldier Spy* are, to be sure, sophisticated variations on this central theme, serving mainly to solidify anti-Russian fears and not challenge them or their source.

Notes

1. Masha Gessen, *The Future Is History: How Totalitarianism Reclaimed Russia* (New York: Riverhead, 2017); Arkady Ostrovsky, *Inventing Russia* (New York: Penguin, 2017).

2. Arkady, *Inventing Russia*, 292.

3. Andrew Kaufman, "Rightwing Attacks 'Tinker Tailor Soldier Spy' as Anti-Western, Too Complex?" *IndieWire*, December 11, 2011, https://www.indiewire.com/2011/12/rightwing-attacks-tinker-tailor-soldier-spy-as-anti-western-too-complex-134424/.

4. Daniel C. Hellinger, *Conspiracies and Conspiracy Theories in the Age of Trump* (New York: Palgrave, 2019), 98.

5. Steven Lee Myers, *The New Tsar: The Rise and Reign of Vladimir Putin* (New York: Penguin, 2014). It would be wrong to suggest that Americans alone share these biases; an article by Steven Abrams begins with a quote from Charles Baudelaire stating, "The neatest trick of the devil is to make us believe he doesn't exist." Steven Abrams, "Beyond Propaganda: Soviet Active Measures in Putin's Russia," *Connections QJ* 15, no. 1 (2016): 5. "The devil," for Abrams, is either Putin or the KGB.

6. Eric Morgan, "Whores and Angels of Our Striving Selves: The Cold War Films of John le Carré, Then and Now," *Historical Journal of Film, Radio and Television* 36, no. 1 (2016): 88–103; Geraint D'Arcy, "'Essentially, Another Man's Woman': Information and Gender in the Novel and Adaptations of John le Carré's *Tinker Tailor Soldier Spy*," *Adaptation* 7, no. 1 (2014): 275–90; Sarah Barrow, "Morality Tales? Visions of the Past in Spielberg's History Plays," in *A Companion to Steven Spielberg*, ed. Nigel Morris (Malden, MA: Wiley-Blackwell, 2017), 307–19.

7. Melvyn Leffler, *The Specter of Communism: The United States and the Origins of the Cold War, 1917–1953* (New York: Hill and Wang, 1994).

8. Les K. Adler and Thomas G. Paterson, "Red Fascism: The Merger of Nazi Germany and Soviet Russia in the American Image of Totalitarianism, 1930's–1950's," *American Historical Review* 75, no. 4 (1970): 1046–64.

9. Bruce Cummings, *The Origins of the Korean War*, vol. 2 (Princeton: Princeton University Press, 1990).

10. Melvyn Leffler, *A Preponderance of Power: National Security, the Truman Administration, and the Cold War* (Palo Alto: Stanford University Press, 1992), 513.

11. J. L. Gaddis, *The Long Peace: Inquiries into the History of the Cold War* (New York: Oxford University Press, 1987).

12. J. L. Gaddis, "On Moral Equivalence and Cold War History," *Ethics and International Affairs* 10, no. 1 (1996): 133.

13. Peter Steinfels, *Neoconservatives: The Men Who Are Changing America's Politics* (New York: Simon and Scnuster, 1979).

14. Some examples are Charles Krauthammer, *Cutting Edges* (New York: Random House, 1985); Irving Kristol, *Neoconservatism: The Autobiography of an Idea* (New York: Free Press, 1995). Both books are essay collections.

15. Noam Chomsky argued that "moral equivalence . . . was invented . . . [by] Kirkpatrick . . . to prevent criticism of foreign policy and state decisions." But "there is no moral equivalence what so ever . . . [simply] many different dimensions and criteria. For example, there's no moral equivalence between the bombing of the World Trade Center and the destruction of Nicaragua or of El Salvador, of Guatemala. The latter were far worse, by any criterion. So there's no moral equivalence. Furthermore, they were done for different reasons and they were done in different ways. There's all sorts of dimensions." James Crossley, *Jesus in an Age of Terror* (London: Routledge, 2009), 89.

16. Jeane Kirkpatrick, *Legitimacy and Force*, vol. 1 (New Brunswick, NJ: Transaction Books, 1988), 77.

17. Seth Hettena, *Trump / Russia: A Definitive History* (Brooklyn: Melville House, 2018), 199. Data by Don Levin found that from 1946 to 2000, comparing Russia and US, the US was twice as interventionist as Russia.

18. Kirkpatrick, *Legitimacy and Force*, 78.

19. Kirkpatrick, *Legitimacy and Force*, 79.

20. Gessen, *The Future Is History*, 292–96.

21. A lengthy critique and history is given by Abbott Gleason in *Totalitarianism: The Inner History of the Cold War* (New York: Oxford University Press, 1995).

22. Michael Geyer and Sheila Fitzpatrick, eds., *Beyond Totalitarianism: Stalinism and Nazism Compared* (Cambridge: Cambridge University Press, 2009).

23. Abel was in fact highly incompetent. He is not the superspy the film portrays. Giles Whittell, *Bridge of Spies: A True Story of the Cold War* (New York: Broadway Books, 2010). See also Michael R. Beschloss, *Mayday: Eisenhower, Khrushchev and the U-2 Affair* (New York: Harper & Row, 1986).

24. The man is never identified.

25. Spielberg, *Bridge of Spies*, emphasis added.

26. Molly Haskell, *Steven Spielberg: A Life in Films* (New Haven: Yale University Press, 2017), 38.

27. For evidence of intolerance, see James L. Gibson, "The Political Consequences of Intolerance: Cultural Conformity and Political Freedom," *American Political Science Review* 86, no. 2 (June 1992): 338–56. A small minority of blacks (13 percent) admitted to being reluctant to speak about politics, believing "that the government might find out about me" (342). Whites in general felt confident that their views would be tolerated.

28. Kai Bird, *The Good Spy: The Life and Death of Robert Ames* (New York: Broadway Books, 2014), 256.

29. Brian Godawa, "*Bridge of Spies*: A Conspiracy of Boredom" *Thus Spake Godawa* (blog), January 21, 2016, https://godawa.com/tag/tom-hanks/.

30. Scott Holleran, "Movie Review: *Bridge of Spies*," *Scott Holleran: Writer* (blog), October 14, 2015, https://scottholleran.com/movies/movie-review-bridge-of-spies/. Another reviewer, Tony Medley, saw the film as having "moral equivalence," but the review is too short to bear detailed analysis. It does, however, confirm how strongly this framework was used. Tony Medley, "*Bridge of Spies*," TonyMedley.com (website), http://www.tonymedley.com/2015/Bridge_of_Spies.htm.

31. Peter Bradshaw, "*Bridge of Spies* Review," *The Guardian*, October 5, 2015, https://www.the guardian.com/film/2015/oct/05/bridge-of-spies-film-review-tom-hanks-steven-spielberg-cold -war-gary-powers-u2.

32. Bradshaw, "*Bridge of Spies* Review."

33. Seth Lipsky, "*Bridge of Spies* and the Urge to Rewrite Cold War History," *New York Post*, October 21, 2015, https://nypost.com/2015/10/21/bridge-of-spies-and-the-urge-to-rewrite-cold -war-history/.

34. Holleran, "Movie Review: *Bridge of Spies*."

35. Godawa, "*Bridge of Spies*." This error is especially weird as the torturers are speaking Russian, not Spanish. But the error—assuming Powers was tortured by Cubans and not Russians—is Godawa's.

36. Godawa, "*Bridge of Spies*."

37. Roger Ebert, "I Knew I Would Lose Friends Over This," *Daily Telegraph*, January 1, 2006, https://www.telegraph.co.uk/news/worldnews/1506765/I-knew-I-would-lose-friends-over-this -film.html.

38. Kyle Smith, "Bridge of Lies: How and Why Hollywood Distorts History by Filming It with a Leftist Lens," *Commentary*, January 16, https://www.commentarymagazine.com/articles /kyle-smith/bridge-of-lies/.

39. Smith, "Bridge of Lies."

40. Holleran, "Movie Review: *Bridge of Spies*."

41. John J. Mearsheimer writes that US nuclear policy was based on "'massive preemption' rather than massive retaliation. Regardless, the key point is that during the 1950s, the United States was committed to gaining nuclear superiority over the Soviet Union." *The Tragedy of Great Power Politics* (New York: W.W. Norton & Co., 2018), 224. It is a myth that both Russia and the US adopted mutually assured destruction (MAD), one ironically popularized by Kubrick's *Dr. Strangelove* and which Spielberg accepts. For more documentation on Soviet weakness, see Leffler, *A Preponderance of Power*.

42. Fully comparing Russia to the US is not possible here, but some comparable cases do exist. Perhaps the closest one is comparing US actions in Timor to Russian actions in Ukraine. Kiernan estimates 150,000 Timorese died in a civil war with the US aiding Indonesia, who were responsible for the vast majority of massacres. President Ford and Henry Kissinger explicitly authorized Suharto, the ruler of Indonesia, to invade Timor. They also advised him to try to ally with the Pol Pot regime in Cambodia. In comparison, Stalin's terror applied to Ukraine resulted in an estimated one to four million people dead or 10 to 15 percent of the population. But Steven Rosefielde admits that the famine in Ukraine may not meet strict definition of genocide. East Timor, in contrast, meets the criteria of intent to destroy a minority in part or total. For Timor, see Ben Kiernan, "War, Genocide, and Resistance in East Timor, 1975–99: Comparative Reflections on Cambodia," in *War and State Terrorism: The United States, Japan, and the Asia-Pacific in the Long Twentieth Century*,

ed. Mark Selden and Alvin Y. So (Lanham, MD: Rowman & Littlefield, 2003), 199–233. Ties between the CIA and Indonesia's fascist military were strong for decades. See Geoffrey Robinson, *The Killing Season: A History of the Indonesian Massacres, 1965–6* (Princeton: Princeton University Press, 2018). For Ukraine, see Steven Rosefielde, *Red Holocaust* (London: Routledge, 2009), 43–44. But one could argue that internal repression should be compared. Yet clearly the Native Americans suffered as badly as any Russian minority. See David Stannard, *American Holocaust* (Oxford: Oxford University Press, 1992).

43. Morgan, "Whores and Angels of Our Striving Selves," 96.
44. Mark Riebling, *Wedge, From Pearl Harbor to 9/11* (New York: Touchstone, 2010), 98.
45. Morgan, "Whores and Angels of Our Striving Selves," 95.
46. There is no canonical work on the Third World and the Cold War but some good treatments are Marilyn Young, *The Vietnam Wars, 1945–1990* (New York: HarperPerennial, 1991); Stephen Schlesinger and Stephen Kinzer, *Bitter Fruit: The Untold Story of the American Coup in Guatemala* (Garden City, NY: Anchor Press, 1983); Gabriel Kolko, *Confronting the Third World: United States Foreign Policy 1945–1960* (New York: Pantheon Books, 1988); Chalmers Johnson, *Blowback: The Costs and Consequences of American Empire* (New York: Henry Holt, 2000).
47. Morgan, "Whores and Angels of Our Striving Selves," 99.
48. Alfredson, *Tinker Tailor Soldier Spy*.
49. Alfredson, *Tinker Tailor Soldier Spy*.
50. Alfredson, *Tinker Tailor Soldier Spy*.
51. Alfredson, *Tinker Tailor Soldier Spy*.
52. Morgan, "Whores and Angels of Our Striving Selves," 99.
53. Alfredson, *Tinker Tailor Soldier Spy*.
54. Morgan, "Whores and Angels of Our Striving Selves," 99.
55. Peter Wilson, "Moral Equivalence in the New *Tinker Tailor Soldier Spy*," *American Thinker*, December 9, 2011, https://www.americanthinker.com/articles/2011/12/moral_equivalence_in_the_new_tinker_tailor_soldier_spy.html.
56. Andrew Roberts, "*Tinker Tailor Soldier Spy*: Almost Perfect, but for the Politics," *Daily Beast*, December 12, 2011, https://www.thedailybeast.com/tinker-tailor-soldier-spy-almost-perfect-but-for-the-politics.
57. Wilson, "Moral Equivalence."
58. Caroline Elkins, *Britain's Gulag: The Brutal End of Empire in Kenya* (London: Jonathan Cape, 2005).
59. Roberts, "*Tinker Tailor Soldier Spy*."
60. Wilson, "Moral Equivalence."
61. Roberts, "*Tinker Tailor Soldier Spy*."
62. Daniel Ellsberg, *The Doomsday Machine: Confessions of a Nuclear War Planner* (New York: Bloomsbury, 2017).
63. For extensive documentation, see Cummings, *The Origins of the Korean War*; Leffler, *A Preponderance of Power*, Robinson, *The Killing Season*. Other works could be easily listed, but considerations of space prevent one from citing detailed counterevidence to Roberts's statements.
64. James Bowman, "*Tinker Tailor Soldier Spy*," January 10, 2012, https://jamesbowman.net/reviewdetail.asp?pubid=2133.
65. Alfredson, *Tinker Tailor Soldier Spy*.
66. Abrams, "Beyond Propaganda," 11.

UNACKNOWLEDGED REALIGNMENT
Representations of US-Russia Relations in Recent American Cinema

Thomas J. Cobb

The two years between Donald Trump's inauguration in January 2017 and the release of the Mueller Report evidenced a reconfiguration in American politics. Collusion with Russia was a political sin attributed to the Democrats at the heights of the Cold War in the 1950s and under Ronald Reagan in the 1980s. In the aftermath of the 2016 presidential election, it became a millstone around the Republican Party, owing to reports of Russian hacking of Democratic Party emails.

Although Cold War narratives have returned in American cinema, portended by the pre-Trump releases of *Bridge of Spies* (2015) and *Hail, Caesar!* (2016), this essay argues that recent representations of US-Russia relations have lacked reification of one of the Trump era's signature ideological heterodoxies. *The Shape of Water* (2017) excoriates the social illiberalism that blighted early Cold War America, yet its magical realist narrative avoids critique of a right wing convergence with Russian interests. It instead adopts a stance of anti-McCarthy liberalism, averting the liberal antipathy toward Russia lampooned by the alt-right. My exploration of del Toro's Oscar-winning picture emphasizes its debts to the films of Douglas Sirk and its evocation of an American fascism redolent of the political dynamics created in *Pan's Labyrinth* (*El laberinto del fauno*, 2006). I establish connection between this and the social attitudes cemented in the populist takeover of the Republican Party, a synergetic focus that nevertheless neglects the remolded right wing perceptions of Russia augured by Trump's election victory.

The critically maligned *Red Sparrow* (2018), which concerns the subject of Russian "sexpionage," also declines to interrogate evident alterations in East-West relations. Despite its storyline possessing affinity with the allegations against Trump posed by the Christopher Steele dossier, Francis Lawrence's film avoids overt invocations of the current state of US-Russia relations. Rather, its storyline focalizes the "culture war" aspects of Putinism's rejection of the West and a vein of sexual exploitation that chimes in with the Me Too scandals impacting American political discourse. I additionally posit that *Red Sparrow*'s convoluted plot conveys a sensibility of cognitive dissonance, lending credence to liberal internationalist and neoconservative agendas of democratization in Russia.

Evaluating these two disparately received films, I postulate that critical renditions of the underpinnings behind Cold War II and the connections forged between American conservatism and Russia have been absent in post-2016 American pictures that depict US-Russia relations. Concluding with a reflection on *Black Panther* (2018), a comic book adaptation that considers collisions of isolationism and internationalism relevant to Cold War II, I posit that its allegory delineates superior ways of understanding the new international relations dynamics created by Trumpism.

The Shape of Water and the America of Donald Trump: Socially Aligned, Diplomatically Disconnected?

The dramatic final moments of Jack Arnold's *Creature from the Black Lagoon* (1954), a picture director Guillermo del Toro considered seminal in inspiring his 2017 production of *The Shape of Water*, purvey capitulation to American ideological supremacy.[1] Capping a narrative focused on the conflict between a merman and a group of American geologists researching links between land and sea animals on an expedition through the Amazon, *Creature from the Black Lagoon* concludes with an affirmation of US might. The climax, which accentuates this hegemonic emphasis, an effort by protagonist Dr. David Reed (Richard Carlson) to rescue his love interest Kay Lawrence (Julie Adams) from the merman, cements divides between an informal American imperialism and indigenous self-determination. Brazilian crewmen hired and co-opted by the scientists arrive to shoot the merman multiple times and leave it to die in the black lagoon of the film's title, delimiting resistance to the American invaders.[2]

Sixty-three years later, del Toro would invert the political hierarchy in this ending to provide a suitable coda for *The Shape of Water*, a magical realist commentary on American foreign and domestic policy during the Cold War.

In the ending of del Toro's film, the merman (Doug Jones), who has a love interest in laboratory cleaner Elisa Esposito (Sally Hawkins), repudiates the xenophobia encoded in Arnold's original picture.

This climax initiates with Colonel Richard Strickland (Michael Shannon), the cruel figure charged with guarding the amphibious creature, tracking the merman and Elisa to the Chesapeake and Delaware Canal. Upon arrival, he knocks Elisa's homosexual neighbor Giles (Richard Jenkins) to the ground, deceptively building toward a conclusion loyal to the narrative of *Creature from the Black Lagoon*. Indeed, the colonel next shoots the merman and Elisa, partially replaying the events of Arnold's film. The remainder of the epilogue, however, conspires against any reprise of dramatic convention. A conscious Giles retaliates and immobilizes Strickland while the merman recovers from his wounds, a resilience that stems from inexplicable healing powers absent in *Creature from the Black Lagoon*. After Strickland remarks, "You are a god," the merman cuts his throat and heals Elisa in the Chesapeake and Delaware Canal, reassuringly ending a film derisive of America's much-hallowed postwar Pax Americana. A final voiceover narration by Giles delivers a poem rumored to have been found by del Toro "in a book of Islamic poetry."[3] Giles recites, "Unable to perceive the shape of you, I find you all around me. Your presence fills my eyes with love; it humbles my heart. For you are everywhere."[4] There are numerous narrative and thematic differences between *The Shape of Water* and the original template of *Creature from the Black Lagoon* that elicit saliences and the imprimaturs of a progressivism antithetical to the politics of Trumpism. The mise-en-scène of *The Shape of Water*, which encompasses the bigotries and shortcomings of Kennedy-era Baltimore, reverses the adventurism of *Creature from the Black Lagoon*. Del Toro's nods to issues of sexual identity (connoted in Elisa's homosexual neighbor Giles) and the injustices of pre-civil rights America bring to mind the dispositions of Hollywood melodrama director Douglas Sirk, infusing the B movie subject matter with a permissive conscience. Yet, in one dimension, del Toro's film lacks synergy with the liberal animi of contemporary American life.

The unorthodoxies of the modern Republican right's alignment with Russia are denied exhibition in a narrative fixated on a repressive American social conservatism and the horrors of the deep state castigated by the United States' current president. *The Shape of Water*'s opening scene presages these priorities of scrutiny, illustrating political conflicts given symmetry and resolution by the conclusion. Del Toro pans through an apartment submerged in water, a sublime chaos mirrored by the fantastical inflections of Giles's voiceover. As in the epilogue, Giles speaks allusively, referencing a "fair prince's reign" on a "small city near the coast, but far from everything." The focal figure of his introduction is, however, "the princess without a voice," who encounters a "tale of love and loss" and "the monster who tried to destroy it all."⁵ The gendered spheres illuminated in this voiceover, dichotomized in the mentioning of the ruling prince and disenfranchised princess, foreshadow a narrative hinging on identity politics, contrasting the marginalized with the hegemonic. This couples with hints of del Toro's earlier body of work. Elisa's regal title of "princess" appears redolent of Ofelia's (Ivana Baquero) adulation of Princess Moanna in del Toro's *Pan's Labyrinth*, an identification that poignantly culminates in a magical realist conclusion. But the Cold War setting of *The Shape of Water*, suffused by specifically twenty-first-century culture wars and intertextual homages to the most subversive aspects of postwar Hollywood cinema, generates significant differences, as well as similarities, with *Pan's Labyrinth*'s 1940s Spanish Civil War milieu.

The Shape of Water's "silent princess" turns out to be a mute who communicates through sign language and works for a secret Baltimore laboratory managed by the Cold War's white, patriarchal overseers. Yet for all of Elisa's immersion in this reactionary paternalism, the opening sequence offers a clear counteraction to the soullessness of the Cold War warriors' vision. Del Toro segues from Elisa's morning routine to shots of the 1960 biblical epic *The Story of Ruth* playing in a theater below Elisa's apartment and a glimpse of the 1935 musical *The Little Colonel* on neighbor Giles's black-and-white TV, portending a storyline of eclectic dissent.⁶

The invocation of *The Story of Ruth*, a film adaptation of the biblical book of Ruth, subtly indicates the heterodox sensibility. Henry Koster's historical romance is a seemingly conventional rendition of a story that celebrates divine providence and the transcendence of sectarian divides, embodied in the journey of the titular Ruth (Elana Eden), who flees her position as a pagan idolatress of the tribe of Moab to join the Judeans and enter into a pact with monotheism. Both the original Old Testament story and the film adaptation deal with themes that possess relevance for the iniquitous positions of women and ethnic minorities in early 1960s American society, emphases repeated in *The Shape of Water*. Indeed, Kirsten Nielson perceives the ultimate salience of the book of Ruth to be in its implications of inclusivity. She posits that the book of Ruth highlights that "it was through a foreign woman, the Moabite Ruth, that God chose David and his family to sit on the throne of Israel."⁷

It is possible to interpret del Toro's reference to this somewhat integrationist story as a kind of mockery against the allegedly Christian mores of a reactionary postwar American society, foreshadowing a broader critique. Yet the more melancholic lesbian subtext to be mined from the original book of Ruth also proves relevant and portentous for *The Shape of Water*'s central romance between forbidden other and human. It also undercuts the presentation of American domestic policies and the reflection of US-Russia relations. Emily

McAvan writes on "the heterosexual melancholia of foreclosing a potential same-sex love," a thematic trope enshrined in Ruth's pact with her mother-in-law, Naomi (Peggy Wood), who joins her on her journey to Judea after her two sons die in Moab.[8] When Ruth eventually marries and sires a child with the wealthy landowner Boaz, a development that represents a "piece of *Realpolitik*" to Nielson, a vicarious connection crystallizes with Naomi.[9] Naomi "replaces her sons with Ruth's new son," eliciting "traces of queer desire and same-sex love," which "emerge but are ultimately thwarted."[10]

Much of this foreclosing could be said to apply to *The Shape of Water*, which, in its depictions of diplomatic and romantic tumult, alternates between dispositions of egalitarianism and capitulations to racial and gender inequality. Del Toro soon juxtaposes the vitality of Elisa's apartment with the gray melting pot of the laboratory where she works shifts, a supremacist and chauvinist environment where African American and women cleaners toil for white scientists and military hardliners. This is emphasized in a scene where Strickland calls Elisa into his office and harasses her, threatening that he can make her "squawk a little."[11] The workplace silence against Strickland's oppressive behavior is of course brutally literalized in Elisa's disability, reflecting American patriarchy at its most nefarious.

To John Richardson, Strickland's transgressions attest to an anti-Trump allegory, undercutting nostalgic views of America's postwar economic and cultural hegemony. Richardson defines Elisa, Giles, and Zelda (Octavia Spencer) as the "Americans who live lives of quiet oppression in the past-tense America that shimmers, mythical and revered, at the heart of the Trump campaign promise."[12] He goes on to posit that "the film both upholds and undermines the old mythologies that can provide comfort and reassurance to people whose lives have been disrupted by global trade, population movements and the emergence of AI in the workplace."[13] The figure of Strickland emblematizes the toxic methods for addressing this dysphoria, a populist cipher "designed as a bridge to Trump's present-day political toxicity" who "boasts about his power to sexually assault women."[14]

For this reading to be fully applicable, however, it would have to be reconcilable with *The Shape of Water*'s production context and humanist portrayal of Russian spy Robert Hoffstetler (Michael Stuhlbarg)—a character discussed later in this essay—factors that mean del Toro's critique of white chauvinist nationalism fails to broach one controversial facet of Trump's presidency. The filming period for *The Shape of Water* took place from August 15, 2016, to November 6, 2016, a time that coincided with the dramatic final months of the American presidential race.[15] Nevertheless, del Toro started working on the script in 2012, a time long predating Trump's campaign and presidency.[16] Even if one considers the filming period as a time potentially inflected by the more debased attitudes of Trump's presidential campaign, it is unlikely that del Toro willingly assimilated these animi to deliver a full-blown allegory in anticipation of the Trump era. It is likely that del Toro's targets in *The Shape of Water*, hatched as they were in 2012, are aimed at conservatives rather than Trumpists, delineating the perniciousness of the modern Republican agenda. Acknowledgment of this preproduction context would explain the omission of allusions to Russiagate, marginalized in favor of castigating an insidious traditionalism. Yet Russiagate's absence is also a natural product of the film's shooting schedule—narratives of Russian collusion surrounding Trump's presidential campaign didn't abound until three weeks before the Democratic National Convention in July 2016 and only became fully resonant in the aftermath of the shocking election result later in November.[17]

The homages of *The Shape of Water* to the Hollywood melodramas of Douglas Sirk, a German American film director whose oeuvre in the 1950s and 1960s dealt with issues of race and sexuality, nevertheless compound an ambiguity of satirical focus, shifting between portraits of American social policy and Cold War statecraft. Sirk's imprimatur is detectable in the whimsy of Elisa and Giles's bonding, a platonic variant on the idiosyncratic relationship between bourgeois widow Cary Scott (Jane Wyman) and the unconventional gardener Ron Kirby (Rock Hudson) in *All That Heaven Allows* (1955). In *The Shape of Water*'s second half, a dream sequence depicts Elisa singing in a black-and-white dance musical with the merman she falls in love with, feats of transcendence that recall the theatrical ambitions of protagonist Lora Meredith (Lana Turner) in *Imitation of Life* (1959).[18]

Del Toro's employment of color also invites comparison with Sirk. Giles, who works as an advertising illustrator, has his paintings rejected for prioritizing red colors over green because "green is the color of future," an arbitrariness echoed in the green-hued furniture of a café where he pines, unrequitedly, for a male member of staff. The green styling that envelops scenes featuring Strickland hints at an emblem for a vulgar, shallow consumerism, associations tangible in items as narratively inconsequential as the sweets he eats and a car he buys. The contrast with red, established in the rejection of Giles's art work, allegorizes a world riven between stultifying bourgeois convention and nonconformist, bohemian passion.

French New Wave director François Truffaut's praise for Sirk's 1957 film *Winter on the Wind*, which revolves around the dissipations of an oil-rich Texan family, attributes a politically holistic character to Sirk's tropes.[19] Truffaut cites an aesthetic powerfully comprehensive, eliciting "colors of the twentieth century, the colors of America, the colors of luxury civilization, the industrial colors that remind us that we live in the age of plastics."[20] Thomas Elsaesser reinforces this catharsis by invoking an elaboration by Sirk on color's purpose for the wounded family's portrayal in *Winter on the Wind*, accentuating the "inner violence, the energy of violence, which is all inside them and can't break through."[21]

These amorphous emphases make it arguable that Sirk's sensibility is an essential part of *The Shape of Water*'s magical realist blend and serves to complement its presentation of the Strangelovian aspects of the Cold War, pertaining to the global and domestic. Such a synthesis of concern permeated facets of liberal Hollywood at the beginning of the Cold War. Andrew Justin Falk outlines the efforts of groups like the HDC (Hollywood Democratic Committee) in the mid-1940s to "identify the nation's postwar mission," a journey that tested "the viability of multilateralism" and catalyzed agitation for "antidiscrimination legislation," heightened in the wish to "promote internationalism and democratic principles."[22] Falk goes on to note that "Hollywood's internationalists looked at the postwar world with unbounded optimism" and sought to "globalize liberal humanism."[23] The homages utilized by del Toro are perhaps evocative of this progressive animus, alluding to a domestic and international mise-en-scène in need of liberal alleviation.

Reasons to interpret such interplay become convincing toward the end of the first act, when Elisa begins her romance with the merman who is the prisoner of the secret laboratory. This relationship unites Sirk's concerns for the repression of minorities with warnings against the exigencies of Cold War militarism, portraying pathologies at the heart of America's social and foreign policy orthodoxies. Implications of the merman's presence manifest when Zelda and Elisa witness Strickland emerging from a top-secret room with his hand bleeding, a Sirkian color contrast that undermines the soulless sterility of the scientific base. The first few scenes featuring the merman intertwine the melodrama of Sirk with the cruelty of Cold War Realpolitik. Elisa's initial courtship of the merman alternates with her witnessing his torture and electrocution by a vengeful Strickland, acts of inhumanity soon established as mere means for American ideological supremacy. General Frank Hoyt (Nick Searcy), a figure who could easily encapsulate the excesses of contemporaneous US Air Force chief of staff Curtis LeMay or *Dr. Strangelove*'s (1964) Brigadier General Jack D. Ripper (Sterling Hayden), embodies this self-interest, openly expressing his wish for the merman to be vivisected to give the United States an advantage in the space race. His callousness emerges when he warns Strickland that decency is superfluous in the geopolitical climate, rationalized with the line, "We sell it because we don't use it."[24]

This insensitivity finds reverberation in the treatment of laboratory scientist Robert Hoffstetler, an undercover Russian spy whose real name is Dimitri Mosenkov. In spite of his vocal opposition, Hoffstetler's Soviet superiors oblige him to euthanize and abduct the merman for vivisection in Russia, plot dynamics synergetic with the moral equivalency arguments cited by Cold War historians such as John Lewis Gaddis as intrinsic to debate over twentieth-century history.[25] Employees such as Elisa and the far more privileged Hoffstetler are mere cogs for the heartless military-industrial complexes of their countries, conscientious objectors in a capricious Cold War consensus. References by Hoffstetler's Soviet bosses to "surf and turf" and the frivolities of 1960s America echo Strickland's vulgarity, showing that the real divide in the world of the 1960s is not between communism and capitalism, but between a staidness of conservative hierarchy and a radical, sensitive, egalitarian dissension.[26]

These parallel plot threads unite strains of nonconformity with a repudiation of superpower politics, encouraging dissidence. For all the combativeness of this blend, however, it hinges on a moral equivalence that distances *The Shape of Water* from the contemporary zeitgeist, a model of allegory that does not address the modern Republican right's ignoring of Russian interference. Uncomfortable affinities with Trump's castigation of a deep state, or what J. Silverman categorizes as "a garrison state" and "militarized oligarchy" with roots "in the early days of the Cold War," stem from skepticism of the military and secret government institutions and date *The Shape of Water*'s critique, numbing the partisan fervor of its Sirkian dimension.[27]

The manner in which *The Shape of Water* borrows from two follow-ups to *Creature from the Black Lagoon* indicates the refrains against social injustice and deep state dominance. The Cold War context that surrounds the torture of the merman results in a combination of B movie and polemic that conjures a resensitized version of *Revenge of the Creature*'s (1955) first act, a sequel in which the Gill-man, having survived the events of *Creature from the Black Lagoon*, languishes in captivity for study in a Florida oceanarium.[28] *Sight and Sound* reviewer Kim Newman affirms this narrative reimagining, noting how *The Shape of Water* "riffs on Arnold's lesser-known follow-up, *Revenge of the Creature* (1955), as well as Jack Sherwood's unusually plotted *The Creature Walks Among Us* (1956)."[29]

Newman declines to detail how tropes of the latter film recur in *The Shape of Water*. Yet elements of *The Creature Walks Among Us* are detectable following Elisa, Zelda, and Hoffstetler's rescue of the merman. This emancipation remolds elements taken from the third act of the 1956 film, engendering off-color scenarios where the merman learns and violates the conventions of human society for the first time. These experiences range from the grotesque, such as a lethal scrap that kills Giles's cat, to the sensual, embodied in a scene where the merman enjoys intercourse with Elisa.

Offering a different tone than *The Creature Walks Among Us*, *The Shape of Water* nevertheless universalizes the melancholy of the original merman's failure to integrate with human society. In John Sherwood's final entry in the Gill-man saga, the merman enters a state of depression when a group of nefarious American scientists attempts to enable him to live among humans in a San Francisco scientific institution. A fight between the merman and a group of mountain lions held at the facility, parodied in *The Shape of Water*'s battle between merman and cat, compounds the merman's dejection, damning him in front of his American observers.[30] The moments that succeed the horrific cat encounter in del Toro's film instead reflect a grander allegorical purpose, attested to when the merman escapes the apartment and enters the downstairs theater. *The Story of Ruth* again plays on screen, revisiting thematic notions peddled in the beginning montage. Watching a scene where Judeans suffer enslavement under the Moabites, the merman stares appreciatively, connoting a vicarious understanding of the world's downtrodden. The pathologies of the monster movie become standbys for a commentary on human repression, overt displays of otherness that could represent the lived experience of women and African Americans.

The liberal politics of Hoffstetler indicate that this outlook salvages older motifs raised by del Toro in *Pan's Labyrinth*, betraying distance from the Russia revisionism that has emerged on both the left and right in the aftermath of Cold War II. Hoffstetler is a character who essentially reprises the role of heroic martyr inhabited by the undercover rebel Dr. Ferreiro (Álex Angulo) in *Pan's Labyrinth*, helping recite dichotomies of fascist chauvinism and leftist solidarity. Like Ferreiro, who mercifully euthanizes a rebel tortured at the hands of the fascistic Captain Vidal (Sergi López), he emblematizes a vanguard of rationalist compassion, stonewalling his Soviet paymasters so the merman can remain alive. Hoffstetler's death at the hands of Strickland, who discovers the spy's identity after tailing him to a rendezvous point in rural Maryland, is the best evidence of del Toro's evocation of orthodox fascist/left wing polarities.

Hoffstetler's death recycles mise-en-scène and body horror imported from the darkest scenes of *Pan's Labyrinth*, a lineage that reinforces dichotomic convention. The pathetic fallacy that encircles Hoffstetler's rendezvous location, a torrent of rain and thunder, recalls analogous clichés from the demise of Ferreiro, who performs a defiant "death march" from Vidal against a backdrop of pouring rain. Strickland, who arrives to find that Hoffstetler has already been mortally wounded by his Soviet bosses, enacts barbarities on the scientist that further demonstrate incorporation of elements which surround Ferreiro's martyrdom. In a grotesqueness redolent of the dental torture Vidal employs on his rebel prisoner and the facial trauma the fascist captain himself suffers when he has his face mutilated by rebel employee Mercedes, Strickland inserts his finger inside a bullet hole in the face of a still-conscious Hoffstetler, playing with and torturing the spy via the wound. Hoffstetler eventually concedes Elisa and Zelda's involvement in the merman's emancipation before Strickland shoots him, capping a sequence indebted to *Pan's Labyrinth*'s gritty political brutality.[31]

It is this recurrence of motif which perhaps makes clear that, for all its greater fixation on identity politics, *The Shape of Water* shares a key novelty with *Pan's Labyrinth*, the addressing of what Kam Hei Tsuei calls "the nonmythical" approach to fascism in Hollywood. Tsuei notes the capacity of "true story" films such as *Schindler's List* (1993) and *The Pianist* (2002) for reassuring audiences that fascism was something foreign and alien, a catharsis that "de-universalizes and then sublimates the bourgeois roots of fascism."[32]

The crude real-world environments of Vidal and Strickland, which contrast the escapist worlds of Ofelia and Elisa, celebrate socially conservative spaces that simultaneously demonstrate synchronicity with predilections of sexual and militaristic intimidation. In *The Shape of Water*, such strains of patriarchal malevolence emerge in an early scene depicting Strickland's domestic life. In this aside, Strickland, who is still recovering from a defensive attack by the merman, has intercourse with his wife while his children attend school. He tells his wife to be silent about his finger bleeding during sex, a warped synthesis of carnality and violence. The ease with which Strickland reconciles suburban mores with his own brutality hints at a far-right amorphousness fostering and festering in spaces of American traditionalism. Fascistic chauvinism is possible anywhere, especially in the milieu of 1960s Americana, a broadness of commentary that broaches the atavistic nostalgia of Trumpist Republicanism, if not its diplomatic heterodoxy.

The Sirkian aspect of *The Shape of Water* heightens the affinity between traditionalism and political authoritarianism, engendering ideological congruities synergetic with the Trump administration's socially conservative elements and Democratic opposition to the president's agenda. But the connection between this political demonology and modern political configuration is offset by the foreign policy or moral equivalence slant of the drama, a framing out of kilter with the inversions of the 2016 election. In the next section, I argue that the espionage thriller *Red Sparrow*, although marketed as a sophisticated take on the corruption of Putin's Russia, repeats tropes of this misalignment, eliding exploration of the mercurial allegiances that made the 2016 presidential election so transformative.

Misalignments in *Red Sparrow*

If *The Shape of Water* purveys partisanships of Democratic social liberalism and Republican social Darwinism, *Red Sparrow* seems, on the surface, comparatively ideology-free, lacking in frequency the political bipolarity that conditioned the Cold War and dominates America's current culture wars. Its opening nevertheless presents an intersection of the foreign and domestic not entirely unlike the competing spheres contained in del Toro's film, intertwining diplomatic intrigue with personal disarray.

Director Francis Lawrence crosscuts between two separate figures in contemporary Russia, professional ballerina and Russian citizen Dominika Egorova (Jennifer Lawrence), and American CIA operative Nate Nash (Joel Edgerton). Their initial appearances are low-key. Dominika packs in preparation for a ballet performance and supports her ill mother, while Nate answers a phone call, writes down a code, and moves incognito through the streets of Moscow. A saturnine mood escalates during Dominika's ballet performance at the Bolshoi, where an abrupt halt to the performance crystallizes a zero-sum Cold War politics, replicating the morose sensibilities of espionage novelist John le Carré for the twenty-first century. While Nate fails to converse with a mole in Gorky Park due to the arrival of Russian police, Dominika's male dance partner jumps on and breaks her leg, ending her ballet career. Lawrence crosscuts in the wake of these misfortunes, paralleling Dominika's leg operation with the fallout from Nate's botched effort to converse with the mole.

If there is a thread which connects Nate and Dominika, it is an experience of institutional caprice that belies both their home countries' historic reputations as confident superpowers, somewhat echoing the moral equivalency slant of *The Shape of Water*. Dominika's recruitment into the Russian foreign intelligence service (called the SVR) pervades this dualism through set pieces proximate to the Me Too scandals in the United States, presenting scenarios multifaceted in political symbolism. Shortly following Dominika's recovery from injury, she is approached by her uncle Ivan (Matthias Schoenaerts), who happens to be deputy director of the SVR. In a sudden turn of events which hints that the ballet "accident" may have been foul play, Ivan pressures Dominika to seduce a Russian gangster in return for her mother receiving private medical care. The mission turns nightmarish, culminating in Dominika's rape and the death of the Russian gangster at the hands of another SVR operative. As the only witness to the execution, Dominika is obliged by Ivan to continue working for the SVR as a Sparrow, an operative who uses sex to entrap enemy agents.[33]

Ted Jorgensen of the right wing *American Thinker* magazine links *Red Sparrow* with the hysteria surrounding the Christopher Steele dossier in January 2017, a document which leveled accusations of collusion against the Trump administration and contained lurid allegations that the president paid Russian prostitutes to urinate on him in a Moscow hotel. Jorgensen condemns the "scenes of violence and shocking vulgarity" of *Red Sparrow*, elements that signal Russia as a country of "pure, nauseating evil" and play to a "Russia-is-bad narrative."[34] Ultimately, *Red Sparrow* embraced a sophomoric outlook "ignorant of Trump's past and of Cold War history," which "diverts us from dealing today with a new Russian challenge" and "the horrific failures of our foreign policy establishment."[35]

Jorgenson ignores the literary origins of *Red Sparrow* in a 2013 book by Jason Matthews, a work long predating the 2016 election and the Christopher Steele dossier. Lead actress Jennifer Lawrence's rationale for *Red Sparrow*'s sexual content further complicates Jorgenson's interpretation by lending a parochial dimension to the transgressive subject matter. Lawrence explained her decision to take the role of Dominika and the inclusion of a later nude scene where she exposes the impotency of a rapist SVR member as a kind of retort to the 2014 4chan photo hack that disseminated explicit photos of her across the internet, a method of "getting something back that had been taken away from me."[36] Although *Red Sparrow* was shot prior to the revelations of sexual abuse and harassment by Hollywood producer Harvey Weinstein, a figure Lawrence dismissed in an interview promoting *Red Sparrow* as a "sadistic monster," its instances of exploitation engender a synergy with the Me Too scandals that started to unfold in late 2017.[37] This subtext, contained in scenes where Dominika must collude with harassment and assault in order to prove her worth to the Russian state, also comes coupled with moments acutely political, generating association with Russian president Vladimir Putin's regime and its championing by Trumpist Republicans.

The sequences that depict Dominika's training for the SVR signal affinity between Putinism and a traditionalist, transatlantic conservatism described as the "Alt-Right International" by *Atlantic* journalist Mike Lofgren.[38] In addresses to the Sparrows in training, the Matron (Charlotte Rampling) in charge of their desensitization propounds that the "Cold War did not end . . . it shattered into a thousand pieces." She further attacks the multicultural and materialist trappings of the West, bemoaning a social fabric oriented around hedonistic individuals "drunk and shopping on social media" and "torn apart by hatred between the races." Because of this, "the world is in chaos" and "only Russia is willing to make the sacrifices required for victory."[39]

The apocalyptic language possesses similarity with Bryn Upton's listing of the tropes that enveloped the Hollywood of the "Cold War era," illuminating "the constant threat of war posed by an external enemy" and "the end of the world coming in the form of manmade destruction."[40] But the Matron's derision of Western culture elucidates more contemporary diplomatic realities, underlining Cold War II as a kind of culture war. Despite the libidinous and depraved methodology undergirding the patriotism, the Matron's rhetoric recalls what M. Steven Fish calls the "traditionalist social agenda" of Putinism, which "prioritizes the maintenance of the status quo while evincing hostility towards potential sources of instability."[41] Her resentment of shallow American consumerism and ethnic diversity additionally conjures notions of the congruities between the modern Russian state and Trumpian figures such as the Republican isolationist Pat Buchanan, who lauded Putin as the voice of "conservatives, traditionalists and nationalists of all continents and countries who seek to stand up against the cultural and ideological imperialism of what Putin sees as a decadent West."[42]

Trump's 2016 campaign arguably echoed this sensibility for a domestic and foreign policy context, warning of a Democratic consensus of open borders and a cultural imperialism inappropriately directed toward Russia. In language that recalls the observations of Fish, James Curran writes on an American nationalism expressing "hostility to foreign entanglements and hostility towards illegal immigration.... Trump's version of America First is driven not so much by a conviction in America's divine providence, but primarily by grievance, the perception that his country is being exploited by others."[43] *Red Sparrow* declines, however, to consummate this overlap of ideology, instead emphasizing social malaise over diplomatic malfeasance. This negation of polemic is detectable soon after the SVR sends Dominika to Budapest to seduce Nate, begetting a sexual relationship that allows her to become a double agent for the Americans and exploit a target who, in a more forthright picture, would typify collusion between Republican Party and Russian circles.

Before analyzing this avoidance of partisan critique, it is first worth contextualizing the plot dynamics that precede and surround the most obvious manifestation of *Red Sparrow*'s neutrality. The interests of the Americans and Russians intersect in Dominika's discovery of a chief of staff to a US senator with a sexual interest in women, named Stephanie Boucher (Mary-Louise Parker), who wants to sell secrets to the Russians. Dominika takes on this assignment when the SVR murders her partner Marta (Thekla Reuten) as a warning against double-crossing, an admonishment ignored when the former ballerina opts to collaborate with the Americans on the Boucher case. In a setup redolent of the paranoia in Francis Ford Coppola's *The Conversation* (1974), Dominika must obtain floppy disks from Boucher in a hotel room under CIA surveillance, gaining information for the Russian state but also illustrating a traitor at the heart of US congressional government.

The equivocal nature of Dominika's mission corresponds with the ideologically shallow quality of Boucher, who betrays the image of clueless opportunist rather than Trumpian ideologue or left wing saboteur. At the beginning of the hotel exchange, she establishes that she is willing to give information on a Star

Wars–style satellite defense system in return for money to pay for her daughter's tuition. She adds that she is "not doing this because I'm an ideologue or pacifist," an insouciance that contrasts with the presence of Dominika's fervent SVR Budapest station chief Colonel Maxim Volontov (Douglas Hodge). Boucher's frivolity amplifies the tonal variation. She drunkenly jokes to Volontov that all Russian men "look like toads," while the women are "sexy."[44] The brief moments of levity are counteracted by the aftermath, which nullifies any operational success. Scared by the sight of CIA agents outside the hotel, Boucher stops in the middle of a road and gets hit by a truck, compromising Dominika and making explicit the presence of American surveillance. Director Lawrence crosscuts between Volontov's discovery of Boucher's death and the CIA's panic, connoting the danger resultant from the accosting of the American traitor.

The sequence's spectacle and its subsuming of the more ideologically significant element of Boucher's treason elicit the salience of David Holloway's concept of an "allegory lite," a cinematic disposition that crystallized in the years following 9/11. Holloway, addressing the treatment of the 9/11 terrorist attacks and ensuing War on Terror in American film, gauges spirits of centrist compromise that perform "the tricky commercial maneuver of appealing simultaneously to multiple audiences, alienating as few customers as possible, while transferring responsibility for any 'politicising' of films to viewers themselves."[45] Using examples as diverse as Jonathan Demme's 2004 *The Manchurian Candidate* remake and Steven Spielberg's *War of the Worlds* (2005), Holloway's analysis speaks to a defusing purpose that "gestures towards political conflict and controversy, but only to marginalise, override, or obscure it, helping generate maximum audience share by depoliticising what begin as ostensibly political interventions."[46]

Red Sparrow's narrative trajectory increasingly represents this animus of elision, recoiling from and neutering overt displays of politicization. In the third act, Dominika survives the torture rituals of the SVR and finds out that SVR head General Vladimir Andreievich Korchnoi (Jeremy Irons) is the mole sought at the beginning by Nash, plot developments that dissipate any acerbic commentary on Russian and American collusion.

In the first plot development, a bricolage emerges that offsets the geopolitical specificity of the narrative, showcased in scenes as much redolent of George W. Bush–era "torture porn" films like *Hostel* (2006) as the comparatively subdued recent pictures that have revisited the Cold War, such as *Bridge of Spies* (2015). In a succession of torture scenarios, Dominika endures showers of freezing cold water, deafeningly loud rock music, and routine threats of execution by the SVR. In the twist that reveals Korchnoi's true identity, equilibrium arrives that contrasts the initially dysphoric opening, belying the bold framing of a moral equivalence standpoint. Deciding against the notion that she should arrest Korchnoi in order to advance within the SVR and allay suspicions surrounding her own political loyalties, she instead fingers her pernicious uncle Ivan as the mole, resulting in his execution. While Korchnoi remains as SVR head and mole, Dominika returns to live with her mother and receives a phone call from an unidentified person who plays Grieg's Piano Concerto, a piece previously used by Nash as a signal to her.

The effect of this closure nullifies the febrile emphasis on a US-Russia culture war conveyed by the Matron, eclipsing these allusions with the liberal internationalism rekindled through Korchnoi's subversion. In an epilogue relatable to the long-term resonance of Holloway's "allegory lite" reading, *Red Sparrow* succumbs to a resolution that attempts to "displace or supersede the political allegory for audiences," cementing "conventional aesthetic patterns that reflected incoherent—but quite traditional—Hollywood political commitments."[47] American espionage in Russia, which in the opening appeared hubristic, becomes noble in light of the narrative U-turn and rationalizes the provocation of revanchist backlash. Employing a narrative framing oppositional to the ideological fervor of *The Shape of Water*, *Red Sparrow*'s plot contortions attest to the relevance of Guy Westwell's concept of a Hollywood that seeks "hegemonic reconciliation between politically irreconcilable positions," a cognitive dissonance that leads to a configuration where "the allegorical dimension may license an aggressive and expansive foreign policy."[48]

Black Panther: The Most Accurate Encoding of International Relations in the Trump Era

The presidential campaign of Donald Trump and the attendant controversies of Russian collusion fostered realignment in American politics. It led to a political climate where the Democratic Party became stereotyped as a party of militant internationalists, nefarious progeny of the neoconservative acolytes in the George W. Bush administration who prosecuted the Iraq War. Andrew Bacevich, whose 2005 book *The New American Militarism* delineates a progressive perspective on military power incarnate from the Democratic Party of the Clinton era, writes of the "Wilsonian moment" that percolated the post–Cold War decades, regnant even in "left-liberal activists," whose "reflexive anti-militarism of the 1960s has given way to a more nuanced view."[49] Trump, rebelling against this bipartisan sanctification of intervention and democratization, used the defense of Russia as a central leitmotif in his campaign, stressing the need for warmer relations with Putin and the potential for a united front against ISIS.⁵⁰ H. W. Brands's dichotomy of exemplarism and vindicationism captures the change of emphasis augured by Trump's isolationism.

In his January 2017 inaugural address, Trump lamented an America that had "defended other nations' borders" at the cost of its own domestic security, an iniquity compounded by a free-trade policy that "made other countries rich while the wealth, strength, and confidence of our country has disappeared over the horizon."⁵¹ Jettisoning the Wilsonianism prevalent in the arms buildup of Reagan's first term and echoed in subsequent Republican administrations, Trump's speech matches the "exemplarist" model of American power. According to Brands, this realist philosophy remonstrates that "Americans should tend their own business in a world bent on destruction" and that US power should hinge on keeping American values "safe at home" rather than engineering them for "export."⁵² The unusual stances of Trump's campaign, especially in regard to Russia, placed the Democratic Party on the side of the "vindicationists," adhering to interventionist facets of US foreign policy that went beyond the idea of America "as a beacon to the world," viewing foreign policy as a battle between "freedom and slavery."⁵³

Films that have depicted US-Russia relations in Trump's first term have lacked the ideologically inverse qualities conspicuous in Cold War II. In the case of *The Shape of Water*, what Tony Shaw defines as a postwar American "hedonism mixed with social Darwinism" permeates characters like Strickland, explicating a hypocritical conservatism marinated in the bipolarities of the twentieth century's Cold War.⁵⁴ *Red Sparrow* at first hints at pointing out the vagaries of contemporary US-Russia relations but fails to consummate its bold premise in the third act's instances of elision, resulting in a picture that lacks assessment of the political demarcations created by the Trump era. Perhaps, however, analyzing recent Hollywood films that explicitly reference US-Russia relations is an unnecessary way of finding encodings of the foreign policy landscape remolded by Trumpism.

2018's *Black Panther* contains no inclusion of Cold War politics or Russia in its narrative, yet it nevertheless purveys political collisions that resemble the schisms wrought by the 2016 election. The hero of Ryan Coogler's film is T'Challa (Chadwick Boseman), the ruler of an African kingdom known as Wakanda. Disguised as a Third World country while harboring technology far superior to the West, Wakanda safeguards its wealth through a completely isolationist foreign policy, seeking noninvolvement with the United States and declining to intervene in the affairs of impoverished, neighboring African states. These policies become vulnerable after the arrival of T'Challa's long-lost cousin, Erik Stevens (Michael B. Jordan), nicknamed "Killmonger." A former US black ops soldier, Killmonger's political positions are fundamentally internationalist, expressed in his wish to use Wakandan technology "to arm oppressed peoples all over the world." References to the dilemmas of choosing between exemplarism and vindicationism surround this drama, connoted in T'Challa's contemplation of whether to adopt policies of "refugee programs" and "foreign aid."[55]

Black Panther resolves these concerns with a final embrace of allegory lite's centrism, showcased in the defeat of Killmonger and T'Challa's decision that Wakanda should engage with the outside world. But the synergy with the ideological polarities resultant from the policies of Russian collusion remains a marking distinction of Coogler's film, obviating its radical endorsements of black autonomy and self-determination. Reviews that champion *Black Panther*'s "prismatic perspectives on black life and tradition" are mischievously counteracted by the alt-right commentators who draw parallels between Wakanda's isolationism and their own conservative worldview of a globe governed between mutually respectful, culturally homogenous ethnostates.[56] A Breitbart piece labels *Black Panther* "President Donald Trump's big screen avatar," citing the "healthy form of nationalism" visible in Wakanda.[57] The YouTube user and alt-right figure "Black Pigeon" notes that Wakanda is a "hereditary monarchy . . . they don't believe in democracy" and an "anti-globalist society with little interest in sharing its wealth and resources."[58] These postulations ignore that *Black Panther* eventually moves in the opposite direction to this vision. In the third act, T'Challa chastises past kings for their isolationism and opens an outreach center in Oakland, where Killmonger's father was killed. An endorsement of internationalism manifests in a mid-credits scene where T'Challa addresses the UN and says that "the wise build bridges while the foolish build barriers," embodying a dramatic repudiation of Trump's nativism.[59]

The awkward ideological incongruities tangible in *Black Panther*, a purportedly progressive superhero blockbuster, go further in illustrating the realignments thrust on American politics by Republican rationalizations of rapprochement with Russia than films containing diegetic representations. Scenes that juxtapose the autocratic isolationism of Wakanda with the radical internationalism of Killmonger chime with the crosscurrents emergent from Trump's rejection of neoconservativism and liberal interventionism, highlighting fissures exposed by the alt-right's defense of Putinism. The absolving of Trump by Special Counsel Robert Mueller in March 2019 hints that the scandal of Russiagate may be of ephemeral significance. But as long as American pictures that explore US-Russia relations stay fixated on the iconic bipolarities of the 1960s and 1980s, respectively conveyed in *The Shape of Water*'s Kennedy era and *Red Sparrow*'s final signaling of democratic capitalism's victory, the ramifications of Trumpian diplomacy and the wider underpinnings of Cold War II will lack cinematic reification.

Notes

1. Tim Gray, "Love and Danger on the Water Front," *Variety*, January 10, 2018, https://variety.com/2018/film/awards/shape-of-water-inspiration-from-monster-movie-1202659976/.

2. Jack Arnold, *Creature from the Black Lagoon* (Universal City, CA: Universal Studios, 1954).

3. This claim first appeared in a review by Jude Noel and was later expounded in greater detail in an online article by Peter Armenti. Jude Noel, "Review: Guillermo del Toro's *The Shape of Water*," *The Northerner*, November 25, 2017, https://www.thenortherner.com/arts-and-life/2017/11/25/review-guillermo-del-toros-the-shape-of-water/; Peter Armenti, "Who Wrote the Poem at the End of *The Shape of Water*?," *From the Catbird Seat* (blog), Library of Congress, March 9, 2018, https://blogs.loc.gov/catbird/2018/03/who-wrote-the-poem-at-the-end-of-the-shape-of-water/.

4. Guillermo del Toro, *The Shape of Water* (Los Angeles: Fox Searchlight Pictures, 2017).

5. Del Toro, *The Shape of Water*.

6. Henry Koster, *The Story of Ruth* (Los Angeles: 20th Century Fox, 1960); David Butler, *The Little Colonel* (Los Angeles: 20th Century Fox, 1935).

7. Kirsten Nielson, *Ruth (1997): A Commentary* (Louisville: Presbyterian Publishing Corporation, 1997), viii.

8. Evan McAvan, "Queer Mourning and Melancholia in the Book of Ruth," *Berfrois*, October 16 2013, https://www.berfrois.com/2013/10/naomi-ruth-boaz/.

9. Nielson, *Ruth (1997)*, vii.

10. McAvan, "Queer Mourning and Melancholia in the Book of Ruth."

11. Del Toro, *The Shape of Water*.

12. John Richardson, "*The Shape of Water*: An Allegorical Critique of Trump," *The Conversation*, March 18 2018, https://theconversation.com/the-shape-of-water-an-allegorical-critique-of-trump-93272.

13. Richardson, "*The Shape of Water*: An Allegorical Critique of Trump."

14. Richardson, "*The Shape of Water*: An Allegorical Critique of Trump."

15. IMDb, "*The Shape of Water* (2017): Filming & Production," accessed January 5, 2019, https://www.imdb.com/title/tt5580390/locations?ref_=ttfc_ql_5#filming_dates.

16. Del Toro began working on the script after buying the idea of *The Shape of Water* from Daniel Kraus, his coauthor of the book *Trollhunters*. Jenna Marotta, "*The Shape of Water*: Why Guillermo del Toro and Vanessa Taylor Speak While Writing Their Film," *IndieWire*, January 12, 2018, https://www.indiewire.com/2018/01/the-shape-of-water-screenwriter-vanessa-taylor-1201915351/.

17. Jonathan Masters, "Russia, Trump, and the 2016 U.S. Election," Council on Foreign Relations, February 26, 2018, https://www.cfr.org/backgrounder/russia-trump-and-2016-us-election.

18. Douglas Sirk, *All That Heaven Allows* (Universal City, CA: Universal Pictures, 1955); Douglas Sirk, *Imitation of Life* (Universal City, CA: Universal Pictures, 1959).

19. Douglas Sirk, *Written on the Wind* (Universal City, CA: Universal Pictures, 1959).

20. Francois Truffaut, *The Films in My Life*, trans. Leonard Mayhew (New York: Simon and Schuster, 1978), 149; quoted in Barbara Klinger, *Melodrama and Meaning: History, Culture and the Films of Douglas Sirk* (Bloomington: Indiana University Press), 4.

21. Thomas Elsaesser, "Tales of Sound and Fury: [Observations on] the Family Melodrama," *Monogram* 4, no. 3 (1972); quoted in Warren Buckland, "Theorizing Melodrama: A Rational Reconstruction of 'Tales of Sound and Fury,'" in *Mind the Screen: Media Concepts According*

to *Thomas Elsaesser*, ed. Jaap Koojiman, Patricia Pisters, and Wanda Strauven (Amsterdam: Amsterdam University Press, 2008), 32.

22. Andrew J. Falk, *Upstaging the Cold War: American Dissent and Cultural Diplomacy* (Amherst: University of Massachusetts Press, 2010), 60–62.

23. Falk, *Upstaging the Cold War*, 61–62.

24. Del Toro, *The Shape of Water*.

25. John Lewis Gaddis, "On Moral Equivalency and Cold War History," *Ethics & International Affairs* 10, no. 1 (1996): 3.

26. Del Toro, *The Shape of Water*.

27. Jacob Silverman, "Is There a Deep State, and If So What Is It?," *New Labor Forum* 27, no. 3 (2018): 28.

28. Jack Arnold, *Revenge of the Creature* (Universal City, CA: Universal Pictures, 1955).

29. Kim Newman, "Film of the Week: *The Shape of Water* Swims in Lagoons of Love and Horror," BFI, February 16, 2018, https://www.bfi.org.uk/news-opinion/sight-sound-magazine/reviews-recommendations/shape-water-guillermo-del-toro-lagoons-love-horror.

30. John Sherwood, *The Creature Walks Among Us* (Universal City, CA: Universal Pictures, 1956).

31. Guillermo del Toro, *Pan's Labyrinth* (New York: Picturehouse, 2006).

32. Kam Hei Tsuei, "The Antifascist Aesthetics of *Pan's Labyrinth*," *Socialism and Democracy* 22, no. 2 (2018): 238.

33. Francis Lawrence, *Red Sparrow* (Los Angeles: 20th Century Fox, 2018).

34. Ted Jorgenson, "Trump, Russia, and the Red Sparrow," *American Thinker*, March 3, 2018, https://www.americanthinker.com/articles/2018/03/trump_russia_and_the_red_sparrow.html.

35. Ted Jorgenson, "Trump, Russia, and the Red Sparrow."

36. Katherine Cusamano, "Jennifer Lawrence on Doing the Explicit *Red Sparrow* After the 2014 Nude Photo Hack: I Felt Like I Was Getting Something Back That Had Been Taken from Me," *W*, November 21, 2017, https://www.wmagazine.com/story/jennifer-lawrence-nude-photo-hack-red-sparrow.

37. Katherine Cusamano, "Jennifer Lawrence on Doing the Explicit *Red Sparrow*."

38. Mike Lofgren, "Trump, Putin, and the Alt-Right International," *The Atlantic*, October 31, 2016, https://www.theatlantic.com/international/archive/2016/10/trump-putin-alt-right-comintern/506015/.

39. Lawrence, *Red Sparrow*.

40. Bryn Upton, *Hollywood and the End of the Cold War* (Lanham, MD: Rowman & Littlefield, 2014), 13.

41. M. Steven Fish, "The Kremlin Emboldened: What Is Putinism?," *Journal of Democracy* 28, no. 4 (2017): 61.

42. Pat Buchanan, "Is Putin One of Us?," *Townhall*, December 17, 2013, https://townhall.com/columnists/patbuchanan/2013/12/17/is-putin-one-of-us-n1764094.

43. James Curran, "Americanism, Not Globalism: President Trump and the American Mission," Lowy Institute, July 3, 2018, https://www.lowyinstitute.org/publications/americanism-not-globalism-president-trump-and-american-mission-0.

44. Lawrence, *Red Sparrow*.

45. David Holloway, *9/11 and the War on Terror* (Edinburgh: Edinburgh University Press, 2008), 83.

46. Holloway, *9/11 and the War on Terror*, 83.

47. Holloway, *9/11 and the War on Terror*, 82.

48. Guy Westwell, *Parallel Lines: Post-9/11 American Cinema* (New York: Columbia University Press, 2014), 94–95.

49. Andrew Bacevich, *The New American Militarism: How Americans Are Seduced by War* (Oxford: Oxford University Press, 2005), 25.

50. Alexander Burns, "Donald Trump Reaffirms Support for Warmer Relations with Putin," *New York Times*, August 1, 2016, https://www.nytimes.com/2016/08/02/us/politics/donald-trump-vladimir-putin-russia.html.

51. Donald J. Trump, "Remarks of President Donald J. Trump—As Prepared for Delivery Inaugural Address," WhiteHouse.gov (website), January 20, 2017, https://www.whitehouse.gov/briefings-statements/the-inaugural-address/.

52. H. W. Brands, *What America Owes the World: The Struggle for the Soul of Foreign Policy* (Cambridge: Cambridge University Press, 1998), 4.

53. Brands, *What America Owes the World*, 2.

54. Tony Shaw, *Hollywood's Cold War* (Edinburgh: Edinburgh University Press, 2009), 170.

55. Ryan Coogler, *Black Panther* (Burbank, CA: Walt Disney Studios, 2018).

56. Jamil Smith, "The Revolutionary Power of *Black Panther*," *Time*, February 19, 2018, http://time.com/black-panther/.

57. John Nolte, "Nolte: Pro-Trump 'Black Panther' Breaks Box Office Records without Breaking New Ground," Breitbart, February 20, 2018, https://www.breitbart.com/big-hollywood/2018/02/20/pro-trump-black-panther-breaks-box-office-records-without-breaking-new-ground/.

58. Black Pigeon Speaks, "Black Panther: A Hero the #AltRight Deserves?," June 18, 2017, YouTube video, 3:54, https://www.youtube.com/watch?v=POZCF9t9FUI&t=133s.

59. Coogler, *Black Panther*.

RED SPARROW
Cold War Redux and the Treatment of Corruption

Donna A. Gessell

Examining why many US citizens fail to see President Donald Trump as corrupt, Peter Beinart, in an August 2018 article for *The Atlantic*, argues that "what the president's supporters fear most isn't the corruption of American law, but the corruption of America's traditional identity."[1] With this concept of corruption in mind, American viewers of the Russia-set film *Red Sparrow* may recast our interpretation of the movie to examine how it comments on current US politics, even in light of its overt critique of current Russian politics. As an example of the recent wave of second Cold War films, *Red Sparrow* suggests that, in a time with traditional identity values at stake, the two current governments are more alike than different, both operating at the expense of the individual.

Viewers familiar with first Cold War films are initially comforted by seemingly familiar images of Russia: a dismal gray concrete city filled with people downtrodden and stunted by limited rights and opportunities—a scene often used to contrast communist culture with that of a capitalistic democracy. Soon, however, we realize that Dominika Egorova, a disabled former ballerina turned spy, is acting with values we associate with ourselves: a freethinking individual, she exhibits a sense of patriotism and duty to family that looms large among her other values. These values force her to protect herself by combating the corruption of the Russian government, made personal in the criminal actions of her uncle, the deputy director of Russia's external intelligence agency, the SVR. Because her values align with our dearly held conception of the ethos of the United States, American viewers identify with Dominika and, as a result, must confront the implied necessity of maintaining our values by fighting corruption in our own government.

Thus, this essay argues that *Red Sparrow* compels US viewers to look not outward but inward. Like a mirror, the film manipulates our longtime fascination with Russia to direct our gaze at ourselves, to evoke a reevaluation of how we maintain traditionally held values, including concepts of duty and patriotism, even if that loyalty demands contesting our own corruption.

Where *Red Sparrow* Truly Roosts

Red Sparrow, directed by Francis Lawrence, features Jennifer Lawrence as Dominika Egorova, a ballerina who is trained as a "Sparrow"; Joel Edgerton as Nate Nash, a CIA operative in Moscow and later Budapest; Matthias Schoenaerts as Dominika's uncle and also deputy director of the SVR; Charlotte Rampling as the Matron at the Sparrow School; and Jeremy Irons as General Vladimir Andreievich Korchnoi, also of the SVR.[2] The film, released in 2018, has provoked mixed reviews. Scoring 46 percent on Rotten Tomatoes,[3] the film's critics disparagingly comment on it as "intended to be a sexy thriller"[4] that only rises to "trash . . . the garbagy essence of most Hollywood movies."[5] Others call it "a sordid spy story for those who relish the genre's escapist titillation,"[6] noting its "few lurid episodes, abundant lust,"[7] and its "high-gloss highly sexualized espionage claptrap with an overlay of faux female empowerment."[8] Few critics look past the "sexy" veneer to consider it as a serious political film. Even Christy Lemire dismisses the film's treatment of Cold War II themes, observing only a minimal treatment of those themes:

> Rampling's character, known only as Matron, gives a speech to the class about how the West is weak, tearing itself apart with racial divisions and social media obsessions, and how it's Russia's time to step in and assert itself as the ultimate world power. This is about as close as "Red Sparrow" comes to addressing the renewed Cold War between Russia and the United States. (I guess a whole movie in which Jennifer Lawrence sits in a Moscow office building pumping out anti-Hillary Clinton Twitter bots would've been hard to market.)[9]

He also focuses the majority of his comments on the sexual desire for and brutality toward the character that Lawrence plays, saying that it "feels more like a cheap exercise in exploitation than a visceral tale of survival."[10]

Tomas Trussow, author of *The Lonely Film Critic*, does provide an intriguing counterperspective in his review:

> With Russia being in the news so often now, a film like this was bound to come along eventually: one that essentially paints the country as a terrorist state which trains an arsenal of espionage agents to do its bidding. Except, in this iteration, those agents are mostly attractive women who learn to use their bodies to entice their victims into giving them what they want. A lot of it is farfetched to be sure, but one can still imagine something like this existing. After all, Russia seems to be capable of anything these days (including poisoning ex-spies with military-grade nerve agents), and weaponizing female bodies is hardly an impossible task. The "whore school" Jennifer Lawrence's character attends, for instance, is not as unconventional as it first sounds. I can totally see it existing somewhere in the hinterlands, desensitizing its cadets to shame and moral decency so that they can go out into the world and sow their discord. That's what I found interesting about this. It fools you at the outset into thinking you're going to be seeing another pulpy spy thriller, and then presents you with strangely feasible scenarios that, coupled with the graphic violence and sexual content, make you fear for the world you're living in.[11]

In fact, Jason Matthews, the author of the 2013 novel that is the basis for the film, is a retired CIA officer. In a *New York Times* article, "Shadowing Jason Matthews, an Ex-Spy Whose Cover Identity Is Author," Charles McGrath discusses the genre of spy thrillers written by "real-life spies" and suggests that Matthews combines current events with "old school" spy novels, incorporating "James Bondian touches" and "traditional tradecraft." Matthews, whose official job was diplomat, worked as a CIA officer for thirty-three years, using his cover for "his real job, [which] was recruiting and then managing foreign agents often in places where such activity was forbidden." He claims that his work "is all fiction, but it's an amalgam of people I've known, of things I've done, of stuff I've lived."[12] The book *Red Sparrow* is the first of his Red Sparrow trilogy, which also includes *Palace of Treason* (2015) and *The Kremlin's Candidate* (2018), the very titles of which suggest second Cold War themes.

To tap into the film's more subtle critique, viewers must focus on how the movie illuminates the second Cold War instead of fixating on its sexuality as an end in itself. The connection between sexuality and waging war may not at first be clear to people still thinking in terms of first Cold War tactics showcasing military might and the constant exchange of bluster regarding possible nuclear war. After all, Matthews portrays not only how operatives currently work, but also how Russia is fighting the new Cold War, using material that is collected by security agencies and used against individuals to blackmail them into activities or to create negative publicity to disempower them. Although the term for these tactics, *kompromat*, was coined during the Stalin era, it is once again in currency in Putin's Russia and has been expanded to include cybercrime and materials especially sexual in nature.

Another reason that critics may misunderstand the film is that many are unaware (or willfully ignorant) of the new Cold War. For at least the last decade, however, journalists and political analysts have warned about our slide into this renewed nonviolent conflict with Russia. Casimir Dadak, in "A New 'Cold War'?," published in the Summer 2010 issue of the *Independent Review*, traces the demographics and economics of world powers, noting, "Some observers perceive that the world is sliding into a new 'cold war.'"[13] He traces the conflict to the Russian economic recovery from its 1998 default by the government. Likewise, Stephen F. Cohen, in his "Cold War Follies," published February 4, 2013, in *The Nation*, leads by warning, "With the full support of a feckless policy elite and an uncritical media establishment, Washington is slipping, if not plunging, into a new cold war with Moscow."[14] After suggesting that "Russian officials (and perhaps their family members) [are] alleged to be guilty of 'gross violations of human rights' in their own country," using terminology such as "Russia's political class" and "Putin's 'authoritarian regime,'" he goes further to suggest that the "'democratic' US mainstream media," including "leading American newspapers and television and radio outlets, have been cheerleaders for a new cold war."[15] In fact, he ends his commentary by arguing that the ending of the Cold War "forever," which had previously been proclaimed, is now impossible: "Too much may have changed—in the quality of leadership, in the political elites of Washington and Moscow, and in US media practices—for it to happen again."[16]

Even though many acknowledge that we are in a new Cold War, the point remains contentious because disagreement exists about how and when this war started. Although Michael Lind acknowledges that "the historians of the future may engage in a similar debate [to that of when the first Cold War began or when it ended] about when Cold War II started in earnest," he does affirm categorically that "the cold peace of the 1990s and 2000s is over. Cold War II is here."[17] The challenge in locating its starting point is discerning the direct causes. Daryl McCann argues for three ways to avoid a new Cold War, while attributing its potential cause to Putin's "deeply held grievance about what he considers to be the loss of the Soviet Union," and thus his need for revanchist strategies.[18] He warns that the FSB has taken over the tactics once used by the KGB, saying that it is "now operating straight out of the old KGB handbook."[19] He quotes Putin, "justifying Russia's unrestrained brutality in Chechnya":

It's like with a dog, you know. A dog senses when somebody is afraid of it, and bites. The same applies here. If you become jittery, they will think that they are stronger. Only one thing works in such circumstances—to go on the offensive. You must hit first, and hit so hard that your opponent will not rise to his feet.[20]

He blames Putin and his "reconfigured version of Russian exceptionalism" for the new Cold War," calling him "the upstart KGB opportunist who has exploited the fears and disappointments of the Russian people in order to satisfy his despotic impulse *and* resuscitate the darkest aspects of Russian history: imperial ambition and xenophobia."[21] Dave Majumdar, writing for the *National Interest*, opens his comments by stating, "With relations at the lowest point in decades, the United States and Russia have embarked on what appears to be a new Cold War," and then argues that "it is a new conflict—but one that is rooted in the ashes of the old struggle between the United States and the Soviet Union."[22] He suggests that the war started after the events in Ukraine in 2014, Syria in 2015, and the United Kingdom in 2018, all places that threaten a country whose geography makes its borders difficult to defend, except by extending them. Edward Lucas puts the blame for the new Cold War directly on Putin while placing its start at a time before Putin took leadership. In the 2008 version of his book, he reports, "My shorthand term for the new era of uneasy confrontation between the West and the Kremlin is the New Cold War."[23]

No matter when it started or how, most analysts agree that the new Cold War has the potential to be more dangerous than the first Cold War. After all, between the first and second Cold Wars are decades of great change, especially in technological developments, spawning new applications of artificial intelligence, including social media as well as hacking, allowing the surreptitious and remote manipulation of any system electronically. It is true, however, that the new Cold War depends on what Lucas identifies as "a tactic from the last Cold War: 'admit nothing, deny everything, make counter-allegations.'"[24]

Rather than a focus on conventional military operations, the new confrontation, Majumdar warns, will be "over the long term." He further warns that "deeply insecure" Russia is "much more prone to acting provocatively than the Soviet Union was during much of the original Cold War." He then argues that "the Kremlin focuses on achieving its victories though [*sic*] political warfare, special operations, and other indirect means."[25] Dadak asserts, "Russia is unprepared to fight a modern, high-technology war," citing the Russian military's lack of conventional warfare equipment, but also its "significant weaknesses in command, control, and communication."[26] These conditions explain Russia's logic in pursuing digital-sabotage tactics rather than building military power. Lind points out that in addition to nuclear posturing, "Cold War II is also underway in the realms of espionage and sabotage.... The United States is threatened by cyberattacks from Russia and China, as well as Iran and North Korea."[27]

Cold War II, then, despite its few major military events, has strong ideological impacts, with indirect consequences both in Russia and abroad. After summarizing how the new Cold War is "shaping up to be every bit as dangerous as the old one," pointing to recent actions of US and Russian militaries, Katrina vanden Heuvel, writing in the April 30/May 7, 2018, edition of *The Nation*, details how "Cold wars are bad for progressives. They empower the military-industrial complex and the worst forces on both sides. Nationalist fervor rises, diplomacy is sidelined, and the space for dissent closes," with the result that "Cold War tensions have been used to suppress independent voices in that country."[28] "That country," in this case, is Russia. Lucas amplifies these ideas by arguing that "the Kremlin's propaganda reflects its ideology, in which Russia is the champion of cherished, age-old values, beset by a sinister and decadent West."[29] Dadak points out that "the present-day Russian nationalist movement has a close relationship with the Orthodox Church. Putin intensely promotes membership in this congregation, and many of his closest collaborators show affinity for this church. This affiliation can be an attractive way to mobilize ethnic Russians around Putin's United Russia Party."[30] He details how the "Russian political structure is highly centralized and run by a small number of people not held accountable for their decisions because ... the judiciary is subordinated to the government." He then draws the conclusion that "Russia has reverted to the czarist system—all decisions are made by the president, and other top institutions depend on him."[31] Lind even goes a step further in diagnosing the crisis: "Some claim that Cold War II involves global ideological struggle pitting liberal democracy against a new authoritarianism, symbolized by Vladimir Putin and Xi Jinping—and Donald Trump."[32] He goes on to say that because of the "long-term rise of China and the diffusion of wealth and power from the West[, which] inevitably diminished American influence ... the United States enjoyed only a brief window of opportunity to shape a world to American values and interest."[33] Even within the US pundits debate whether or not America has similarly entered a new era of American authoritarianism at the expense of democracy and individual freedom.

It is the ideology of the second Cold War and its resulting social consequences that *Red Sparrow* so well addresses, by showing that the sociopolitical beliefs of Russia and the US, and the ways those beliefs are integrated into the two cultures, are much more similar than different. For the purposes of this essay, Lucas's careful analysis of the new Cold War tactics will be employed because of its thoroughness in considering the indirect social consequences of Putin's "threat to the West." In the 2014 introduction to his revised book,

Lucas details how "the old Cold War will not return ... analogies with it are anachronistic and outdated."[34] He further describes how Russia has fallen "into the hands of those driven by selfish desire for money and power, not an idealistic desire to make their country prosperous and free," doing so as "the intelligence and security services came creeping back from the shadows, bringing their own Soviet-era values and habits: authoritarianism and xenophobia."[35] He states that "the real threat is a different one. . . . The New Cold War is fought with cash, natural resources, diplomacy and propaganda."[36] He notes the oppressiveness: "The Kremlin is always right. At home, any challenge, any resistance, will be crushed by brute force of money and the levers of state power."[37] He bemoans the lack of reaction to the country's corruption, which he terms "the lack of a public fuss about official crookedness," and pronounces that "the ideological conflict of the New Cold War is between lawless Russian nationalism and law-governed Western multilateralism."[38] Comparing Putin to Yuri Andropov, he claims,

> Like Andropov, Mr Putin believes that ruthless discipline is the key to economic recovery. Like him, he places great weight on the use of the secret police, both to collect information and to intimidate opponents and backsliders. Like him, he believes that the West is both weak and hypocritical and can be easily faced down with a mixture of threats and selective arm-twisting.[39]

The importance of the film's commentary on contemporary authoritarian ideology for a US audience is evident in its prerelease. Two weeks before its March 2, 2018, release, *Red Sparrow* premiered at the Newseum in Washington, DC. The Newseum is much more than a museum featuring exhibits on news reporting; rather, it is also a venue housing a 501(c)(3) public charity with the mission "to increase public understanding of the importance of a free press and the First Amendment."[40] Its educational programming includes interactive exhibits and a free online platform. That the Newseum premiered *Red Sparrow* confirms the film's importance in educating its audience about US politics in the second Cold War, an audience largely still steeped in first Cold War tactics both on and off the screen.

Lingering First Cold War Nostalgia

American audiences, for generations schooled in Cold War tactics both from news sources and pop culture, including books and films, have grown to expect more conventional measures for achieving world dominance, so they may feel that they can ignore the current disruptive behaviors. Through a variety of manipulative tactics, Russia is undermining its competitors psychologically to make them more vulnerable. *Red Sparrow* challenges US audiences to emerge from their blindness to see the power shift. It does so subtly, ironically by first introducing the audience to traditional tropes from the Cold War genre, including various Russian settings that might reassure an audience that the Soviet ethos still undercuts the current Russian society.

 The opening montage consists of shots shifting back and forth between Dominika, a Russian, and Nate Nash, who, we later learn, is a CIA operative. Both are in Moscow, but the scene cuts introduce ambiguity that may at first confuse the audience as to who is experiencing what. Because the viewer has no context for each of the characters' actions, we cannot fully interpret them. The effect is to see these characters living parallel lives, even though they live different ideologies, at least superficially. We see Dominika first privately, in her bedroom, listening to music on headphones; we learn later that she is rehearsing mentally for the ballet she will perform that evening at the Bolshoi. Next we see Nate in his apartment. He too is decoding abstract signals to make sense of them as he receives instructions from his Russian informant as to where to meet him. In the next two scenes, we see Dominika interrupted by her duty to her disabled mother, still domestic; this is paralleled by Nate, who has left his apartment for a café, eagerly checking for possible tails. Dominika leaves her apartment, the external scene shots revealing blocky Soviet-style architecture; the next shot is in the Bolshoi Theater of Russia, offering sharp contrast, with its imperial décor recalling the splendor of nineteenth-century czarist Russia. This scene is at odds with the previous scenes of domestic Dominika; her gray existence is as transformed as the vividness of her communist-red evening dress, the opulence of the Bolshoi, and the words of her uncle: "Tonight, you are the pride of Russia." This first sustained dialogue of the film introduces the audience to the tension in her life between the personal and public, as well as her loyalty as she pleases her uncle, Ivan Vladimirovich Egorov, who we later learn is the deputy director of the SVR. She reluctantly acquiesces to a photo with the plutocrat whom her uncle has introduced, even as the obviously married stranger crosses boundaries by inappropriately pressing his thumb into her bare back. The tension is heightened with the interspersed cuts of Nate, who also is now performing for his state, showing where his duty and values lie, as he prepares to meet his informant in Gorky Park, a place name that uses its effect on a US audience to recall the 1983 Cold War film of the same name, a thriller that traded on the common spy tropes of the first Cold War, especially in its bleak depictions of Soviet life in Moscow. We see Dominika performing as prima ballerina, her brilliant red costume once again in stark opposition to the gray costumes of the corps de ballet. The montage ends as both of the main characters encounter actions that go incredibly wrong: on stage Dominika's partner brutally knocks her down, leaving her leg at an unnatural angle, and Nate, in sight of his informant, fires a pistol to distract the police and then escapes on foot in a police chase through Moscow. Dominika is removed to a hospital, and Nate narrowly escapes to safety on US embassy property. The credits end and the film begins in earnest, with both characters forced into new identities: Dominika's broken leg has ended her career as ballerina, and with the compromise of his cover, Nate has lost the connection to his informant and must leave his Moscow posting.

Several months pass before the next scenes; however, both characters are still largely depicted against first Cold War backdrops. If a US audience watches only the scenery, we can be comforted by a Russia that has not emerged from its Soviet stupor. A long shot of Dominika shows her walking with a cane, surrounded by the blocky gray buildings of Moscow housing both government offices and civilian apartments. After a domestic scene in her apartment, we are returned to the Bolshoi stage. However, this time we are in the dark shadows, watching a rehearsal, and then in the steamy grayness of the women's locker room. The subsequent scenes—a shot on a commuter train, a call from a pay phone, another shot of her apartment, and the boxy buildings where she meets her uncle—all contribute to the feeling of everyday dullness. Even the contrast of the splendor of the hotel decorated in lavish imperial style and Dominika's beaded dress is strikingly reassuring in response to any of our thoughts of post-Soviet Russian excess, thoughts that are reinforced by scenes at the SVR headquarters. Its bleak Soviet style reinforces expectations that the SVR is, after all, just an updated KGB with another acronym.

Current terminology for the Russian military services, as well as their scope of power, may be yet another unknown for a US audience. Among others, successors to the KGB include the SVR, which oversees external operations, including intelligence and espionage activities. Appointing the directors of each agency, the president of Russia ultimately directs the organization, which is responsible to him. *Red Sparrow* focuses on the SVR, whose members' identities, including staff, informers, and agents, are protected by secrecy. The powers are far-reaching, as Lucas explains:

> The FSB, which was once restricted to dealing with security threats inside Russia, now has a full legal license to operate abroad. As well as promoting disinformation and manipulating public life, these two agencies [including the SVR] and the GRU all try to penetrate the central institutions of state in the ex-Soviet countries.[41]

Of the scenes that might inspire nostalgia for the old notions of the Soviets in the first Cold War, perhaps the most striking emotionally is the one that follows those just described: when Dominika is on her way to the State School 4, the Sparrow training school. In the gray of a snowstorm, a panoramic shot of a snow-covered, absolutely flat field, the horizon in the far distance is only broken by the two straight wheel tracks left by the solitary car. For an American audience, the landscape invokes similar scenes from *Doctor Zhivago*, a 1965 film depicting the received ethos of the Russian Revolution: individual sacrifice at the expense of the state. These expectations are reinforced as we next see the car arriving at the prerevolutionary country manor that has been converted into a massive governmental institution, now run-down and snow-covered. The dark sandstone of the entrance, contrasted with the otherwise white exterior, invokes the repurposing of aristocratic structures by the Soviets to serve the state by housing the masses in overcrowded tenements. The mansion's classical style suggests formalism's emphasis of form over content, of ritual and rules trumping meaning and truth. The architectural shots reconfirm what many in a US audience may believe, that "Russia is still living off the conscripted brilliance and perverse sacrifices of the past."[42]

These strong images are reassuring for an American audience harboring almost romantic recollections of the Cold War: after all, it was the West that won with the fall of the Berlin Wall and the dismantling of the Soviet empire. If the audience is paying attention to the plot and the characterization of Dominika, however, they are being challenged to shift away from their comfort to notice the differences in what is motivating the individual Russians. The tension created against the almost romantic backdrop depicts the reality of contemporary Russia and the second Cold War, a reality that differs significantly from received notions held by many in the US.

Cold War Redux: "A Thousand Different Pieces"

Analysis of the plot of these scenes shows that difference. In the first, the long shot shows gray buildings, but the close-up shows Dominika smoking a cigarette, indicating her complete acceptance that her dance career has ended. Although the audience understands that she has come to terms with the loss of her career, they learn that she has yet to negotiate the loss of her protection by the state. Not only has the Bolshoi provided the apartment for Dominika and her mother; her mother's medical care has also been paid for by the state. The external shot is followed by a domestic scene as her uncle compliments Dominika for her determination to recover: she is walking much sooner than the doctors had predicted. We learn that he has not been involved with Dominika or her mother since her father's death, underscoring the lack of support they must endure but also making it clear that he is related to her by her father and so has little interest in the welfare of her mother, only in how it influences Dominika's actions. To lead her into his control, he reveals that the accident that ended her career was intentional. Further manipulating her, he reassures her that "I've come to help," yet he reminds her that the apartment rental and her mother's medical coverage, both paid for by the Bolshoi, will soon be curtailed. As he leaves her an envelope, the contents of which will incriminate both her dance partner and her replacement, he claims, "There are no accidents; we create our own fate," words that will prove to have stinging verbal irony for all of the main characters in the film, and even for its audience.

After Dominika and the audience review the photographs and experience the incriminating conversations recorded on a burner phone, we realize that her previous partner and her replacement, who she now knows are lovers, successfully carried out a premeditated "accident" while she was performing live, intentionally breaking her leg and ending her professional career. In the next several scenes, the plot becomes seemingly predictable in its use of violence, employing Cold War techniques of brutality to depict revenge: we see Dominika in the women's locker room of the Bolshoi Theater, bludgeoning with a golf club the two dancers who have ruined her career. At first we may misunderstand her character, seeing her as motivated by selfishness, jealousy, and revenge because her uncontrolled actions display the violence we expect. However, rather than seeing the attack as predictably "Soviet," the audience must consider how deeply she has been wounded. Because her injury during the ballet was not accidental but an attack by her partner, the audience can best understand the film's point by appreciating the enormity of the breach of trust, a key part of the relationship between the principal dancers, that the attack signifies. Not only has she lost her career, which is her livelihood and her means of caring for her disabled mother, the attack has shattered the basic values of the ballet—values she had internalized, which depend on individual and collective strength and trust.

In the ensuing train scene, the blood on her hands that reminds her of who she is, how she has trained, and what her career means, so she disembarks to find a public phone to anonymously call in the attack. She is a trained professional from the beginning, and that training instills the values most US audiences would consider traditionally American: hard work, individual exceptionalism, and trust in the system and the values it incorporates. After all, she is trained as a ballerina, and she is so successful that she has earned prima ballerina status at the Bolshoi Ballet, a company that enjoys one of the foremost reputations in the world for its training of dancers. For the careful viewer, the film, in its development of the motivations of Dominika, has begun its argument that warns the audience that it must be careful in its assumptions, just as the world needs to evaluate its assumptions carefully. We must let go of dated notions of the Cold War and instead recognize how Cold War II is being fought. What becomes important is the role of the individual in that fight.

When Dominika returns to her apartment, her mother is lying on the floor, and we learn that the Bolshoi has formally withdrawn its support. It is then that the audience should consider the new Russian values as enumerated by Lucas:

> The dominant value is not freedom but economic stability, protected not by the rule of law, but by strong government. Consensus replaces the electoral mandate. The powers that be are accountable to history, not to the citizenry. Opposition is disloyalty at best, and outright treason if it is supported from abroad. The individual is a means to an end, not a bearer of inalienable rights; justice is a tool, not an ideal. The mass media are an instrument of state, not a constraint on its power. Civil society is an instrument for social consolidation, not diversity. Property rights and contract are conditional; foreign policy is solely about the promotion of national interest. Intervention to protect human rights is hypocrisy. The *raison d'état* rules.[43]

True, we do not know yet how worldly and experienced Dominika is; however, her uncle, who represents the government, uses both her weaknesses as well as her strengths. He uses the strength of their emotional bond as well as her weakness in needing to provide housing and medical care for her mother to entrap her into once again being a pawn for the government, saying, "You can stay in your apartment as long as I can show that you are of value to the state."[44]

When her uncle sends her to her first assignment in the grand opulence of the hotel, the plutocrat's words sting as he dispels the American myth of the self-made individual: "My father died at forty-three and left us with nothing; now I could buy this place. Is this just luck?" Dominika agrees: "There is no such thing as luck." We see her depart from the script she has been given to embrace one of exceptionalism: even before attaining eminence as a dancer, she recognized that she is not like other people, that she is special. The plutocrat's attraction to her is perverse in his fascination with her scar, an imperfection that he calls "a crack in the vase." The blood we witness in the ensuing murder is virginal, not that of her sexuality or hers at all; however, for her uncle's purposes, the stronger blood tie is her complicity in the murder. In Cold War II, it is this blood tie that binds, not one of relation, despite his continuous sentimental reminders to her of their experiences together during her childhood.

His appeal to their relationship generates dramatic irony because, in fact, it is his sentimentality that blinds him to her true motivations. For him, as with the plutocrat, she has become a commodity, one valuable for the Russian state because Uncle Ivan knows that she understands manipulation: "You have potential, great potential.... You told him what he wanted to hear."[45] He offers her the opportunity to make herself better with hard work, a system over which she has mastery, which others do not yet recognize. In fact, the film copies the modus operandi of the Kremlin. As Lucas concludes after reporting a string of murders attributed to the Kremlin, "The message of all of this is 'be quiet.' If you annoy the rich and powerful, you face threats, beatings, or death."[46] Her uncle is emblematic of what Lucas describes as "the Kremlin's diet of crony capitalism and secret police rule."[47] Instead of offering Dominika freedom through individual choice or self-determination, her uncle offers her his coin in trade. Without understanding her true values, which she honed in the ballet, he reinforces his own values of cronyism with his offer to send her to Sparrow school to learn how to work secretly against Russia's opponents. Dominika, however, remains true to her values, rejecting the corruption of her uncle. The first clue that this will happen is her mother's advice, shown in a flashback after the *Doctor Zhivago*-like snow scene. In contrast to that scene, which many would argue recalls individual sacrifice, her mother says, "You hold something back. Don't give him all of you." Despite the fact that Dominika is told repeatedly that she does not own herself and that her life always has belonged to the government, she has learned to assert her individuality.

After all, she is not an inexperienced young woman, but an established prima ballerina, one who has been perfected by years of training—both intrinsically and extrinsically motivated—to be a paragon of persistence, discipline, and obedience to her art. The opening scene of the film has introduced us to that person; however, it is before the credits and followed by the splendor of the Bolshoi Ballet and her ensuing accident, which is coupled with the tense scene in Gorky Park and Nate's ensuing narrow escape to the US embassy. The tension of both the ballet sequence and the Gorky Park sequence serves to erase the opening shots from the audiences' memories, scenes that include the discipline of her bedroom meditation, when she mentally rehearses her every ballet movement while listening to the music on her headphones. Before the two life-changing incidents, the audience witnesses the sweeping grandeur of the ballet, performed in the renowned Bolshoi Theater of Russia with its imperial Russian décor and the ornateness of the classical costumes. We experience the artistry of Dominika as a prima ballerina, whose mastery of skills has far surpassed that needed to be in the corps de ballet, as evidenced by her superiority contrasted with the younger, less experienced ballerinas in their troupe, fading to the background in their gray, military-colored costumes, serving as foil to her prima ballerina role and her red tutu. Psychologically, the strict discipline of the ballet has taught her to compete not only with others, but also with herself.

Furthermore, her status as the prima ballerina for the Bolshoi invites the audience to make inferences about her classical ballet training at the Bolshoi Ballet Academy, with all that such classical ballet training entails, beginning at age two to four: rigorous dance exercises, which train and strengthen all of her muscle groups; music theory, which shapes her sense of timing; history of the ballet, which includes its complex political aspects mirroring Russian history; acting methodology, which includes character development and understanding motivation, teaching her to subvert her emotions in favor of that of the role she is portraying. Above all else, classical ballet training demands that a ballerina learn what might be the most difficult lesson: trust. She must learn to surrender herself to her partner and trust that she will be supported and caught during complex movements, including lifts, jumps, and difficult poses. Before the action of the film starts, Dominika has already mastered all of these physical, mental, and emotional strengths.

Therefore, when Dominika goes to Sparrow school, the Matron's mistaken appraisal of Dominika's situation as being one of catch-up is almost believable. With her prior training in mind, the appraisal is a clear miscalculation of Dominika's potential. The Matron, knowledgeable of the cronyism of Dominika's uncle in landing her there, challenges her, saying, "You're not like our usual recruits; most of them come from the military with training already. You'll have to work hard to catch up."[48] Rather, her training at Sparrow school is an issue of adapting her ballet training, which in some ways may be superior. Indeed, as a prima ballerina, she has learned to trust herself as an individual and become a paragon of idealized behavior.

It is during the Sparrow school scenes that—if an American audience is paying close attention—we begin to understand that Russia's way of fighting in the Cold War has changed. Instead of depending on conventional military might with large standing armies and expensive weaponry, it now largely avoids direct armed conflict, instead using targeted attacks with artificial intelligence and other less costly strategies, such as the Sparrows, to destabilize other governments. A Red Sparrow, like the common sparrow (which on its own seems powerless, if even noticed, but in large flocks, with persistence, can devastate crops) promises to be an especially effective weapon because it can be used with precision to undermine a particular enemy target. The Sparrow school's ideology is encapsulated in the Matron's classroom lectures: "The Cold War did not end; it shattered into a thousand different pieces."[49] She explains:

The West has grown weak, drunk on shopping and social media, torn apart by hatred between the races, and as a result is in chaos. Only Russia is willing to make the sacrifices required for victory. For there to be peace, we must once again place ourselves at the head of nations. From this day forward, you will become Sparrows, weapons in a global struggle for power.[50]

The "normal" expectations for recruit training include "psychological manipulation," training that allows a Sparrow "to determine a target's weakness, to exploit that weakness through seduction to extract information." Recruits are told, "Your body belongs to the state. Since your birth, the state nourished it; now the state asks something in return. You must learn to sacrifice for a higher goodness, to push yourself beyond all limitation."[51] The Russian government is shown over and over again to take a whole person's life—not those of Sparrows, but also spies, and even ballerinas in the state-run arts program.

However, this message is something that Dominika has learned through her prior experience at the Bolshoi and with her uncle. She makes that knowledge abundantly clear in Sparrow school during the scenes that contain nudity or sexual acts, scenes that critics have misunderstood, taking them only as gratuitous sexualization. When she refuses to strip, the Matron tells her, "You must sacrifice for a higher goodness, to push yourself beyond all limitation, and forget the sentimentality with which you were raised."[52] Dominika's refusal is not out of unwillingness to sacrifice but out of self-preservation. She understands that an intact self is more important than blind obedience.

Dominika avoids being sexualized, subverting the Sparrow school teachings for her own individual good. The Matron has preached to "forget the sentimentality with which you were raised." Obviously, Dominika has already done so; however, when ordered to seduce a soldier who is home on leave, she chooses a young man, a "boy," and by being "sweet, sentimental, maintains control."[53] The latter appraisal comes begrudgingly from the Matron, who has begun to recognize Dominika's individualism.

When Dominika later strips in front of the class, offering herself for sex with a classmate, she has beaten the Matron at her own game. The Matron has instructed the class, "Every human being is a puzzle of need. You must learn to intuit what is missing. Become the missing piece and they will give you anything."[54] Dominika knows that her classmate does not want sex; he wants power over her and so her offering of sex will be refused. The scene, rather than showcasing nudity and sexual acts for prurience or for their own sake, conveys her power as she undermines the state's authority. She has already violently beaten the classmate for his unwanted advances in the shower, and now she subverts her punishment. When she is questioned in front of the Matron and

General Korchnoi—"And your honor is worth depriving Russia of a promising cadet?"—the answer is clear to everyone in the room. She "has potential" even after "only three months in Sparrow school."⁵⁵ What she has learned is not from the training-scene montage showing jogging, target shooting, lock picking, and using invisible chemical-tracking compounds, nor from watching pornography. She has claimed her individual identity, honed in the Bolshoi and reinforced by her long-held belief in her own exceptionalism. She is not representative of the Russian values that the World Council of Russian People enumerated in 2006, as reported by Lucas:

> The Council took particular exception to the focus on individual rights, which it blamed for both moral relativism and the deprival of the interests of others. "There are values that are no less important than human rights," the concluding statement said. "These are faith, ethics, [national] sacraments, Fatherland."⁵⁶

When told that she is leaving Sparrow school, Dominika misunderstands the motivation and says, "I have done everything you asked of me." The Matron replies, "On the contrary, you have done nothing I've asked, but my superiors think otherwise."⁵⁷ Dominika has become a freethinking individual, yet she is able to act ambiguously, reserving something for herself, as her mother coached her, though appearing to conform to the government's ethos.

Back at her Moscow apartment, she spends only a few minutes with her mother before her uncle summons her. He thinks he owns her, still playing the sentimental game by taking her to a restaurant she loved as a child. She, however, is not playing games and asks him directly, "What do you want, Uncle?" a question that the audience now knows is meaningless because she already knows the answer. He also knows that she understands him all too well, even though he doesn't act accordingly. He tells her that the "whore school," as she calls it, has "made you special again. You have a gift, like me. You see through people; you see them for who they really are; and you always stay one step ahead. Do this for me, and I'll let you go if you want; I feel you won't. This is what you were meant to do."⁵⁸ He mistakenly believes that her motivations are similar to his own.

The film reconfirms traditionally held beliefs about Russians. The beliefs are startlingly similar to those that Lucas attributes to agents in the former KGB:

> They harbored a sense of great superiority over the shabby, humdrum and ill-informed lives of the ordinary citizen. For many, that sense was stoked by special training in psychological tricks: how to manipulate strangers, to gain their trust or break their resistance. The result was more like a cult than a government bureaucracy: omniscient, omnipresent and omnipotent.⁵⁹

What the US audience should recognize, however, is that Dominika's strength as an individual is not because of anything learned at the Sparrow school. She has always known that she is special, and it has been reinforced through her rigorous training and life experience.

In that regard, Dominika turns out to be much more in line with Americans' idea of themselves: freethinking, preserving herself at the cost of the state, doing the "right" thing. She achieves what Americans would consider to be the traditional order, where good should overcome evil, even if it means becoming selfish, betraying family, and bending what it means to be a patriot. She has internalized the "American" values of putting individualism and family first, questioning big government, and trusting few individual relationships. She may operate in the SVR world with the same wiliness that her uncle does; however, she does so not for loyalty to the state or to patriarchal family, but for loyalty to herself and to her mother. She has already promised her mother that she will find a way to get away from her uncle, and the rest of the film is largely her plan to do so put into action. Unwittingly, he has heightened her individual agency by giving her new credentials, a new passport, and a new name. He has empowered her further by ordering her to get close to Nate Nash so that she will discover the mole within the SVR. Knowledge is power, and Dominika acts to gain that power and then use it to her own advantage.

Waging the Second Cold War

The remainder of the film largely takes place outside of Russia. Repeatedly, we see Dominika applying the lessons that she has learned throughout her life as she puts into action a plan to free herself from her uncle. An audience already trained to consider the film as a second Cold War vehicle will not be taken in by the ambiguity of her actions. Although she is seemingly in accord with the Russian government, she is acting on her own plan, which will ultimately benefit not only her own individual values but also those claimed by American viewers. We see her seeming to erase her identity by becoming a blonde because that is what attracts Nate. Yet, she keeps her true name and trusts no one, including her roommate, who is also a Russian Sparrow, and her immediate supervisor, who is blatantly out for sex to compensate for his own inadequacy. Even though she befriends the American, becoming his lover, she keeps herself emotionally distant, even passing a lie detector test as she supposedly defects to the American side. What allows her success is her ability to read what others lack and to give it to them, sometimes even when they do not want it.

For American audiences, the biggest issue in the second half of *Red Sparrow* may be the torture scene, with its excessive violence. The brutality in the face of an otherwise socially intelligent message cannot be excused as we encounter the sadism of the torturer, who seems to derive pleasure from violence, which is not just a business for him.

However violent, it is a successful plot device: the outcome of the torture scene is that both Dominika and Nate are hospitalized, making it possible for the mole in the Russian government to communicate with her face-to-face without compromising himself to anyone but her. Politics have seemingly pitted them against each other, but the audience is able to see them not as traitors but as fighters against political ideologies that they commonly abhor. Consequently, by doing what might commonly be considered bad, each is fighting against evil for the good of the common person and for themselves. Dominika is doing so primarily for her own good; the mole is doing so primarily for the good of his ideal of his country, and now at great expense to himself, as he has made himself vulnerable to her.

Through Dominika and Nate's interaction and its aftermath, the audience must examine what constitutes patriotism and what sacrifice they would personally be willing to make to preserve their country. They must consider whether a person can maintain individually aligned notions of morality rather than commonly held ideas of morality. They must also reason out for themselves what circumstances allow an individual to break laws if a larger good is served. Several times throughout the film, Dominika is asked, "Are you a patriot?"[60] As an audience, we have to ask what that means. Thus, rather than viewing this second Cold War narrative as solely detailing the corruption of the Russian government, the viewer becomes aware of a narrative centering on America's values. In fact, it is more about American values, as we realize that Dominika embodies ideals of freedom. As Lucas claims, "The paradox is that so many Russians seemingly want to live in a system that curtails their freedom" despite having lived under the Soviet system for nearly eight decades.[61]

In her quest to attain personal freedom while keeping her mother safe, Dominika's actions at first seem to abrogate individualism, patriotism, and duty to family, and the US audience is forced to examine her motives and in the process to question their own. Dominika does manipulate those around her to escape her uncle and preserve her mother's well-being. However, because of her respect for the value of trust, she also preserves the mole's identity and her love for Nate. In the process, however, her government recognizes her for being a true Russian patriot. Ironically, she has earned the designation by doing what she has always done best: telling people what they want to hear and fighting for her own individual freedom.

Ultimately, the film raises questions about the process of perceiving which reality is valid. It becomes a problem of perception: the world seems black and white, but in the manner of the first Cold War comic strip *Spy vs. Spy* (1961–), which ambiguously dressed the two spies in black or white, making it impossible to identify either one—or his ethos—as being "the good guy" or "the bad guy." Our own methods of observing reality are questioned. The second wave of Cold War films demonstrates how our view can be clouded by the confusion caused by the shifting forms of power from within both the Russian government and our own. We can no longer hold onto outdated notions of power or how power is expressed. Instead of expecting the strong physical threat of traditional warfare created by the communist government of the first Cold War or by the chaos of plutocracy and mobsterism in the interim, we have to recognize that the current Cold War uses tactics created by Vladimir Putin's brand of fascism, which insidiously destabilize what we want to hold as constants.

Red Sparrow also raises questions about whether or not the two cultures are as separate as traditional Cold War films have depicted, or whether the true nature of our obsession is that we are more alike in our willingness to sacrifice our patriotism to uphold strongly held ideas of democratic nobility and ultimately of the nation. Rather than serving solely as a critique of current Russian politics in its evolution from plutocracy to dictatorship of Putin, *Red Sparrow* critiques current US politics as well. For both, the situation is no longer about wealth, even wealth concentrated in the hands of a few, but about concentrated power, which can lead to abuse and corruption, especially after achieving full control.

Corruption: Disruption of the Individual or the Whole?

Corruption, the disruption of other systems for individual benefit, looms large. However, not only is the US audience largely unaware of how Russia's Cold War tactics have changed, it is also unaware of how its ideas about American identity have become encoded in US politics. Peter Beinart upholds his argument that Trump supporters are more afraid of the corruption of what they *perceive* as American traditional values than corruption of the law itself. He does so by arguing about how "corruption" is defined, citing a quotation from *How Fascism Works* by Jason Stanley, a Yale University philosophy professor:

> Corruption, to the fascist politician, is really about the corruption of purity rather than of the law. Officially, the fascist politician's denunciations of corruption sound like a denunciation of political corruption. But such talk is intended to evoke corruption in the sense of the usurpation of the traditional order.[62]

Red Sparrow so missed the mark with its US audience, however, that a perceptive critic might have to wonder if the Sparrow school Matron has it right about the American public: "The West has grown weak, drunk on shopping and social media, torn apart by hatred between the races, and as a result is in chaos."[63] Has America become self-obsessed, consumed with social media and shopping and ignoring larger truths? Lucas comments:

> Russia is reverting to Soviet behaviour at home and abroad, and in its contemptuous disregard for Western norms. Yet the outside world has been inattentive and complacent, partly thanks to greed and wishful thinking, and partly because of serious distractions elsewhere. Western public opinion and policymakers alike find it hard to focus on more than one or two problems at a time.[64]

After all, "Mr Putin has swung from citing Western countries as objects of envy to denouncing the West for hypocrisy and arrogance."[65]

The US audience, through the abstract experience of watching the film, is meant to question its direct experience with corruption, looking past traditional notions of identity to understand the dire effects of corrupting American law. As Lucas asserts, "The foundation of freedom is justice."[66] The real message, then, of *Red Sparrow* for its US audience is to safeguard our systems of justice so that the individual does not have to safeguard them for herself. Just as Lucas argues, "It is one thing for the authorities of a corrupt country to misuse the legal system to grab assets and imprison opponents. It would be dismal indeed if they were indirectly helped in this by those who are meant to be the international guardians of financial integrity."[67] Lucas sets up the real problem:

> If you don't believe that capitalism is a system in which money matters more than freedom, you are doomed when people who don't believe in freedom attack using money. Russia has spotted that the weakest link in the Western approach to life is inattention to the moral and ethical basis of capitalism: if only money matters, then why is the Kremlin's money worse than anyone else's?[68]

We may be able to agree with his statement that "a truly stable system is also a transparent one, where people outside politics can easily see what is going on. In Russia political decision-making is shrouded in secrecy, and abrupt changes ... prompt agitated speculation about the Kremlin's real intentions."[69] Yet, are we able to grasp the true state of our own government? *Red Sparrow* insists that we take responsibility for our own freedom despite what the government and popular opinion insist.

If nothing else, the film, when closely examined, develops a tension to accept a more realistic worldview, one that is urgently needed. As Lucas concludes his 2014 introduction by summarizing the situation:

In short: the West is losing the New Cold War, while having barely noticed that it has started. Mr. Putin and his allies have seized power in Russia, cast a dark shadow over the eastern half of the continent, and established formidable bridgeheads in the main Western countries. And the willingness to resist looks alarmingly feeble.[70]

The words of Dominika's uncle resound: "There are no accidents; we create our own fate."[71]

Notes

1. Peter Beinart, "Why Trump Supporters Believe He Is Not Corrupt," *The Atlantic*, August 22, 2018, https://www.theatlantic.com/ideas/archive/2018/08/what-trumps-supporters-think-of-corruption/568147/.
2. Francis Lawrence, *Red Sparrow* (Los Angeles: 20th Century Fox, 2017).
3. Rotten Tomatoes' page for *Red Sparrow*, accessed February 9, 2019, https://www.rottentomatoes.com/m/red_sparrow.
4. Rex Reed, "'Red Sparrow' Really Makes You Question Jennifer Lawrence's Career Choices," *Observer*, March 8, 2018, https://observer.com/2018/03/review-jennifer-lawrence-and-joel-edgerton-fizzle-in-red-sparrow/.
5. Armond White, "*Red Sparrow*'s Dirty Dossier Is Rotten at the Core," *National Review*, March 2, 2018, https://www.nationalreview.com/2018/03/red-sparrow-film-review-corrupt-core-loveless-exposes-hollywood-cynicism/.
6. Andrew Wyatt, "The Lens Review: *Red Sparrow*," Cinema St. Louis, March 1, 2018, https://www.cinemastlouis.org/the-lens/red-sparrow.
7. Filipe Freitas, "*Red Sparrow* (2018)," *Always Good Movies*, March 26, 2018, https://alwaysgoodmovies.com/reviews/2018/3/26/red-sparrow-2018.
8. Peter Rainer, "'Red Sparrow' Is All Grim Oppressiveness," *Christian Science Monitor*, March 2, 2018, https://www.csmonitor.com/The-Culture/Movies/2018/0302/Red-Sparrow-is-all-grim-oppressiveness.
9. Christy Lemire, "*Red Sparrow* (2018)," RogerEbert.com (website), March 2, 2018, https://www.rogerebert.com/reviews/red-sparrow-2018.
10. Lemire, "*Red Sparrow* (2018)."
11. Tomas Trussow, "*Red Sparrow* (Lawrence, 2018)," *The Lonely Film Critic*, October 17, 2018, https://thelonelyfilmcritic.com/?s=red+sparrow.
12. Charles McGrath, "Shadowing Jason Matthews, an Ex-Spy Whose Cover Identity Is Author," *New York Times*, May 27, 2015, https://www.nytimes.com/2015/05/28/books/shadowing-jason-matthews-the-ex-spy-whose-cover-identity-is-author.html.
13. Casimir Dadak, "A New 'Cold War'?," *Independent Review* 15, no. 1 (Summer 2010): 90.
14. Stephen F. Cohen, "Cold War Follies," *The Nation*, February 4, 2013, 7.

15. Cohen, "Cold War Follies," 8.
16. Cohen, "Cold War Follies," 8.
17. Michael Lind, "Welcome the Cold War II," *National Interest*, May/June 2018, 6.
18. Daryl McCann, "The Looming Prospect of a Second Cold War," *Quadrant*, June 2014, 5.
19. McCann, "The Looming Prospect of a Second Cold War," 6.
20. McCann, "The Looming Prospect of a Second Cold War," 9.
21. McCann, "The Looming Prospect of a Second Cold War," 10, italics in original.
22. Dave Majumdar, "The Rise of Russia's Military," *National Interest*, July/August 2018, 36.
23. Edward Lucas, *The New Cold War: Putin's Russia and the Threat to the West* (London: Palgrave Macmillan, 2009), 4.
24. Lucas, *The New Cold War*, 107.
25. Majumdar, "The Rise of Russia's Military," 40.
26. Dadak, "A New 'Cold War'?," 99.
27. Lind, "Welcome the Cold War II," 11.
28. Katrina vanden Heuvel, "Cold War II," *The Nation*, April 30/May 7, 2018, 3.
29. Lucas, *The New Cold War*, xix.
30. Dadak, "A New 'Cold War'?," 97.
31. Dadak, "A New 'Cold War'?," 101.
32. Lind, "Welcome the Cold War II," 14.
33. Lind, "Welcome the Cold War II," 16.
34. Lucas, *The New Cold War*, 7.
35. Lucas, *The New Cold War*, 8.
36. Lucas, *The New Cold War*, 13.
37. Lucas, *The New Cold War*, 17.
38. Lucas, *The New Cold War*, 18.
39. Lucas, *The New Cold War*, 20–21.
40. Newseum, "The Newseum's Mission," Newseum.org (website), accessed February 9, 2019, https://newseumed.org/newseums-mission.
41. Lucas, *The New Cold War*, 202.
42. Lucas, *The New Cold War*, 249.
43. Lucas, *The New Cold War*, 269–70, italics in original.
44. Lawrence, *Red Sparrow*.
45. Lawrence, *Red Sparrow*.
46. Lucas, *The New Cold War*, 84.
47. Lucas, *The New Cold War*, 173.
48. Lawrence, *Red Sparrow*.
49. Lawrence, *Red Sparrow*.
50. Lawrence, *Red Sparrow*.
51. Lawrence, *Red Sparrow*.
52. Lawrence, *Red Sparrow*.
53. Lawrence, *Red Sparrow*.
54. Lawrence, *Red Sparrow*.
55. Lawrence, *Red Sparrow*.
56. Lucas, *The New Cold War*, 137.
57. Lawrence, *Red Sparrow*.
58. Lawrence, *Red Sparrow*.
59. Lucas, *The New Cold War*, 26.

60. Lawrence, *Red Sparrow*.
61. Lucas, *The New Cold War*, 89.
62. Beinart, "Why Trump Supporters Believe He Is Not Corrupt."
63. Lawrence, *Red Sparrow*.
64. Lucas, *The New Cold War*, 3.
65. Lucas, *The New Cold War*, 154.
66. Lucas, *The New Cold War*, 93.
67. Lucas, *The New Cold War*, 126.
68. Lucas, *The New Cold War*, 130.
69. Lucas, *The New Cold War*, 120.
70. Lucas, *The New Cold War*, 22.
71. Lawrence, *Red Sparrow*.

ABOUT THE CONTRIBUTORS

Thomas J. Cobb completed his PhD at the University of Birmingham in 2018. His dissertation discussed how various American films during the late 1990s and the War on Terror allegorized contradictions within US foreign policy. The combination of international relations with film studies is central to Thomas's research, and he is currently under contract to write a monograph, titled *American Cinema and Cultural Diplomacy: The Fragmented Kaleidoscope*, for Palgrave Macmillan based on his thesis. He has published articles in *MHRA Working Papers in the Humanities* and *Film International*. Thomas currently works as an academic writing tutor at Coventry University.

Donna A. Gessell is professor of English at the University of North Georgia, where she teaches courses in linguistics, pedagogy, and literature, including courses on John Milton, Jane Austen, plague literature, and the literature of Australia and New Zealand. Her most recent publications include work on the fiction of Judith Ortiz Cofer, Gabriel García Márquez, and Flannery O'Connor, as well as a cowritten chapter in *The Routledge Handbook of Pacifism and Nonviolence*.

Helena Goscilo is professor of Slavic at the Ohio State University. She has written approximately one hundred articles on topics ranging from Soviet criminal tattoos to male fashion in the 1990s and the Polish operatic contralto Ewa Podleś. The twenty-plus volumes she has published include *TNT: The Explosive World of Tatyana Tolstaya's Fiction*, *Dehexing Sex*, *Preserving Petersburg: History, Memory, Nostalgia* (coedited with Stephen Norris), *Cinepaternity: Fathers and Sons in Soviet and Post-Soviet Film* (coedited with Yana Hashamova), *Putin as Celebrity and Cultural Icon* (coedited with Vlad Strukov), and *Fade from Red: Screening the Cold War Ex-Enemy, 1990–2005* (coauthored with Margaret Goscilo). Her current monographs are *Graphic Ideology: The Soviet Poster from Stalin to Yeltsin* and a study of contemporary Polish film cowritten with Beth Holmgren.

Cyndy Hendershot (1968–2020) was professor of English at Arkansas State University. She is the author of *The Animal Within: Masculinity and the Gothic* (University of Michigan Press), *Paranoia, the Bomb, and 1950s Science-Fiction Films* (University of Wisconsin Press), *The Cold War, Eroticism, and 1950s Horror Films* (University of Wisconsin Press), and *Anti-Communism at Mid-Century* (McFarland Press). She also wrote numerous articles on the Cold War and genre fiction and film.

Christian Jimenez has recently published "Cynical Toleration," in *Bonds of Brotherhood: Essays on Gender and Masculinity in Sons of Anarchy*, edited by Susan Fanetti (MacFarland, 2018), and "Strategies of Containment: Sexual Liberation and Repression in the Sci-Fi Genre in Cuarón's *Gravity* and Kubrick's *2001*," in *Women: Issues of Exclusion and Inclusion*, edited by Alka Singh (YKing, 2018). Future publications include encyclopedia entries "Al Jazeera" and "Framing," in *Conflict in the Modern Middle East: An Encyclopedia of War, Revolution and Regime Change*, edited by Jonathan K. Zartman, and "Cinema from World War II to 1980," in *Encyclopedia of African American Culture*, edited by Omari Dyson. His research interests include narrative, especially apocalyptic narrative, myth, gender, race, and transnational cinema.

David LaRocca is the author, editor, or coeditor of ten books, including *The Thought of Stanley Cavell and Cinema: Turning Anew to the Ontology of Film a Half-Century after The World Viewed*, *The Philosophy of War Films*, and *The Philosophy of Documentary Film: Image, Sound, Fiction, Truth*. He has held visiting research and teaching positions in cinema, English, and philosophy at Binghamton, Cornell, Cortland, Harvard, Ithaca College, and Vanderbilt and has participated in a National Endowment for the Humanities Institute, a workshop with Abbas Kiarostami, Werner Herzog's Rogue Film School, and the School of Criticism and Theory at Cornell University. More information is available at www.DavidLaRocca.org.

Lori Maguire is professor of British and American studies at the University of Paris 8 (Vincennes-St. Denis). She has published extensively both in French and English. Her main focus has been on the political history and foreign policy of Britain and the United States as well as on the presentation of the Cold War in popular culture. Her most recent book is *The Cold War and Entertainment*

Television (Cambridge Scholars, 2016). She is currently working on a new project on France and the American war in Indochina.

Tatiana Prorokova-Konrad is a postdoctoral researcher in the Department of English and American Studies, University of Vienna, Austria. Her current project examines representations of the environment and climate change in fiction since the Industrial Revolution. She holds a PhD in American studies from the University of Marburg, Germany, a European joint master's degree in English and American studies from the University of Bamberg, Germany, and a teaching degree in English and German from Ryazan State University, Russia. She was an Ebeling Fellow at the American Antiquarian Society (2018) and a visiting scholar at the University of South Alabama, USA (2016). Her research interests include war studies, ecocriticism, gender studies, and race studies and are reflected in her publications in academic journals and edited collections. She is the author of *Docu-Fictions of War: U.S. Interventionism in Film and Literature* (University of Nebraska Press, 2019) and a coeditor of *Cultures of War in Graphic Novels: Violence, Trauma, and Memory* (Rutgers University Press, 2018).

Ian Scott is senior lecturer in American studies at the University of Manchester. He is the author of numerous books, including *American Politics in Hollywood Film*, 2nd ed. (Edinburgh University Press, 2011), and *The Cinema of Oliver Stone: Art, Authorship and Activism* (Manchester University Press, 2016), coauthored with Henry Thompson. As well as writing extensively on political movies and Hollywood's relationship with Washington, he also works in documentary film, and his first collaboration with Docdays Productions in Berlin, *Projections of America*, won awards and appeared at various film festivals and on television throughout the world during 2015–17. A book of the film, *A Better Tomorrow: Transatlantic World War II Propaganda*, is currently being finished. He is also currently writing a brand-new radio series for BBC Radio 4 looking at Hollywood and California that will be broadcast in 2020.

Vesta Silva is associate professor in the Department of Communication Arts at Allegheny College. Her work focuses primarily on questions of power and authority in public discourse, including ideas about race, health, science, and policy in the contemporary US.

Lucian Țion is a theater studies PhD candidate in his final year at the National University of Singapore. His research interests include East European cinema, Chinese cinema, and postcolonial/nationalism studies. His PhD thesis explores the similarities and contrasts between East European and Chinese cinemas in the socialist and the postsocialist eras. His articles have been published in *Studies in Eastern European Cinema, Senses of Cinema, East European Film Bulletin,* and *Acta Universitatis Sapientiae: Film and Media Studies.*

Dan Ward is lecturer in media & cultural studies at the University of Sunderland. His PhD focused on representations of masculinity in US crime drama, and his previous publications include work on sports documentaries, fantasy TV, and the use of social media in contemporary Hollywood stardom.

Jon Wiebel is assistant professor in the Department of Communication Arts at Allegheny College. His work focuses on American politics and culture, particularly related to questions of immigration policy, nationalism, and identity.

INDEX

abjection, 87
action heroine, 20, 112, 113, 118, 120
aesthetics, 5, 18, 19, 20, 69n51, 90n15, 93, 95–99, 101–8, 110n23, 116, 117, 123, 125, 208, 217, 221n32
Afghanistan War, 9, 33, 47nn22–25
Air Force One (1997), 3, 58
al-Nusra Front, 124
al-Qaeda, 33, 124
Alias (2001–6), 118
aliens, 11, 112, 166, 168, 178
All That Heaven Allows (1955), 208, 220n18
Allegiance (2015), 161, 180n6
allegory, 23, 177, 204, 207, 208, 210, 216, 217, 219
Allied nations, 6, 37, 40, 98, 132, 193
American Dream, 13, 26n47, 148
Americans, The (2013–18), 4, 22, 109, 117, 159–79, 179n2, 180nn4–5, 180n7, 180n9, 180n11, 180n19, 180n22, 182
Andropov, Yuri, 229
anti-Americanism, 4, 16, 58, 77, 136, 191
anti-Russian fears/feelings, 4, 13, 199
arms race, 7, 11, 12, 109, 141
art, 8, 20, 22, 68n49, 69n51, 86, 106, 107, 162, 163, 176, 208, 235
artificial intelligence (AI), 207, 227, 236
Atomic Blonde (2017), 4, 18, 20, 30, 34, 35, 37, 39–40, 42–45, 59, 96, 103–9, 110n19, 112, 113, 116–20, 125, 127n26, 129
authoritarianism, 14, 19, 74, 75, 83, 85, 88, 98, 212, 226, 228, 229
Avengers, The (1961–69), 18, 50, 57
Avengers, The (2012), 50

Axis allies, 6
Azov Battalion, 124

B movie, 11, 129, 134, 205, 210
Barber of Siberia (*Sibirskiy tsiryulnik*, 1998), 58
Barton Fink (1991), 144
Bay of Pigs, 7, 137
Beatles, 52
Beginning or the End, The (1947), 11
Ben-Hur (1959), 21, 144
Beria, Lavrentiy, 149–51, 155n21
Berlin, 6, 7, 19, 20, 37, 39, 40, 42, 45, 57, 62, 63, 95, 97, 98, 99, 100, 102, 103, 104, 108, 116, 117, 119, 120, 142; Berlin Blockade, 57, 184; East Berlin, 7, 43, 62, 98, 103, 189; West Berlin, 7, 40, 43, 57, 98, 189
Berlin Express (1948), 97
Berlin Station (2015–19), 102, 103
Berlin Wall, 3, 7, 8, 19, 29, 30, 41, 42, 43, 58, 64, 117, 135, 142, 189, 190, 232
Black Panther (2018), 23, 204, 217–19, 222nn56–58
body, 20, 21, 103, 112, 121, 122, 123, 125, 137, 211, 237
Bolshevik Revolution (1917), 5, 9, 132, 183, 232
Bolshevism, 73, 79, 87
bomb, 10–11, 17, 30, 98, 146, 184, 200n15
Bond, James, 12, 18–19, 50, 51, 55, 57, 58, 59, 61, 64, 65n1, 66n5, 100, 105, 147, 193, 225
Bourne, Jason, 58, 59, 100
Bourne Supremacy, The (2004), 58
Bowie, David, 102–4, 106, 110n16
Breach (2007), 59
Brexit, 88

Brezhnev, Leonid, 66n2, 95, 151
Bridge of Spies (2015), 4, 18, 20, 22, 23, 30, 34, 35, 36–39, 40–46, 102, 129, 144, 154n7, 182, 186–92, 193, 199, 200n23, 201nn29–36, 201n40, 203, 216
Buchanan, Pat, 215
Budapest, 97, 215, 216, 224
buddy film, 54, 76, 144
Bullwinkle Show, The (1959–63), 182
Bush, George W., 29, 30, 32, 33, 46n1, 96, 115, 216, 217
Butch Cassidy and the Sundance Kid (1969), 54
Butina, Maria, 59

Call Me by Your Name (2017), 64
Cambodia, 201n42
capitalism, 4, 6, 8, 71, 72, 73, 74, 76, 78, 86, 113, 117, 142, 146, 154n6, 210, 219, 235, 242
Castro, Fidel, 7
Chapman, Anna, 59
Chepiga, Anatoliy, 59
China, 75, 82, 89n1, 90n11, 228
Churchill, Winston, 51, 57, 66n13, 74
CIA, 20, 38, 39, 41, 42, 43, 45, 62, 96, 102, 105, 113, 114, 115, 116, 118, 120, 121, 122, 123, 124, 125, 126, 127n10, 127n19, 127n21, 127nn24–25, 128n29, 128n33, 128n35, 128n37, 128n39, 128n41, 159, 161, 187, 188, 189, 190, 191, 193, 202n42, 213, 215, 216, 224, 225, 230
civil rights, 131, 205
Clinton, Bill, 175, 217
Clinton, Hillary, 14, 15, 224
Cohn, Roy, 137, 139n24
Coldest City, The (2012), 37, 118
colonialism, 74, 79, 87, 88, 89n1; anti-colonialism, 77; neocolonialism, 19, 79; postcolonialism, 19, 74, 75, 79
color, 22, 67n17, 89n1, 101, 104, 134, 208, 209
comedy, 12, 21, 54, 140–45, 152–53, 155n18
communism, 3, 4, 6, 7, 8, 9, 10, 11, 12, 13, 17, 21, 25n22, 29, 71, 72–74, 75, 76, 78, 79, 83, 85, 86, 87–88, 132, 137, 140, 141, 142, 145, 186, 189, 190, 196, 197, 199n7, 210; anti-communism, 13, 25n27, 132
Company Business (1991), 58
Comrade Detective (2017), 4, 19, 75–79, 86, 87, 88, 90nn13–16, 90n19
Coney Island (1943), 131

Congress, 32, 128n38, 135
conservatism, 22, 71, 116, 136, 182, 183, 184, 186, 188, 189, 190, 197, 198, 204, 205, 210, 212, 214, 218, 219; neoconservatism, 22, 182, 184, 190, 191, 200n13, 204, 217
Conversation, The (1974), 215
corruption, 4, 5, 16, 18, 22, 23, 73, 83, 84, 112, 137, 193, 196, 212, 223–24, 229, 235, 240, 241–42; anti-corruption, 74
Creature from the Black Lagoon (1954), 11, 21, 129, 130, 204, 205, 210
Creature Walks Among Us, The (1956), 210
Crimea, annexation of, 14, 60, 140
Crimson Tide (1995), 58
Cuba, 7, 189, 190, 197, 201n35; Cuban Missile Crisis, 29, 49; Cuban Revolution, 142
cultural stagnation, 71, 87

Dandy in Aspic, A (1968), 97
Danger Man (1960–68), 50
Deadly Mantis, The (1957), 11
Death of Stalin, The (2017), 19, 21, 75, 79–88, 89n3, 90n12, 90n26, 141, 148–52, 153, 155n20, 155n28
democracy, 4, 5, 6, 9, 14, 15, 19, 59, 72, 73, 74, 75, 78, 79, 82, 83, 84, 85, 87–88, 89nn7–8, 107, 117, 195, 196, 219, 221n32, 223, 228; un-democracy, 82
Democratic Party, 22, 23, 114, 115, 127n13, 127nn15–16, 147, 203, 217, 218
détente, 7, 10, 12, 64, 96
Deutschland 83 (2015), 101, 109, 117
Deutschland 86 (2018), 101, 109
dictatorship, 68n44, 76, 82, 140, 149, 150, 152, 196, 241
diplomacy, 25n37, 106, 108, 191, 219, 221n22, 228, 229
disability, 136, 207, 223, 230, 233
Doctor Zhivago (1965), 232, 235
Dr. No (1962), 12, 18, 50
Dr. Strangelove or: How I Learned to Stop Worrying and Love the Bomb (1964), 3, 12, 80, 89n3, 141, 142, 149, 209

Eastern Bloc, 6, 8, 19, 70, 71, 77, 124, 135, 143, 144
Eastern Promises (2007), 133
egalitarianism, 70, 207, 210
Eisenhower, Dwight D., 187, 188, 200n23

election, 143, 198; Russiagate, 47n31, 208, 219; Russian legislative elections (2011), 14, 15; Russian presidential election (2012), 15; Russian presidential elections (2018), 15; US midterm elections (2018), 114; US presidential election (2016), 3, 9, 14, 15, 16, 23, 26n54, 45, 82, 95, 116, 198, 203, 208, 212, 214, 218, 220n17

elitism, 107

Equalizer, The (2014), 3

espionage, 12, 50, 51, 57, 60, 66nn9–10, 100, 117, 120, 134, 135, 212, 213, 217, 224, 225, 228, 231; secret agent, 53, 54, 60, 63, 160; sexpionage, 23, 204; spy/spycraft/spying, 12, 18, 30, 36, 38, 39, 40, 42, 49, 50, 53, 56, 58, 59, 60, 63, 65, 66n9, 67n29, 69n63, 69n65, 95, 99, 101, 104, 105, 108, 110n18, 111n27, 119, 132, 141, 143, 160, 162, 167, 171, 173, 174, 175, 180n17, 182, 186, 187, 188, 189, 190, 191, 192, 193, 194, 198, 199, 199n3, 200n23, 201n28, 207, 209, 211, 223, 224, 225, 230, 243n12

exceptionalism, 30, 45, 233, 234, 238; American exceptionalism, 30, 31, 35, 37, 40; Russian exceptionalism, 227

fascism, 10, 152, 200n8, 203, 212, 241
fashion, 43, 54, 57, 64, 65, 96, 104, 106, 109, 119
fatherland, 161, 163, 238. *See also* motherland
FBI, 15, 177, 186, 190
femininity, 5
Firefly (2002–3), 161
Flight to Mars (1951), 11
Flight to Nowhere (1946), 11
Forbidden Planet (1956), 11
Ford, Gerald R., 201
Foreign Affair, A (1948), 97
freedom, 9, 11, 14, 15, 22, 29, 37, 42, 44, 66n2, 76, 79, 133, 163, 186, 189, 200n27, 218, 228, 234, 235, 240, 242; Free World, 6, 9, 193
From Russia with Love (1963), 105
FSB, 20, 226, 231
Funeral in Berlin (1966), 97

Gagarin, Yuri, 49, 147
gender, 4, 105, 113, 114, 115, 118, 119, 120, 121, 124, 126, 155n16, 195, 199n6, 206, 207; transgender, 136
Georgia, 14, 140, 144

Germany, Year Zero (1948), 97
Get Smart (2008), 66n9
Girl from U.N.C.L.E., The (1966–67), 50
glasnost, 58
Good Bye Lenin! (2003), 101, 140
Good Day to Die Hard, A (2013), 3
Gorbachev, Mikhail, 7, 42, 58, 103, 144, 155n15
Greece, 6, 66n11, 184
Grenada, 185
Gromyko, Andrei, 49, 185
GRU, 20, 231
Guiana, 197
Gulag, 150, 196, 197, 202n58
Guryeva, Lydia, 59

Hail, Caesar! (2016), 4, 21, 23, 129, 140, 141, 144–48, 149, 152–53, 154n1, 154nn7–8, 155n18, 203
Haiti, 197
HDC (Hollywood Democratic Committee), 209
hegemony, 79, 207
hero, 5, 16, 20, 30, 40, 42, 45, 51, 61, 63, 67n29, 113, 123, 132, 143, 154n4, 191, 199, 211, 218, 222n58; antihero, 175, 176; superhero, 100, 219
Hezb-i-Islami, 124
Hitler, Adolf, 6, 85, 183, 195
Hollywoodland (2006), 145
Homeland (2011–20), 116
homophobia, 130, 131, 138n5
Hoover, John Edgar, 135
Hostel (2006), 216
How and Why (2014), 161
HUAC (House Un-American Activities Committee), 12, 17, 141, 144, 148, 153
Human Stain, The (2000), 175
humor, 12, 21, 22, 54, 55, 56, 62, 63, 81, 141, 149, 150, 151, 152
Hunt for Red October, The (1990), 12, 58, 147

I Married a Communist (1949), 11, 25n20
I Spy (1965–68), 18, 50, 61
I Spy (2002), 50, 54
idealism, 23, 45, 192
identity, 4, 5, 12, 23, 31, 37, 38, 39, 40, 44, 48n62, 53, 55, 79, 100, 101, 110n18, 114, 119, 121, 124, 126, 160, 161, 164, 170, 184, 205, 206, 211, 212, 216, 223, 225, 238, 239, 240, 241, 242, 243n12

Imitation of Life (1959), 208
imperialism, 184, 185, 186, 190, 196, 204, 215; anti-imperialism, 77
In the Loop (2009), 81, 149
individualism, 119, 189, 237, 239, 240
Indonesia, 201n42
Inhofe, James, 29, 30
Interview, The (2014), 199
Invasion U.S.A. (1985), 25n27, 183
Iran, 197, 228
Iraq, 9, 32, 47n18, 116, 217
Iron Curtain, 11, 40, 57, 70, 71, 100, 102, 109, 142
Iron Man 2 (2010), 3
ISIS, 14, 218
isolationism, 8, 14, 130, 169, 204, 215, 218, 219
It Came from Beneath the Sea (1955), 11
It Came from Outer Space (1953), 11

Jackal, The (1997), 58
Jet Pilot (1957), 51, 132
John Wick (2014), 37, 104, 118
Johnson, Lyndon, 136
Jumpin' Jack Flash (1986), 143

Kaczyński, Lech, 73, 74
Kaganovich, Lazar, 150–51
Kara-Murza, Vladimir, 68n43
Kennedy, John F., 7, 18, 49, 65–66nn1–2, 130, 131, 133, 134, 205, 219
Kenya, 164, 196, 197, 202n58
KGB, 20, 40, 43, 59, 62, 63, 64, 104, 147, 177, 183, 198, 199n5, 226, 227, 231, 238
Khrushchev, Nikita, 7, 21, 66n2, 70, 84, 141, 149, 150, 151, 153, 188, 200n23
King and I, The (1956), 19
Kingdom, The (2007), 199
Kissinger, Henry, 201n42
kompromat, 96, 226
Korean War, 29, 200n9, 202n63
Kosovo, 32
Kremlin, 15, 59, 141, 151, 152, 155n20, 194, 221n41, 225, 227, 228, 229, 235, 242

laughter, 21, 88, 141
le Carré, John, 100, 110n14, 190, 192, 193, 195, 196, 197, 199n6, 213
LeMay, Curtis, 209

Lenin, Vladimir, 63, 98, 101, 140, 146, 152, 155n15, 182
liberalism, 4, 18, 19, 23, 59, 66n2, 71, 72, 73, 74, 75, 79, 87, 89n8, 109, 115, 116, 117, 119, 120, 124, 125, 184, 185, 190, 203, 204, 205, 209, 211, 212, 217, 219, 228; neoliberalism, 71, 79, 87, 126
Libya, 124, 128n40
Life Is Worth Living (1952–55, 1955–57), 145
Little Colonel, The (1935), 130, 206
Litvinenko, Alexander, 59, 140, 153
Lives of Others, The (2006), 101
London, 37, 40, 45, 97, 99, 101, 103
Long Kiss Goodnight, The (1996), 105

Mafia, 3, 5, 145
magical realism, 23, 203, 204, 206, 209
Magnitsky, Sergei, 59
Malenkov, Georgy, 149–52
Man Between, The (1953), 97
Man from U.N.C.L.E., The (1964–68), 18, 19, 50–56, 60–62, 66n3, 66nn9–12, 66n14, 67nn16–18, 67n23, 67nn25–27, 67n30, 67nn33–34, 68nn38–39
Man from U.N.C.L.E., The (2015), 4, 18, 19, 50, 59–60, 62–65, 68n46, 69nn57–58, 69nn63–64
Man of Steel (2013), 64
Manchurian Candidate, The (1962), 100
Manchurian Candidate, The (2004), 216
Manhattan Project, 10
Maoism, 71, 75, 85, 89n2
Marshall Plan, 6, 57
Marxism, 79, 106, 185
masculinity, 5, 131, 132, 154n4, 155n16
Matthews, Jason, 95, 120–23, 128n33, 214, 225, 243n12
Max Payne (2008), 104
McCarthy, Joseph, 11, 23, 29, 134, 135, 136, 137, 189, 203; McCarthyism, 25n15, 134, 141, 154n12; second Red Scare, 21, 135, 141
Me Too, 204, 213, 214
Medinsky, Vladimir, 151
Miami Vice (1984–89), 90n15
military-industrial complex, 142, 144, 210, 228
Mishkin, Alexander, 59
MI6, 37, 62, 99, 103, 117, 142
Mission: Impossible (1966–73), 18, 50, 59, 65

Mission: Impossible—Ghost Protocol (2011), 3
Mission: Impossible—Rogue Nation (2015), 65, 69n66
Mister Ed (1958–66), 131
Molotov, Vyacheslav, 149–51
moral equivalence/equivalency, 22, 182–86, 189–91, 194, 196–98, 200n12, 200n15, 201n30, 202n55, 210, 212, 217
Moscow, 65n2, 101, 124, 140, 147, 178, 213, 224, 226, 230, 231, 238
motherland, 22, 163, 168, 176, 179. *See also* fatherland
Mueller Report (2019), 3, 45, 203, 219
Munich (2005), 191
music, 8, 43, 44, 53, 56, 80, 96, 102, 103, 104, 105, 106, 109, 145, 148, 149, 163, 206, 208, 216, 230, 235, 236
My Son John (1952), 51

nationalism, 15, 82, 89n1, 89n8, 91n43, 133, 186, 189, 195, 196, 207, 215, 219, 229
NATO, 6, 14, 15, 121, 143, 196
Nazism, 5, 6, 10, 11, 15, 62, 63, 124, 128n37, 185, 195, 200n8, 200n22; neo-Nazism, 124, 128n38
NCIS (2003–), 56, 68n37
Nemtsov, Boris, 59
Nena, 119
Never Say Never Again (1983), 57
New Tsar: The Rise and Reign of Vladimir Putin, The (2014), 183, 199n5
Nikita (1990), 105
9/11 (September 11, 2001), 9, 32, 33, 44, 115, 202n44, 216, 221nn45–46, 222nn47–48
Ninotchka (1939), 3, 9, 89n3, 141, 142
Nixon, Richard M., 137
NKVD, 151
nomenklatura, 73
North Korea, 82, 199, 228
nostalgia, 18, 19, 20, 21, 30, 31, 35–37, 45, 46, 46n3, 47n36, 48nn37–38, 48n40, 48n43, 56, 88, 103, 130, 141, 152, 154n7, 207, 212, 229, 232
Notorious (1946), 11
November Man, The (2014), 59

Obama, Barack, 5, 14, 60, 96, 130, 176
Octopussy (1983), 57

Oh! What a Lovely War (1969), 80, 81
oligarchy, 4, 16, 210
On the Beach (1959), 100
Orbán, Viktor, 73, 74, 77, 82
Our Man in Havana (1959), 142

Pan's Labyrinth (*El laberinto del fauno*, 2006), 203, 206, 211, 212, 221n32
parody, 85, 55, 77, 211
patriotism, 4, 12, 15, 18, 22, 23, 81, 109, 118, 126n3, 134, 137, 152, 161, 162, 168, 178, 179, 183, 186, 187, 188, 192, 194, 195, 214, 223, 224, 239, 240, 241
Pax Americana, 205
Pentagon, 114, 120, 121, 127n10
perestroika, 58, 103
Pianist, The (2002), 212
Pol Pot, 201n42
politburo, 84
Politkovskaya, Anna, 59
populism, 15, 73, 74, 77, 80, 81, 88, 89n8, 106, 203, 207
Power of Positive Thinking, The (1952), 131, 132
Prisoner, The (1967–68), 18, 50, 66n5
propaganda, 10, 17, 26n43, 51, 55, 57, 75, 76, 77, 78, 80, 81, 82, 84, 85, 88, 98, 99, 110n1, 121, 130, 138n6, 142, 185, 186, 190, 191, 193, 199, 199n5, 228, 229
Pussy Riot, 140
Putin, Vladimir, 3, 5, 14–16, 19, 20, 23, 26n48, 26n53, 26n59, 34, 47nn30–31, 58, 59, 60, 64, 68nn43–44, 95, 96, 97, 106, 107, 108, 109, 121, 130, 141, 152, 153, 155n31, 155n33, 161, 183, 185, 198, 199n5, 204, 212, 214, 215, 217, 219, 221n38, 221nn41–42, 222n50, 226, 227, 228, 229, 241, 242, 243, 244n23

Rambo: First Blood Part II (1985), 143, 154nn4–5
Rambo III (1988), 133, 154n4
Rasputin and the Empress (1932), 132
Reagan, Ronald, 7, 23, 42, 103, 117, 132, 134, 135, 143, 154n4, 159, 203, 218
Realpolitik, 23, 106, 108, 190, 207, 209
Red Danube (1949), 12
Red Dawn (1984), 77, 132
Red Dawn (2012), 199

Red Heat (1988), 144
Red Menace, The (1949), 11, 132
Red Nightmare (1957), 51
Red Scorpion (1988), 147
Red Snow (1952), 11
Red Sparrow (2018), 4, 20, 23, 95–96, 102, 103, 105, 107, 109, 110n18, 111n27, 113, 118, 120–24, 125, 128n29, 128nn31–34, 204, 212–17, 218, 219, 221n34, 221n36, 223–24, 228–43, 243nn3–9, 243n11
Red Sparrow trilogy (2013–18), 225
Republican Party, 23, 29, 46n2, 135, 203, 205, 208, 210, 212, 214, 215, 218, 219
Return of the Man from U.N.C.L.E.: The Fifteen Years Later Affair, The (1983), 56–57, 59, 66n4, 68n40
Revenge of the Creature (1955), 210
revisionism, 117, 184, 187, 194, 211; post-revisionism, 184, 188
Robertson, Pat, 136
Rocky IV (1985), 77, 112, 143, 147, 154n5
rogue states, 30
Roman Holiday (1953), 142, 154n1
Romania, 19, 75, 76, 88, 90n13, 90n18
Romanoff and Juliet (1961), 143
Rosenbergs, 135, 186
Route 66 (1998), 54
Russia House, The (1990), 3, 58
Russian Civil War (1917–22), 148
Russian Revolution. *See* Bolshevik Revolution
Russians Are Coming! The Russians Are Coming!, The (1966), 12, 25n34, 132, 143, 147

Saint, The (1962–69), 18, 50
Saint, The (1997), 50, 58
Salt (2010), 3, 105, 118
SALT I, 7
SALT II, 7
sanctions, 3, 15, 59, 60
satire, 72, 75–77, 79–88, 89n3, 90n12, 91n29, 91n34, 141, 142, 148, 162, 208
Schindler's List (1993), 212
science, 11
Sessions, Jeff, 130
Seven Year Itch, The (1955), 129
Seventeen Moments of Spring (*Semnadtsat mgnoveniy vesny*, 1973), 67n29

sexuality, 20, 103, 119, 120, 131, 136, 173, 174, 208, 225, 234; bisexual, 105, 119; gay, 21, 119, 130, 131, 136, 138n6; heterosexuality, 132, 207; homosexuality, 130, 131, 205; lesbian, 206; queer, 207, 220n8
Shape of Water, The (2017), 4, 21, 23, 129, 133–35, 137–38, 138n1, 138n14, 203, 204–12, 213, 217, 218, 219, 220n3, 220n12, 220nn15–16, 221n29
Sherlock Holmes (2009), 60
Sherlock Holmes: A Game of Shadows (2011), 60
Sicario (2015), 199
Sicario: Day of the Soldado (2018), 199
Skripal, Sergei, 3–4, 65, 68n43
SOA, 137; WHINSEC, 137
socialism, 19, 70, 71, 76, 78, 89nn1–2, 121; postsocialism, 85, 89n8
Song of Russia (1944), 132
South Pacific (1958), 19
Soviet-Afghan War, 8, 143, 185
Spies Like Us (1985), 143
Spinning Boris (2003), 58
Spy vs. Spy (1961–), 241
Spy Who Came in from the Cold, The (1965), 97, 98, 99, 100, 102
Spy Who Loved Me, The (1977), 61
Stalin, Joseph, 6, 16, 19, 21, 75, 76, 79–88, 89n3, 90n12, 90n26, 91n27, 98, 141, 146, 148–52, 153, 155nn15–16, 155nn20–21, 155nn28–29, 155n32, 184, 186, 200n22, 201, 226
Stalker (1979), 105
Star Wars (1977), 51
Starsky and Hutch (2004), 54
State Department File 649 (1949), 11
Steele, Christopher, 23, 204, 213, 214
Story of Ruth, The (1960), 206, 211
Stripes (1981), 143
subaltern, 74, 75, 79, 89n10
Suharto, 201n42
Sum of All Fears, The (2002), 58
SVR, 95, 120, 122, 123, 213, 214, 215, 216, 217, 223, 224, 230, 231, 239
Syria, 14, 124, 128n39, 140, 227
Syriana (2005), 116

Tarantula (1955), 11
technocracy, 15, 116

Tereshkova, Valentina, 49
terrorism, 17, 26n70, 30, 32, 33, 34, 35, 44, 47n21, 47n26, 51, 115, 116, 191, 201n42, 216, 225. *See also* War on Terror
theater, 25n29, 79, 80, 81, 147, 208
Thelma and Louise (1991), 54
Them! (1954), 11
Thick of It, The (2005–12), 81, 83, 84, 86, 91n29, 149
Third Man, The (1949), 97
Thirty Cases of Major Zeman (*Třicet případů majora Zemana*, 1975–80), 90n15
Thunderball (1965), 61
Tinker Tailor Soldier Spy (2011), 20, 22, 96, 100, 101, 104, 105, 106, 108, 109, 110n7, 111n27, 182, 186, 192–98, 199, 199n3, 199n6, 202nn55–56, 202n64
To Russia with Love (1963), 12
Top Secret (1952), 142
Top Secret (1984), 143
totalitarianism, 6, 7, 72, 75, 80, 82, 83, 84, 85, 86, 87, 88, 91n44, 184, 185, 186, 193, 197, 199n1, 200n8, 200nn21–22
Transformers (2007–17), 114
Truman Doctrine, 6, 57
Trump, Donald, 3, 5, 14, 15, 16, 19, 20, 22, 23, 26n48, 26nn53–54, 33, 47n24, 47n31, 77, 82, 85, 88, 95, 96, 97, 106, 107, 108, 109, 111n26, 114, 115, 116, 127n15, 130, 132, 138n5, 138n17, 139n24, 162, 176, 183, 199n4, 200n17, 203, 204, 205, 207, 208, 210, 212, 213, 214, 215, 217–19, 220n12, 220n17, 221n34, 221n38, 221n43, 222nn50–51, 222n57, 223, 228, 241, 243n1
Tunnel, The (2012), 101
Turkey, 6

Ukraine, 3, 14, 15, 18, 47n31, 51, 60, 124, 140, 201n42, 227
UN, 18, 49, 219
United Russia Party, 14, 228

Veep (2012–19), 83, 149
victory culture, 18, 30, 31, 46n4, 47n18
Vienna, 97
Vietnam War, 8, 29, 32, 44, 47n18, 115, 137, 154n4, 184, 202n46

View to a Kill, A (1985), 147
violence, 20, 37, 41, 81, 103, 117, 118, 119, 141, 145, 153, 177, 209, 212, 213, 225, 233, 240
Virus (1999), 58

War of the Worlds (2005), 216
War on Terror, 32, 33, 35, 44, 46, 46n8, 47n21, 115, 216, 221n45. *See also* terrorism
Warsaw Pact, 57, 58, 107
Weinstein, Harvey, 214
What's Up, Tiger Lily? (1966), 77
White House, 111n26, 136
WikiLeaks, 113, 126n7
World War I (Great War), 80
World War II, 5, 6, 10, 12, 15, 30, 31, 47n21, 67n29, 80, 113, 132, 135, 137, 152, 155n31, 194, 195

xenophobia, 88, 205, 227, 229
Xi Jinping, 228

Yalta Conference, 6, 8
Yanukovich, Viktor, 14
Yeltsin, Boris, 58
Yes, Prime Minister (1986–87), 81

Zero Dark Thirty (2012), 116

www.ingramcontent.com/pod-product-compliance
Lightning Source LLC
Chambersburg PA
CBHW030617230426
43661CB00053B/2025